Words and *The W*

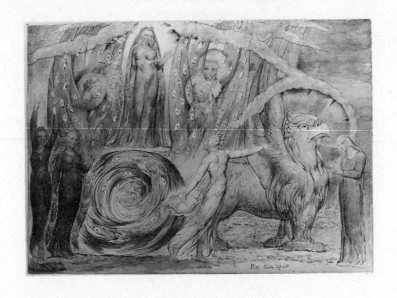

Beatrice addressing Dante from the car
by William Blake
(reproduced by permission of the Tate Gallery, London)

Words and *The Word*

Language, poetics and biblical interpretation

STEPHEN PRICKETT

Professor of English, Australian National University

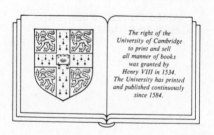

The right of the
University of Cambridge
to print and sell
all manner of books
was granted by
Henry VIII in 1534.
The University has printed
and published continuously
since 1584.

CAMBRIDGE UNIVERSITY PRESS

Cambridge
New York   New Rochelle
Melbourne   Sydney

Published by the Press Syndicate of the University of Cambridge
The Pitt Building, Trumpington Street, Cambridge CB2 1RP
32 East 57th Street, New York, NY 10022, USA
10 Stamford Road, Oakleigh, Melbourne 3166, Australia

First published 1986
First paperback edition 1988

Printed in Great Britain at
the University Press, Cambridge

British Library cataloguing in publication data
Prickett, Stephen
Words and the Word: language, poetics and biblical
interpretation.
1. Bible–Hermeneutics
I. Title
220.6'01'09033   BS476

Library of Congress cataloguing in publication data
Prickett, Stephen.
Words and the Word.
Bibliography.
Includes index.
1. Bible–Hermeneutics. 2. Languages–Religious
aspects. 3. Criticism. I. Title.
BS476.P75 1986   220.6'01   86–8269

ISBN 0 521 32248 0 hard covers
ISBN 0 521 36838 3 paperback

In translating, we must go to the brink of the Untranslatable; it is only then that we really become aware of the foreignness of the nation and the language.

Goethe: 'Aphorisms on Art and Art-History'

Touchstone: . . . I would the gods had made thee poetical.
Audrey: I do not know what 'poetical' is: is it honest in deed and word? is it a true thing?

As You Like It, III, iii, 13–15

Contents

Acknowledgements	*page*	xi
Introduction		1
1	Ways of reading the Bible	
	The problem of the transparent text	4
2	'The peculiar language of heaven . . .'	
	The religious and the poetic	37
	'Primal Consciousness' and linguistic change	68
3	Poetry and prophecy	
	The language of the Great Code	95
	The Book of Nature	123
4	The paradoxes of disconfirmation	
	Elijah and Dante: The *Word* and the 'Voice'	149
	Convention and realism: The shaking of the foundations	174
5	Metaphor and reality	196
Notes		243
Bibliography		283
Index		297

Acknowledgements

To list all those who have helped shape the development of this book would be an impossible task, but it is a pleasure to express at least my thanks to the friends and onetime colleagues at the University of Sussex to whom it owes so much. I am grateful in particular to Tony Nuttall (now of New College, Oxford) for his patient and generous criticism of my arguments, and to John Burrow, not only for his critical insight but also for his permission to make use of his unpublished article 'The Poverty of Methodology'; I have also learnt perhaps more than they realise from the criticism and assistance of Peter Burke (now of Emmanuel College, Cambridge), Christopher Chaffin, Terry Diffey, Charles Martindale, and Michael Wadsworth (now in the Liverpool Diocese). Stephen Medcalf has kindly allowed me to draw on material used in his 1984 paper to the Conference on Religion and Literature at the University of Durham, 'Coleridge's Vision of the Chariot'. To new friends and colleagues at the Australian National University I owe debts no less great. Bill Krebs has generously allowed me to draw on material from his unpublished Ph.D. thesis, 'The Study of Language in Scotland 1760–1810'; Richard Campbell has deepened my understanding of Heidegger; Livio Dobrez has initiated me into the mysteries of St John of the Cross; and, above all, the polymathic Robert Barnes has been of incalculable assistance in guiding me through the subtleties of German theology. I am grateful also to Drina Oldroyd, of Melbourne University, for her assistance on Dante, and for her permission to make use of her unpublished paper, 'Hunting the Griffin in Dante's Purgatorio'. Many others, John Todd (who did so much to encourage me to begin writing), James Mark, John Dancy, Helen Irwin, Marjorie Reeves, Desmond Ryan, John Gillies, Valentine Cunningham, George Mabbutt, and Michael Holquist, have played parts in the writing of this book, and I gladly acknowledge their help and inspiration.

Parts of Chapter 1 first appeared in *Theology*, in November 1977, and in *Ways of Reading the Bible*, ed. Michael Wadsworth, Harvester Press, 1981; part of Chapter 3 appeared in *Images of Belief*, ed. David Jasper, Macmillan, 1984; part of Chapter 4 appeared in *The Journal of European Studies*, December 1972.

Finally I must thank my secretary and word-processor operator, Lesley McRae, without whose endless patience and skill this book would have taken twice as long to write, and been twice as inaccurate.

For the confusions and errors I have been saved from by all the above, I am deeply grateful; for any that remain, I am solely responsible.

Canberra 1985

Introduction

When, in 1809, Baron Wilhelm von Humboldt was given the task by Frederick William III of creating the new University of Berlin, one of his basic principles was to separate theology from the study of the humanities, and to place the latter firmly within the faculty of Arts (*Philosophische Fakultät*).[1] Following the lead given by such eminent academic reformers as Thomasius at Halle and Munchhausen at Göttingen, Humboldt's policy, which aimed at freeing the humanities from the dead hand of the scholastic theology then practised in most German universities, was an essential step in the evolution of the modern idea of the university and of the disciplines of literary studies and philology.[2] For Humboldt, theology (like the natural sciences) was not conducive to the new spirit of *Wissenschaft* that lay at the heart of his conception of what a university should be, and which would find its fullest expression in a faculty of Arts. This notion of the centrality of the humanities to a university was one shared by other contemporary university reformers: Fichte, Schelling, Schleiermacher, and Steffens.[3] It was to have momentous and ultimately unforeseen consequences.

In Germany what Hermann Usener was later in the century to call a 'glacial-moraine' (*gletscherwall*)[4] was created between biblical studies and the study of other literatures, both classical and modern, which (to continue Usener's image) has left today a massive and seemingly natural barrier dividing the cultural landscape. In England, on the other hand, the two disciplines had, if anything, been drawing closer together at the end of the eighteenth century. The work of Robert Lowth had made possible a new aesthetic appreciation of biblical poetry, and the fact that the first generation of English Romantic poets, Blake, Wordsworth, Coleridge and Southey, so far from rejecting Christianity like Humboldt, were devout Christians of one kind or another, helped them to find in the Bible far more powerful sources of inspiration than their German contemporaries or their immediate

1

predecessors of the Enlightenment. But though the Bible might be common ground, in the nineteenth century theology itself could be, and sometimes was, construed as a threat to the development of the other humanities. It underlay the Test Acts that until the 1850s excluded Dissenters and Catholics from Oxford and Cambridge, and the imperial claims assigned to it by Newman in his *Idea of a University* were paralleled in practice by Pusey's Oxford campaigns against Jowett and Max Müller for suspected heterodoxy. Given the prestige of the reformed universities of Germany it is hardly surprising that the new English foundations, such as London, and later the major civic universities, or the reforms in Cambridge and Oxford, tended to follow Humboldt's models of curricula.[5] Moreover, the deservedly formidable reputation acquired by the refounded German theology of the nineteenth century brought with it its own assumptions that only served to strengthen the moraine between biblical and literary scholarship. The fact that there were distinguished and honourable exceptions to this general pattern,[6] does not alter the fact that by the end of the century the same wall that divided German scholarship had been successfully transplanted into English institutions and thought.

The result, latent in the nineteenth-century situation, but often delayed in experience until the twentieth, has been a crisis in biblical hermeneutics that theology by itself seems incapable of resolving satisfactorily. It is significant that in the two most powerful and persuasive accounts of the current dilemma, both Hans Frei and Robert W. Funk find themselves turning towards literary models in their search for a solution.[7] Meanwhile, separated from the biblical and prophetic models that gave the Romantics such confidence in their role and relevance, literature, and in particular, poetry, has also suffered a crisis of meaning in the twentieth century.

This book begins from the suspicion that the current problems of biblical hermeneutics are unlikely to be solved without some historical understanding of how the present situation arose, and that its roots cannot be understood simply in terms of development of theology or of literary theory considered as separate disciplines in isolation, but that they must be approached through their interaction and subsequent separation in the late eighteenth and early nineteenth centuries. As this history unfolds it should become apparent that problems that first surfaced in biblical studies have been, and in many cases still are, paradigmatic of wider hermeneutic, epistemological, and linguistic problems. It is, indeed, hardly an exaggeration to say that the contemporary crises in literary criticism and translation theory also have roots in that same division between biblical scholarship and aesthetics that occurred in the early nineteenth century, and that any lasting attempt to solve these problems must similarly begin with an understanding of how they came into being. It is, for instance, not always recognized that the German Higher Criticism, nineteenth-century English poetic theory, French twentieth-century discussions of the relationship of author to text, and the American Sapir-Whorf hypothesis in linguistics all have common origins in eighteenth-century debates over poetry and hermeneutics. The history of each of these topics would be the subject of a complete study in itself, and this book does no more than indicate, parenthetically, a few of their landmarks; the thread that links them – and my subject here – is the more tenuous but amazingly persistent debate over the past three hundred years on the relationship of poetry to religious language.

What follows is an attempt to tease out certain problems that have lain at the back of my mind for more than fifteen years. They were present when I first wrote on Coleridge and Wordsworth[8] and by the time I came to write on the Victorian Church[9] I was able to refer in the Introduction to a possible further study of religious language on a broader front that that of nineteenth-century England. The result is this book. My earlier work had suggested that many of the assumptions and attitudes of the Victorians towards the Bible and religious language in general could not be satisfactorily explained without reference to the critical controversies of the previous century, and though the eighteenth century was, in many ways, a critical watershed, it, in turn, had inherited a whole complex of ideas and models from earlier centuries – from the Church Fathers, Augustine, Dante and the sixteenth-century Reformers, for instance. Any starting-point is arbitrary. What is contained in the following chapters is, of necessity, a part of the story.

1
Ways of reading the Bible

The problem of the transparent text

Belinda: Ay, but you know we must return
       good for evil.

Lady Brute: That may be a mistake in the
       translation.   (Vanbrugh, *The Provok'd Wife*, 1697, I.i.)

We start with two quotations – both about the Bible. First Coleridge:

> I take up this work with the purpose to read it for the first time as I should
> any other work, – as far at least as I can or dare. For I neither can, not dare,
> throw off a strong and awful prepossession in its favour – certain as I am that
> a large part of the light and life, in which and by which I see, love, and embrace
> the truths and the strengths co-organised into a living body of faith and
> knowledge . . . has been directly or indirectly derived to me from this sacred
> volume, – and unable to determine what I do not owe to its influences.[1]

Our second quotation is from a far more respectable source in its own
time than was Coleridge's *Confessions of an Inquiring Spirit* in 1849: the
Preface to the *Good News Bible* of 1976:

> The primary concern of the translators has been to provide a faithful transla-
> tion of the Hebrew, Aramaic, and Greek texts. Their first task was to under-
> stand correctly the meaning of the original . . . the translators' next task was
> to express that meaning in a manner and form easily understood by the readers
> . . . Every effort has been made to use language that is natural, clear, simple,
> and unambiguous.

Now an observer from another culture – let us say, the man on the
Peking omnibus – might be forgiven for assuming that the tone of
breezy confidence exuded by the translators of the *Good News* in 1976
came from their having understood and resolved the problem that concerned Coleridge. Where he found himself hesitant, tentative, and
uncertain, they, carried forward by the progress of scholarship in the
intervening 150 years, could be knowledgeable and precise. The fruits
of the modern sciences of archeology, anthropology, and linguistics,
together with a more sophisticated notion of history than the early

4

nineteenth century, had, he might suppose, at last given an authoritative biblical text. Yet, of course, our baffled Peking everyman would once again have been deceived by the inscrutable Occident.

The thrust of Coleridge's *Confessions* becomes clearer if we recall that the work was originally entitled 'Letters on the Inspiration of the Scriptures', and that it was his nephew and editor Henry Nelson Coleridge who substituted the personal and subjective title of the published version. Coleridge's hesitancy was in the face of a particular and very complex dilemma: that of cultural relativity in perhaps its most extreme form. His difficulty lay not merely in the enormous problems inherent in translation from one cultural world to another, separated by at least two thousand years, but also in the fact that this cultural relationship was apparently asymmetric. He was uncomfortably aware how many of his basic cultural assumptions might be derived from the Bible in ways that, by definition, were inaccessible to impartial investigation. He had come to consciousness within a society which, while it was clearly very different from anything to be found in the Old or New Testaments, had taken many of its most basic presuppositions from them. The very system of criteria by which he might try to read the Bible as he would 'any other work' was already enmeshed by an almost unravellable tangle of likeness and unlikeness extending from the simplest equivalents down to the most complex unconscious premises. The dual metaphors of the passage, organically connected by a striking Coleridgean ellipsis: 'The light . . . by which I see', the 'life by which I . . . love', suggest the scope of his problem. 'Light' and 'life' are not objects of consciousness or perception, they are their *conditions*. We do not 'see' light, we see other things by it; we are not 'conscious' of life; it is the ground of consciousness – a ground peculiarly resistant to analysis by autopsy – as Wordsworth had succinctly put it, 'we murder to dissect'.

In short, Coleridge perceives the problem of cultural relativity in terms as much existential as analytic: the totality of a cultural world is one that can only be experienced as a participator, from the inside. 'In the Bible,' he admits a few pages later in the *Confessions*, 'there is more that *finds* me than in all other books put together'.[2] There is, and can be, no impartial observer. Hence his final inability to 'determine' what he did 'not owe to its influences' is not so much a disarming admission of failure, perhaps to be solved in due course by the advance of scholarship, as a staking-out of the limits of human enquiry.

By contrast, the translators of the Bible Society's *Good News Bible* appear to be afflicted by no such inhibiting doubts. Their appointed task 'to understand correctly the meaning of the original', though undoubtedly difficult in places, is in their estimation by no means impossible – given the aids of the various sciences hypothesized by our mythical observer, and given also, they would probably feel, the aid of the Holy Spirit, which had providentially ensured that the Bible *was* fully translatable into all languages: a process that could only enhance rather than diminish our understanding of the treasures encoded in the original Hebrew and Greek. Such confidence is, it would seem, rooted in a belief in the text itself as an objective entity over and above any debilitating niceties of cultural relativity and academic debate. Hence their commitment to conveying the 'correct meaning' of the original in 'language that is natural, clear, simple, and unambiguous'. As a gloss on this approach a member of the Bible Society has described the *Good News Bible* as being for 'the unsophisticated' or 'average reader' who 'is likely to be grateful rather than offended at being delivered from theological subtleties', arguing that since God 'stooped to the level of human language to communicate with his people' it was the translators' task to set forth the 'truth of the biblical revelation in language that is as clear and simple as possible'.[3] The *text* has a 'meaning' that is finally independent of our cultural presuppositions.

Yet Coleridge's problem has a way of persisting. Take for example, a well-known story from the Elijah cycle. I quote from the *Authorized Version* of 1611:

And he arose, and did eat and drink and went in the strength of that meat forty days and forty nights unto Horeb the mount of God. And he came thither unto a cave, and lodged there; and, behold, the word of the Lord came to him, and he said unto him What doest thou here, Elijah? And he said, I have been very jealous for the Lord, the God of hosts; for the children of Israel have forsaken thy covenant, thrown down thine altars, and slain thy prophets with the sword: and I, even I only, am left; and they seek my life, to take it away. And he said, Go forth, and stand upon the mount before the Lord. And, behold, the Lord passed by, and a great and strong wind rent the mountains, and brake in pieces the rocks before the Lord; but the Lord was not in the wind: and after the wind an earthquake; and after the earthquake a fire; but the Lord was not in the fire: and after the fire a still small voice.   I Kings xix, 8–12

This is such a well-known story that it is easy to miss how enigmatic and puzzling it becomes once we start looking beyond the bare and stark biblical narrative. We are simply not given any answers to the 'obvious' circumstantial and naturalistic questions. What, for instance, *was* this 'fire'? Was it some kind of electrical storm, or was it a bush fire? Was it connected with the earthquake? What did it burn? Similarly, what was this 'voice'? What is the status of this third-person narrative, anyway? Since Elijah was alone, do we conclude that this is his own account? There is no answer to these and a host of related questions. Stripped of what Erich Auerbach calls 'foreground' detail[4] the story concentrates exclusively on its central theme: that of Elijah's encounter with God.[5] And it is here that we begin to suspect this bare account of extreme complexity. Elijah's long-delayed meeting with God turns out to be not at all what we are told he had expected. Instead, his original assumptions are disconfirmed by a revelation so ambiguous as to resist any modern attempt to reduce it to a direct simple statement. Herein lies the translator's problem.

Translation, especially from one period of time to another, is not just a matter of finding the nearest equivalents for words or syntactic structures. In addition it involves altering the fine network of unconscious or half-conscious presuppositions that underlie the actual words or phrases, and which differentiate so characteristically the climate of thought and feeling of one age from that of another. Thus according to G. B. Caird, the biblical translator always 'runs the double risk either of modernising or of archaising: to modernise is to ignore the culture gap of many centuries and to read the Bible as though its were contemporary literature; and to archaise is to exaggerate the culture gap and to ignore the similarities between the biblical world and our own'.[6] Caird's dilemma, we may suppose, is one common to many modern translators – and our story from the Elijah cycle is apparently a case in point.

What the prophet hears after the earthquake, the wind, and the fire may be literally translated from the Hebrew into English as 'a voice of thin silence'.[7] As we have seen, the King James *Authorized Version* of 1611 renders this curious oxymoron into English as the well-known 'still small voice'. Bearing in mind that in Elizabethan English 'small' could still mean 'thin' (as in Wyatt's 'her arms long and small' or the Shakespearean 'small beer') this is a remarkably accurate translation. In so far as it is obscure and ambiguous, it is an obscurity and ambiguity that is at least faithful to the original. Something very odd had apparently happened to Elijah.

The modern English translations, however, seem to be quite unanimous in *rejecting* any ambiguity or oddity perceived in the original. In the *Good News Bible* what Elijah hears is no more than 'the soft whisper of a voice'. The *New English Bible* hopefully tries reducing the 'voice' to a metaphor, translating it as 'a low murmuring sound', while the Catholic *Jerusalem Bible* outdoes the nascent naturalism of its Protestant rivals by eliminating all suggestion of speech with its 'sound of a gentle breeze' – which is a fair translation of the Vulgate's '*Et post ignem sibilis aurae tenuis*' ('and after the fire, a thin whistling sound of the air'). *Aura* refers literally to motion of the air – either wind or breath according to context. For an age with a typological cast of mind, the associations of the 'breeze' with the Holy Spirit would have been irresistible. The Hebrew word for 'wind' in this passage corresponds to the Greek word for 'spirit' in the Septuagint and the New Testament[8] and so what Elijah hears is made conveniently to prefigure its antitype of the Holy Spirit in the Gospels and the rushing wind of Pentecost. Yet such a chain of associative thinking, almost second-nature until the early nineteenth century, is lost in the modern context. It is interesting to speculate, therefore, why both the translators of the *New English Bible* and the Bible Society, supposedly unhampered by the mistranslation of the Latin tradition, should have been almost as eager as their Catholic peers to produce an implicitly naturalistic reading rather than follow the mysteriously suggestive Hebrew – an impressively accurate translation of which already existed in English.

Part of the answer clearly lies in the cultural milieu of the new translations. A noticeable feature of modern English that increasingly separates it from the critical sensibility of its past is an intolerance of ambiguity. We have come to expect that narrative will convey its own frame of reference so that we know, almost at once, for instance, whether we are reading what purports to be 'fact' or 'fiction' and adjust our mental sets accordingly. Writers who mix their genres are apt to leave us uneasy. Explanations may only operate at one level of our experience. We need to know whether Elijah's theophany was visionary or miraculous – whether the 'voice' is to be understood as 'internal', an event presumed to be *within* Elijah's own mind, or 'external', producing a phenomenon in nature to be detected by the presence of a witness. These distinctions between 'outer' and 'inner', or 'natural' and 'supernatural', are not, of course, biblical categories and the *Authorized Version*'s 'still small voice' should prevent us from applying them to Elijah's mysterious experience. Yet the *New English Bible* offers us no choice: we are given the 'low murmuring sound' as an apparently *natural* if not immediately identifiable phenomenon. There is nothing peculiar or odd about low murmuring sounds, after all. They are as 'natural' as earthquakes, winds, and fires, if somewhat less noisy. If any ambiguity remains, it is only whether that 'murmuring' is a metaphor (as in 'murmuring breeze') or a literal voice – an altogether arbitrary ambiguity which, as we have seen, is quite foreign to the original. (So *that*'s what the sound was: it was just a gentle breeze: no problems with miracles now; no theophany either!) After these, the *Good News Bible* seems positively pietistic in suggesting that what Elijah heard might, after all, have been speech, but its 'soft whisper' is as naturalistic as the other two, and to the secular ear has a conspiratorial or even sexy flavour. Not one of these three major modern translations manages to suggest an inherent peculiarity about the event that might indicate a quite *new* kind of experience. Indeed, it is precisely that oddity or paradox in the original text that the modern translators, themselves responding to the unstated assumptions of the scientific revolution, found either untranslatable, or, more probably, unacceptable. Since our distinctions between 'inner' and 'outer' are un-biblical categories (so the argument appears to run) we can only be 'modern' by treating the whole story at one level: it must be made *either* miraculous *or* natural. The modern mind cannot have an event that does not fit snugly into one of the two categories. Yet such rationalism would seem to strike right at the heart of the original story. Though no record survives of the seventeenth-century translators' attitude to this particular passage, we know from the notes of John Bois, who was both a translator and a member of the final revision committee for part of the New Testament, that he and his committee were careful in general to preserve textual ambiguity. Of the word 'praise', which might refer either to Jesus or the church members, in I Peter i, 7, he comments, 'We have not thought that the indefinite sense ought to be defined.'[9] In this, the King James translators may well have had an eye on the rival Catholic translators of the English *Rheims* and *Douai* Bibles (New and Old Testaments respectively) who had attacked the Protestants for mollifying hard places, whereas they themselves, they claimed, 'religiously keep them word for word, and point for point, for fear of missing or restraining the sense of the holy Ghost to our phantasie . . .'[10] Protestant and Catholic translators alike in the seventeenth century were under no doubt that oddities in the Hebrew or Greek texts were there for a divinely ordained purpose.[11] In contrast, Professor Kenneth Grayston, one of the translators of the *New English Bible*, has described their brief in terms very similar to those set forth by the *Good News* panel:

We have conceived our task to be that of understanding the original as precisely as we could (using all available aids) and then saying again in our native idiom what we believed the author to be saying in his.

'And so,' he continues, 'in equivocal passages, the translators had to come off the fence and say "we think it means this". In ambiguous passages they had to write out the meaning plainly, and in obscure passages, to refrain from reproducing nonsense in translation.'[12] Interestingly, the possibility that something original and altogether new in human experience might be emerging into words in this (or similar) 'ambiguous' passages is not one that Grayston is altogether blind to. Rather, he firmly shuts his eyes to it. That the language of 'Spenser, Sidney, Hooker, Marlowe and Shakespeare' was a richer denser thing than his own he freely admits – but the poetic density of the *Authorized Version* is attributable not to a greater richness of *content*, but to an altogether different and apparently separable thing he calls 'style':

> The *New English Bible* does not compete with the *Authorized Version*, certainly not in language and style: this is not a period of great writers equal to Spenser, Sidney, Hooker, Marlowe and Shakespeare. Modern English, it seems to me, is slack instead of taut, verbose and not concise, infested with this month's cliché, no longer the language of a proud and energetic English people, but an international means of communication. And 'means of communication' gives the game away: it seems to me a repository for the bad habits of foreigners speaking English. This is how we must speak if people are to listen and grasp what we say.[13]

This belief that religious experience, and the historic record of mankind's deepest questionings and insights, can only be adequately described today in the slack, verbose and cliché-ridden language of international communication would be disconcerting if it were not – by Grayston's own admission – so evidently self-defeating. How far it is possible, in the words of the *Good News Bible*'s Preface, 'to use language that is natural, clear, simple, and unambiguous', when the Bible is *not about* things that are natural, clear, simple, and unambiguous? or for the linguistically-enfeebled modern theologians struggling on the *New English Bible* to 'write out the meaning plainly' of what to the taut and concise translators of the seventeenth century was essentially ambiguous and obscure? The answer – in so far as Grayston seems to perceive that this question exists – appears to be 'that the *Authorized Version* was a translation made by men who knew far less than we know'[14]: in short, a matter of the textual and archeological progress correctly supposed by our mythical but puzzled observer on the Peking omnibus. Yet in this instance Grayston's hermeneutical confidence hardly satisfies.

What is quite clear is that the paradoxical 'voice of thin silence', which is the true manifestation of Yahweh, does not belong to the same associative 'set' as earthquakes and the rest. Ancient Hebrew, we are told, had no word for (and therefore no concept of) 'nature': the normal progression of the seasons were seen as being as much the result of God's direct action as the whirlwind that whisked Elijah to heaven.[15] As a result there was no concept of 'the miraculous' either. The relationship between man and his environment was fundamentally different.[16] Yet it is nevertheless clear that there is an essential discontinuity between the old cyclical world of nature–mysticism or 'primal participation' (as expressed in the cult of Baal) and the world of meaningful change, and therefore of History, into which Yahweh was perceived as bringing his people.[17] Let us concentrate on this ambiguous discontinuity for a moment.

The account of Elijah's experiences on Horeb is given a very specific and apparently historical setting. After the rout and slaughter of the prophets of Baal, Jezebel the Queen has threatened his life, and Elijah, believing himself to be the sole survivor of the faithful, has fled to Horeb. The full force of the dramatic disconfirmation that follows depends on our recognizing that Horeb is traditionally associated with Sinai, the 'mountain of the Lord', where Moses himself had encountered God before the burning bush. Elijah had come to Horeb with certain expectations precisely because of that sense of history that was already, in Israel, distinctively the mark of men of God. Before the assembled prophets of Baal he had already vindicated Yahweh in pyrotechnics – proving once again the power of the God who had traditionally manifested himself by fire.[18] Now he had come to receive the divine revelation for which he believed he had been preparing himself. What followed was the more unexpected. Paradoxically, his notion of Yahweh was disconfirmed by a greater display of natural violence than any yet. But Yahweh is *not* a fire God. His presence, when at last it is revealed, is experienced as something mysteriously apart from the world of natural phenomena that had been in such spectacular convulsions. Elijah's own categories are overthrown. What comes is a simple question: 'What doest thou here, Elijah?' He had come expecting one thing and found another – entirely different. To begin with, his own report of the situation turns out to be untrue: there are, apparently, yet seven thousand in Israel who have not bowed the knee to Baal.[19] Elijah is told to return and organize what amounts to two separate *coups d'état*. Hazael is to be made king of Syria, and Jehu King of Israel. History is yet again to be shaped by revelation, just as long before, Moses had been sent back from Horeb by God to lead his people out of Egypt. Finally – and ominously – Elijah is ordered to appoint his own successor.

At every level the ambiguous discontinuity persists. Any attempt at 'explaining' the contrast between the fire and the 'voice of thin silence' is in danger of losing that sense of an immediate but unstated connection between the two that is emphasized even by the very act of dissociation. Yahweh is not a fire God – nor one of winds and earthquakes – yet from whom, if not from him, did these things come? Moreover, what about those modern categories in which, it is true, we are culturally conditioned to think? Are we to interpret Elijah's experience as a 'miracle' (which would, for instance, link it even more closely with the parallel story of Moses and the burning bush (Exodus iii, 1–17), associated with the same place) or are we to understand it as a 'vision' (in the same category, perhaps, as Isaiah's vision of the Lord in the Temple when he, too, is purged by fire (Isaiah vi))? Can we, instead, dispense with the supernatural altogether, as the modern translators unanimously seem to believe, and interpret it as soft whispers in the night, or the wind on the heath? The Hebrew holds us poised at every level between two different kinds of event that cannot, and *must* not, be told in any other way without destroying the meaning – just as Kierkegaard discovered in *Fear and Trembling* that the story of Abraham and Isaac could not be 'interpreted' and re-told. The whole effect of Elijah's mysterious experience seems to be to deny, *and* simultaneously affirm, certain connections. Thus Yahweh *is*, and *is not*, a God of natural phenomena (a paradox more familiar under the theological terms 'immanence' and 'transcendence'); revelation is both 'miraculous' and 'natural'; God is concerned with both the individual and the shaping of history. The story seems to insist that at each level these two modes are both completely discontinuous and yet inseparable.

We could go on; the passage is a rich and fascinating one which as we shall see has attracted many commentators through the ages, but another problem is beginning to intrude itself into our investigation. Something rather strange seems to have happened to the premises from which we started. The modern translators and the Bible Society, confident of understanding 'correctly the meaning of the original' text, have in fact shown very little interest in the *literal* sense of the Bible with its attendant complexity and resonances, and have instead chosen quite blatantly interpretative paraphrases which, it appears, they feel are more cultur-ally acceptable to modern sensibilities. Whatever 'the truth of the biblical revelation' may be, it is clear, at least from this passage, that for the Bible Society it does *not* reside in the text itself, but in a 'theology' which is implicitly variable and conditioned by the spirit of the age. Moreover, Caird's account of the translators' dilemma between the risks of modernizing and archaizing, common-sense as it may sound, begins to look oddly spurious. Of the interpretations of the Elijah story we have been looking at, *which*, after all, is the 'modern' and which the 'archaic'? We may, I think, safely assume that the recent translators believed they were 'modernizing' the still small voice, though they certainly did not 'read the Bible as though it were contemporary literature' – which, though Grayston seems to have missed the fact, is typically problematic, obscure, and attentive to the exact nuances of words. However, the inter-pretation of the passage just suggested, centering specifically on the ver-bal ambiguity of the voice of thin silence, is unquestionably twentieth-century in its concepts, its critical tools, and in the kind of questions it asks of the text. Yet so far from 'ignoring the culture gap of many cen-turies', it is precisely the nature of that gap which is of central inerest to our own historically-minded age.

Even a brief historical survey would reveal how utterly different modern discussions of a text such as this would be from those of the past. We know, for instance, that, following anterior hints in the Old Testa-ment, for the New Testament writers – possibly for Jesus himself – Elijah was seen as the forerunner of the Messiah. Mark ix, 12–13 records Jesus as saying 'How is it that the scriptures say of the Son of Man that he is to endure great sufferings and to be treated with contempt? I tell you, Elijah has already come and they have worked their will upon him, as the scriptures say of him.'[20] Since, we are told, he was taken up into heaven by a whirlwind,[21] Elijah by tradition belonged, with Melchizedek, to the select company of those who had not tasted death.[22] It was therefore ap-propriate that his reappearance should herald the coming of the Messiah.[23] So much was common legend – rather along the lines of the mediaeval English story that King Arthur sleeps at Avalon, waiting to return in his country's direst hour of need. Jesus's coda, 'as the scriptures say . . .' does not, however, appear to refer to this, but to Elijah's suffering and rejection. Now there is no prophecy of Elijah being rejected on his return in either the Old Testament, or, so far as is known, in the Jewish tradition as a whole.[24] The sole reference to his suffering and rejection is this story in I Kings xix. The main source of the 'suffering servant' tradition in the New Testament applied specifically to the Messiah is, of course, Isaiah liii (though whether it carried that connotation in the Old Testament context is a matter of debate). What appears to have happened, therefore, is that Jesus (or the gospel writer)[25] has taken Elijah as the 'type' of the servant of God, or prophet – and even, according to some suggestions, the whole people of Israel themselves, who are drawn into the prophecy in Isaiah. Whether other writings, now missing, or an oral tradition made these links in greater detail we can only conjecture, but from examples elsewhere it is perfectly possible. What we can say is that the New Testament writers had the best authority – that of Jesus himself – for making this double association of Elijah with the Messiah, and with the suffering servant of God.

The key phrase is that twice-repeated 'as the scriptures say . . .' The long and powerful process of scripture making and interpretation which we call by the Hebrew name of 'midrash' was a living tradition in New Testament times[26] and Jesus himself seems to have been the midrashist in his development of the Elijah story. Yet though he seems to have been referring specifically to I Kings xix the 'voice of thin silence' plays no part in this particular exegesis. Nor, in the immense elaboration of typology that followed with the church Fathers and continued through mediaeval Europe to the Renaissance and later, is there a significant shift of interest towards the natural phenomena of the story and the contrast with the 'voice'[27]. Augustine, it is true, based his elaborate typological superstructures upon the most minute and careful respect for the text as the Word of God. As his most recent biographer describes the process:

> The exegete . . . will train himself to listen for the single hidden 'will' that expressed itself in the deliberate selection of every word of the text: for in a sacred text, 'everything was said exactly as it needed to be said.' Thus the first question he must ask is not 'what', 'what was the exact nature of this particular religious practice in the ancient Near East?' but '*why*?' – 'why does this incident, this word and no other, occur at just this moment in the interminable monologue of God; and so, what aspect of His deeper message does it communicate?' Like the child who asked the basic question: 'Mummy, *why* is a cow?' Augustine will run through the text of the Bible in such a way that every sermon is punctuated by 'Quare . . . quare . . . quare . . .' 'Why? . . . why? . . . why?'[28]

Yet Augustine's close questioning of the actual words of scripture does not reveal that he is conscious of a special significance in the contrast between the natural violence and the theophany on Horeb. Following the New Testament and the established Patristic tradition he sees Elijah's forty-day fast and the revelation on Horeb as types of Christ's in the wilderness.[29] The earthquake, the wind, and the fire are of little significance in themselves to early commentators, though not all sense of the curious dichotomy of the story is lost. In the sixteenth century we find St John of the Cross taking the contrast of violence and stillness as a type of the duality of the *logos* itself.[30] When, however, we move on to the eighteenth century we find an interesting shift. The popular biblical commentaries are as firmly typological[31] as ever, but, as befits an age of science, the centre of attention has moved dramatically towards the violence of nature and the contrast with the still small voice. Thus in the *Royal Bible* of 1761 Dr Leonard Howard explains that '*after the fire*, that is, after the storms, thunders, lightnings, and earthquakes, which attended the promulgation of the Law; *came a still small voice*, that is, the gospel, wherein God spoke to us by his son, with the greatest lenity and sweetness, using the most convincing arguments, and the most soft and gentle persuasions'. The *Royal Bible* is something of a *locus classicus* among eighteenth-century family Bibles – no less than 20 editions of it were produced between 1785 and 1800. It is hardly surprising that as late as 1806, we find Mrs Trimmer, that formidable engine of the S.P.C.K. Tract Society, apparently echoing Howard, even to the phraseology:

The LORD'S *speaking in a still small voice*, was a sign that He was graciously disposed to show lenity and forbearance towards the idolatrous people of Israel, and to preserve the land of Israel for those who had not yet bowed the knee to Baal.[32]

Similarly, to take a contemporary example from Germany – the main centre of biblical scholarship in the eighteenth century – even Herder[33], while he draws slightly different conclusions in detail, shares the new emphasis:

The vision would seem designed to teach the Prophet, who, in his fiery zeal for reformation, would change everything by stormy violence, the gentle movements of God's providence, and to exhibit the mildness and longsuffering, of which in the passage above given, the voice spoke to Moses.[34]

Not until the second quarter of the nineteenth century do we find the incident seen in terms of the relationship between 'nature' and 'spirit'. For

John Keble, probably the most ardent Wordsworthian of his generation, the Elijah story is still a source of imagery, but the terms of
reference have been subtly transformed:

> The raging Fire, the roaring Wind,
> Thy boundless power display;
> But in the gentler breeze we find
> Thy spirit's viewless way.[35]

The midrashic process lives on in devotional verse. This looks extraordinarily like the 'gentle breeze' of the *Jerusalem Bible*, but whether or
not Keble was influenced here by the Vulgate, it is not of course an
entirely safe assumption that Keble intended his breeze as a *paraphrase*
of 'the still small voice'. As we have seen, the traditional verbal associations of 'wind' and 'spirit' make the second two lines into a familiar
typological pun – now combined with a nineteenth-century Wordsworthian feeling for the awesome sublimities of nature. Once again, a
shift in sensibility transforms interpretation. In Caird's terminology
Keble is doing what he so often did and 'archaising' the biblical passage
– consciously looking for its mediaeval Catholic resonances.[36] Yet the
result could only be nineteenth-century. Ostensibly he is doing no
more than versifying the familiar typology with the now commonplace
eighteenth-century interest in the natural side of the revelation: the
'gentler breeze' is the more appropriate metaphor for divine 'inspiration' (to use the parallel Latin pun) than earthquakes and storms. But
the emphasis is not between 'natural' and 'supernatural', but on what
Keble's contemporary, Carlyle, was to call 'Natural Supernaturalism'[37]: both are works of God; the supernatural is latent or immanent in the manifestation of nature.[38] In thus making explicit the
implicit typology of the earlier eighteenth-century commentators
Keble is, however, making a point that is now general rather than
specific – applicable not just to a single antitype in the New Testament, but to the universal action of God everywhere. In other words,
for Keble the image has become essentially *symbolic* rather than
typological in the traditional sense.

We could pursue the changing fashions of biblical commentary into
our own century, but so far from giving us an authoritative reading,
they would in fact be of less and less assistance. The standard English
commentaries of the twentieth century are notable mainly for their
reluctance to deal with the central linguistic oddity of the text. Lacking
confidence in the powers of either typology or historical criticism to

deal adequately with the story, they succeed mainly in conveying a profound methodological uneasiness. J. Robinson may be cited as typical:

In the cave at Horeb all the great natural forces which were associated with the exodus tradition passed by Elijah, but the Lord was not in them. They were instruments God had used in the past, but not essential elements in his character. After the symbols of power came a *low murmuring sound*. The Revised Standard Version had kept the well-known translation, 'a still small voice'. *Sound* has a wider range of meaning than voice. We are not told whether or not the *sound* conveyed meaning, but the general point is clear. The God who had revealed himself in the past in wonders and displays of power sought also to reveal himself and his purposes through the minds and personalities of men who were willing to be his servants.[39]

What Hans Frei has aptly called 'the eclipse of biblical narrative', from the combined pressures of historical criticism and doctrinal relativity, has meant that there is now no agreed hermeneutic procedure for such ambiguously miraculous accounts.[40] If corroboration were needed for the soundness of Coleridge's instinctive hesitation over his relationship to biblical texts, we have it here. Even the most intense and detailed textual study does nothing to provide common ground if the pre-suppositions are sufficiently divergent. Maurice Wiles has cited the example of a seventeenth-century English clergyman's attitude towards his son's untimely death (which he saw as a punishment for his own excessive fondness for chess) as evidence for 'changes so profound as to transform Christianity from time to time into almost a different religion from what it was before';[41] now, as we have seen, even for the Bible Society the text of the Bible is culturally dependent. The narratives of the past remain for us strangely enigmatic. If to 'modernize' is to embrace cultural relativity; to 'archaize' is not to choose stability, but merely to opt for a particular (apparently no less culturally variable) reading of history.

Yet the idea of a historical reality somewhere within the enigmatic language of biblical narrative continues to haunt us. The 'principle of analogy' beloved of Higher Critics – the principle that nothing should be believed to have happened in the past of a kind which is never experienced in the present – logically presupposes, *somewhere*, a verifiable historical reality. The mere fact that Elijah found his experience so disconfirming suggests he did not make it up. For some, it is enough that such a reality should exist – however provisionally unrecoverable. Dennis Nineham has castigated as 'saving the appearances' the arguments of those who would claim that if the biblical events could be reconstructed 'as they actually happened' they would prove to have a privileged religious status, and to be religiously revealing and illuminating in a unique way.[42] 'What is happening to theology today', he writes, 'is that it is just becoming aware of what some of the important habitual assumptions of earlier theologians were, and just how contingent, and even arbitrary, they appear from our perspective, once we have isolated them.'[43] Yet though Nineham is properly critical of the assumptions behind over-confident and speculative reconstructions by various schools of historical critics, one can see in his own conclusions the kind of thinking evident in the recent translators' attempts to evade the central ambiguity of the Elijah story:

> Since our totality is so different from that of the New Testament and of most of our Christian predecessors, it may be questioned whether the idea of a divine intervention of the sort in question is not so alien to it that there is no possible way of relating it to the cultural context which will be intelligible to a large proportion of educated people today.[44]

Elaborating this point in the context of the New Tesament writings, he adds:

> I do not mean to suggest of course that any of them (the biblical writers) deliberately sat down and made up these stories as answers to consciously formulated questions. Their stories are unselfconscious expressions of the *corporate* Christian experience of Christianity as it developed during the period after his lifetime, often independently in different Christian centres. For that reason we should not expect in such stories the sort of consistency appropriate to a unified dogmatic theory, or even a coherent attempt to explain rationally the workings of an objective divine intervention . . . we should accept them as stories – imaginative objectifications of the various types of release and freedom their respective authors felt.[45]

This dismissal of the question of 'historical fact' behind the narrative to secondary place is clearly a popular strategy in the present climate of thought. It echoes warnings by both Frei and Caird against confusing 'history-likeness' with historical 'fact', and an over-concentration on the referential aspects of history. Yet, for all its persuasiveness, there are elements here in Nineham's argument that must give us pause. *'Das Volk dichtet'*. The argument is one that, in essence, takes us back aesthetically to Herder and theologically to Schleiermacher.

However is it *really* true, for instance, that St John's Gospel or the Book of Revelation are 'unselfconscious expressions of corporate Christian experience'? Anyone who has read Austin Farrer's fascinating study of the sophisticated image-patterns of the Apocalypse[46] will find this Herderian notion of unselfconscious folk-art distinctly unconvincing. But the inaccuracies of sweeping generalization are, in a sense, easy targets, and may even prevent us from detecting a further implication more difficult to reject precisely because it operates at a level where no evidence of the kind Farrer presents can be brought to bear. Here, in this passage from Nineham, it presents itself as a kind of illegitimate omniscience: the assumption that as twentieth-century critical readers we can *understand* the 'unselfconscious expressions' of the faith of an earlier age, and are capable of sorting the wheat from the chaff; the kerygma from its period wrapping: 'We should not expect in such stories the sort of consistency appropriate to a unified dogmatic theory . . .' – in short, that we can understand the *intentions* of the biblical writers, both conscious and unconscious, and comprehend (in a way they could not) the limitations of their own mental set.

The argument that the biblical writers were unsophisticated 'peasants' (a word suitably loaded with cultural connotations from a quite different social and geographical context) has of course roots as far back as the middle of the eighteenth century in historical critics such as Gesenius, Lessing, and Eichhorn, and in spite of Herder and a whole tradition of literary critics from Blake and Coleridge to Farrer who have given evidence of the complex literary structure of the Bible, it has too frequently been assumed.

Another contemporary biblical scholar in a recent public discussion dismissed a certain theory about the structure of St Mark's Gospel on the grounds that 'it would be ridiculous to look for that kind of literary sophistication among first-century Galilean peasants . . .'[47] When challenged as to his evidence, he was forced to admit that we know very little of the general level of literary sophistication among first-century Galilean peasants except from the gospels – and the complex literary tradition behind them in the shape of the Old Testament and its associated writings. This is a point of which Caird is apparently very conscious:

There is, then, an accumulation of evidence that the biblical writers were not only skilful handlers of words (which is obvious) but were also well aware of the nature of their tools. Yet this conclusion would have been challenged by many Old and New Testament scholars who, whatever their differences of approach, were agreed about one thing: that biblical man was pre-scientific and therefore naïve, that he inhabited a mythical world, and that his intellectual development was at the stage which some of them designated 'the mythopoeic mind'.[48]

Yet, though he scrupulously avoids patronizing the biblical writers in the way that Nineham does, Caird, in his fascinating account of current biblical scholarship, is not free of another kind of omniscience — perhaps more dangerous because clearly unconscious. At first sight the argument for the superiority of modern knowledge looks unimpeachable:

An eighteenth-century artist's reconstruction of the temple of Solomon looked very much like Blenheim Palace; and if today we know better than this, it is because the ground-plans of several other ancient temples have in the meantime been excavated.[49]

No one would doubt that archaeology has contributed greatly to our knowledge of near-Eastern temples, but resemblances to Blenheim are a matter of façades, not ground-plans. It is also worth noting, in passing, that there is some evidence to suggest that the detailing of Blenheim Palace (the work not of Vanbrugh, but of two Huguenot carvers) was directly influenced by contemporary reconstructions of Solomon's Temple. The Lion heads on the kitchen court gate, for example, seem to be straight from one of Hollar's engravings of the Temple, which were, in turn, based on the conjectures of Juan Bautista Villalpando, a Portuguese Jesuit whose prints were widely used in the eighteenth century in both Catholic and Protestant Bibles.[50] If we compare John Martin's[51] early nineteenth-century reconstructions of biblical architecture with those of the eighteenth century what we find is less a development of knowledge than of architectural *fashion*. Martin's megalithic orientalism is as unmistakably 'romantic' and nineteenth-century as Vanbrugh's baroque is eighteenth. Similarly, Sir Arthur Evans's reconstructions of Knossus in Crete reveal to us as much about Evans's own Edwardian taste and his British imperial assumptions about the functions of the royal palace as they do about any historical Cretan King. We are all familiar with the way in which photographs of 1930s 'Roman' plays of Shakespeare instantly suggest to us their twentieth-century period as much as their classical: 1930s 'Roman' is unmistakably different from 1960s 'Roman' — and doubtless from 1990s 'Roman' as well. No doubt our twentieth-century reconstructions of ancient palaces and temples will betray their 'period' and provenance equally unmistakably to twenty-first-century scholars.[52] In other words, *any* act of historical interpretation is conditioned not merely by the available evidence from the period in question, but also by the unconscious assumptions and the cultural context of the period when the interpretation is made. As George Steiner has shown[53] – and our own examples confirmed – this is as true for language and literature as it is for architecture or costume.

Since Kant we have been accustomed to the idea that we cannot know the world apart from the perspective of the knower. The Kantian dialectic would similarly seem to imply that we cannot know the world of the past from an objective standpoint either – and it is not clear what such 'perspectiveless' knowledge might look like. Yet, as Kant also interestingly argues, we are constantly driven by reason itself to attempt the impossible[54] and we aspire to truths that are objective and universal. Certainly we need some such explanation for the extraordinary power and persistence of the notion that, if properly presented, the 'facts' of history (or anything else) will 'speak for themselves'. Take, for instance, the following quotation from Northrop Frye (who should surely know better), written in the context of biblical scholarship, but clearly intended as a general maxim:

> The ideal of the scholar is to convey what he knows as clearly and fully as he can: he lays down his hand and remains dummy, so to speak, while the reader plays it.[55]

Whatever he may have intended, the bridge metaphor inescapably implies the passive Lockeian and empiricist model of knowledge as a series of printed playing-cards of fixed and clearly identifiable value. Thus, by metaphorically assuming a particular epistemology involving a clear separation between 'facts' (the playing-cards) and 'interpretation' (how they are played) Frye has already begged the real question of 'what he knows'. Perception is inseparable from interpretation; but interpretation without common ground in that which is to be interpreted is meaningless. The quest for historical fact has led to the place we might least expect: the ideological battleground of modern epistemology.

Perhaps it is hardly surprising that the strategies that are currently advocated for dealing with this problem seem to raise more difficulties than they solve. Nineham, for instance, draws a close analogy between the problems of the biblical and literary critic, quoting Lionel Trilling from *The Liberal Imagination* on the vexed question of 'What is the real poem?' — adding his own bracketed letters for reference:

Is it (a) the poem we now perceive? Is it (b) the poem the author consciously intended? Is it (c) the poem the author intended and his first readers read? Well, it is all these things, depending on the state of our knowledge. But in addition the poem is (d) the poem as it has existed in history, as it has lived its life from Then to Now, as it is (e) a thing which submits itself to one kind of perception in one age and (f) another kind of perception in another age, as it (g) exerts in each age a different kind of power. This makes it a thing we can never wholly understand — other things too, of course, help to make it that — and the mystery, the unreachable part of the poem, is one of its . . . elements.[56]

The analogy is a revealing one. It implicitly assumes, for example, that biblical language is essentially 'poetic' and therefore best understood through principles derived from literary criticism.[57] It is also explicit about what Nineham apparently takes to be the central critical principle. 'The modern biblical critic', he writes, 'is concerned almost exclusively with (b) and (c) and only with the others so far as they throw light on these.' The conclusion which seems to follow from this is, curiously, that 'there is nothing properly described as "*the* meaning" of the Bible . . .'[58] However, this analogy between religious and poetic language will be a main theme of later chapters; what concerns us here is the idea that 'intention' is the key to understanding the Bible. This view, to be found even as early as Schleiermacher, is not uncommon. Caird, similarly, dismisses Augustine's elaborate allegorical interpretations of Jesus's parables by an appeal not to historical fact, but to authorial intention. 'Most modern readers', he writes, 'would agree with Dodd that this farrago bears no relationship to the *real meaning* of the parable . . . To allegorise is to impose on a story hidden meanings *which the original author neither intended nor envisaged* . . . Here, as in all questions of meaning, *the intention of the author* or speaker is paramount.' (my italics)[59]

In spite of the disagreement between Caird and Nineham over the question of the 'real meaning' or relative literary sophistication of their sources, both critics appear to be united in their agreement to turn away from the quest for historical 'fact' behind the biblical narratives in favour of this search for the authors' intentions. This interpretative method, originating in the early nineteenth century with Friedrich Ast and F. A. Wolf,[60] developing into Schleiermacher and Dilthey's quest for a harmony between the spirit of the author and the reader, has been sharply attacked by, for instance, Paul Ricoeur, who describes it as 'a romantic and psychologising conception of hermeneutics'.[61] It does not appear to occur to Caird that his confidence that he has special insight into the mind of Jesus, denied to, say, Augustine or even apparently the Apostles, is a claim to privileged status far more problematic than that of any historical critic; just as it did not occur to Nineham that his judgement on the unselfconscious expressions of the early Christians involved a similar unsubstantiated claim to understand them better than they understood themselves. To neither does the suspicion apparently occur that their strategy is simply a way of shifting the problem to a different place, rather than solving it. The idea that the certainties that had eluded them in the quest for 'what really happened' could be rediscovered after all by transposing the question to 'what did they *intend*' simply compounds the epistemological problem.

Like Nineham's idea of an 'unselfconscious' corporate authorship creating the New Testament, Caird's idea of a conscious authorial intention is open to criticism both on factual and theoretical grounds. For instance, the evidence is by no means clear that the New Testament authors did *not* 'intend or envisage' an allegorical interpretation of their work.[62] Allegory was a normal part of the midrashic mode of thought in first-century Palestine[63] – and, as we have seen in the specific case of the Elijah story, very probably a part of Jesus's own mental set. At least one modern critic, Birger Gerhardsson, has claimed a quasi-allegorical interpretation from the parable of the Good Samaritan.[64] Similarly (but presumably with the benefit of midrashic hindsight) it seems likely that in the parable of the wicked tenants the reason why the son is killed *outside* the vineyard in Matthew's and Luke's Gospels, rather than on the spot, inside, as in Mark, is that Golgotha was *outside* Jerusalem.[65] So far from being a later personal obsession of Augustine, allegorical interpretation has roots in pre-biblical Babylonian and Egyptian hermeneutics, and, as we have seen, lasts until well on into the nineteenth century.[66] When the King James' translators recorded a sharp disagreement with one of the their number, Andrew Downes (Kings' Professor and lecturer in Greek at St John's College, Cambridge) over 'the interpretation of Augustine . . . concerning the types and figures' of a certain passage, they are not questioning the principle, but only its applicability in that particular instance.[67]

Behind such instances lies a more general point: that just as the content of the Bible has always been a matter of interpretative selection, so that principle of interpretation has historically been based upon criteria of a 'spiritual allegorical sense' rather than upon any modern notion of 'history'. Thus the Old Testament was itself created by 'hermeneutical fiat' out of the Jewish Torah, and (as Frank Kermode puts it):

... as the Old Testament signified the New, so the New Testament signified the Church, which alone had the power to determine its spiritual sense. For the early fifteenth century theologian, Gerson, the spiritual sense so authorized was the true literal sense; there was no appeal against the Church's judgment that could be based on the text itself. So the literal truth of the New Testament could in its turn be superseded.[68]

Ever since W. K. Wimsatt's seminal essay on 'The Intentional Fallacy'[69] we have learned to be wary of the idea that knowledge of an author's 'intention' – even were this possible in a world where we create fictions in our lives as well as in books – would necessarily clarify what is going on in a particular work. A writer may well write, as we say, 'better than he knew'. Did Shakespeare 'intend' a theory of Continental Drift in *Henry IV* Part 2, or 'believe' in a Romantic theory of the imagination in *Midsummer Night's Dream*?[70] Was Milton in *Paradise Lost*, as Blake claimed, 'of the Devil's party without knowing it'?[71] Are *Gulliver's Travels* merely an effective piece of early eighteenth-century political satire (as they were presumably 'intended') or are they universal literature? A writer may well intend one thing, and, by common consent, achieve quite another.

In short, the notion of intention, whether conscious (as assumed by Caird) or unconscious (as supposed by Nineham) looks suspiciously like an internal displacement of our old friend the unmediated 'historical fact'. In each case the assumption is fundamentally the same: a version of what Karl Popper has termed 'methodological essentialism': that is 'the view . . . that it is the task of pure knowledge or "science" to discover and describe the true nature of things, that is, their hidden reality or essence'.[72] In this it is the linguistic equivalent of the pre-Kantian (or even, pre-Lockeian) philosophies.[73] The principle assumes the possibility of knowledge of 'things-in-themselves' which, like Northrop Frye's playing-card facts, will 'speak for themselves' once they have been laid bare by the march of scholarship. This is the kind of belief that underlay the efforts of the eighteenth-century historical critics like Johann Philip Gabler, who argued in his

Altdorf inaugural lecture of 1787 that 'dogmatic theology' had to await the definitive results of the completely historical investigations of 'biblical theology' before it could undertake its own evaluative work.[74] This quest for historical certainty in the eighteenth and nineteenth centuries was in itself partially the result of an earlier failure (especially in England) to give theology the same kind of external certainties as those apparently enjoyed by the natural sciences in the age of the Royal Society and of Newton.[75] In 1668 John Wilkins, then Dean of Ripon and a Fellow of the Royal Society, as a 'digression' in his *Essay Towards a Real Character and a Philosophical Language* offers an exact reconstruction of Noah's Ark from the information and dimensions given in Genesis vi–viii, showing that it was seaworthy and would hold all the animals then known and later discovered plus precisely the right amount of foodstuffs – including an appropriate surplus of sheep (1888 all told) to feed all the carnivores for the forty day voyage. Perhaps even more dramatic were the efforts of John Craig, a mathematician and later prebendary of Salisbury, whose *Theologicae Christianae Principia Mathematica*, 1699, presented the whole of Christian doctrine as a series of *a priori* mathematical propositions reasoned from first principles. In the early years of the eighteenth century there had been a revival of more orthodox natural theology in the form of scientifically presented arguments from design, such as the botanist John Ray's *Wisdom of God in the Creation* (1701) and William Derham's *Physico-Theology* (1713) and *Astro-Theology* (1715) – both were Anglican clergymen and Fellows of the Royal Society. Arguments from design were to remain a flourishing theological tradition in England throughout the century, reaching a climax anachronistically late with William Paley's best-sellers *Evidences of Christianity* (1794), and *Natural Theology* (1802) – which were to earn the scorn of that arch-methodological nominalist, Samuel Taylor Coleridge.[76]

Yet, to be fair, neither Caird nor Nineham, though they are unable to shake themselves free from some of its unconscious assumptions, are out-and-out methodological essentialists. Both, indeed, take care to be on their guard against its worst excesses. It is, rather, as if, like many of their contemporaries, they have not realized fully the ramifications of the position they are consciously rejecting – that the progressive shifting of the theological essentialists' quest for firm ground from 'external' to 'internal', from the natural science of Ray and Derham to the 'science' of history advocated by men like Gabler, and finally to that of psychology or even anthropology, reflects the gradual realization that (as we have seen) the uncertainty and relativity they sought to evade are an integral part of scholarly methodology. As Newman was among the first to recognize in his *Grammar of Assent* (1870), the kind of certainty sought consciously or unconsciously by the essentialists, is not to be found by the human intellect.

Yet this inherent uncertainty of all recorded experience has been found to point towards some unexpected conclusions. Many critics would be happy to accept the gist of George Steiner's dictum, if not its slightly mannered phraseology, that:

The meaning of a word or sentence uttered in the past is no single event or sharply defined network of events. It is a recreative selection made according to hunches or principles which are more or less informed, more or less astute and comprehensive. The illocutionary force of any past statement is diffused in a complex pragmatic field which surrounds the lexical core.[77]

Beyond such a balanced sense of word and historical context against reader and contemporary context there lurks, however, a yet more iconoclastic school of criticism:

. . . a text is not a line of words releasing a single "theological" meaning (the "message" of the Author-God) but a multi-dimensional space in which a variety of writings, none of them original, blend and clash. The text is a tissue of quotations drawn from the innumerable centres of culture.[78]

What Julia Kristeva has called the 'intertexuality' of any piece of writing encloses it within a sealed system from which the possibility of the 'new' is seemingly excluded by definition. As his carefully-chosen metaphor of theology indicates, Roland Barthes is fully alive to the hermeneutical consequences of his proclaimed 'death of the author':

Once the author is removed, the claim to decipher a text becomes quite futile. To give a text an Author is to impose a limit on that text, to furnish it with a final signified, to close the writing . . . literature (it would be better from now on to say *writing*), by refusing to assign a "secret", an ultimate meaning, to the text (and to the world as text), liberates what may be called an anti-theological activity, an activity that is truly revolutionary since to refuse to fix meaning is, in the end, to refuse God and his hypostases – reason, science, law.[79]

Before we read this as a *reductio ad absurdum* – or the ultimate fate prepared for those who would impiously transpose the historical 'fact' of the Bible into authorial 'intention' – there is in this descent into the pit of endless subjectivity a curious corollary. Barthes's use of the term 'theological' in this context is, in one sense, no more than a metaphor for *any* externally imposed reading. Yet the corollary seems to be that without any such externally imposed principles of interpretation 'meaning' itself becomes so elusive and problematic as to slide away into a welter of endless possibility. The Barthesian flux of meaning can, we notice, only be defined in negative terms: as 'an anti-theological activity'. Meaning is thus seen in terms of *choice*, that is, the selection of one reading over another on rational criteria provided by the interpretative schemata of science or of law (whether natural or human). All meaning is, in short, Barthes seems to imply, the creation of what we bring to the text. If we push it back far enough, beyond the practical dictates of reason, science or law, we encounter only Humian scepticism or metaphysics – in other words, God. 'Meaning' is ultimately guaranteed by God. We do not need proofs of God; the concept of 'proof' is itself meaningless without God. Given these premises, Barthes is perhaps right, therefore, to insist however backhandedly that the *creation of meaning* is the central theological activity. The principle of intertextuality, the postulate mentioned above that all writing (indeed, as we shall see in a later chapter, *all* language) exists within a closed-circle of previous meanings, is, therefore, an integral part of his attack on 'theology'. The idea of the new is an inherent quality of the divine prerogative to which Barthes here stands so resolutely opposed.

In case so radical a notion as this is lost by inversion, Barthes elsewhere, in a discussion of the story of wrestling Jacob (Genesis xxxii, 22–32), restates it in positive form:

By marking Jacob (Israel), God (or the Narrative) permits an analogical development of meaning, creates the formal operational conditions of a new 'language', the election of Israel being its 'message'. God is a logothete, the founder of a language, and Jacob is here a 'morpheme' of the new language.[80]

By the equivalent reasoning, it is God, the Barthesian logothete, who, in challenging Elijah on Horeb, breaks into the closed-circle of nature to bring new language out of the 'friction' between the multiple 'intelligibilities' of the earthquake, the wind, the fire, and the still small voice. Barthes's God, (that Great Author in the Sky) may seemingly have more in common with Blake's Urizen than Elijah's Yahweh, but He is still recognizably the originator of the 'Word', who brings meaning out of chaos.

From opposite poles, therefore, somewhat unexpectedly, Barthes and Newman join hands. The problem of hermeneutics is not one peculiar to theology – though the personal demands of religious belief may for some make the questions of certainty more problematic. It is a dilemma that in one form or another faces any study of human experience, be it politics, philosophy, literature or science, when it attempts to hold a dialogue with its recorded past.

Discussing current methodologies of history, John Burrow has suggested that there are two poles to contemporary interpretations of the words of the past: the 'transparent' and the 'opaque'. According to the former, past utterances are intrinsically no more inaccessible than present ones. They may express thoughts with a continuing life and claim on us (the canonical view) or moments on the way to our present condition (usually a progressive view) – or even combine these by a process of selective transmission containing possibilities of renewal and recall (the concept of tradition), but their problems, if there are problems, are those inherent in all communication:

At the opposite extreme from this lies the view epigrammatically expressed as 'the past is another country'. The practitioner of intellectual history approaches the past imbued with a sense of its alienness, of the initial inaccessibility of its meanings, like an early anthropological fieldworker arriving for the first time on the shores of the Andaman or Trobriand Islands . . . Methodology is one's intellectual survival kit, the only reassurance in the face of the wholly unfamiliar and incomprehensible, a remedy for culture-shock, giving one a rule and a task . . . There is then an intrinsic connection between methodological self-consciousness and the sense . . . of unfamiliarity; the former is a life-support capsule for aliens. At this point, it seems to me, the upholder of the transparent view might begin to point out that the insulating implications of the last metaphor are, from the historian's point of view, rather disturbing: that the methodological self-consciousness which offers to make the unfamiliar intelligible does so on terms which actually place a screen of current methodological concerns between us and the past.[81]

As Burrow recognizes, his extremes may be caricatures but they are not without exempla – not least, one might add, in theology. While on the one hand fundamentalists tend to see the biblical texts as 'transparent' communication, those with a strong sense of their opaqueness have tended to betake themselves to holistic methodologies that guarantee their results. Edmund Leach's structuralist analyses of Genesis would be one such extreme example.[82] Between these poles what we tend to find is an area of modified or confused essentialism

- mirrored by the confusions and uncertainties of contemporary translation theory. Just as there is no longer an agreed hermeneutic procedure for interpreting the Old Testament, so, correspondingly, there is no universally applicable theory of translation. As Louis G. Kelly has pointed out, theories of translation depend upon theories of language:

> Linguists' models assume that translation is essentially transmission of data, while hermeneutic theorists take it to be an interpretative recreation of text. It is hardly surprising then, that each group, sure it has the whole truth, lives in isolation from the other.[83]

The result in practice is perhaps more surprising. Given this division of theory, it seems to be those who see translation essentially in terms of data-transmission who turn most readily to paraphrase, while those who think in interpretative terms tend to cling more faithfully to the actual words of the original text. Literal translation is a form of hermeneutics.

The lines of contemporary debate go back at least as far as Dryden. In his *Preface to Ovid's Epistles* (1680) he wrote:

> All translation, I suppose may be reduced to these three heads.
> First, that of metaphrase, or turning an author word by word, and line by line, from one language into another. Thus, or near this manner, was Horace in his *Art of Poetry* translated by Ben Jonson. The second way is that of paraphrase, or translation with latitude, where the author is kept in view by the translator, so as never to be lost, but his words are not so strictly followed as his sense, and that is to be admitted to be amplified, but not altered. Such is Mr Waller's translation of Virgil's Fourth Aeneid. The third way is that of imitation, where the translator (if he has not now lost that name) assumes the liberty not only to vary the words and sense, but to forsake them both as he sees occasion; and taking only some general hints from the original, to run division on the ground - work as he pleases. Such is Mr Cowley's practice in turning two odes of Pindar, and one of Horace, into English.[84]

As Steiner has pointed out, nothing in Dryden's analysis was particularly original, though his has become the classic statement;[85] as Charles Martindale has pointed out, the three-fold division is calculatedly tendentious: it is the keystone of a defence of paraphrase as the virtuous Aristotelian mean between the vicious extremes of freedom and metaphrase.[86] Implicit in his exposition is the assumption - soon to be associated with the name of Locke, but already widely current in the late seventeenth century - that words correspond to an underlying substratum of 'ideas' (either things or concepts), and that therefore

translation should not seek to match what might, by analogy, be called
the 'secondary qualities' of individual words, which in any particular
language or culture may be subject to irrelevant associative idiosyn-
crasies, but should, as it were, look for the basic 'primary qualities' of
the ideas themselves. For Dryden, there was a legitimate sense in
which paraphrase could be seen as more 'accurate' than metaphrase. As
his examples show, his argument is fundamentally an *aesthetic* one,
grounded in standard neo-classical assumptions about the nature of
poetry.

It was precisely these notions, both of the basic equivalence of ideas
and about aesthetics, that were to come under fire from the Romantics,
such as Herder, Humboldt, and Coleridge a century later. The traditional notion of the word as index to a concept was reversed; it was the
word that shaped the concept.[87] A language was inseparable from the
particular and peculiar experience of a people and a culture; though
there may be similarities to a greater or lesser degree, there are no
equivalencies. A statement, or work of art, was unique to the language
in which it found expresion. Nineteenth-century anthropologists
surveyed mankind from China to Peru: though Mr Casaubon found
evidence for his key to all mythologies and Sir James Frazer his golden
bough, others saw not so much uniformity as endless variation and
radical divergence. Translations, meanwhile, continued to be made –
even by those who denied the possibility. Herder wrote on Hebrew
poetry in German and Coleridge translated Schiller into English.

In fact, of course, of Dryden's three kinds, as he half admits, only
the first two, metaphrase and paraphrase, concern translation proper.
His examples, moreover, are specifically non-biblical. For dealing with
the Word of God the seventeenth century had no doubt that *only*
metaphrase was valid; the frequent, and often splendid, biblical
paraphrases of the hymnographers and devotional poets of the period
were essentially a different kind of exercise which presupposed a
knowledge by the reader of at least the King James' Bible, if not the
originals. George Herbert's or John Milton's version of the Psalm 23
invite reference to the *Authorized Version*; they do not attempt to sup-
plant it. The difference is crucial: metaphrase aims to render the
original in all its starkness and oddity, it does not imply *mastery*.
Paraphrase implies, at least in some degree, comprehension – in the
ancient and full meaning of the word.

This is a distinction which it is difficult to find in the modern advocates of paraphrase. For Eugene A. Nida, for instance, the problem for translation reveals it simply in terms of 'finding the closest equivalence':

> Translating consists in producing in the receptor language the closest natural equivalent to the message of the source language, first in meaning and secondly in style . . . By 'natural' we mean that the equivalent forms should not be 'foreign' either in form . . . or meaning. That is to say, a good translation should not reveal its non-native source.[88]

For Nida, there are basically two kinds of equivalence, which he calls 'formal' and 'dynamic'. Formal equivalence, in his words, 'focuses attention on the message itself, in both form and content. In such translation one is concerned with such correspondences as poetry to poetry, sentence to sentence, and concept to concept.'[89] Its purpose is to reveal as much of the source language as possible. Dynamic equivalence, on the other hand, is what he is describing above: its purpose is to create in the receptor language an equivalent effect to that existing in the source language. This, according to him, is the proper activity of the biblical translator. Nida is explicit that this process of 'interpretation of a passage in terms of relevance to the present-day world, not to the Biblical culture' is esentially one of 'exegesis' not of 'hermeneutics'.[90] The principle of dynamic equivalence means that when there is conflict, for instance, between meaning and style, 'the meaning must have priority over the stylistic forms'.[91]

In view of this confidence in the basic equivalence of concepts between languages, it comes as no surprise to discover that Nida is one of the prime movers behind the American Bible Society, and hence behind the Anglo–American *Good News Bible*. We remember the certainties of its Preface. That the 'message' of the original might, in itself, be problematic enough to warrant metaphrase is not for a moment considered; what problems there are, are those of the host language, not the source. Hence the appropriateness of paraphrase: the methodology of the twentieth-century essentialist.

More disconcerting is the understanding of linguistic history implicit in Nida's approach. So far from biblical translation being best achieved by finding appropriate 'equivalencies', it has been precisely in those cases where there was *no* appropriate equivalent that the greatest impact on the host language has resulted. The first major biblical translation, that of the *Septuagint*, probably in the third century B.C., revealed its 'non-native source' in a way that was to have a profound effect on the subsequent development of Greek. Because, for instance, the Hebrew word 'kabod' (whose root had meant 'weight' but which had at some stage since the time of Ezekiel come to mean also 'glory') was translated by the Greek word 'doxa' (which had originally meant something more like 'appearance' or 'reputation') the Greek term rapidly gained the added connotations of 'radiance' and 'splendour' – even in other contexts, such as in Egyptian pagan texts.[92] Jerome's translation, of the Bible[93], was to have a similar modifying effect upon the development of Latin. The subsequent ingestion of these Hebrew, Greek, and Latin sources into English sensibility was to give scripture a more important role in the development of the language than in that of any other European community – an effect, Steiner notes, that 'would not have occurred had the scholars and editors of 1604–11 laboured to be "modern" '.[94] In short, translation, where there is no effective equivalent, is one of the major sources of change and enrichment in a living language. A language develops in range and subtlety of expression *not* by means of receptivity to translation, but through its *resistance* to new words and concepts. It is not equivalencies, but *dissimilarities* that force the modification and change necessary to accommodate new associative patterns of thought.

Yet the real problem raised by the Nida theory of paraphrase is not that it makes a nonsense of the actual previous history of biblical translation, but that it tacitly denies a vital function of language itself: the creative. Steiner's thesis 'that translation . . . is a special, heightened case of the process of communication and reception in any act of human speech',[95] is here convincing. What, then, of those cases – of which the story of Elijah on Horeb may stand for our paradigm example – where there is *no* 'equivalence', because what is being said is strange and without parallel, struggling to painful birth in the original language? What about the 'new'? Faced with an event without precedent, that which breaks existing boundaries, and reshapes thought – the irruption of the numinous, the holy, the 'otherness' of religious experience – the whole notion of 'understanding the meaning' of a passage tacitly implied by essentialist assumptions and by easy notions of 'equivalence' starts to disintegrate. We may, indeed, be better off attempting to define the 'new', in this sense, by *inverting* Nida's principle of dynamic equivalence thus: *the 'new' may be said to occur when there is no adequate translation available.* 'Translation' here covers transference from one language into another; from different synchronic culture-groups within the same language; and diachronically between different historical periods in the same language. If we construct our definition like this we avoid the problem of whether every original verbal formulation (such as a new poem) is actually the creation of new meaning. Clearly, there *is* a very real sense in which no two ways of expressing anything in words are saying exactly the same thing; every act of reading or listening *is* a new translation in Steiner's sense. But in so far as we 'understand' a poem or passage of prose it is also familiar: in our sense it is 'translatable'. It is when it cannot be intelligibly rephrased, when we remain baffled and are forced to search through clearly inadequate alternatives to illuminate the problem, that we can be said to have encountered the really 'new'.

How, after all, *do* we begin to 'understand' an event such as that given by the Elijah story? As did Augustine? or St John of the Cross? Mrs Trimmer or Dr Robinson? And are such passages really fundamentally different in kind from those of more obviously 'translatable' meaning where theories of data-transmission and paraphrase might seem more appropriate? In view of what we know about the cultural variability of our conceptual framework – by definition most powerful when we are least conscious of it – the idea that the story is one of a minority of atypical instances is difficult to sustain with confidence. So far from being an exception to a general rule, the stubborn oddities of metaphrase may turn out to be, on examination, paradigmatic of biblical language as a whole.

What this debate has done, however, has been to focus attention in a quite new way on theories of language itself – and on the relationship between language and religious experience. One contrast in particula: that recurs over and over again in such discussions is that between the theoretical constructs of linguistics and the natural organic movement of language as it is actually spoken by a culture or community. It is, as we shall see, a contrast implicit in John Dennis's reaction against Wilkins's *Essay*; it lies at the very heart of the revolution in biblical studies initiated by Lowth's *Sacred Poetry of the Hebrews* in the middle of the eighteenth century and is underpinned by his later translation of Isaiah and his immensely popular *Short Introduction to English Grammar*; it is crucial to Coleridge's rejection of Hartley's theory of language and the corresponding empiricist views of the mind in the early nineteenth century; it is even present in the very metaphor of a 'Grammar' of a living language by which Newman sought to elucidate the psychology of belief. Nor is the metaphorical contrast between a 'natural' and an 'artificial' language exhausted in the twentieth century. It occurs again, for instance, in the focal image of a recent book by Maurice Wiles:

Religion, like language itself, is to be found not in one universal form, but in a multiplicity of diverse forms. Artificial attempts to create a single religious esperanto are as lifeless as the linguistic case. It may be that there is some deep structure, some universal grammar of religion, but if so it is as inaccessible to us as its equivalent in language.[96]

It is also, as we shall see, the guiding simile in John Burrow's secular discussion of how we are to approach the thought-processes of the past.

Much of the rest of this book will be concerned with the variations of this extended family of linguistic models and their corresponding metaphorical applications over the past three hundred years and more. In spite of obvious differences, these Romantic and proto-Romantic theories and metaphors characteristically have in common the belief that language is the paradigm for all forms of human communication – verbal or non-verbal. In particular we find that 'poetry' is commonly assumed to be *the* basic art-form, and the word 'poetic' used by analogy as a term of approval in the whole range of non-verbal arts – and even sometimes for the Church itself. As in the Coleridge quotation with which we began, language is not seen as something that can be created *ab initio*, or even defined by *a priori* or essentialist methodology; it constitutes rather a collective and cultural context within which human beings come to consciousness and self-discovery.

In accepting a particular biblical story – such as, say, that of Elijah on Horeb – as primarily a *verbal* event, a linguistic happening, one also necessarily accepts it as a 'historical' event in the sense that it comes to us with a subsequent critical history. In what it implies about nature and transcendence, for instance, it may well be taken to indicate a decisive and even historic shift in human consciousness that would take centuries (or even millennia) of commentary, midrash, and translation, to be assimilated into the cultural life of the community – in this case, of course, affecting no longer a single linguistic group, but eventually the whole of Judeo-Christendom (considered as a single cultural-linguistic entity). Thus we do not fully understand the Elijah story until we have also read Wordsworth's *Prelude* and Tennyson's *In Memoriam*. In this example, we note, it is not a question of what modern code or mental set the story must be translated into to bring out its meaning, but rather of the conditioning assumptions brought by the modern reader to the text itself. For the Bible Society, these pre-conditioning assumptions were, it seems, primarily those of a popular 'scientific' and materialist culture ill-at-ease with mysterious or ambiguous events that threaten to break the conventional categories of experience; for Coleridge, the assumptions were more to do with the history of the reader's own consciousness – having grown up into a language and culture in part framed and formed by the Bible. In the one the *Zeitgeist* is paramount; in the other, the two-sided nature of communication – the text and the reader, each with its own history – is central. Both are concerned with historical reality. Both are culturally variable, but whereas the former, by tacitly denying the problem, tends to move towards a pseudo-essentialist position on the pretext that it is moving ever-nearer 'historical truth', the latter, by focusing on it, ends by looking in detail at the one concrete fact in its possession: the text itself.

Thus, it seems, we now find ourselves in the position of needing to refine Burrow's apparently common-sense distinction between 'transparent' and 'opaque' modes of textual interpretation. As his own analysis suggests, it is conventional to assume that the distinction implies the deployment of a 'realist' critical approach to the former and a 'formalist' to the latter. The obvious corollary would seem to be that the record of human religious experience (as represented in this instance by the biblical narratives) is, as it were, a free-standing entity, an expression of truths best perceived by taking the stories at their face-value, and obscured by the interposition of too much attention to its formal, structural, or historical matrix. Yet this antithesis turns out to be more complex than might appear at first sight. Though the Bible Society's approach is presented in terms of simple 'transparency', it is in fact covertly as 'opaque' as that of Nineham or Bultmann. On the other hand, the kind of reading of the Elijah story we have been examining, for all its attention to the linguistic, structural, and historical context, is in effect far more uncompromisingly *literalist* than any of the other readings proposed by twentieth-century critics. We are left with the paradox that an apparently 'transparent' approach to the Bible turns out to be, in reality, severely (if unconsciously) formalist and 'opaque', while an apparently 'opaque' technique seems to be the only way to restore a genuinely 'transparent' reading. To put it another way, it is those who would look *through* the text, who, disconcertingly, see least; those who would look at it and study the detailed patterning of its surface as an artifact, who discover most. For the former, the text has become evermore transparent — revealing nothing behind; for the latter, the text's apparent opacity has become evermore richly revealing.

As we shall see in the following chapters, this is no new paradox, but one rooted in the biblical criticism of the past few hundred years, and in our processes of understanding language itself. Our understanding of religious language depends upon our view of language as a whole; a sense of the relationship between words and reality is, consciously or unconsciously, the precondition of all other theological and biblical studies. Fortunately, though language is endlessly complex, and in a constant state of flux and development, we find we are already speaking it.

2
'The peculiar language of heaven . . .'

The religious and the poetic.

If the twentieth century has become increasingly uneasy and hesitant in dealing with the status of biblical narrative, it has seen a corresponding efflorescence of theories and studies of religious language. I say 'corresponding' because it might seem reasonable to suppose that the growth of the latter was in some way stimulated by the problems presented by the former. Though this may be the case, it is nevertheless observable that the 'answers' so produced tend to be curiously tangential to the original 'questions' – as if the problems never quite permit themselves to be resolved into the terms implied by the suggested solutions. One is left with that uneasy feeling sometimes encountered when an apparently impressive argument has left some vital factor out of account, or contains a nagging contradiction that temporarily eludes analysis, but would be obvious if once pointed out. It is even, perhaps, analogous to the state of mediaeval cosmology just before Copernicus, desperately trying to 'save the appearances' by more and more elaborate epicycles, or that of biology immediately pre-Darwin. The tangled relationship between the 'religious' and the 'poetic' seems to be a case in point.

The concept of 'religious language' is a significantly recent one. The notion that the actual words used to talk about religious experience should be seen as constituting a historical or epistemological problem of a special or even unique kind is rather less than three hundred years old. There have always been, it is true, philosophers and theologians who have tended to view language *per se* as a somewhat sloppy and ineffective medium for precise communication. Aristotle carefully warns his auditors that we cannot be more precise in our classifications than the subject and the limitations of language will permit.[1] Augustine saw all post-Babel communication as cripplingly limited by the fallen state of the human intellect which could now only communicate via the clumsy artifice of language.[2] Calvin builds his *Institutes* on a foundation of even more dogmatic articulatory pessimism; while Locke suspected that, limited though the human understanding might be in general, it was noticeably ill-served and further unnecessarily hampered by the lamentably metaphorical state of our language in particular.[3] None of these authorities, however, was inclined to view the language used to describe religious experience as presenting a *special case* – a different order of problem from the perennial one of 'words and things' as a whole. Such a suspicion was scarcely voiced before the beginning of the eighteenth century, and then was voiced, not as one might expect in connection with the peculiar problems raised by biblical narratives, but in relation to the current critical passion for classification of literary kinds.

Longinus, who seems to have been a Greek pagan literary critic writing some time in the early Christian era, had picked out the opening of Genesis for special mention as an example of his category of the 'sublime'.[4] This endorsement of the Bible's aesthetic qualities was (and was to remain until the beginning of the eighteenth century) a controversial point. Jerome, for instance, had found the style of the scriptures in comparison with the classics 'harsh and barbarous',[5] and he warned his readers not to expect in his translation any Ciceronian 'eloquence': 'a translation made for the Church, although it may indeed have some literary merit, ought to conceal and avoid it, so as to address itself, not to the private schools of the philosophers with their handful of disciples, but rather to the whole human race'.[6] Augustine had, similarly, been repelled alike by the style and obscurity of the Old Testament.[7] Though Longinus was known in Western Europe apparently from the late fifteenth century, he only became widely influential with the translation into French by Boileau in 1674, and his praise for the sublimity of Genesis had, even then, to be defended by Boileau against Huet and other critics.[8] Nevertheless, within a few decades of the beginning of the eighteenth century the growth of his prestige had helped to transform the critical climate all over Europe. Though his actual reference to it was fleeting enough, through Longinus it now could seem that the classical world had acknowledged not merely the moral but the aesthetic supremacy of God's Word. Thus Isaac Watts declares the manifest inferiority of the (classical) 'Gentiles . . . when brought into Comparison with MOSES, whom LONGINUS himself, a *Gentile* Critic, cites as a Master of the sublime Stile, when he chose to use it'.[9] By the end of the century the aesthetic sublimity of the scriptures had become a critical commonplace. In 1810, for instance, we find no less a figure than Dugald Stewart, the formidable Professor of Moral Philosophy at Edinburgh, in an essay on the Longinian tradition, commenting specifically on 'the influence which the sacred writings must have had, all over the Christian world, in adding solemnity and majesty' to the natural sublimity of the ideas of Eternity, Immensity, Omnipresence and Omniscience. [10]

In England in particular, the question of the status of scripture posed problems of peculiar, even unique, urgency and complexity. A hundred and fifty years of Protestant/Catholic controversy had produced no decisive hermeneutical outcome, – but rather, a growing awareness of the ultimate subjectivity of biblical interpretation. As a Dutch commentator had observed in the middle of the sixteenth century, 'The scripture is like a nose of wax that easily suffereth itself to be drawn backward and forward, and to be moulded and fashioned this way and that, and howsoever ye list.'[11] The phrase was at first part of the polemic – the Papists 'make the scriptures a nose of wax, and a tennis ball', (Roger Hutchinson, 1550)[12] – but to less committed observers the image could be seen to suggest the flexibility of the basic material as much as the clownlike antics of the opponents. As Dryden summed up the interminable debate:

> After long labour lost, and times expence,
> Both grant the words, and quarrel for the sense.
> Thus all disputes for ever must depend;
> For no dumb rule can controversies end.
> Thus when you said tradition must be try'd
> By Sacred Writ, whose sense yourself decide,
> You said no more, but that yourselves must be
> The judges of the Scripture sense, not we.
>
> *The Hind and the Panther*, Bk II, 200–7

Dryden, we note, was writing on the Catholic side, that of the Hind, not the Protestant Panther. Yet it is part of the peculiar poise of *The Hind and the Panther* that it values the political stability of England, Europe's most powerful Protestant state, above sectarian controversy. Dryden was, after all, a friend of Charles II. Unlike Germany, Britain was a unitary state; unlike France, it contained a multitude of rancorously divided sects, each with its own self-justifying system of biblical interpretation. The search for a resolution to the hermeneutical debate was intimately associated with the quest for a fresh political consensus. Though one answer seemed to lie with the new spirit of enquiry expressed through the foundation of the Royal Society, the 'scientific' approach to the Bible of men like Ussher, Wilkins, and Craig, was also liable to lead dangerously towards empiricism and deism, and a growing scepticism about miracles of all kinds.

Partly as a reaction to Wilkins's reconstructions of Noah's logistics and Craig's Euclidian theology, the idea that the Bible was of value primarily for its overwhelming 'sublimity' of expression (supported, however dubiously, by the classical authority of Longinus) seemed to another way of thinking to offer a tactical sideways move, and the hint of a new approach to the current stalemate. That approach was the concept of the 'poetic sublime'.

In 1704 John Dennis, in an essay entitled *The Grounds of Criticism in Poetry*, cited the authority of Longinus to show 'that the greatest sublimity is to be deriv'd from Religious Ideas'.[13] 'Poetry,' he concludes, 'is the natural Language of Religion'.[14] It is the form through which the most profound human passion finds expression, and at the same time it makes plain by its own 'regularity' – that is, its expression of order by fulfilling the rules and laws of its being – 'the works of God', which like poetry, 'tho' infinitely various, are extremely regular'.[15] For Dennis, poetry was not just the predominant language of the scriptures, it was an agent of Natural Law itself:

The great Design of Art is to restore the Decays that happen'd to human Nature by the Fall, by restoring Order . . . Poetry . . . is an Art, by which a Poet excites Passion (and for that very cause entertains Sense) in order to satisfy and improve, to delight and inform the Mind, and so make Mankind happier and better: from which it appears that Poetry has two Ends, a subordinate, and a final one; the subordinate one is Pleasure, and the final one is instruction.[16]

It is, therefore, almost a tautology to say that religious language is poetic:

In the first Ages of writing among the *Grecians*, there was nothing writ but Verse, because they wrote of nothing but Religion . . . and Nature had taught them, that Poetry was the only Language in which they could worthily treat of the most important parts of Religion.[17]

The Bible was, therefore, to be treated as belonging to a higher, more sublime order of discourse than prose: an inferior and late medium fit only for describing the mundane and practical world of everyday affairs.

But as soon as Religion was sufficiently imprinted in the Minds of Men, and they had the leisure to treat of human things in their Writings, they invented Prose, and invented it in imitation of Verse . . . but after that Prose was invented by them, never any of them treated of their Gods or their religious Matters in Prose, before the Age of *Socrates*, because they found that way of writing was by no means proper for it.[18]

Dennis, though by no means uncontroversial, was a critic of considerable stature and influence. Isaac Watts singled out his 'noble Essay' for special praise.[19] A contemporary literary historian, Giles Jacob, confidently described him in 1720 as 'The greatest Critic of this Age'.[20] His argument was to constitute a watershed in critical history. Joseph Trapp, the first Oxford Professor of Poetry, writing only a few years after Dennis, accepts the obvious affinities between poetry and religion, but is committed to the common-sense thesis that prose, being simpler, is more ancient than the complexities of verse. As a result, the relationship between poetry and religion can only be one-way: poetry 'owes its increase and Progress' to Religion . . . 'as nothing is so suitable to Poetry as the *Marvellous*, nothing can afford more matter for it than the *Christian* Religion, which so much abounds with Miracles'.[21]

James Thomson, however, in his 1726 Preface to 'Winter' for the second edition of his *Seasons*, is clearly with Dennis in his affirmation that poetry is 'that divine art' which 'has charmed the listening world from Moses down to Milton' constituting 'The sublimest passages of the inspired writings themselves and what seems to be the peculiar language of heaven'.[22] Since Moses was assumed to be the writer of the Pentateuch, and therefore, arguably at least, the first author, it is clear that Thomson, like Dennis, sees poetry as the primal linguistic form. What is perhaps, with hindsight, more significant is his confident Longinian assumption that the Pentateuch's sublimity makes it 'poetic' without it having to conform to the conventional structures of verse.

This was the starting-point for Robert Lowth's epoch-making *Lectures on the Sacred Poetry of the Hebrews*. Delivered as the Oxford Poetry Lectures in 1741, they were first published in Latin in 1753, and were to achieve wide circulation with their English translation in 1787. As we shall see in the next chapter, they were to redefine the conception of Hebrew poetry; less obviously, but perhaps no less significantly in the long run, they were to redefine the notion of 'poetry' itself. For Lowth, 'poetry' was the natural expression of prophetic utterance. The poets of ancient Israel were also the prophets.[23] He implicitly rejects the stilted conventions of Augustan poetic diction, and praises instead the 'simple and unadorned' language of Hebrew verse, that gains its 'almost ineffable sublimity' not from elevated terms, but from the depth and universality of its subject-matter. This is a theme that was to recur, with many variations, in Burke, Smart, Cowper, Blair, Blake, and Wordsworth. Yet already we can detect two very different strands to this tradition.

Dennis had drawn a sharp and explicit distinction between the language of poetry, the proper vehicle of the sublime, and that of prose. With apparently convincing *a priori* logic he had argued 'that all those parts of the Old Testament which were writ in Verse, ought to be translated in Verse, by Reasons which may have force enough to convince us, that Verse translated in Prose is but half translated'.[24] But this common-sense distinction between two orders of language, differing in kind rather than degree, collapses with Lowth for the simple reason that, as he makes clear from his study of Hebrew prosody, biblical poetry worked by means of structural 'parallelisms' rather than by the devices of verbal sound familiar in all European poetry. In the wake of this discovery it could be appreciated for the first time how *little* of the Hebrew poetry was in fact lost through the normal processes of translation. Whereas contemporary European verse, which relied heavily on the essentially untranslatable auditory effects of alliteration, assonance, rhyme, and metre, was extremely difficult to render in another language with any real equivalence of tone and feeling, Hebrew poetry was almost all translatable. According to Lowth:

> . . . a poem translated literally from the Hebrew into the prose of any other language, whilst the same form of the sentences remain, will still retain, even as far as relates to versification, much of its native dignity, and fair appearance of versification.[25]

Translated into Greek and Latin, however, with essentially different and inflexible word-orders, 'having the conformation of the sentences accommodated to the idiom of a foreign language', it 'will appear confused and mutilated'. We may, perhaps, hear in this the convictions of the man who was later to publish one of the most highly acclaimed translations of Isaiah.

The point was not missed by succeeding critics, who noticed also the corollary, that, contra Dennis, Hebrew poetry was actually *better* translated into prose than verse. As Hugh Blair, Professor of Rhetoric and Belles Lettres in the University of Edinburgh, and one of Lowth's most influential admirers, put it in 1783:

> It is owing, in a great measure, to this form of composition, that our version, though in prose, retains so much of a poetical cast. For the version being strictly word for word after the original, the form and order of the original sentence are

preserved; which by this artificial structure, this regular alternation and correspondence of parts, makes the ear sensible of a departure from the common style and tone of prose.[26]

Though Lowth may not have foreseen the consequences of his line of argument, its effect was all but to obliterate the traditional distinction between prose and poetry as separate literary 'kinds'. The term 'poetic' could now apply, with scholarly rectitude rather than metaphorical licence, as easily to prose as verse.

Blair's own poetics bear this out. 'Our first enquiry', he writes, 'must be, what is poetry? and wherein does it differ from prose?' His answer, is, as it now has to be, that 'it is the language of passion, enlivened imagination'.[27] If this sounds like an uncanny anticipation of Wordsworth's Preface to the *Lyrical Ballads*, it is because Wordsworth patently took much of his famous formulation directly from Lowth and Blair. Though his insistence that 'there neither is nor can be any essential difference' between 'the language of prose and metrical composition'[28] was strikingly original in context, it stands in a tradition which, if it reaches back as far as Aristotle, has immediate roots in the revived interest in biblical poetics.

For Dennis, the link between poetry and religion was that both relied on passion and supernatural persuasion to restore the inner harmony disrupted by the Fall.[29] Above all, the insistence upon religious language as 'poetic' takes the debate away from the unarguable fanaticisms engendered by theories of inspiration, and places it firmly within the realm of aesthetics and psychology. Comparing the sublimity of Psalm 18 with that of Virgil in the first book of the *Georgics*, he argues for the superiority of the Bible, not on grounds of its inspired truth, but its greater poetic power and passion.[30] Literary criticism is substituted for revelation as the guarantee of authenticity. Behind this redefinition of poetry in terms of passion lay an essentially psychological theory of how the head and heart, representing the most powerful human faculties, combined to produce through art a unique form of psychic integration.[31]

If Coleridge was later to express doubts about Wordsworth's conflation of the languages of poetry and prose,[32] this underlying postulate of the psychically integrative function of poetry was to remain central to the development of his whole aesthetic theory. For him, as for Dennis, the language of the scriptures was the *locus classicus* for the 'poetic'. The narratives of the Bible, he says, are:

. . . The living *educts* of the imagination; of that reconciling and mediatory power, which incorporating the Reason in images of the Sense, and organising (as it were) the flux of the Senses, by the permanence and self-circling energies of the Reason, gives birth to a system of symbols, harmonious in themselves, and consubstantial with the Truths, of which they are the *conductors* . . . Hence . . . The Sacred Book is worthily intitled *the* WORD OF GOD.[33]

The argument is an interesting one, but like all Coleridge's statements, it requires some unpacking.

Biblical narrative is distinguished from contemporary secular history with its stress on such trivialities as political economy (the products of an 'unenlivened generalised understanding') by the fact that it 'lives' as extensions of the creative or 'poetic' imagination. They supply concrete body and form from the world of sense-perception (the Kantian realm of the 'Understanding') to the Kantian 'Reason', – those innate ideas of God, Freedom, and Immortality which we all possess, but which, since they are 'regulative' only, in themselves lack content. By means of poetic symbols the scriptures bridge the gap between the 'Understanding' and the 'Reason', and create, through art, a wholeness and unity that is otherwise lacking in fallen man – an impressionistic, but perhaps not altogether unfair deployment of ideas from Kant's *Critiques of Pure Reason* and *Aesthetic Judgement*.[34] Hence the poetic symbol is essentially 'bi-focal':

It is characterised by a translucence of the special in the Individual, or of the General in the Especial, or of the Universal in the General. Above all by the translucence of the Eternal through and in the Temporal. It always partakes of the Reality which it renders intelligible; and while it enunciates the whole, abides itself as a living part in that Unity, of which it is the representative.[35]

A symbol is thus the opposite of a generalization. The latter is a kind of lowest common denominator, deduced by the understanding from outward events according to the dead arrangement of a mechanical philosophy. In contrast, to describe a symbol, he uses the metaphor of a lens: it is 'translucent' – focusing the universal generality through the concreteness of a particular example.[36]

What is interesting here is to see how Coleridge goes beyond Dennis in his claim for the poetic nature of the Bible. Poetry, Coleridge explains in a parallel discussion written at almost the same period, 'brings the whole soul of man into activity'[37] 'reconciling opposite or discordant qualities' into a new and health-giving harmony. We recognize that authenticity of biblical inspiration from its poetic and symbolic power, that is, from the evidence of its inward effect on ourselves, rather than from any external authority. This does not mean that the Bible is merely to be apprehended as aesthetic, or that the blurring of the distinction between prose and verse means that *all* prose is poetic. In a clear reference to Lowth's translation he writes:

The first chapter of Isaiah (indeed a very large proportion of the whole book) is poetry in the most emphatic sense; yet it would be not less irrational than strange to assert that pleasure, and not truth, was the immediate object of the prophet.[38]

The Aristotelian ends of poetry distinguished by Dennis, 'pleasure' and 'instruction', are not to be lost sight of now that 'truth' is a matter more of inward 'recognition' (in the Platonic sense) than external instruction. On the contrary, it merely means that there is an inherent *psychological* link between the two. Coleridge's theory of the imagination[39] stressed that all knowledge was acquired by an active integrating mental process; the passive receptivity assumed by the Lockeian and empiricist notion of the 'tabula rasa' model of the mind was an impossibility. Thus in reading poetry we are not receivers of the word, we are, by definition, *participators* in it. When Coleridge wrote of the Bible that in it 'there is more that *finds* me than in all other books put together',[40] he is deliberately using the biblical image of *dialogue*, the process of call and response that is the hallmark of God's dealings with man from Genesis to Acts, as a metaphor of the process of reading itself. Poetry is, as it were, characterized and known by this image of 'election' in the theological sense. The Bible is '*the* WORD OF GOD' because it exemplifies most overtly what is everywhere true of poetry. The *logos* is poetic.

The inward and re-integrative power of poetry as the vehicle of religious experience is taken a stage further by John Keble: the best-selling poet of the nineteenth century. His *Lectures on Poetry*, delivered between the years 1832–41, when he was Professor of Poetry at Oxford, were published in 1844. Unfortunately their public impact was somewhat muted since Keble published as he lectured, in Latin. *De Poeticae vi Medica* was not translated into English until 1912. The Lectures were dedicated 'to William Wordsworth, true philosopher and inspired poet, who by the special gift and calling of Almighty God, whether he sang of man or of nature, failed not to lift up men's hearts to holy things . . .' In them, Keble puts forward what is, in effect, the most thoroughgoing exposition ever devised of poetry as the spontaneous overflow of powerful feelings. But whereas, for Wordsworth, the metaphor clearly implied a natural spring or fountain of water, for Keble it seems to suggest something more like the safety-valve of a steam engine. To his old college friend, J. T. Coleridge (the poet's nephew) he wrote: 'My notion is to consider poetry as a vent for over-charged feelings, or a full imagination, and so account for the various classes into which Poets naturally fall, by reference to the various objects which are apt to fill and overpower the mind, so as to require a sort of relief.'[41] For Keble, poetry is essentially the product of tension or repression. The man who under emotional stress utters his feelings easily and without reserve, is no poet.[42] As he put it in his 1828 review of Lockhart's *Life of Scott*, 'poetry is the indirect expression in words, most appropriately in metrical words, of some overpowering emotion, or ruling taste, or feeling, the direct indulgence whereof is somehow repressed.'[43] Following the line we have seen developing from Lowth onwards, Keble denies that the 'poetic' is a quality peculiar to verse. Where he goes far beyond Coleridge or Wordsworth is in his claim that it is essentially common to *all* art-forms – including music, sculpture, painting, and architecture.[44] The traditional genres of poetic criticism that had persisted since the time of Aristotle are at a stroke swept away: clearly 'there will be as many kinds of poems as there are emotions of the human mind'.[45] The tendency begun by Wordsworth, to see poetry through the state of mind of the poet, is here carried to its logical conclusion. Keble classifies poetry by the emotions of the writer, who seeks relief and health by disguised utterance and strange socratic irony.[46] Poetry is, above all, the healing art – and as such it is not a quality confined to literature. 'Each several one of the so-called liberal arts, contains a certain poetic quality of its own, and . . . this lies in its power to heal and relieve the human mind when agitated by care, passion, and ambition.'[47] This is such an unexpected inversion of normal Romantic aesthetics that it is easy to miss just what Keble is actually saying here. He does not believe that it is one of the powers of 'the poetic' that it can heal and give relief to the person under stress; he believes that we can actually *define* 'the poetic' by the presence of this healing power. Moreover, it is clear both in this passage and elsewhere that 'healing' and 'soothing' are very closely related in Keble's thought. Wordsworth, in his *Immortality Ode*, had openly delighted in what he calls the 'soothing thoughts that spring/out of human suffering' – and in so doing had touched a chord that continued to reverberate in a host of lesser nineteenth-century sensibilities, including that of Keble. It is to the 'soothing' power of poetry that Keble tries to lead us with what the modern often feels is quite indecent haste. In his 1827 Advertisement to *The Christian Year* he calls our attention to the poems on the Occasional Services of the Prayer Book which he had added at the end of his collection (including one on the Commination Service!). These, he tells us, 'constitute, from their personal and domestic nature, the most perfect instance of that *soothing* tendency in the Prayer Book, which it is the chief purpose of these pages to exhibit'. Nor is it merely the prime purpose of *The Christian Year* to 'soothe' the jaded reader: the title of the poem for the Fourth Sunday after Epiphany gives us explicitly the full strength of this word for Keble – and presumably also for his readers. It is entitled *The World is for Excitement, The Gospel for Soothing*. Clearly the power of 'soothing' is absolutely central to Keble's understanding of religious experience. Keble was a good enough philologist to know the older meaning of the word 'soothe': 'to prove and show to be true'; 'to assert or uphold a truth'; and 'to give support', 'encourage' and 'confirm' – by which it comes by its weaker modern sense of 'to calm' and even, 'to tranquillize'. Yet this weak sense had come to co-exist with the older, stronger one by the seventeenth century, and by the nineteenth it was undoubtedly the primary meaning.

We can, I think, best understand the force of the word for Keble if we link it with the Aristotelian notion of 'catharsis' – the release of tension in tragedy through the emotions of pity and terror. The 'poetic', for him, involves a build-up of unresolved tension between intense private emotion and the constraints of public expression which finally finds utterance in some veiled and even ironic form. But the poet is healed and set at rest not in any mere anodyne sense: 'soothing' here involves 'asserting and upholding the truth' even in the hidden symbolic forms of poetry. The Prayer Book and the Gospel are essentially 'poetic' because they compellingly assert the truth. What Keble has done, in effect, with his poetic theory of religious language, is to bring together two very different stands in biblical hermeneutics. On the one hand, he has preserved the ancient Augustinian and typological tradition of reading the scriptures in terms of hidden layers of meaning only to be unravelled by the patient reader with prayers and study. On the other hand, in line with the common movement of Romantic aesthetics, he has shifted the *origins* of this encoding process from the inscrutable workings of God, and the Fall, to the mind of the human biblical writer. He has, in effect, *psychologized* typology, thus providing a direct link between Augustine and Freud. Typology is not now the cryptic structuring of the Holy Spirit, but the basic mode of the unconscious mind. At the same time,

Keble has, in a typical nineteenth-century way, made *feeling* central to religious experience.

What then, *is* the relationship between poetry and religion for Keble? He seems to think of it at two levels. Historically, and perhaps also in the development of the individual, poetry prepares the ground for theology. The classic poets, philosophers, and historians 'may all be considered poets, so far as they are wont to elevate the mind by the clear light either of memory or lofty speculation'.[48] 'Men come to realise that the various images and similies of things, and all the poetic charms, are not merely the play of a keen and clever mind, not to be put down as empty fancies: but rather they guide us by gentle hints and no uncertain signs, to the very utterances of Nature, or we may more truly say, of the Author of Nature.'[49] The Christian is the rightful fulfiller of the dream that our imaginative longings should, somehow, be discovered to be more true than the apparently real world. We are reminded of Keats's Platonism: 'The Imagination may be compared to Adam's dream – he awoke and found it truth.'[50] 'It would be hard to believe,' declares Keble, that poetry and theology 'would have proved such true allies unless there was a hidden tie of kinship between them'.[51] But that hidden tie is not merely one that binds matter and spirit, nature and the supernatural, phenomena and noumena, but also operates in the very structure of language itself. 'Poetry . . . supplies a rich wealth of similies whereby a pious mind may supply and remedy, in some sort, its powerlessness of speech.'[52] Poetry makes religion live in the human imagination, just as, at another level, religion makes the imagination live in another world. This is a line of thought, we notice, that owes more to Coleridge than to Wordsworth. Poetry, for Keble, is the medium or vehicle of religious experience, revealing its meaning not so much by direct statement (which would be impossible, given the limitations of language) but through the very organic creativity of its form. The symbol, with its hidden meanings, is an expression of the inwardness of religious feeling. The echoes here of *The Statesman's Manual* are unmistakable:

In short, Poetry lends Religion her wealth of symbols and similies: Religion restores these again to Poetry, clothed with so splendid a radiance that they appear to be no longer symbols, but to partake (I might almost say) of the nature of sacraments.[53]

The presence of Coleridge behind Keble's feeling for a symbolic and sacramental universe is no surprise, and it gives us a clue to one of the most difficult problems in Keble's aesthetics: the meaning he attaches to that much-overworked word, 'poetic'. On the one hand the word serves narrowly and conventionally as an adjective from 'poetry'; on the other, it is – as we have seen – applied with reckless abandon to the entire range of the liberal arts, before being somewhat ambiguously defined in terms of its healing power. What seems to happen in the first half of the nineteenth century is that Coleridge's pseudo-Kantian use of 'Imagination' is largely ignored and forgotten, and the word is instead increasingly used in the context of the dream-worlds of Victorian poetry.[54] As a result, the word 'poetic' tends to rise in status, and to take on many of the qualities Coleridge had ascribed to the 'Imagination'. Keble appears to have been a key figure in this semantic shift. In 1852, for instance, we find F. W. Robertson, a Brighton clergyman and preacher of some distinction, lecturing on 'The Influence of Poetry' to a class of working men. Robertson was an avowed admirer of Coleridge, and as a Broad Churchman no friend to Keble and the Tractarians, yet his whole theory of poetry is modelled very closely on Keble's. In particular, the words 'imagination' and 'poetic' have undergone much of the semantic shift predicated. 'Poetry,' he writes, 'is not imagination, but imagination shaped. Not feeling, but feeling expressed symbolically: the formless suggested indirectly through form.'[55] The 'imagination', for Robertson, is no longer the 'esemplastic' force in Coleridge's sense that it shaped the unity of the material; that process, by which the 'leading idea' and the organic unity of the work are revealed, is now a quality of 'poetry' itself.

If Keble's aesthetics are in some ways peculiar to himself, many of the individual elements – the stress on feeling, for instance, or the belief in the poetic nature of language *per se* – are common not only to other English Romantics, but to their German contemporaries. During the mid-years of the eighteenth century there had been a spate of translations of English criticism into German. Lowth's commentary on Isaiah was translated into German the year after its English publication in 1778. His *Lectures* had been reprinted in the original Latin at Göttingen in 1758 with extensive notes by the pioneer biblical scholar Johann David Michaelis, and had been partially translated into German by C. B. Schmidt in 1793.[56] Michaelis's notes were translated into English and reprinted in subsequent English editions. The *Lectures* were to be a major influence on the new generation of German biblical critics and historians such as Eichhorn, Gesenius, Lessing and, above all, Herder, who explicitly acknowledged in the preface how much his own seminal work, *The Spirit of Hebrew Poetry*, had owed to Lowth.[57] Though by far the most significant,[58] Lowth's was only one of a number of English works to fuel the German critical revolution. Others included Thomas Blackwell's *Enquiry into the Life and Writings of Homer*,[59] John Brown's *Dissertation on the Rise Union and Power, the Progressions, Separations and Corruptions of Poetry and Music*[60] and Robert Wood's *On the Original Genius and Writings of Homer.*[61] Blackwell, who was probably also an influence on Lowth, had supported the view that poetry pre-dated prose, but unlike Dennis, makes his case on sociological rather than aesthetic grounds. The customs, language, and destiny of a people were indivisible: a poem like Homer's could only be understood within its social and historical contexts. This spate of translations was to affect the whole development of the German literary revival. The two central books of western culture, the Bible and Homer, were now set by Blackwell, Lowth, and Wood, in a quite new perspective – hitherto blocked by ideas based upon the principles of Natural Law, which had seen both books primarily as timeless didactic works.[62] In the context of the intense Germanic nationalism of Hamann and Herder, and the efforts of Goethe, Schiller, Wieland, Voss, Hölderlin, Kleist, and others to recreate the German language by returning to its cultural roots, and forging a new literature, the idea of the 'poetic' as the expression of the life of a people took hold and flourished as it never could in the less theoretical climate of England.[63]

England, however, was not the only foreign source to influence the late eighteenth-century German renaissance. Giambattista Vico's *New Science (Scienza nuova)* had been published in Naples in 1725. In it he had specifically selected German for attention as a 'mother language', comparable to those of the ancient Chaldeans, Scythians, and Egyptians, but which, unlike them, had survived from 'remote antiquity',[64], and which was accordingly more 'poetic' than other modern, or even classical European languages. Vico's own definition of the 'poetic' is a striking, even paradoxical one. It is the word he chooses to describe the most primitive of what he sees as three stages of language.[65] For him, the origin 'both of languages and of letters lies in the fact that the first gentile peoples, by a demonstrated necessity of nature, were poets who spoke in poetic characters'.[66] This 'discovery' Vico saw as the 'master key' to his new science of mankind. To understand 'the poetic nature of these first men' required a mental leap of enormous difficulty – for Vico himself, it was the product of a lifetime's research – yet, aided by imagination, it was possible. This was the vital clue to unravelling the mysterious origins of art, mythology, and religion (Vico prudently excludes from consideration the origins of Hebrew religion and Christianity, since these are the result of direct Revelation). Isaiah Berlin summarizes his use of the word thus:

> By 'poetical' he means – what, following the Germans, we tend to attribute to the people or 'folk' – modes of expression used by the unsophisticated mass of the people in the early years of the human race, not by the children of its old age – self-conscious men of letters, experts or sages.[67]

But the German parallel, useful as it may be for a later understanding of Herder or Niebuhr, is an oversimplification of the complexity of Vico. For one thing, the idea of the *Volksgeist* is, for the author of the *New Science*, a much less attractive one than it is for Herder. The life of the natural man in the period following the Flood is, for Vico, Hobbesian in its barbarism – nasty, brutish and short. Vico has a recurrent image of primitive man ranging 'the great forest of the earth, pursuing shy and indocile women, and fleeing from the wild animals . . .' It took the imagined wrath of Jove – thunder – to drive them into caves and substitute for promiscuity 'religious and chaste carnal unions' and so found families. This natural and poetic religion, founded wholly on fear, has little to recommend it or its products:

> The first nature, by a powerful deceit of imagination, which is most robust in the weakest at reasoning, was a poetic or creative nature, which we may be allowed to call divine . . . This nature was that of the theological poets, who were the earliest wise men in all the gentile nations . . . it was a nature all fierce and cruel; but, through that same error of their imagination, men had a terrible fear of the gods they themselves had created . . .

> The second was heroic nature, believed by the heroes themselves to be of divine origin. . . The third was human nature, intelligent and hence modest, benign, and reasonable, recognising for laws conscience, reason, and duty.[68]

Yet in case we should be tempted to take this definition of the 'poetic' as in some sense metaphorical, Vico is also at pains to stress that once human language had got beyond the presumed initial stage of monosyllabic grunts, it was 'poetic' in the quite literal sense of being *verse*. 'Heroic verse', he informs us, 'is the oldest of all, and spondaic the slowest; . . . heroic verse was originally spondaic.' Iambic is the most sophisticated and latest form because it is 'the closest to prose'.[69] That this primitive language is poetic is no guarantee of its greater truth – indeed, rather the opposite. Certainly it is not the 'peculiar language of heaven' lauded by Thomson:

The first language, spoken by the theological poets, was not a language in accord with the nature of the things it dealt with (as must have been the sacred language invented by Adam, to whom God granted divine onomathesia, the giving of names to things according to the nature of each), but was a fantastic speech making use of physical substances endowed with life and most of them imagined to be divine.[70]

Indeed, it is this very conceptual weakness that makes it the better as poetry. With increasing civilization there comes a progressive and inevitable decline of poetry as an art form:

. . . it has been shown that it was a deficiency of human reasoning power than gave rise to poetry so sublime that the philosophies which came afterward, the arts of poetry and of criticism, have produced none equal or better, and have even prevented its production.[71]

Similarly, what Vico calls 'poetic wisdom' is only a passing stage in human culture, which, while it originally embraced every sphere of activity, is gradually superseded and dispensed with:

. . . we must trace beginnings of poetic wisdom to a crude metaphysics. From this, as from a trunk, there branch out from one limb logic, morals, economics, and politics, all poetic; and from another, physics, the mother of cosmography and astronomy, the latter of which gives their certainty to its two daughters, chronology and geography – all likewise poetic.[72]

Thus 'poetic theology' gives way by an inevitable progression to 'natural theology' and, finally, to the revelation of Christian theology.[73]

Whereas the idea of the *Volksgeist* in German suggests positive and even admirable qualities, Vico's 'poetic', while constituting a necessary stage of mental development, is from our point of view almost wholly retrogressive. Almost – but not quite. As in other European languages, the root of the Italian *poesia* comes from the Greek verb to 'make'. For Vico, steeped in classical philology, the 'poetic' is the natural and spontaneous mode of human thought: it is *how* the mind creates. Rejecting the traditional Aristotelian and neo-classical notion of poetry as a means of adorning and communicating intellectual truth, he claims it instead as the precondition for the perception of any truth. According to Croce, the central importance of Vico is that by returning to this root he invented a quite new concept of the 'aesthetic':

Poetry is not esoteric wisdom: it does not presuppose the logic of the intellect: it does not contain philosophical judgements. . . Poetry is produced not by the mere caprice of pleasure, but by natural necessity. It is so far from being superfluous and capable of elimination, that without it thought cannot arise: it is the primary activity of the human mind.[74]

For Vico, the basic division between kinds of human knowledge lies not between art and science in our modern senses of the words, but between what we make for ourselves, which includes not merely art and history, but also mathematics, and what we can know only from the 'outside' – as we know, for instance, the natural world. The Feuerbachian and Marxist distinction between creativity and alienation has its origins in Vico. Poetry is the evidence of man as an animal who *creates*.

Now for Vico, as a good (or, at least, a prudent) Catholic, this basic creative drive in mankind is at the very opposite pole from theology – which in its Christian form is strictly a matter of divine Revelation. Yet, though history may be regarded as man's supreme creation, there is at work in its processes another shadowy quality – a kind of 'immanent will' – manifesting itself through human affairs. Partly because of his resolute avoidance of biblical history and Christian theology, it is never clear from the *New Science* whether this power is more akin to the impersonal forces of Marxist history (which have an undoubted Vichian origin) or whether it represents a direct, if covert, incarnational theology – the ancestor of Matthew Arnold's 'not-ourselves which makes for righteousness'.[75] Though it would be possible to think of this force as a kind of external manipulation of human destiny by God, it is far more consistent with the whole tenor of Vico's thought if we see it, rather, as a divine spark inherent in the very depths of human creativity itself; that in the act of 'making' – that is, in the poetic apprehension of things – humanity is resonating with the divine will that created the world *ex nihilo*.

As has been suggested, Vico's influence leads in a number of very different directions. Whether or not his (somewhat ambiguous) admiration for the 'poetic' qualities of German assisted the spread of his ideas in that language, we know that he was read by Hamann, Herder,

Goethe, and Jacobi; in France by Montesquieu, de Maistre, and above all by Michelet; in England by Coleridge, Thomas Arnold, and F. D. Maurice – not to mention Mazzini when in exile. The real question of influence is, however, much more problematical than this list might suggest. Neither Hamann nor Goethe seem in fact to have been impressed by the *New Science*, and Herder, who is in many ways closest to Vico in spirit, seems, incredibly, to have formulated his most 'Vichian' ideas long before reading it. J. G. Robertson's vision of Vico as not merely a major factor in the development of German thought in the eighteenth century but also as a precursor of the Darwinian concept of evolution in the nineteenth, however persuasive, is difficult to sustain in terms of hard evidence.[76]

Yet, even though, as Isaiah Berlin admits, the parallels between Vico and Herder are, if accidental, astonishingly close, they differ markedly over the definition and function of the poetic. For Herder, language is the expression of the collective experience of the group (to think and speak in words is to 'swim in an inherited stream of images . . .' which we accept on trust)[77] that makes the *creation* of language by the poet an act paralleling divinity. Of Adam naming the beasts in Genesis, he writes:

> In giving names to all, and ordering all from the impulse of his own inward feeling, and with reference to himself, he (Adam) becomes an imitator of the Divinity, a second Creator, . . . a creative poet. Following this origin of the poetick art, instead of placing its essence in an imitation of nature, as has generally been done, we might still more boldly place it in an imitation of that Divine agency which creates, and gives form and determinateness to the objects of its creation.[78]

Whereas Vico had postulated a clean break between the divinely-inspired 'onomathasic' language of Adam and the re-invention of words after the Flood, Herder sees language as a continuum. Behind this lies a Protestant tradition, going back at least as far as Luther, that saw in the emphasis on the study of the 'word' – the actual biblical language, rather than the typological interpretations of the Fathers – a rediscovery of the original relationship between language and creation disrupted by the Fall and Babel.[79] It was a common seventeenth-century view, held for instance with differing degrees of literalness by figures as different as Leibniz and Boehme, that underlying all known languages was the original radical and primitive language of Adam.[80] In spite of the Fall, Adam remained the first and greatest philosopher and etymologist because he alone had 'known' all creatures according to their true essences, and for him words had corresponded directly with things in a way never possible again.[81] As Boehme had put it:

Now, that Adam stood in the image of God and not that of the beasts is shown by the fact that he knew the property of all the creatures and gave names to all the creatures according to their essence, form, and property; he understood the language of nature as revealed and articulated word in all essence, for the name of each creature has its origin there.[82]

For Herder, then, the Adamic language is 'poetic' because, as the true language of nature, it corresponded with the essential inner quality of things. How far, at this stage in his writing, he believed literally in an Adamic origin to poetry is questionable. Steiner has argued that in the 1772 Prize Essay *On the Origin of Language* Herder never quite shakes himself free from the enigma of whether language had natural or divine origins.[83] In fact in the *Essay* Herder explicitly disassociates himself both from Süssmilch's thesis that language was the divine and miraculous gift of God,[84] and from the theories of Condillac and Rousseau that it had evolved from the noises of animals.[85] But, as Hans Aarsleff has pointed out,[86] many other aspects of Herder's argument, including his psychological stress on the 'totality of the organisation of all human powers, the entire economy of man's perceptive, cognitive, and volitional nature',[87] follow Condillac closely rather than rejecting him. It becomes clear as the argument of the *Essay* unfolds that questions of historical origins (the obligatory theme of the prize essay set by the Berlin Academy) are in fact less interesting to Herder than its *psychological* origins. For him, the essence of language lies not in external sounds, but in the internal genesis of words as symbols not so much for communication as for thought.[88] It is man's internal dialogue with himself as an integral part of consciousness that is, for him, the distinguishing quality of human language. Similarly, in the later *Spirit of Hebrew Poetry*, Herder is oddly poised, like many of his generation, between literalist and metaphorical readings of the Bible. Yet as his references to the story of Babel 'as a poetic fragment of the archeology and history of the human race' in the *Essay on the Origin of Language* make clear, he is in little doubt over the essentially symbolic nature of the Genesis accounts.[89] Thus in the passage quoted, any question of the historical status of the Creation-naming is clearly secondary to the aesthetic. He is implicitly stepping aside from questions of imitative versus expressive theories of language, or of its divine versus natural origin, and claiming instead, by bold analogy, the internal aesthetic autonomy of the word – echoing Vico's conclusion, if not his way of reaching it. It anticipates by a generation Coleridge's description of the imagination as 'a repetition in the finite mind of the eternal act of creation in the infinite I AM.'[90]

This movement away from expressive and imitative theories of language towards notions of its artistic autonomy is, of course, most fully developed by Wilhelm von Humboldt – perhaps the greatest of the Romantic linguistic theorists.[91] For him, as for Keble later, the shaping powers of the intellect are inherent in language. Language is *itself* essentially poetic – a more comprehensive work of art than its own artifacts. It was the pioneer work of Sir William Jones on the relationship between Sanskrit and the classical European languages that was to inspire the new science of comparative philology in Germany and it is no accident of grouping that C. B. Schmidt should have published his translation of Lowth's *Praelectiones* together with extracts from Jones and Herder.[92] Jones's *Third Anniversary Discourse on the Hindus* (1786)[93] had, in the words of Fredrich von Schlegel, 'first brought light into the knowledge of language through the relationship and derivation he demonstrated of Roman, Greek, Germanic and Persian from Indic, and through this into the ancient history of peoples, where previously everything had been dark and confused'.[94] Jones's initial insights elaborated in his essay, *On the Origins and Families of Nations*,[95] were taken up and developed by German philologists of the early nineteenth century: Franz Bopp, the Schlegels, Jacob Grimm, and Humboldt himself.[96] The details of the amazing growth of comparative philology during this period do not concern us here.[97] What is of interest is the attempt by a group of Anglo-German scholars in the mid-years of the nineteenth century to relate the new philology to some of the traditional concerns of theologians and, in particular, to the idea of the 'poetic'.

J. W. Donaldson's *The New Cratylus* (1839) was an attempt to revitalize classical study in England by setting it in the context of comparative philology. A Fellow of Trinity College, Cambridge, and a member of the Hare–Thirlwall circle of liberal Anglicans,[98] Donaldson had also a strong theological motive: to reject materialism (in particular the reductionist philology of Horne Tooke)[99] and to show the essential identity of philosophy with philology. Language is thought, so the history of language is nothing less than the history of thought.[100] Once again he takes up the theme of the primacy of poetry: primitive man was naturally poetic, in contrast to 'the careful but barren elegancies of logical prose'.[101] Donaldson's arguments, together with those of Renan in France, and the German philologists, were taken up by F. W. Farrar, the future Dean of Canterbury, in his *Essay on the Origin of Language* (1860) and in *Chapters on Language* (1865). But the twenty years separating Donaldson and Farrar had seen a radical change in possible attitudes towards the primitive. As a result of the dramatic advances in archaeology and prehistory the old Biblical time-scale of a world only six thousand years old (still being officially clung to in the Cambridge Theology Tripos as late as the 1840s) was no longer possible. With it went much of the emotional force behind belief in noble and poetic forebears of modern man. In 1860 Farrar could still write scornfully of 'the error of man's slow and toilsome development from an almost bestial condition' and proclaim that 'the dawn of language took place in the bright infancy, in the joyous boyhood of the world'.[102] But by 1865, as John Burrow points out,[103] he had lost much of this confidence, and admits the probable savage state of prehistoric man: 'a miserable population . . . forced to dispute their cave-dwellings with the hyena and the wolf'.[104]

Though intelligent and learned, Farrar was not a notably original thinker. Others had faced this crisis before him, and others – many more – would have to come to it after him. It was, in many ways, a minor example of the genus of Victorian religious crisis. Yet the problem it poses, and which Farrar's volte-face epitomizes so convenient-ly, is significant: the *historical* discussion of the 'poetic' could no longer be confused with the *aesthetic*. For Dennis and Trapp, debating the primacy of poetry over prose, the distinction between historical primacy or logical, and aesthetic, primacy is never fully worked out. If, for Dennis, poetry is the more ancient art, that also means it is of a fundamentally superior *kind*; nearest, as it were, to the language of Eden itself, and Thomson's 'peculiar language of heaven'. There are still traces of this belief in an Adamic language in Farrar's 1860 *Essay*. From mid-Victorian times, though it was, and still is, possible to claim in some senses that the 'poetic' use of language is far older than the literal and prosaic, questions of the status of literary forms, and their relative value, had to be entirely separate for the historical question of their age. Fact had to be desynonymized from value.

The ambivalence towards primitive man that this differentiation came to produce in Farrar, is also noticeable in the last two examples of this great period of Anglo-German cooperation that concern us here: Baron Bunsen, onetime Prussian Ambassador to London, and his protégé, Max Müller, who became the first Professor of Comparative Philology at Oxford.

For the German romantics, as for the English, the links between religion, prophecy, and poetry were almost a critical commonplace. 'The poetizing philosopher, the philosophizing poet, is a prophet', wrote Friedrich Schlegel.[105] For him, religion is apprehended by the poets 'as a variety of poetry', and, indeed, 'poetry and philosophy are, depending on one's point of view, different spheres, different forms, or simply the component parts of religion'.[106] Similar connections are predicated by both Tieck and Solger,[107] but whereas the romantic aestheticians share the same spirit of latent anti-clericalism already seen in von Humboldt, and argue from a lofty and generalized philosophic idealism, by aphorism and fragment, rather than from the more practical historical premises of Lowth and Herder, Bunsen combines the two traditions in a manner at once systematic, universal, and historical. The titles of his two major works convey his concerns with almost a parody of teutonic precision: *Outlines of the Philosophy of Universal History applied to Language and Religion* (2 vols. 1854) and *God in History, or the Progress of Man's Faith in the Moral Order of the World* (3 vols. 1868). For Bunsen, Christianity is continuous with the ancient religions of India and Egypt and the specifically Jewish element is correspondingly played down. Matthew Arnold noted approvingly that:

Bunsen used to say that our great business was to get rid of all that was purely semitic in Christianity, and to make it Indo-Germanic, and Schleiermacher that in the Christianity of us Western nations there was really much more of Plato and Socrates than of Joshua and David.[108]

The key to understanding this progressive spiritual development of 'the Indo-European genius' is, of course, philology. 'The structure of thought revealed by its deposits in language', writes Bunsen, 'precedes all other coinage of the human intelligence.'[109] According to him, primitive man, though ascending culturally, still trailed some clouds of glory: 'linguistic enquiry shows that the languages of savages are degraded decaying fragments of nobler formations'.[110] There is, therefore, a sense in which civilization is a route whereby we may regain the original Paradise lost – the Miltonic metaphor is Bunsen's own.[111] Thus the history of mankind revealed by the study of language is one of deepening religious insight:

The power of the mind which enables us to see the genus in the individual, the whole in the many, and to form a word by connecting a subject with a predicate, is essentially the same which leads man to find God in the Universe and the Universe in God. Language and religion are the two poles of our consciousness, mutually presupposing each other.[112]

Though, for Bunsen, the *word* 'poetic' itself remains relatively narrow, and, in factual terms, faintly suspect, conveying something of the same connotations of exaggeration and figurative inaccuracy that we find in an earlier generation of German critics, such as Eichhorn and Lessing,[113] we find that the idea of 'language' *as a whole* has taken its place as the vehicle of revelation. Bunsen has, in effect, used the new science of comparative philology (however illegitimately) and Hegelian idealism to claim that *all* language, prose and poetry, is religious language simply because it is inescapably charged with history. If the argument's German origins in the writings of Schelling, Hegel, von Humboldt, and others is most immediately obvious, there is also a strikingly Wordsworthian element in the universality of Bunsen's claim for language. Wordsworth had come close to asserting that all language was poetic. Bunsen now caps this with the assertion that *all* language is religious. For both, the primitive sources of power lost in the corruptions of society are to be rediscovered through further sophistication. The significance of this basic premise can be seen by comparing Bunsen with Müller. Both shared common roots in German idealism and in English liberal Anglicanism; both shared a belief in language as the key to understanding history. Where Müller goes way beyond Bunsen is in his knowledge of comparative religion: his early work was on the Hindu sacred books of the *Rig-Veda*, and as Professor of Comparative Philology at Oxford he was to give both four series of Gifford and the Hibbert Lectures.[114] He is, however, much more acutely aware than Bunsen apparently is of the philosophical problems engendered by language. He toys with the idea of an unambiguous language of precisely defined terms, but is too conscious of the difference between natural and artificial languages to pursue this idea. The ghost of the old idea of the Adamic 'natural' language still lurks behind his notion of a prehistoric 'metaphorical period' when the simple language of early man suddenly blossomed into poetic complexity.[115] Finally he comes to the conclusion that the 'meaning' of a word was equivalent to its whole etymological history.[116] Indeed, for him 'History, if properly understood can take the place of philosophy'.[117] In one sense this is little more than an extension of Bunsen's equation of the spirit of religion with its history (a belief that Müller shared)[118] but in another it involves one of the most extraordinary admissions ever made that an idea had ran out of steam. As John Burrow and Garry Trompf have shown, there are a number of ways in which Müller was outpaced by intellectual developments, in particular in anthropology, towards the end of his life,[119] but from our perspective in the history of religious language, we can see all too clearly another reason.

Max Müller is the end of one line in the long tradition we saw begin with Dennis claiming the 'poetic' status of religious language. Aided by associations with the Greek root *poesis* ('a making') the word had grown from a simple adjective derived from a particular literary kind to conquer as its field the Bible and religion generally then the whole of literature, the fine arts, the performing arts, and architecture, then hardly pausing in its headlong career, as 'religion' it had subsumed most of the rest of human learning – history, prehistory, anthropology, mythology, and language itself.[120] After such a growth in less than two hundred years, it is small wonder if the value of the word had almost collapsed from inflation, and the central idea from which it had started – that of 'sublimity' – had been almost lost in its imperial expansion. Müller's attempt to rediscover the precise meaning of a word in its total etymological history is, seen in this light, a final admission of failure for the original attempt to solve the problem of biblical hermeneutics through the concept of poetic language.

Yet, as we saw earlier, this extensive or 'imperial' meaning to the word 'poetic' represents only one of a number of possible developments of Dennis's original idea of the 'poetic sublime'. Dennis, we recall, had made a fundamental distinction between poetry and prose. Edmund Burke, in his seminal treatise *On the Sublime and the Beautiful*, refined this distinction still further, by insisting that the two qualities, both essentially 'poetic', were fundamentally opposed to each other. Burke had no doubts that the Longinian tradition is correct in seeing religious language as the very essence of the sublime, but by that token it cannot also be beautiful. The Bible exemplifies *par excellence* the qualities of 'fear', 'obscurity', 'power', 'privation', 'vastness', 'infinity', and all the other sensations that awe the mind into a recognition of sublimity. The Book of Job is invoked as the *locus classicus* of the sublime.[121] In contrast, the 'beautiful', for Burke, exemplifies the more 'feminine' qualities of the 'small', the 'smooth', the 'delicate', and the clarity of the Hogarthian 'line of beauty'.[122] In his final section, 'On Words', Burke spells out the implications of his thesis on language:

> . . . very polished languages, and such as are praised for their superior clearness and perspicuity, are generally deficient in strength . . . whereas the languages of most unpolished people, have a great force and energy of expression . . . Uncultivated people . . . are more affected with what they see, and therefore express themselves in a warmer and more passionate manner.[123]

The distinction between clarity and strength of expression has an important bearing on the problem of biblical translation noted in the last chapter; for Burke, an attempt to create simple, clear, and unambiguous language from that of the Old Testament would have been a monstrous violation of literary decorum. The *Enquiry* was published in 1757, a few years after Lowth's *Praelectiones*, but twenty-one years before Lowth's *Commentary on Isaiah* (which repeats in English many of the arguments in the Latin *Praelectiones*). Though the common ground with Lowth, and later with Wordsworth, is obvious, it is clear throughout that Burke finds the religious sublime a narrow and relatively rare linguistic category – certainly much narrower than that of 'the poetic' in general.

For others in the eighteenth century, of course, the word 'poetic' had never been much of a compliment. We have already considered Vico's use of it. Similarly, however much Johann Gottfried Eichhorn may have been influenced by Lowth's historical methodology, he takes a fundamentally opposed view of art. For him, art represents conscious artifice. When he praises Ezekiel as the greatest artist among the prophets he is purporting to defend him against the deist argument that he was deliberately dishonest. Yet in so far as he was an artist, he was a composer and not a visionary: 'All these raptures and visions are in my judgement mere cover-up, mere poetical fancies'.[124] In the same commentary on the Old Testament Eichhorn wrote of Jeremiah, 'In order to give this simple stuff prophetic dignity, Jeremiah made use for his poetic fiction of a conversation with Jehovah.'[125] For others, such as Lessing, and later, Feuerbach, the idea of 'the poetic' suggested immediately 'that which is not true'.

For the English philosophical radicals, such as Bentham and the elder Mill, who had, by temperament as much as intellectual inclination, no interest in either poetry or religion, the equation of either, or both, with lies, wishful thinking, or the dangers inherent in figurative language, was a simple enough matter. For John Stuart Mill, however, the problem of defining 'poetry' had a private urgency. The accounts of poetry given or implied by previous empiricists, Locke, Hartley, and Hume, as well as Bentham and his own father, had totally failed to live up to the complexity of his personal aesthetic experience. After his breakdown at the age of 21 it had been the experience of reading Wordsworth that had done most to restore the sense of value and meaning in his own life. From thenceforth, poetry was for Mill an essential ingredient of human existence: an expression of, and the means for, the cultivation of the feelings.[126] Like Keble, he insists that poetry is not confined to verse, but is present in prose, music, sculpture, painting, and architecture − in short, it is 'the better part of all art whatever, and of real life too'.[127] But though this looks at first glance like Keble's 'extensive' view of poetry, as Mill quickly makes clear, this is a *qualitative* rather than a *quantitative* judgement. His idea of poetry is essentially 'intensive' rather than 'extensive'. In his essay, *What is Poetry?*, first published in 1833, he answers the question of the title by saying it is neither more nor less than 'feeling' or emotion − to be 'distinguished from what Wordsworth affirms to be its logical opposite, namely not prose, but matter of fact or science'. That Wordsworth had not quite said this is beside the point.[128] Mill continues:

The one addresses itself to the belief, the other to the feelings. The one does its work by convincing or persuading, the other by moving. The one acts by presenting a proposition to the understanding, the other by offering interesting objects to the sensibilities.[129]

There are, Mill concludes, two very different kinds of 'truth': the one is essentially irrational and subjective, expressing the inner world of human feeling; the other is intellectual, objective, and concerned with the external world of things.[130] Thus poetry has not merely to be contrasted with science, but also with *fiction*. 'The truth of poetry is to paint the human soul truly: the truth of fiction is to give a true picture of *life*. The two kinds of knowledge are different, and come by different ways, come mostly to different persons . . . '[131] In so far as verse contains *narrative* of any kind, it ceases to be poetry; poetry is simply the expression of emotion: properly speaking, it cannot refer to the world of material things. Though phrased in terms remarkably similar to his contemporary Wordsworthian, Keble, Mill's definition of poetry is one of the most narrowly intensive ever devised: if it contains 'the better part . . . of real life', few Desert Fathers could have propounded a more world-renouncing doctrine.

Interestingly enough, the religious implications of Mill's idea of poetry are entirely congruent with those of Burke. Since it, too, has no cognitive content in a positivist sense, but is simply a matter of feeling, religion is deeply poetic. For the Catholic – clearly the most 'poetic' form of Christian for Mill – 'the Deity' is 'wrapped up in vagueness, mystery, and incomprehensibility'[132] – and is therefore truly sublime.

In 1873, the same year as Mill's *Autobiography*, Matthew Arnold published *Literature and Dogma*. It is commonly assumed, in spite of his half-hearted disclaimers, that he had drawn mainly on German sources (notably Lessing and Feuerbach) when writing it, but in one respect his ideas appear as a clear continuation of those of Mill. Like Mill, he effectively denies any public cognitive content to the traditional language about God. It is, Arnold insists, essentially 'poetic'. It was a product of that familiar phenomenon of *Aberglaube* or, as he translates it into English, 'extra-belief': the encrustation of miraculous legend, superstition, and fairy-tale that had grown up around the basic moral truths of Christianity, and by the nineteenth century were in danger of strangling them. '*Aberglaube*', he explains, 'is the poetry of life.' It is part of an entirely natural process of innocent self-deception rather than fraud:

> That men should, by help of their imagination, take short cuts to what they ardently desire, whether the triumph of Israel or the triumph of Christianity, should tell themselves fairy-tales about it, should make these fairy-tales the basis for what is far more sure and solid than the fairy-tales, the desire itself – all this has in it, we repeat, nothing which is not natural, nothing, blameable . . .[133]

Unlike Eichhorn, Arnold insists that this process of miraculous accretion is an unconscious one involving no deliberate fabrication; unlike Feuerbach he insists that this unconscious process is essentially 'poetic'. The problem, of course, is to decide what Matthew Arnold, the well-known poet and man of letters, means by 'poetic' in this context. In *God and the Bible* (1875) he spells out what were his basic principles in *Literature and Dogma*. These were, firstly, the Bible requires nothing for its basis except what can be verified; and, secondly, that its language is not scientific, but literary: 'that is, it is the language of poetry and emotion . . .'[134] Like most of his Victorian contemporaries, Schleiermacher and Feuerbach, Mill and Keble, Arnold assumes that religion is essentially a matter of 'emotion' and 'feeling'.[135] What is much more significant is his willingness to abandon the idea of psychic unity at the centre of the Wordsworth/Coleridge idea of poetry as a union of thought *and* feeling[136] in favour of Mill's view of poetry as a matter of pure feeling opposed to 'science' and cognitive content. 'Poetry' continues Arnold, is 'language not professing to be exact at all . . . We are free to use it and not to use it as our sense of poetic propriety may dictate.'[137] Thus:

We have to renounce impossible attempts to receive the legendary and miraculous matter of scripture as grave historical and scientific fact. We have to accustom ourselves to regard henceforth all this part as poetry and legend. In the Old Testament as an immense poetry growing round and investing an immortal Truth, 'the secret of the Eternal': *Righteousness is salvation*. In the New, as an immense poetry growing round and investing an immortal truth, the secret of Jesus; *He that will save his life shall lose it, he that will lose his life shall save it.*[138]

Arnold is not saying here that 'poetry' is simply a decorative fiction that is untrue, because he is also committed to the view that poetry can and often does embody profound truths.[139] The power of its emotions brings those truths to life in our hearts.[140] Yet in the last resort 'poetry' (that is, 'feeling') and 'truth' (that is, here, ethics) can and must be separated. The kernel can be extracted from the shell. It is − to continue his own image of a nut − the husk that protects the seed, carries it safely to its destination, and nourishes it. But in order that the seed of truth may grow, the husk must sooner or later be dispensed with − break down or decay. If, at first, poetry gives life to new truths, at a later stage it can be a source of confusion, misunderstanding, 'delusion and error'. If poetry is not itself 'untrue', it is because it is not itself concerned with ideas at all: it is merely a *mode* of expression − a figurative, unscientific, and − here consciously echoing Vico − it must be said, primitive mode of expression. For Arnold, the tragedy of modern man is that 'soon enough will the illusions which charmed and aided man's inexperience be gone; what have you to give him in the place of them?'[141]

The real paradox of Arnold as a poet-theologian is that he has in effect *narrowed* the concept of the 'poetic' more radically than any of his predecessors, including the utilitarian atheist, Mill. For Mill at least the *whole* of religion, considered as 'feelings of devotion', was poetic; because Arnold wishes to salvage some ethical and cognitive kernel from that feeling, he is forced in the end to define as 'poetry' the useless residue. Worse, he has, as poet, found himself forced to consign by definition almost everything that is attractive to that residue. Like some strict eighteenth-century Lockeian who has discovered the unreality of secondary qualities,[142] or a Kantian forbidden to take pleasure in moral duty, Arnold has boxed himself into a corner where 'reality' is totally stripped of human emotion:

> ... For the world, which seems
> To lie before us like a land of dreams,
> So various, so beautiful, so new,
> Hath really neither joy, nor love, nor light,
> Nor certitude, nor peace, nor help for pain. . .[143]

– nor, incidentally, *Dover Beach* itself, since that, after all, is poetry.

This was a paradox seized upon by George Tyrrell, the Catholic Modernist, who was in many ways Matthew Arnold's closest successor. With brilliant inversion, worthy of Blake's comment that Milton was 'of the Devil's party without knowing it',[144] Tyrrell commented that what Arnold really 'hoped for was, roughly speaking, the preservation of the ancient and beautiful husk after the kernel had been withered up and discarded'.[145] If he could recognize more clearly than many of his contemporaries the contradictions between head and heart in Arnold, it was because Tyrrell shared something of that tension. Starting as a Jesuit from an orthodox Catholic position, he had until about 1899 believed that revelation must imply supernaturally communicated propositional truth,[146] and it was only slowly and reluctantly that he came to accept the idea of a clear distinction between the language of religion and that of science. When he did so, it was to attempt a reconciliation between the two ways of understanding the poetic that, as we have seen, had come to dominate nineteenth-century thought. 'All language', he wrote in 1907, 'is poetical in origin. It tries to express the whole inner state – not merely the truth, but the emotions and feelings in which the truth is embedded; for the so-called "faculties" – mind, will, feeling – have not yet been marked off from one another by abstract thought.'[147] In the Preface to the same book, *Through Scylla and Charybdis*, he had written:

> Were it possible to show that underneath the obvious sense of revelational and dogmatic utterances there lay a deeper sense, a truth of an entirely different order; were it possible, in the light of the comparative study of religions and of an immensely deepened psychological insight, to give a more real and undeniable value to the notion of "prophetic truth" than I can claim to have done, then it seems to me we might perhaps be able to reconcile perfect fidelity to the ancient principles of Catholic tradition with an equal fidelity to the fullest exigencies of scientific truth and moral truthfulness.[148]

As a solution to the problem presented by the Arnoldian split between 'poetry' and 'science', Tyrrell's idea of 'prophetic truth' has some appeal:'

> "Prophetic" truth is analogous with poetic, artistic, dramatic truth in that the religious and moral values of its utterances, like the aesthetic values of artistic utterances, are to a certain extent independent of the fact-values or historical values.[149]

Here a separation is implied between poetic and religious language; 'prophetic' language is *analogous* to the poetic, but differs from it in that its symbols express the 'ancient principles of Catholic tradition'. The problem, of course, is how are we to know when language is being merely poetic, and when it is being actually prophetic?

This was the problem with which John Henry Newman had already attempted to grapple. It was, as he had seen perhaps more clearly than any of his contemporaries, the unsolved question latent in Coleridge's religious aesthetics. In an early essay on *Poetry, with Reference to Aristotle's Poetics* (1829) Newman's use of the word 'poetry' is strikingly similar to that of Keble — even to the suggestion of its healing power.[150] Since this essay was written a good five years before Keble's lectures it is even possible that Keble was partly influenced by Newman. Yet, though Newman is ostensibly discussing Aristotle, the fundamental bias of his thinking is consistently more platonic than Keble's was ever to be. 'The metrical garb' and 'metaphorical language' of poetry are 'but the outward development of the music and harmony within'. There is here a strong suggestion that like Coleridge, Newman at this stage held that true poetry is somehow self-authenticating — revealing in words the hidden reality and harmony of the Platonic forms. Coleridge's idea of a symbol, we recall, was at once universal and concrete. Though Newman appears on occasions to be taking a similar position in the *Essay on the Development of Christian Doctrine* (1845) this is not in fact the case. The test by which one can know 'genuine development' from decay and corruption is the organic 'life' of the whole. A 'living' idea is not received passively by men, 'but it becomes an active principle with them, leading them to an ever-new contemplation of itself, to an application of it in various directions, and a propagation of it on every side'.[151] The source of true judgement is indeed the living body of the Catholic Church, but only because that body is infallibly guided. To interpret rightly is not a gift of the imagination unaided: 'such aspects are often unreal, as being mere exhibitions of ingenuity, not of true originality of mind'.[152] His conclusion is not that there is no objective truth, but rather that 'there is something deeper in our differences than the accident of external circumstances; and that we need the interposition of a power greater than human teaching and human argument to make our beliefs true and our minds one'.[153] This 'Power' is, of course, the Roman Catholic Church – but *not* in its expression through the dogmatic powers of the papacy or even of the great Councils. As Karl Rahner has pointed out about Newman,[154] the establishment of 'truth' by dogmatic ruling, however unexceptionable it might be in terms of doctrine, would violate the internal 'life' of the mind central to all his thinking. In Newman's own terminology from the *Grammar of Assent*, it would produce a 'notional' assent, mere passive acceptance, rather than the active 'real' assent which engages the imagination.

For Newman, as for Lowth, Vico and Herder, the metaphorical frame of reference of any language cannot be understood apart from the communal life from which it has grown.[155] But the price of thinking and speaking in any particular language is that we are also *enclosed* by 'the framework on which the working of our language is based'.[156] This is as true of religious language as of any other. Newman's increasing distrust of formal syllogistic logic (especially after his first visit to Rome) turned him more and more towards an interest in analogy, metaphor, and symbol as the appropriate vehicles of the living ideas of a community. It is the deliberate purpose of formal logic to *shed* the richness and vitality of actual experience in order to promote an artificial clarity. In a passage which is almost a direct inversion of Matthew Arnold, he writes:

> Words which denote things, have innumerable implications, but in inferential exercises it is the very triumph of that clearness and hardness of head, which is the characteristic talent for the art, to have stripped them of that depth and breadth of associations which constitute their poetry, their rhetoric, and their historical life, to have starved each term down till it has become the ghost of itself . . .[157]

The Catholic Church is, in the last resort, safeguarded from error not by official pronouncements of Popes and Councils (necessary as these are) but by the living organic structure of the whole body. How then may we describe that richness of historical tradition, of language, ritual, and emotional association that we experience in the organic life of the Catholic Church? Newman repeats the answer that he had already given in his 1846 essay on Keble: the life of the Church is *poetic*. 'The Church herself is the most sacred and august of poets . . .'[158] If the language of the Church is 'poetic' it is because the Church itself, the body of Christ, is the model from which we gain our idea of what a 'poet' is. Coleridge's definition of poetry as a 'reconciling of opposite and discordant qualities' is literally true – but he sought his certainty in the wrong place: aesthetics is to be understood by analogy with religion, not religion from aesthetics.

There is no doubt that Newman's was the most subtle, the most satisfying, and the most comprehensive solution to the problem of the relationship of the religious to the poetic that the nineteenth century was to see. In it the 'intensive' and the 'extensive' views of poetry were to find some measure of reconciliation. Unlike Arnold, Newman never conceived of Truth simply as a body of knowledge, but always understood that knowledge is inseparable from the knower, and the way of knowing. For Tyrrell, however, there was a major flaw. The Church that Newman had held to be the most sacred and august of poets was to dismiss Tyrrell from the Jesuits in 1905 and was to condemn his views under the blanket term of 'Modernism' in the decree 'Lamentabili' and then the Encyclical 'Pascendi' in 1907. Ironically, the Catholics were not yet ready for the ideas being thrust upon them by England and Germany. It was the Anglicans who were to read and debate the ideas of Newman, Arnold, and Tyrrell, and to question the conflicting ideas of the poetic, thrown up in the course of the two hundred year old debate since Dennis.

'Primal Consciousness' and linguistic change

The twentieth century's ideas of the 'poetic' reflect much of the confusions and polarization of meaning engendered by the nineteenth. In Germany, Hölderlin had applied Herder's revolutionary ideas of language by attempting, through translation, to incorporate what he saw as the creative energies of great foreign writers into his own culture. Behind languages, he believed, lay 'Language' – a kind of platonic absolute manifested in particular concrete works.[159] Though no Platonist, Heidegger, one of Hölderlin's most influential twentieth-century admirers, similarly describes language as the 'House of Being' – with all the peculiar force he attached to that last word. Language is one of the ways in which Being is articulated in a particular epoch. Humboldt's belief that it is only speech that makes man properly human becomes in Heidegger's hands the paradoxical maxim: '*Language speaks*'. [160] It is not to be understood as an expressive or representational activity of human beings; it is, rather, an autonomous force that cannot be grounded in anything outside of itself. Thus two elements, both already present in nineteenth-century German Romanticism, but later to become prominent via Saussure in twentieth-century French structuralism, are also present in Heidegger's thought: the notion of language as a self-referential closed circle, and the corresponding autonomy of the text:

We do not wish to ground language in something else that is not language itself, nor do we wish to explain other things by means of language . . . In its essence, language is neither expression nor activity of man. Language speaks.[161]

What is spoken purely is the poem . . . Who the author is remains unimportant here, as with every other masterful poem. The mastery consists precisely in this, that the poem can deny the poet's person and name.[162]

But Heidegger's notion of the 'poetic' is much more inclusive and fundamental than any specific aesthetic genre, however broadly conceived. He is always conscious of the Greek etmyology of the word. For him, human existence is itself fundamentally 'poetic' in a sense that is immediately familiar:

Poetry is not merely an ornament accompanying existence, not merely a temporary enthusiasm or nothing but an interest or amusement. Poetry is the foundation which supports history, and is therefore not mere appearance of culture . . . it is poetry which first makes language possible. Poetry is the primitive language of a historical people. Therefore, in just the reverse manner, the essence of language must be understood through the essence of poetry.[163]

The echoes of Vico and Croce are unmistakable. The link between this view of language and biblical hermeneutics is central to the understanding of much twentieth-century German theology. For Gerhard von Rad, for instance, Old Testament typology is essentially a poetic and analogical mode of thinking whose characteristics are common both to other Near Eastern mythologies and to the modern European poetic tradition.[164] It would be over-simple to describe Rudolf Bultmann, Ernst Fuchs, Gerhard Ebeling or Hans-Georg Gadamer as 'Heideggerians', but all four have in common with him certain existential and phenomenological premises rooted in ideas from Husserl and, beyond him, from German Romanticism, and share in their own ways Heidegger's notion of language as that which brings the world into existence.[165] Maurice Merleau-Ponty and Paul Ricoeur in France, and John Macquarrie in England are rooted in a similar existential linguistic tradition. Ricoeur emphasizes that the study of language is 'the common meeting-ground' of all forms of philosophical investigation.[166] In poetry, philosophical analysis encounters an older and more basic function of language than that of description:

. . . poetic language alone restores to us that participation in or belonging-to an order of things which precedes our capacity to oppose ourselves to things taken as objects opposed to a subject. Hence the function of poetic discourse is to bring about this emergence of a depth-structure of belonging-to amid the ruins of descriptive discourse.[167]

Poetry is thus a link between the historically original function of language, as Heidegger and Ricoeur conceive of it, which is one of primal participation with an animate cosmos, and the modern Saussurian notion of the autonomy of language in a literary text:

. . . the poetic function recapitulates in itself the three preparatory concepts of the autonomy of the text, the externality of the work, and the transcendence of the world of the text. Already by means of these three traits an order of things is revealed that does not belong to either the author or the original audience. But to these three traits the poetic function adds a split reference by means of which emerges the Atlantis submerged in the network of objects submitted to the domination of our preoccupation. It is this primordial ground of our existence, of the original horizon of our being-there, that is the revelatory function which is coextensive with the poetic function . . . Religious discourse is poetic in all the senses we have named. The style of its literary genres gives it the externality of a work. And the intended implicit reference of each text opens onto a world, the biblical world, or rather the multiple worlds unfolded before the book by its narration, prophecy, prescriptions, wisdom and hymns.[168]

Though the influence of Husserl, Heidegger and Saussure all mark such a statement as unmistakably twentieth-century, its provenance is not difficult to identify. From our point of view it belongs clearly to the 'extensive' tradition of poetics reaching back to a fundamentally Romantic nexus of ideas that we have traced through both Herder and Wordsworth. In place of the eighteenth-century debate over genres, and over the relative antiquity of prose and verse, we have a recognition that it is not literary 'kinds', but their structural function in a particular context that is of determining significance. For Ricoeur, the participatory function of language (i.e. the 'poetic') is more basic and fundamental than the descriptive (or 'prose' to reapply Dennis's terminology).

This is not, of course, a new idea. Northrop Frye traces this functional account of language back as far as Vico's three-fold distinction between the 'poetic', the 'heroic' and the 'vulgar',[169] – or, to use Frye's own terminology, the 'hieroglyphic', the 'hieratic', and the 'demotic'. In pre-Platonic and pre-biblical Greek and Near Eastern writing, Frye claims, language tended to be poetic and hieroglyphic. Words were essentially signs that *linked* subject and object, rather than distancing them from one another. Abstract words were in this sense still intensely physical. With Plato, Frye sees a shift to a more 'hieratic' use of language by an intellectual elite. As he graphically puts it: 'what Homeric heroes revolve in their bosoms is an inseparable mixture of thought and feeling; what Socrates demonstrates, more especially in his death, is the superior penetration of thought when it is in command of feeling'.[170] The language of this elite is, he argues, 'metonymic' or analogical: words are now the outward expressions of an inner reality. Socrates's 'celebrated "irony"' was a momentous step in transforming the use of language: it implied renouncing the personal possession of wisdom in favour of an ability to observe it'.[171] This metonymic use of language is associated with the development of continuous prose, and, significantly, parallels the growth of interest in mathematics. Thus Frye sees its high point coming with the philosophy of Kant, where the phenomenal world is made metonymically to 'stand for' the unknowable world of things-in-themselves.[172] The third stage, Vico's 'vulgar' or Frye's 'demotic', occurs when language is primarily used for description. Frye assumes that this way of using language had always been present, but dates its cultural dominance from the time of Locke and the scientific revolution of the seventeenth century.[173] In the case of religious language, he argues, we need to distinguish the language of immanence, which is founded on metaphor, and belongs to the first, the poetic, stage, from that of transcendence, which is founded on metonymy, and from descriptive language which is the backbone of scientific and narrative prose.

Though Vico may well be Frye's inspiration for this three-fold development, it is clear that the interpretations of each stage are largely Frye's – and are, again, unmistakably twentieth-century. They are, moreover, historically dubious. How, for instance, would he account for the fact that the very earliest written documents we possess, from Sumeria, are a form of business records[174] – by this classification, surely 'vulgar' in the extreme? Similarly, Aristotle's theories of language are totally ignored.[175] Yet Frye's scheme has a strangely familiar ring. The more we try to tease out, for instance, the distinction between poetry as the original language of primal participation and that of modern descriptive prose, the more we become aware that this is, in essence, a distinction at least as old as Dennis in the field of biblical studies. Moreover, as we found with Dennis, it is one that does not *quite* solve the problem of defining kinds of biblical language for which it was originally invoked. With a curious *volte-face* Frye himself recognizes this:

The linguistic idiom of the Bible does not really coincide with any of our three phases . . . It is not metaphorical like poetry, though it is full of metaphor, and it is as poetic as it can well be without being a work of literature. It does not use the trancendental language of abstraction and analogy, and its use of objective and descriptive language is incidental throughout. It is really a fourth form of expression, for which I adopt the now well-established term *kerygma*, proclamation.[176]

We are back to Bultmann with a bump. Indeed, the idea of the *kerygma* (leaving aside for the moment the not-obvious question of *what* that *kerygma* is) takes us back beyond Bultmann to a much older tradition of 'demythologizing' in German thought stretching back to the Enlightenment rationalism of Eichhorn and Lessing, and which we have already seen exemplified in England with Matthew Arnold. The basic problem remains that this view of the 'poetic' as the language of primal participation suggests also its primitive and non-discursive qualities. Whatever we decide in the end to be the *kerygma* must, somehow, be separated from its poetic matrix. The result, as we have seen in translations of the Elijah story, is an almost irresistible nisus or pressure to paraphrase or reinterpret the Bible to suit the contemporary idiom – unconsciously to continue the process of midrash in what purports to be the demotic language of neutral description. This is a problem to which we must return. I want here, however, to call attention to another, perhaps more unexpected, pressure revealed in the course of this argument.

That is that there appears to be a strange tendency for the 'extensive' claim for the 'poetic' to collapse surreptitiously and without warning into its opposite – the 'intensive'. Thus Ricoeur's assertion that biblical language is essentially the 'poetic' language of primal participation can almost imperceptibly be rephrased by the statement that it is essentially emotive rather than cognitive – in effect, the position of Arnold and Mill rather than Herder. This process can be seen even more dramatically at work in the writing of Heidegger's most distinguished theological disciple in England: John Macquarrie.[177] 'The problem,' he writes, 'is that of God-talk' – literally, theology:

To put it briefly, this problem is to show how in a human language one can talk intelligibly about a divine subject-matter. There are two obvious approaches to the problem. One would be to begin from the side of human language in its ordinary intelligible uses, and would enquire whether and how this language can legitimately be stretched so that one can use it to talk about God. The obvious advantage of this approach is that it sets out from the solid ground of something that is familiar and intelligible. The second line of approach would begin by positing the reality of God and would then bear in mind that if we do concede God's reality, then we must think of him as coming before everything else and as making possible everything else, including any knowledge of him or talk about him. So the inquiry would begin from God, and would ask what conditions would have to be fulfilled if the divine reality is to fall, at least to some extent, within the scope of human language.[178]

Such a distinction between two fundamentally different kinds of religious language, that of what Macquarrie calls 'ordinary intelligible usages' which must be 'stretched' to talk about God, and that of divine revelation, which must be brought within the 'scope of human language', sound a common-sense starting point – especially since he is careful to add that neither approach is, by itself, satisfactory. Yet, perhaps because of this no-nonsense flavour, it is in fact not immediately clear what this distinction involves. We may, I think, take it that the disconcertingly empiricist tone owes more to its intellectual provenance (mid twentieth-century Oxford) than to any notion of producing a positivist account of revelation. More plausible is the assumption that 'the ordinary intelligible usages' of language are the 'vulgar', 'demotic', and 'descriptive' that we have already encountered in Frye and Ricoeur, and that the language of revelation that posits God as before and behind everything else is to be associated with the language of primal participation so central to the Heideggerian idea of the 'poetic'. As if in confirmation of this, another modern English theologian, Peter Baelz, has developed this theory of 'two languages' more explicitly:

In speaking of the significance of Jesus Christ for the Christian faith we must indeed use two languages, the one human and historical, the other divine and mythological, each with its own distinctive function and logic.[179]

Here the distinction, though recognizably the same as Macquarrie's, is made specifically between the language of history and that of mythology – in short, between prose and poetry. Yet there is an important addition. Each, we are told, has its own distinctive 'function and logic'. Now the idea that language can have, according to context, distinctively different functions is not a difficult one; the idea of different *logics* – in the plural – is much more mysterious, since it seems to imply that the process of reason itself, as distinct from the premises of a system of thought, has fundamentally different rules according to the area of knowledge to which it is being applied. But if, considered rigorously, the proposition is an odd one, it is also not unfamiliar. It is, in essence, a restatement of the distinction between 'science' and 'poetry' put forward by Mill. The one

deals with discursive fact; the other affirms human participation in a pur-
posive and divinely-charged universe. We do not look to the Bible for
information on history or science, we find within it – so that argument
runs – a metaphorical and 'poetic' account of the growth of the spiritual
consciousness of mankind. The idea of different 'logics' is a recognition
that the two kinds of language belong to two utterly different modes of
awareness.

Once again, the 'extensive' claim for the 'poetic' has collapsed towards
the 'intensive'. Cognitive content has been edged towards the periphery
and in its place we find the 'poetic' interpreted as a form of pre-critical
affirmation (or 'proclamation'). Though the point is rarely made
specifically, such formulations seem tacitly to assume that the whole of
the Bible belongs to the realm of the 'poetic' or metaphorical in this sense
– in spite of Frye's engaging admission that such distinctions are less
helpful than they might appear when dealing with its linguistic idiom. It
is significant, for instance, that Macquarrie manages to write his entire
book on God-talk almost without reference to the language of the Bible,
even though substantial passages of both the Old and New Testaments
clearly come under the heading of 'theological discourse' – a category
which, for him, is self-evidently very different from narrative. His most
lengthy illustration is taken from Athanasius's *De Incarnatione*. 'Simply
to go to such a text,' he writes, 'examine and analyse it, and discover what
patterns of discourse are employed in it, would be a big step forward in
coming to grips with the syntax of theological discourse.'[180] The implication seems to be that the major problems of theology or religious
language are to be found typified in discursive texts such as this. We
might, not unfairly, compare such a methodology with that of discussing
Shakespeare by means of comparing his critics without reference to the
actual texts of his plays – or their performance.

Yet neither Macquarrie not Baelz set out to evade the problems of
biblical language. They are, on the contrary, pursuing what clearly
seems to them to be a method of analysis that is at once intellectually
rigorous and yet sensitive to literary nuance. The distinction between
'two languages' appears to offer a historically and linguistically valid way
of treating important areas of human experience that are otherwise very
difficult to give a satisfactory account of in the normative terms of a post-
Lockeian world. But what in the end amounts to an attempt to define and
defend the 'poetic' as a primal and non-intellectual mode of knowledge
launches them inexorably onto a course of more and more

desperate manoeuvres to save the appearances. Thus Macquarrie's vague initial sense of the inadequacy of human language to express divine reality in contrast to the 'ordinary intelligible usages' of everyday language, seems to impel Baelz towards clarification by the further claim that mythological language is even possessed of a different 'logic'.

This is an assumption that is made sufficiently frequently for it to merit some examination. What it usually seems to mean is that the narrative structure of mythological stories is recognizably different from that of so-called 'realistic' or historical narrative. If we take the Epic of Gilgamesh, for instance, or the stories of Greek mythology, the Norse myths, or the fairy-tales of Grimm and Perrault, this is clearly true. The seemingly universal presence of metamorphosis and arbitrary magic creates a quite unmistakable narrative frame. Myth and fairy-stories *do* have a recognizable 'logic' of their own. The problem, once again, is that the Bible, even at its most miraculous, does not fit into this genre. Its characters insist on behaving according to the conventions of realistic narrative, not fairy-stories. They tend to be nonplussed, astonished, and even at times made sceptical by the miraculous. They rarely live happily ever after. Metamorphosis does not happen.[181] Though monsters get a mention, they are natural not sentient. Gods do not take animal form, let alone mice turn into footmen or pumpkins into coaches. The exceptions – Adam and Eve and the serpent, for instance – are so obvious as to prove the general rule. Whatever the resemblances between the Sumerian myths and Genesis, or solar myths and the story of Samson, *in terms of literary genre* the overwhelming majority of the biblical narratives are firmly 'realistic'. Even those that are clearly intended as fiction – Jonah, for instance, or Job – are, significantly, much more like novels in their narrative technique than they are like myths.

In *The Rule of Metaphor* (1975), Ricoeur suggests a solution to the difficult problem of this relationship between the 'two languages' – or, as he calls them, 'speculative' and 'poetic discourse'. Though he is careful to distinguish between 'poetry' as an art-form and the wider category of 'poetic discourse', he nevertheless gives full weight to what he accepts as a fundamental difference between the two modes of discourse. His answer, following and extending the thesis of Douglas Berggren's seminal essay, *The Use and Abuse of Metaphor*,[182] is that poetic and speculative discourse exist in a *tensional* relationship to one another – each, in fact, being dependent on the other while, as it were, pulling in opposite directions.[183] Though he does not seem aware of it, this is a model already prefigured by Blake, who, in one of the most sweepingly imperial claims for the poetic ever made, nearly two hundred years before had made uncompromisingly explicit what was, perhaps, latent in Vico, and suggested that the poetic was central to all cognitive thought:

If it were not for the poetic or Prophetic character the Philosophic and Experimental would soon be at the ratio of all things, and stand still, unable to do other than repeat the same dull round over again.[184]

The analysis is a crucial one, and after trying to set it in its wider intellectual context in the next chapter, we shall be returning to it much later. Here, however, what is puzzling is the way that Ricoeur apparently fails to apply his own insight when specifically dealing with biblical texts. In *Toward a Hermeneutic of the Idea of Revelation*, published only two years after *The Rule of Metaphor*, he proceeds to define the 'poetic' in univocal rather than tensional terms. The inference is clear: biblical narratives relate to their historical context only as fiction relates to its social setting. Questions of 'historical fact' do not apply. For him it is axiomatic that any truth-content in religious, and, in particular, biblical language, must be metaphorical rather than literal. As he puts it: 'when language most enters into fiction . . . it most speaks truth . . . *mythos* is the way to true *mimesis*'.[185] At a stroke this solves the problem of the status of biblical narrative by cutting the Gordian knot that seemingly bound what Frei calls 'fact-likeness' to 'factuality'.[186] Thus there is no need to confine the 'poetic' to myth and fairy-story, or to suggest that it has a logic of its own. The 'fact-like' narratives of the Bible, *whether or not they are 'factual'*, are to be read as 'fact-like' in the sense that they bear the same relation to reality as a naturalistic novel does to its ostensible setting. Again Frye echoes Ricoeur's point: 'if anything historically true is in the Bible, it is there not because it is historically true but for different reasons'.[187] With a neat and, I suspect, not unconscious irony, he inverts Matthew Arnold: so far from being a basic moral message encrusted with the *Aberglaube* of mythical accretions, 'it has been obvious for at least a century that "mythical accretions" is what the Bible is: it is the bits of credible history that are expendable'.[188] In short, the claim is here that we need to read the Bible as poetically 'true' in the same sense that we might accept that a novel presents a more 'accurate' portrait of its society than any actual history – as we might say, for instance, that George Eliot's *Scenes of Clerical Life* tells us more about the privations of Victorian rural clergy than Victorian biographies are ever likely to. We do not enquire as to accuracy of detail; we ask if it is 'true-to-life'.

But if this seems to solve one problem, it raises others, even more complex. *Scenes of Clerical Life* (to continue our own analogy) purports to be historical narrative. The narrator claims to have known the characters personally and uses a number of rhetorical devices to add verisimilitude to this claim.[189] The fact that it is *not* 'history' is not because George Eliot was misinformed, nor because there were conceptual confusions in her mind between fact and fiction, nor even that she held a quite different idea from ourselves as to what constituted 'history', but simply that she was writing within a particular literary convention – that of the 'realistic novel' – in the nineteenth century, and that both she and her readers understood perfectly well that one of the prime conventions of this art form was that the narrative should *seem* to be about real persons in a real place. Now, as it happens, every one of the three stories in the *Scenes* is substantially true. To the consternation of the locals, they were recognizably based on incidents in the lives of actual clergy in the Nuneaton area where George Eliot had lived.[190] It might be very difficult to explain to an observer from Mars, or a historian from the fortieth century for whom the *Scenes* is one of a small number of books to have survived from the nineteenth, that the narrator's frequent stress on the truth of the story was an entirely conventional mode of fictional construction, bearing no relation to the fact that they happened to be true. Yet we know that this is so – indeed, what caused the scandal in Warwickshire when the stories were published was that the unknown author's claim to be recording 'history' turned out to be *true*, and not false.

The point of this circumstantially extreme example should be obvious. If it is correct to say of the *Scenes of Clerical Life* that if anything in it is historically true, it is there not because it is true but for other reasons, it cannot also be true to say it of the Bible *in the same sense*. It might, admittedly, be difficult to prove conclusively that the authors of the narratives in Kings, or Samuel, or the Gospels did not subscribe to a similar literary convention to that of the nineteenth-century novel, but we must, I think, assume they did not. We only have to compare them with Jonah to see the difference. As we have seen, the principle of midrash is essentially one of interpretation, not the creation of 'fact-like' fiction. However different the biblical authors' notions of 'history' may have been from our own, we have no reason to suppose that they did not believe that they were relating 'fact' and not 'fact-likeness' in Frei's sense. Even if one were to argue (as one might) that the effect of midrashic interpretation was closer, in fact, to *our* idea of 'realistic fiction' than it is to *our* idea of 'history', it would still be unsatisfactory to describe the historical narratives of the Bible as deliberate creations of fiction. We can, in short, interpret the 'poetic' nature of biblical narrative *neither* in terms of myth (in its traditional sense) *nor* in terms of mimetic art.[191]

It might seem at first sight as if this argument is an example of precisely the 'intentionalist fallacy' rejected in the last chapter. There are two ways of replying to this. The first is to point out that it is in fact the exact converse of the assumptions made by Nineham and Caird. Whereas they were prepared to assume a knowledge of the biblical authors' intentions as a principle of interpretation, here the argument is that we have no evidence for making any assumptions about authors' intentions beyond what is explicit in the texts themselves. The second follows from this, but has much more far-reaching implications. It is that, for Ricoeur, the notion of the autonomy of the literary text implies that the conventional ideas of authorial intention, even were we to know them, are simply irrelevant. According to this view, the text, once created, has an independent existence that transcends the worlds of either author or reader,[192] and constitutes an autonomous entity that is in the normal sense neither 'fact' nor 'fiction'. Since (on Kantian principles) it is impossible for us to know 'things-in-themselves', and there can be no such thing as 'knowledge' or 'facts' free from the interpretation of the knower, the difference between what we mean by 'history' and 'fiction' is a matter of degree, not kind. Both depend upon the creative interpretation of the human mind, and its expression through the semi-autonomous medium of language. We are thus freed from the necessity of asking meaningless questions as to the 'factual' or 'fictional' status of a narrative, and are able to look at the text itself and at what *that* can disclose. Ricoeur's idea of the 'poetic' is that it thus constitutes a third term that is neither 'fact' nor 'fiction' but transcends both in its metaphorical representation of truth.

This approach is valuable in that it permits us at least to look at the text itself for what it says, rather than try to extrapolate from it what it leaves out. But the price is a high one. By including everything, this new 'third term' explains nothing. Under the old literary categories it was clear that the different genres of the Bible – Ricoeur himself divides them loosely into narration, prophecy, prescriptions, wisdom, and hymns[193] – stood in conventionally different relationships to the world of presumed 'fact'. The reader learned to 'read' statements in the Song of Solomon in a different way from those in the Acts of the Apostles. But if *both* belong to the same metaphorical level, then this process of conventional discrimination is altogether lost. Once again, the unintended effect of the 'extensive' claim for the 'poetic' has been to collapse meaning towards a single linguistic category: in this instance the metonymic and descriptive functions of language seem to have been subsumed by the historically more primitive 'metaphorical'. Though it would be a mistake to see Ricoeur's position as reductionist in the normal sense, since he is fully aware of the interrelations and complexities of the biblical genres in relation to the reader, the effect of this inclusiveness is to suggest that there is no 'speculative' or 'descriptive' element in biblical narrative – that it operates solely at a level analogous to fiction, and that we cannot there entertain an idea of 'history' that is not identical with that of 'poetry'.

In reaction to this general tendency to blur genres by extending the territory of the 'poetic', certain twentieth-century English critics have sharply attacked the whole notion. In his 1948 Bampton Lectures, *The Glass of Vision*,[194] Austin Farrer devotes a whole lecture to distinguishing between 'poetry' and 'prophecy' in the Revelation of St John – denying, or at least, sharply modifying the close identification first suggested by Lowth and elaborated by Tyrrell. It is a theme he returns to again in his essay on 'Poetic Truth'.[195] For Farrer, the 'poetic' is always primarily a quality of *poetry*, or, by extension, of 'poetry-likeness'. That implies, almost by definition, that it is fundamentally different from other kinds of writing – such as prose. Thus he is constantly sensitive to changes in style and mode not merely between one biblical writer and another, but within the works of a single writer. In *A Rebirth of Images*, for instance, he argues that St John of Ephesus was in fact author of the Apocalypse, the Gospel, and the epistles traditionally ascribed to St John – probably in that chronological order.[196] Of these, however, only the Apocalypse is 'poetic' in any meaningful sense. It is, he writes, 'the one great poem which the first Christian age produced, it is a single and living unity from end to end, and it contains a whole world of spiritual imagery to be entered into and possessed'.[197] These qualities of organic and aesthetic unity, combined with a pattern of imagery related to that unity are, for him, characteristic of 'poetic' as distinct from other forms of writing. His interest in patterns of poetic imagery is not that of an anthropologist or a structural mythologist, but quite specifically that of the traditional literary critic:

The images (of God) are not through all ages absolutely invariable, and there is no historical study more significant than the study of their transformations. Such a transformation finds expression in the birth of Christianity; it is a visible rebirth of images . . .[198]

This poetic rebirth of images, central as it is to the creation and transmission of Christianity, is however, only *one* of the literary achievements of the New Testament:

St John was making a new form of literature: it happens that he had no successor. St Mark performed the same unimaginable feat, and he was followed by others . . . students of St Mark ought to ask the same question as we here are about St John . . . To us the idea of writing a memoir or a biography is perfectly familiar, and the literary men of the Hellenistic world had some notion of it too. But it is unlikely that St Mark had ever read such a work, and in any case his gospel had no resemblance to their efforts.[199]

For Farrer, there is, quite properly, nothing particularly 'poetic' about the gospels (though one might argue the Fourth Gospel is somewhat more 'poetic' in Farrer's sense than the synoptics). They are another, quite different, and highly original literary form, and naturally employ a different style and narrative technique.

In a paper delivered to the Oxford Socratic Club in 1944 entitled 'Is Theology Poetry?', C. S. Lewis had raised similar objections to the blanket use of the idea of the 'poetic',[200] but his most famous and dramatic onslaught, aimed principally at Rudolf Bultmann and his followers, was in 'Fern Seeds and Elephants', written in 1959:

In what is already a very old commentary I read that the fourth Gospel is regarded by one school as a 'spiritual romance', 'a poem not a history', to be judged by the same canons as Nathan's parable, the book of Jonah, *Paradise Lost*, 'or, more exactly, *Pilgrim's Progress*'. After a man has said that, why need one attend to anything else he says about any book in the world? Note that he regards *Pilgrim's Progress*, a story which professes to be a dream and flaunts its allegorical nature by every single proper name it uses, as the closest parallel. Note that the whole epic panoply of Milton goes for nothing. But even if we leave out the grosser absurdities and keep to *Jonah*, the insensitiveness is crass – *Jonah*, a tale with as few even pretended historical attachments as *Job*, grotesque in incident and surely not without a distinct . . . vein of typically Jewish humour. Then turn to *John*. Read the dialogues: that with the Samaritan woman at the well, or that which follows the healing of the man born blind. Look at its pictures: Jesus . . . doodling with his finger in the dust; the unforgettable ἦν δὲ νύξ (13:30). I have been reading poems, romances, vision-literature, legends, myths all my life. I know that not one of them is like this. Of this text there are only two possible views. Either this is reportage – though it may no doubt contain errors – pretty close up to the facts; nearly as close as Boswell. Or else, some unknown writer in the second century, without known predecessors or successors, suddenly anticipated the whole technique of modern, novelistic, realistic narrative. If it is untrue, it must be narrative of that kind. The reader who doesn't see this has simply not learned to read. I would recommend him to read Auerbach.[201]

What was significant about this attack on the loose employment of the concept of poetry in the hermeneutics of biblical narrative is that it does not come from an empiricist or philistine quarter. As well as being Professor of Renaissance English Literature, Lewis was a distinguished novelist and poet; though Farrer's training was more conventionally in philosophy and theology, he too was a Greats scholar, and noted for the 'poetic intensity' of his writings and for his skill as a literary critic.[202] Their criticism is basically that those who are most liable to invoke the 'poetic' as a tool of biblical exegesis are too frequently those who know least about poetry. Lewis again:

> . . . whatever these men may be as Biblical critics, I distrust them as critics. They seem to me to lack literary judgement, to be imperceptive about the very quality of the texts they are reading . . . If (a critic) tells me that something in a Gospel is legend or romance, I want to know how many legends and romances he had read, how well his palate is trained in detecting them by the flavour . . .[203]

Lewis puts his finger with unerring skill on the greatest weakness of the whole 'Heideggerian' school of 'poetics' in biblical criticism: its distance from, and, in many cases, its lack of understanding of, actual poetry. Though Heidegger does in places argue from close readings of specific poems – notably those of Hölderlin[204] – it is clear that he is not concerned with poetry as a genre, nor with its structural or aesthetic qualities; rather he meditates on isolated fragments of texts that can serve as foci for his own thoughts. At the same time, both Farrer and Lewis reveal, in their turn, little understanding of the wider concept of primal participation through metaphor that is central to Heidegger's idea of the 'poetic', and they never seriously consider the possibility that for their opponents the word 'poetic' might connote much more than simply an adjective derived from 'poetry'.

Right at the outset, therefore, we find that the two sides of the debate are lacking a common terminology. Whereas the continental theologians we have cited are rooted in a particular tradition of phenomenology and existentialism, their English critics of the 1940s and 50s address the problem from the context of a very different philosophical orthodoxy – that of a context demarcated by Ayer on one side and Wittgenstein on the other. Secondly, and perhaps even more significantly, whereas the English critics are either themselves poets, or close to their contemporary literary culture, the continental writers are primarily philosophers. Even the apparent exceptions conform to this general pattern. Thus the English Heideggerians, such as Macquarrie, lack the literary training of the earlier generation of Farrer and Lewis, while the French literary critics, such as the structuralists, with whom Ricoeur is most obviously associated, are themselves notably remote from the text as the English critics would have understood the notion. This obvious contemporary gap in understanding is, in turn, symptomatic of a much more profound historical gulf in literary experience that separates England from Germany.

Hans Frei has called attention to the curious way in which the fictional and critical techniques in these two countries, where discussion of biblical narrative was most intense during the eighteenth century, tended to polarize:

In England, where a serious body of realistic narrative literature and a certain amount of criticism of the literature was building up, there arose no corresponding cumulative tradition of criticism of the biblical writings, and that included no narrative interpretation of them. In Germany, on the other hand, where a body of critical analysis as well as general hermeneutics of the biblical writings built up rapidly in the latter half of the eighteenth century, there was no simultaneous development of realistic prose narrative and its critical appraisal.[205]

This absence of a tradition of realistic prose fiction and criticism meant that right from the beginnings of modern biblical hermeneutics in Germany the idea of the 'poetic' was able to occupy territory that in England would naturally have seemed the domain of prose. Thus, somewhat disconcertingly to the English ear, Friedrich Schlegel praises Goethe's prose novel, *Wilhelm Meister*, by eulogizing: 'it is all poetry – high, pure poetry. Everything has been thought and uttered as though by one who is both a divine poet and a perfect artist. . .'[206] Similarly, comparing Cervantes with Shakespeare, Tieck takes it for granted that both are poets working in a common medium: *Don Quixote* was 'genuine poetry' which 'set the tone for the whole age . . . Cervantes, with great understanding and the most delicate and graceful touch, was trying to provide poetry in its orphaned state with a safe course and steady support in real life.'[207] For J. H. Voss, the acknowledged master of Greek translation, there was, Humboldt records, but one standard of literary judgement: 'Whatever is excellent is also Homeric'.[208] Even more disconcertingly, Novalis actually praises Schlegel's literary criticism in the same vein: 'Schlegel's writings are philosophy as lyric. His [essays on] Forster and Lessing are first-rate minor poetry, and resemble the Pindaric hymns.'[209] Within the framework of this kind of critical vocabulary, prose realism could, at best, only come across as a technically uninteresting sub-genre of poetics. Added to this was another equally paradoxical feature of German thought as it developed at the end of the eighteenth century.

On the one hand, historicism was an apprehension of the specificity and irreducibly historical particularity of cultural change. But on the other hand as a movement in German thought it led to the very opposite of this apprehension, to a vast universalization in defining the content of historical change. One reason why historicism failed to move toward realistic depiction was the enormous universalizing tendency we have observed in Herder and which reached its philosophical epitome in Hegel's descriptive explanation of spirit or reason as the unitary moving force of history. In a more moderate form this spiritualising, universalizing tendency, for which life, spirit, self-consciousness, or some other mode of man's self-grasp as generically unique is the subject of culture and history, has remained the same ever since.[210]

Translation from German to English was further hampered by the presence in German of two adjectives both of which must be rendered into English by the single word 'poetic'. The word from poetry, *dichterisch*, refers more specifically to verse and imaginative writing in a technical sense, and corresponds most accurately to the restricted meaning in which Farrer and Lewis, for instance, tend to use the word in English, while *poetisch* rapidly acquired the universal, abstract, and spiritualized flavour that, as we have seen, is so typical of the 'extensive' use of the word in the nineteenth and twentieth centuries. Whereas the former word would naturally apply to discussions of Hebrew verse, such as the Psalms, it is the latter that tends to be used for discussions of the 'poetic' quality of the scriptures as a whole, the 'poetic' foundations of language, and its function in affirming primal participation. Because of the relative lack of development of realistic prose fiction in eighteenth- and even much of nineteenth-century German literature, and its consequent lack of prestige, it was natural for German theologians, inheritors of this universalizing and generalizing cast of thought (now built into the very structure of their language) to think of biblical prose narrative in terms of the 'poetic', and, consciously or unconsciously, to seek models drawn from anthropology and mythology rather than from contemporary realism.[211]

Frei's claim that Lowth's *Lectures on the Sacred Poetry of the Hebrews* and his subsequent commentary on Isaiah failed to establish 'a historical or literary-critical tradition of the biblical writings in the author's native land'[212] is, as we shall see in the next chapter, one that needs further qualification. What tends to happen in England at the end of the eighteenth and beginning of the nineteenth centuries is a widening split between the poets and literary critics on the one hand, and the theologians on the other. The critical ideas of the former, including Blake and Coleridge, were either unknown or increasingly suspect to a generation of religious apologists which, with honourable exceptions, was more concerned to debate with Hume and Gibbon than with Lowth. When the idea of the 'poetic' was reintroduced into English biblical criticism in the later nineteenth century it owed more to the German *poetisch* than it did to English critical experience. The presence of a vigorous minority tradition stemming from Coleridge and including Julius Hare, F. D. Maurice, and Newman, did little to change the course of nineteenth-century theology in the short term, influential though it was in sowing the seeds of a new integrative pattern in the long run.[213] It is to that tradition and its twentieth-century heirs that we must now turn.

Ricoeur's model of the process of primal participation as metaphorical and 'poetic' is, we notice, essentially a historical one. He is careful not to suggest, however, that because it is historically prior to descriptive uses of language and in some sense more fundamental, it is necessarily more primitive in the sense of being crude.[214] What the 'poetic' use of language in this sense offers twentieth-century man is a deep structure of 'belonging-to' amid what Ricoeur sees as 'the ruins of descriptive discourse'.[215] It is not difficult to guess why a philosopher of his intellectual background might see 'descriptive discourse' as reduced to 'a ruin' by late twentieth-century critical movements – the very idea of 'deconstruction' actively encourages the metaphor. Nevertheless, announcements of the death of descriptive prose may turn out to be much exaggerated. Certainly the concomitant idea that the autonomy of the literary artifact offers a return to a pre-descriptive and even authentically biblical modes of participatory consciousness seems dubious in the extreme – and it is doubtful if Ricoeur would wish his words to be construed in quite this manner.[216] Nevertheless, one does not get the impression that Ricoeur has thought much about the fundamental differences that, for better or worse, have come to separate twentieth-century poetic discourse from its biblical counterpart. This is not a matter of the obvious differences in scientific and philosophic world-picture that would automatically change the connotations of so many words, important as these clearly are, but of a much more fundamental development in *language* itself—any modern European language. The distinctions between the various modes of discourse on which Ricoeur bases his notion of primal participation go back, as we have seen, at least as far as Vico, and were elaborated by both Herder and Coleridge. Both saw the development of language in terms of an unfolding of human consciousness – a growth of consciousness expressed primarily in the poetry and imaginative literature of any period. As Coleridge put it:

. . . few there have been among the critics who have followed with the eye of the imagination the imperishable, yet ever wandering, spirit of poetry thro' its various metempsychoses, and consequent metamorphoses, or who have rejoiced in the light of clear perception at beholding at each new birth, at each rare avatar, the human race form itself a new body, by assimilating to itself the different materials of nourishment out of the then circumstances, and new organs of power and action appropriate to the new sphere of its motion and activity.[217]

Though this generalized 'spirit of poetry' may sound at times more like *poetisch* than *dichterisch*, a detailed acquaintance with Coleridge's thought nearly always shows that he has actual examples of poetry in mind. Here there is a marked resemblance to Wordsworth's Preface to the *Lyrical Ballads*. The 'spirit of poetry' is not a random reification, but the mainstream of developing human consciousness embodied in particular concrete form. The word '*avatar*' is, of course, an Indian one describing the descent of a Hindu deity to earth in a particular incarnation – in this case, therefore, in a particular work of poetry.[218] It is an idea we have become familiar with in the twentieth century through T. S. Eliot's argument that 'tradition' in poetry does not involve *imitation* of existing forms, but *changing* them.[219] For twentieth-century English literary criticism the idea of the 'poetic' necessarily involves a sense of it as a historical process of growing and developing consciousness.

Owen Barfield has called attention to the revolution in the perception of nature and the external world that reached its climax with the

Romantic movement – in particular to what he describes as 'a sharp divergence in the behaviour of two broad classes of words':

Of those which refer to nature, or what we now call nature we observe that *the further back we go*, the more they appear to connote sentience or inwardness. Of those on the other hand which refer to human consciousness, the opposite is the case, and their meaning, if I may put it so, becomes more and more outward. Nature, as expressed in words, has moved in the course of time from inwardness to outwardness; consciousness, as expressed in words, has moved from outwardness to inwardness.[220]

In an earlier work, *Saving the Appearances*, he had sketched in the corresponding change in human consciousness that he saw accompanying this historical shift in meaning:

The elimination of original participation involves a contraction of human consciousness from periphery to centre – a contraction from the cosmos of wisdom to something like purely brain activity – but by the same token it involves an *awakening*. For we wake, out of universal into self-consciousness. Now a process of awakening can be retrospectively surveyed by the sleeper only after his awakening is complete; for only then is he free enough of his dreams to look back on and interpret them. Thus, the possibility to look back at the history of the world and achieve a full waking picture of his own gradual emergence from original participation, really only arose for man . . . in the nineteenth century.[221]

To put it another way: the *idea* of a language of primal or original participation in this sense is only possible to an age that no longer possesses it. Whether or not it is true, as Ricoeur claims, that poetry restores modern man to that sense of belonging, it must be clear at the outset that any such self-conscious restoration is necessarily very different from the original unselfconscious participation. The very words used by a twentieth-century writer have irreversibly shifted their ground – not just in the sense of having changed their meanings, but also in the more complex sense that *the nature of those meanings* themselves has radically changed.

Barfield examines some of the effects of this phenomenon in an essay entitled *The Meaning of 'Literal'*.[222] Many of our words, he points out, are the result of deliberately coined metaphors. The Latin *scrupulus*, for instance, from which we get our English word 'scruple', meant a small sharp stone – of the kind that gets into your shoe and makes walking uncomfortable. To take this word and apply it for the first time not to a physical sensation, but to a *moral* qualm was a strikingly bold piece of wit – or insight. In English we have now completely lost the root meaning, and 'scruple' has ceased to be a metaphor and become for us literal once again, but literal now with an 'inner' qualitative meaning, and no longer a physical one. But this kind of deliberate metaphorical wit is rare in history of word-formation. If we take the word 'spirit' (whose root, in Hebrew, Greek, and Latin meant 'wind' or 'breath') we seem to be faced with a very different kind of case. If we assume that 'spirit' is a dead metaphor in the same sense that 'scruple' is, then we must also assume one of two things. *Either* that it was a metaphor for something that could also be said literally (which we know to be untrue), *or* that it was coined deliberately to express something that needed to be described and for which no adequate word yet existed – much as Baird coined the word 'television' for his new invention for transmitting pictures. But if we look at this notion we can see that it, too, must be false, since in its earliest usages (unlike the word 'scruple') it is impossible to tell the 'outer' and 'inner' meanings of *ruach* or *pneuma* apart. We have to say instead that for the ancient Hebrews the wind was an essentially numinous force. The very idea of 'wind' was for them inseparable from 'breath' and, therefore, from a ghostly, magical, and mysterious immaterial presence for which the word *also* stood. The act of breathing was associated with Life itself. But, if we allow this, the whole carefully-constructed modern distinction between 'literal' and 'metaphorical' has been turned upside-down. 'Literalness', for words such as these, is not the starting point but the final stage. It was only after 'wind' and 'spirit' had finally been separated from each other that the modern meaning of 'wind' could emerge. The original word, Barfield argues, since it meant both 'wind' *and* 'spirit' cannot have meant *either* in modern senses. It is impossible for us now to re-enter that linguistic word of primal participation and think of it in that undifferentiated third sense that meant both. In other words, literal meanings (for terms like these) are not the starting point, but the end of a long process of linguistic differentiation or 'desynonymy' which can only come about once the world of primal participation has been left behind.[223]

Though it is possible for us to understand this process after the event, we cannot share in it in the Old Testament sense. When, for instance, Wordsworth writes at the beginning of *The Prelude*, 'O there is blessing in this gentle breeze . . .' he is well aware of the history of the metaphor he is using, but simply *because* he possesses that historical consciousness he is using the word metaphorically, and not in its original undifferentiated Old Testament meaning. Precisely the same is true for the modern words 'earthquake' and 'fire'. The phenomena are presumably the same for us as for the author of I Kings xix, but the fact that we also have a word for, and therefore a concept of, 'nature', means that they lack that 'inner' numinous quality they had for him. Similarly when Gerard Manley Hopkins, theologically an arch-conservative, wrote in 1877:

> The world is charged with the grandeur of God
> It will flame out, like shining from shook foil,

he is consciously recreating images in Farrer's sense; he is not restoring primal participation in the sense in which Ricoeur seems to intend it.

Indeed, the whole nexus of ideas underlying the Heideggerian notion of poetry as 'the primitive language of a historical people' raises complex problems. Behind it there seems to lurk the idea, exemplified in various forms in the late eighteenth and early nineteenth centuries in such thinkers as Winckelmann, Herder, Schiller, and even Marx, that there is to be found in the language of classical Greece and the Old Testament a pure and primitive freshness denied to the writers of later generations.[224] The combination of sophisticated literary form and a language yet un-sullied by cliché and staleness had, it was believed, given these first writers opportunities for vividness and originality never again granted to the civilized world, and it was they who had the privilege of giving primal shape to the fundamental human impulses. Such a theory is, of course, dubious in the extreme. The transformation in time-scale that came with the collapse of the biblical chronology for the history of man has helped us to realize how long a linguistic history must lie behind even the very earliest literary works.[225] The implicit suggestion that the linguistic world of primal participation was one of stasis is, of course, equally im-probable. We have no reason to assume that even the pre-literate worlds of the Greeks and Hebrews did not involve successive rebirths of images as language and thought modified and reshaped one another in the light of imagination and experience. The slow movement of desynonymy separating nature from consciousness described by Barfield can be traced in detail through the history of the written word.[226] Unlike, say, the great vowel-shift in late Middle English, it was not a comparatively sud-den event that happened at the end of the eighteenth century with the Romantic movement, but rather what we loosely call 'Romanticism' was the culmination of a complex change in consciousness that reached back over hundreds of years, involving a number of significant changes in im-agery, and which even occurred at different times in different European languages.[227] Frye, for example, sees that process beginning in England at least as early as the Renaissance, and achieving dominance with the scientific revolution of the seventeenth century and the empiricist philosophy of Locke. In so far as the language of primal participation is one of actually definable semantic meanings rather than a mystical assertion of being, then we must think of it not in terms of primitive freshness of perception or pre-literate stasis, but one of change and growth which, however slow, followed fundamentally the same kind of developmental processes we can observe at work today.

But there is a corollary to this progressive development of meaning. This is that language itself is not as 'neutral' a medium as some have come to assume since the rise of so-called 'demotic' or descriptive prose. One obvious and very tempting conclusion to be drawn from Vico's model of language-development is that the movement from primal participation to modern descriptive prose has been one from language charged with implicit value-judgements to a language of objectivity and 'neutrality' – in other words that scientific descriptive prose is 'value-free'. Examples to the contrary can be dismissed merely as evidence that the process is as yet incomplete – that so fundamental a shift cannot be achieved in a period of a few generations. In fact, few philosophers of science would today support such a view of value-free descriptions.[228] If Barfield is right – and his detailed linguistic evidence is difficult to resist – descriptive prose is neither 'value-free' (nor in the process of becoming so) but is no less value-charged than the language of primal participation but *at a different level of consciousness*. In this respect it does not differ from the language of poetry.

Any viable modern definition of the 'poetic' must therefore take account not merely of its original participatory function but also of the process of developing consciousness in its subsequent evolution. Thus a contemporary English poet and critic has chosen to define 'poetry' primarily in terms of "an extension of the possibilities of language'. 'Poetry', he argues,

is an attempted evocation by conventional symbols of a state of mind sometimes called mystical . . . writing may be poetic without being either moral or didactic . . . primarily poetry is an exploration of the possibilities of language. It does not aim directly at consolation or moral exaltation, nor at the expression of exquisite moments, but at an extension of significance.[229]

There are, we observe, two basic contentions here, positive and negative, and they seem at first sight at odds with each other. The first posits qualities vaguely described as 'mystical' concerned with 'an extension of significance'; the second involves a denial of any necessary 'moral or didactic' content to poetry. The author's ambiguity here is understandable – and is not untypical of such attempts to define or describe 'poetry'. He finds himself forced simultaneously both to affirm and deny that value-structures are inherent in poetry. The apparent contradictions of this position are partly, but only partly, masked by the device of using strong and weak terms for the two statements: poetry is *not* 'moral or didactic', it *is* 'mystical' and concerned with 'significance'. Yet the reader is not, I think, left with the impression that he wants to establish some kind of middle-ground between two extremes (i.e. 'poetry is a little bit concerned with values in a general kind of way, but it must not be too precise or heavy-handed about it . . . '). In fact, Roberts is here very honest with his own experience, and the curious ambiguity of his definition reflects that honesty. Poetry *is* concerned with values and meaning, but they are less a matter of authorial attitude or ostensible topic than a willingness to exploit and highlight values *already* inherent in language itself – and, as we have seen, those 'possibilities of language' are, at any one historical moment, in a constant process of growth and change.

An extended example may illustrate the point. Take what looks like the same image in two major devotional poets just over a hundred years apart. First George Herbert:

> When God at first made man,
> Having a glass of blessings standing by,
> 'Let us,' said he, 'pour on him all we can.
> Let the world's riches, which dispersed lie,
> Contract into a span.'   (*The Pulley* 1633)

The crux, of course, lies in that last line: 'Contract into a span'. 'Contract' at this period was still used primarily in its legal sense, especially in marriages, and the connection with 'riches' in the previous line suggests the idea of a dowry – a wedding-present from God to Adam. But, of course, that meaning is at once overtaken by the contrast with 'dispersed'. The use of 'contract' to mean 'to draw the parts together' is first recorded by the O.E.D. in 1602, and 'to reduce to smaller compass by drawing together' does not occur until 1626. In other words, what may seem to us the obvious and primary meaning of the word is in fact a very new one in Herbert's own time, and is being deliberately played off against the word's traditional meaning.[230] The primary meaning of 'span' is, of course, a unit of linear measurement: an outstretched hand from the tip of the thumb to the end of the little finger (conventionally taken to be nine inches). From this it takes its obvious figurative meaning of 'a small extent', either of space or time. Just as relevant for Herbert's purposes is a sixteenth-century use of the word as a verb 'to harness or yoke' two things together – in this case God and man. The biblical echo of Christ's 'my yoke is easy . . . ' might well be at the back of Herbert's mind in the context of this poem about a 'pulley'. From here it takes another, technical, meaning of the rope or cable by which a ship is moored. The riches of the world, drawn all together in the little compass of human life will (because man lacks 'the rest') eventually bind man back to God.

Just over a hundred years later, in 1746, Charles Wesley returned to Herbert's image:

> Let earth and heaven combine,
>   Angels and men agree,
> To praise in songs divine
>   The incarnate Deity,
> Our God contracted to a span,
> Incomprehensibly made man.

(Nativity Hymns 1749)

The echoes of Herbert (whose work Wesley knew well) are clearly deliberate. For Herbert's riches of the world, Wesley has, however, substituted the riches of God himself. His theme is not man turning to God, but God turning *into* man. For the first Adam we substitute the second. In the first, something ('the rest') is left over; in the second, 'incomprehensibly', nothing. The boundless and infinite is reduced in the miracle of the Incarnation to the quantifiable and tiny. The primary meaning of 'span' in this context is the traditionally allotted period of human life. But the unit of linear measurement is as important: the length of a tiny new-born baby has become the standard by which all creation is to be measured. But in the century since Herbert the word 'span' had acquired other meanings. New in Wesley's time (1725: O.E.D.) is its use for the span of a bridge: here the leaping arch which joins earth to heaven in a new unity – in the words of a later stanza of the same hymn, 'Widest extremes to join'. Older Christian images of bridge-building can now be incorporated in the new synthesis: in place of the Pope as 'supreme Pontiff', for the Protestant and passionately anti-Calvinistic Wesley, *all* may have access to God through Christ. Whereas for Herbert, at least a quasi-Calvinist,[231] the poet stands solitary before his God, for Wesley 'angels and men' may join in collective and universal hymns of praise.

Similarly the word 'contracted' has itself undergone changes of meaning in the period. Though the idea of the divine Covenant is not absent from Herbert's poem, and is subsumed within the image of a dowry, with Wesley the shift to the New Testament makes the New Covenant in Christ central. God, by his own contract, is bound to his 'span'. This shift in theological emphasis is reinforced by the word's new, early eighteenth-century meaning of 'restricted' (1710: O.E.D.) that had become current in the period. The Incarnation is a self-imposed restriction on divinity. No wonder, then, that the making of God into man is 'incomprehensible' – both in its modern sense of 'not to be understood' *and* in the still-current older meaning of 'not to be grasped' (physically, not even by the outstretched 'span' of a hand) and the figurative, 'not to be contained within limits'. The original meaning of 'span', the verb, is to 'to grasp'[232] in a sense that corresponds exactly with this physical sense of 'comprehend' – as in John i, where it says, speaking of the Incarnation, 'the light shineth in darkness and the darkness comprehended it not'. Jesus, the 'incarnate Deity', is the shining of the light that could not be understood or extinguished. The syntax of Wesley's penultimate line has now become very ambiguous indeed. Is 'made', for instance, active or passive? Is God merely allowing himself to be made into man, and by that 'contract' through obedience, making a true man for the first time – the doctrine, in short, of the second Adam – or is he, by that act, to be seen as *actively* 'making' mankind afresh?

Behind this last question lies another important linguistic development that had taken place in the middle years of the seventeenth century. As Coleridge pointed out[233], as late as the time of Charles I there was no substantive distinction made between 'compelled' and 'obliged' – a fact which could enable Hobbes in *Leviathan* (1651) to maintain that there was in fact no such thing as guilt. The case provides a perfect illustration of Barfield's generalization on the progress of words describing human consciousness from 'outer' to 'inner' meanings. It would not have been possible for Herbert to raise the question implied by Wesley as to whether the 'contract' compelled God to a course of action under the outward sanctions of the 'law', or whether he acted from an inner moral compulsion. What is foreshadowed by such questions, of course, is the eventual collapse of the whole system of legal imagery that had been such an integral part of Christian theology from Paul to Calvin. Once the distinction between moral and legal obligations had become part of linguistic experience, it was difficult for either the legal ideas of the Covenant or for the Ransom theory of the Atonement to retain their old force in theology. In short, another rebirth of images was under way.

One could continue: both Herbert and Wesley are great poets, and both poems are rich and complexly allusive works. But, as we have seen, the difference between them is not merely that which separates two great, but very different poets, nor yet simply a matter of the ways in which individual words have desynonymized or changed their meanings; what has changed is also a world-picture. The apparent simplicity of Herbert's verse-parable may be deceptive, as all good parables are, but it belongs to a world still in touch with the mythological framework of the Bible in at least one respect. Man still occupies the centre stage as of right. Between Herbert's time and that of Wesley stand Newton and Locke, and the whole imaginative shift of key encapsulated by the phrase 'the scientific revolution'. For Wesley the Incarnation is no less a miracle than for Herbert, but because the physical universe has expanded and achieved a different kind of objective reality for the eighteenth century, the nature of a 'miracle' has changed too. One senses in almost every line of Charles Wesley's hymn an awe at God's intervention in the regulated order of nature. Herbert would not have claimed to have 'understood' the Incarnation, but he would not have described it as 'incomprehensible'. In the post-Newtonian universe the gap to be spanned between man and nature was more consciously mysterious; the 'widest extremes' had grown wider.

In doing so, of course, the idea of 'poetry' and the 'poetic' had also changed. Wesley's images of extremes conjoined by grace anticipate with extraordinary prescience Coleridge's idea of *poetry* 'reconciling opposite or discordant qualities' and 'bringing the whole soul of man into activity'. The Romantic idea of 'poetry' is itself rooted in the new theological images of the Wesleyan revival.[234]

To sum up, therefore: the debate over the past three hundred years as to the cloudy relationship between the religious and the poetic has, as it were, crystallized into three quite distinct, if related, ways of understanding the word – each with its own implied epistemology. At the root of all three we have the view that 'poetry' represents a basic mode of human consciousness, either in historical or psychological terms, or both. It expresses a state of primal and undifferentiated being; a felt unity with all things. From this notion of the poetic primal language of mankind stem the three distinct but often intermingled traditions of thought. In the first, the 'extensive' tradition, the poetic came to embrace the whole of human language, and therefore all mankind's manifold linguistic activities, including history and religion. The second, the 'intensive', stressed rather the non-cognitive and emotive aspects of this presumed primal state, and in the twentieth century has tended to insist that it constitutes a quite separate 'language-game', distinct from prose, and complete with its own peculiar associative, pre-rational, or magical 'logic'. The third, which is to be found most prominently in the tradition of such Romantic poets as Wordsworth and Coleridge, sought to define the poetic as a peculiar and indissoluble union of thought and feeling, productive of psychic health and wholeness, which though primal was not pre-rational but *historical* in its mode of consciousness.

It is to that tradition that we must now turn in greater detail.

3
Poetry and prophecy

The language of the Great Code

It is a historical commonplace that the course of Western thought since the Renaissance has been one of progressive secularization, but it is easy to mistake the way in which that process took place. Secular thinkers have no more been able to work free of the centuries-old Judeo-Christian culture than Christian theologians were able to work free of their inheritance of classical and pagan thought. The process – outside the exact sciences at any rate – has not been the deletion and replacement of religious ideas but rather the assimilation and reinterpretation of religious ideas, as constitutive elements in a world view founded on secular premises.[1]

Abrams's theme is the gradual displacement of 'traditional concepts, schemes, and values which had been based on the relation of the Creator to his creature and creation' and their reformulation 'within the prevailing two-tier system of subject and object, ego and non-ego, the human mind or consciousness and its transactions with nature'.[2] The original ambiguity of Carlyle's phrase 'Natural Supernaturalism', poised between the divinization of nature and the naturalizing of the miraculous is conveniently resolved by making it the label for the latter. With the coming to consciousness of secular man, the emotions of awe and wonder previously invoked by the Creator are relocated in the created world – 'to naturalize the supernatural and humanize the divine'.[3]

As he admits at the outset, Abrams's thesis *is* something of a historical commonplace. It was not new when Feuerbach used it. Another variant is the widely held Marxist version of Romantic religious language that sees in the religious and apocalyptic terminology of, for instance, Blake and his millenarian contemporaries of the 1790s, the embryonic secular language of social protest. 'Blake uses the religious idiom', writes Jack Lindsay, boldly ignoring Paine, Godwin, and a whole school of pro-French Revolutionary secular controversialists, 'because there was no other idiom of his day . . .'[4] For him, Blake's 'struggle' was 'to secularize millenary religion without losing what was vital and improving in it'. Similar arguments are to be found in E. J. Hobsbawm and

95

E. P. Thompson.[5] Nevertheless, the very thoroughgoing comprehensiveness of Abrams's great work, *Natural Supernaturalism*, has tended to give added academic weight and a seal of orthodoxy to what was before often little more than an unexamined assumption. Moreover, he has specifically elevated this process of displacement and secularization to the status of *the* distinguishing hallmark of Romanticism. This act alone would make Abrams's thesis central to any discussion of the development of ideas of religious language.

In a crucial passage Abrams compares two versions of the traditional Christian concept of the *Liber Naturae* – the 'book of nature' – a dialogue between the individual and the landscape. The first is from Augustine's *Confessions*; the second from Wordsworth's *Prelude* (Bk III, 83–194)[6] The Augustine passage is as follows:

> And what is God? I asked the earth and it answered: 'I am not He'; and all things that are in the earth made the same confession. I asked the sea and the deeps and the creeping things, and they answered: 'We are not your God; seek higher' . . . I asked the heavens, the sun, the moon, the stars, and they answered: 'Neither are we God whom you seek.' And I said to all the things that throng about the gateways of the senses: 'Tell me of my God, since you are not He. Tell me something of Him.' My question was gazing upon them, and their answer was their beauty. And I turned to myself and said: 'And you, who are you?' And I answered: 'A man.' Now clearly there is a body and a soul in me, one exterior, one interior. From which of these two should I have enquired of my God? . . . The inner man knows these things through the ministry of the outer man: I the inner man knew them, I the soul, through the senses of the body.   *Confessions*, Bk X, vi.

Augustine, Abrams notes, 'has three points of reference':

> God, the natural creation, and man . . . Of the three, God (figured here as speaking through His creation) retains all initiative, as the first, efficient, and final cause of nature and soul. In Wordsworth's passage God has not quite dropped out, but He is mentioned only after the fact, and given nothing to do except to be spectator of a completed action . . . But if God has become a nonparticipant, it is with this peculiar result: His traditional attributes and functions . . . survive, to be inherited (together with the appropriate sentiments of wonder and awe) by the two remaining components of Augustine's triad, nature and the human 'soul', or 'mind'.[7]

Before we turn to the comparison with Wordsworth, it may be useful to observe the Augustine passage from another perspective. This approach to nature as a thing separate from the self, at once not-God, but to be read as bearing witness to Him, is a significant development away from the undifferentiated primal consciousness discussed in the last chapter. The insight represented so dramatically by the story of Elijah on Horeb has here been taken a step further. There – perhaps recorded for the first time in human history – the forces of nature were experienced as being both 'not-God' and yet somehow also representative of Him; for Augustine, under the influence of Plato, Plutarch, and Porphyry, this separation but yet intimate relationship has become more sharply defined in the form of the *via negativa*. For the modern, post-Romantic, reader, accustomed to a long literary tradition of such dialogues[8] the only surprise is the unexpected parenthetical explanation: 'My question was my gazing upon them, and their answer was their beauty.' It is the very *self-consciousness* of the extended metaphor behind the whole passage that is startling. We are far removed now from the psalmist's 'the Heavens declare the glory of God . . .' That was a statement of a divinely-charged universe; this, for all its Platonism, is something much more of a metaphorical conceit – a conscious exploration of Augustine's own state of mind. The all-revealing parenthesis fatally undermines Abrams's easy assumption that in this passage 'God . . . retains all the initiative.' That view, it seems to me, implies a fundamental misapprehension as to the nature of any literary narrative (including a spiritual autobiography). 'God', in the *Confessions* is a 'character', or more specifically, an 'actant', in the story told by Augustine. If He is described as retaining the initiative, it is because *Augustine*, as author, ascribes that initiative to Him.[9] Moreover Augustine is not Elijah. Here he is, in his own way, as fascinated as Wordsworth by the movements of his own consciousness.

Which brings us back to Wordsworth and God. Wordsworth's theme in *The Prelude* is not of divine action, as in his great forerunner, Milton, but human: 'The growth of a poet's mind.' What is extraordinary about the poem is not its difference from Augustine's *Confessions* (1,400 turbulent years separate the two writers) but its *similarity*: a similarity to which the reader is carefully alerted by the 1805 *Prelude*'s arrangement into thirteen books, the same number as the *Confessions*, with Wordsworth's crisis over the French Revolution placed as a clear structural parallel with Augustine's conversion. Moreover, what strikes the reader about the *Prelude* is not so much its secularity, as a kind of disconcertingly inappropriate religiosity that suddenly obtrudes itself into the narrative for no very obvious reason. If one compares it not with Augustine but with poems about nature from the early part of the eighteenth century – *Windsor Forest*, for instance, or *The Seasons* – the contrast is startling.

In Book XIII of the 1805 text, for example, after describing his vision
of the 'sea of clouds' by moonlight from the top of Snowdon, Wordsworth goes on to use it as the culminating symbol of the poet's mind
– a magnificent pre-Freudian intuition of the power of the unconscious mind in artistic creativity.[10] But having made his disclosure
with admirable economy, he then proceeds to labour the point with
what seem like abstract pieties:

> Such minds are truly from Deity,
> For they are powers; and hence the highest bliss
> That can be known is theirs – the consciousness
> Of whom they are, habitually infused
> Through every image and through every thought,
> And all impressions; hence religion, faith,
> And endless occupation for the soul,
> Whether discursive or intuitive;
> Hence sovereignty within and peace at will,
> Emotion which best foresight need not fear,
> Most worthy then of trust when most intense;
> Hence chearfulness in every act of life;
> Hence truth in moral judgements; and delight
> Thus fails not, in the external universe.   (lines 106–19)

Most critics omit this passage when discussing the Snowdon scene.
Its grandiose and pious abstractions do not seem to belong to the unconscious as we have come to think of it. The notorious egotistical
sublime seems to have gone over the top a bit. We feel about it,
perhaps, as we do about Shelley's claim in the *Defence of Poetry* that
the poet ought to be, and is, 'the happiest, the best, the wisest and the
most illustrious of men'.[11] Yet, for Wordsworth, the passage was
clearly of some importance since in the 1850 text of *The Prelude* the
tone is even more overtly religious, and a number of extra lines were
added to reinforce the point, concluding:

> Hence, amid ills that vex and wrongs that crush
> Our hearts – if here the words of Holy Writ
> May with fit reverence by applied – that peace
> Which passeth understanding, that repose
> In moral judgements which from this pure source
> Must come, or will by man be sought in vain.   (lines 124–9)

Abrams's own position over such pieties is uncompromising:

. . . it is not enough to list the passages in which reference is made to God;
for the essential matter is, 'What does God *do* in the Poem?' And to this the

answer is patently, 'Nothing of consequence.' In *The Prelude* of 1805 (and this fact is only thinly overlaid with pious phrases in Wordsworth's later revisions and additions) God is at intervals ceremoniously alluded to, but remains an adventitious and nonoperative factor; if all allusions to deity were to be struck out of *The Prelude*, there would be no substantive change in its matter or development.[12]

But in fact the question, 'What does God *do* . . .' is rather an odd one. God *does* far more in *Paradise Lost*, for instance, than in Augustine's *Confessions*. Given the subject-matter of *The Prelude*, the interesting question is not so much what does God do, but *why* does Wordsworth so obstinately insist on dragging God in at all? Again, a comparison with his immediate neo-classical forerunners, Pope or Johnson, rams home the *oddity* of what Wordsworth is doing. Did *they* so labour the divine status of the poet's task? And what about Rousseau's *Confessions* – to which *The Prelude* is sometimes compared?

The relative absence of God from neoclassical critical theory was paralleled by a similar absence in other areas of public life – including that of the Church of England itself. Accounts such as the following, from the *Edinburgh Review*, were a commonplace:

The thermometer of the Church of England sank to its lowest point in the first thirty years of George III. Unbelieving bishops and a slothful clergy, had succeeded in driving from the Church the faith and the zeal of Methodism which Wesley had organised within her pale. The spirit was expelled and the dregs remained. That was the age when jobbery and corruption, long supreme in the State, had triumphed over the virtue of the Church; when the money-changers not only entered the Temple, but drove out the worshippers; when ecclesiastical revenues were monopolized by wealthy pluralists: when the name of curate lost its legal meaning, and instead of denoting the incumbent of a living, came to signify the deputy of an absentee.[13]

Statistics bear out this general impression of religious indifference.[14] On Easter Day, 1800, there were a mere six communicants at St Paul's Cathedral in London – the principal church of the largest Christian city in the world. In 1807 (the first year for which we have any figures) out of some 10,000-odd benefices of the Church of England, no fewer than 6,145 (61%, or nearly two-thirds) were non-resident. The years when Wordsworth was at work writing the early drafts of *The Prelude* were described by Thomas Mozley, a Victorian clergyman, as a time when 'thousands of livings were without parsonages, and with incomes so small as not to admit of building or even renting'. Consequently, 'non-residence was almost the rule in some districts, and . . . even the pastoral duties of which all clergymen are capable and which are always welcome, were discharged intermittingly and cursorily'. 'Church fabrics fell into disorder and even decay . . . bishops and dignitaries made fortunes, and used their patronage for private purposes.'[15] The general temper of the Church, and the nation at large, was one of conventional scepticism:

This growing indifference was the great fact of this day. It was a public fact, a social fact, an academic fact, a domestic fact. A man might avow any phase of unbelief, and any contempt of religion, without loss of character, in the service of the state, in society, at Oxford, and at home. It was expected of every young man in 'the world' . . . For everything short of fanatical and intolerant atheism, there was not only condonance, but certain degree of admiration.[16]

According to the Wordsworths, the curate at Grasmere was frequently drunk. Wordsworth declared to his rather startled sister Dorothy, in 1812, that he would gladly 'shed his blood' for the Church of England – but, upon her expressing scepticism, agreed that he did not know when he had last been inside the local church: 'All our ministers are such vile creatures.'[17]

It is against this social and religious background that we must approach Wordsworth's religiosity in *The Prelude*. The effusive claim for the religious role of the poet comes from a man who only shortly before had rejected the profession of a clergyman and against a background a general religious laxity and indifference far more widespread and dramatic than anything the twentieth century has yet seen.

We may get some clue to the origins of his spontaneous overflow of pious feelings if we look back to the previous book of *The Prelude* where he addresses his friend, Coleridge, on the 'genius of the Poet':

> Dearest Friend!
> Forgive me if I say that I, who long
> Had harboured reverentially a thought
> That poets, even as prophets, each with each
> Connected in a mighty scheme of truth,
> Have each for his peculiar dower a sense
> By which he is enabled to perceive
> Something unseen before . . .
>
> (Book XII (1805) lines 298–305)

This claim, that the poet is a prophet, who, like those of the Old Testament, proclaims the great hidden Truths of human existence, is one of the central tenets of Romanticism.

As we mentioned in the last chapter, William Blake, in an early work polemically entitled *There is no Natural Religion* (1788), argues (incidentally on sound Kantian lines) that not merely religion, but *all* knowledge of whatever kind is ultimately dependent upon the poetic or 'prophetic' leap of the imagination:

If it were not for the poetic or Prophetic character the Philosophic and Experimental would soon be at the ratio of all things, and stand still, unable to do other than repeat the same dull round over again.[18]

The same year, 1788, in another piece with the equally aggressive title *All Religions are One*, Blake's 'Voice of one crying in the Wilderness' announced that 'The Religions of all Nations are derived from each Nation's different reception of the Poetic Genius, which is everywhere call'd the Spirit of Prophecy.'[19]

Shelley goes even further than the first generation Romantics. In his *Four Ages of Poetry* his friend Thomas Love Peacock had ironically described the poets of ancient times as being:

not only historians but theologians, moralists, and legislators: delivering their oracles *ex cathedra*, and being indeed often themselves regarded as portions and emanations of divinity: building cities with a song, and leading brutes with a symphony: which are only metaphors for the faculty of leading multitudes by the nose.[20]

Shelley's reply, in his *Defence of Poetry*, was to out-top all previous claims for the status of the poet, supporting his assertion that 'poets are the unacknowledged legislators of mankind' with reference to their traditional prophetic role:

Poets, according to the circumstances of the age and nation in which they appeared, were called, in the earlier epochs of the world, legislators or prophets: a poet essentially comprises and unites both these characters.[21]

Moreover, as rapidly becomes clear, Shelley, the atheist, is not using the word 'prophet' in any merely figurative sense. The main thrust of the rhetoric of the *Defence* is towards a scarcely metaphorical language of divine inspiration. The phrases tumble over each other: 'poetry lifts the veil from the hidden beauty of the world . . . A man to be greatly good, must imagine intensely and comprehensively . . . The great instrument of moral good is the imagination . . . Poetry strengthens the

faculty which is the organ of the moral nature of man, in the same manner as exercise strengthens a limb . . . Poetry is the sword of lightning,
ever unsheathed, which consumes the scabbard that would contain it
. . . Poetry is indeed something divine.' Here indeed, if anywhere, is
apparently the 'secularization' sought by Abrams. But what exactly is
it that is being secularized?

Though it is argued just a little too vehemently to be a critical commonplace, the identification of the poet with the prophet of old so
permeates Romantic thought that it is easy to lose sight of just how
dramatic a critical revolution lies behind it. As with most 'new' ideas,
its roots can be traced back a long way. Sidney, in his *Apologie for
Poetry*, remarked that 'Among the Romans a Poet was called Vates,
which is as much a Diviner, Fore-seer, or Prophet . . .'[22] and noted
that the Delphic oracles were delivered in verse. Thomas Percy, the
antiquarian collector of poems, and, if truth be told, part-composer of
the anthology published under the title *Reliques of Ancient English
Poetry*, added to it an 'Essay on the Ancient Minstrels in England' in
which he dilates upon the 'northern SCALDS, in whom the characters
of historian, genealogist, poet, and musician, were all united'. These
Norse 'Scalds' 'professed to inform and instruct, and were at once the
moralists and theologues of their Pagan countrymen'.[23]

Alongside this pagan tradition was another, specifically Christian
concept of the election of the prophet as poet and orator which finds
expression in, for instance, Milton's prose works and even in Blake's
Jerusalem. It was, as we have seen, Dennis who was to give this idea
a new impetus in the early eighteenth century. His argument that
'Poetry is the natural Language of Religion' . . . was supported by his
historical belief that 'the Prophets were Poets by the Institution of their
Order, and Poetry was one of the Prophetick Functions'.[24] Though
the strands of thought between pagan and Christian, Homer and the
Old Testament, cross and re-cross throughout the eighteenth century,
their essential difference is, once again, beautifully illustrated by Wordsworth in the *Prelude*.

From his meditation on the poet as prophet in Book XII he goes on
at once to what he calls a 'reverie', first of ancient Britons, 'with shield
and stone-axe' striding 'across the wold', and then of Druid sacrifices:

> . . . fed
> With living men – how deep the groans! – the voice
> Of those in the gigantic wicker thrills

Throughout the region far and near, pervades
The monumental hillocks, and the pomp
Is for both worlds, the living and the dead.   (lines 331–6)

At other times, he tells us, he saw before him 'on the downy Plain':

Lines, circles, mounts, a mystery of shapes
Such as in many quarters yet survive,
With intricate profusion figuring o'er
The untilled ground, (the work, as some divine,
Of infant science, imitative forms
By which the Druids covertly expressed
Their knowledge of the heavens . . .)   (340–6)

But though Wordsworth hopes to catch 'a tone/ An image, and a character' from these 'bearded teachers', he distances it all as an 'antiquarian's dream'. They may well be in a historical sense his spiritual ancestors, but, though he recognizes the connections, he does not cast himself as a new 'Druid' – the reference to the screaming victims being burnt alive in the wicker cages are sufficient reminder of the gulf between the ancient Celtic bards and the modern poet. If we want to find in Wordsworth echoes of the same tone of high seriousness and sense of divine meaning to the high calling of the poet that so obtruded themselves in the lines with which we began, we must look, for instance, to the passage in Book IV of *The Prelude* where the young Wordsworth is coming home after an all-night dance. As he walks across the fields in the first light of dawn he is caught up in a sudden mood of exaltation:

Ah, need I say, dear friend, that to the brim
My heart was full? I made no vows, but vows
Were then made for me; bond unknown to me
Was given, that I should be – else sinning greatly –
A dedicated spirit.   (lines 333–7)

The contrast in language with the previous passage about the pagan bards is total. He is not now concerned with the poet as guardian of esoteric mysteries, or with the sense of tradition that inspired an 'antiquarian's dream', but with personal commitments, 'vows' and 'dedication'. Nor, in spite of the title of a recent book centering on Wordsworth's 'natural methodism',[25] is this the language of contemporary Methodist or Evangelical conversion. Though to break those vows would be 'sinning greatly', they are not ones that he himself has made; he has, rather become aware of them as an existing condition that

affects his entire life. This is not the language of the northern bards
and Druids, nor that of the classical world: it is that of a specific
minority tradition running from the Old Testament through certain
kinds of individual experience into the later tradition of the Church.
It is that of St Augustine in the *Confessions*, and behind him the stories
of Samuel, of David, and of Hosea. The vows made for the infant
Samuel by his mother, Hannah, are echoed by Monica's prayers for her
son, Augustine, and now, metaphorically, by Wordsworth's 'foster-
mother', Nature, for her dedicated child. Though Wordsworth was
well aware of the pagan and classical antecedents for the divine status
of the poet, his stress is not on the powers bestowed by the gift of prophecy on the poet, but on the process of *election*.

At the risk of labouring the matter, it needs to be said (*pace* Abrams)
that this is, given its historical context, not so much the language of
secularization, but of religious revival. It matters little, it seems to me,
whether God is seen as 'acting' directly here, or whether we accept the
implied parallels between St Monica and Nature. Certainly it is true
that for Augustine election is not a matter of metaphor, but of plain
fact, but what matters is that Wordsworth should have chosen to reject
what was by then a perfectly adequate secular aesthetic vocabulary in
favour of overtly religious and Augustinian language to describe his experience of being 'chosen' as a poet. Moreover, it would be, I think,
over-simple to label the passage simply as 'metaphorical'. The fact that
Wordsworth is describing what he knows to be a psychological experience does not mean that he really believed he 'chose' *himself*, any
more than it would be true to say that because Augustine attributed his
conversion to the action of God, he was not intensely interested in the
psychology of religious experiences. Once again, given the historical
gulf that inevitably separates them, what is astonishing about
Augustine and Wordsworth is not their differences, but their
similarities — and that Wordsworth should have so consciously
recognized them. To put it another way, there are themes in
Augustine's *Confessions* (Nature, time, and the unconscious, for instance)
which were not touched on again with the same sensitivity until *The
Prelude*, and are, therefore, mediated to us *by* Wordsworth. We understand Augustine through the Romantics.

Wordsworth stands at a peculiar, and, in some ways, a unique moment
in the history of biblical criticism. To understand something of the

complexity of his aesthetic vision we need to turn back to the middle of the eighteenth century: to the publication of Lowth's *Lectures on the Sacred Poetry of the Hebrews* – the book that was to transform biblical studies in England and Germany alike, and which was to do more than any other single work to make the biblical tradition, rather than the neo-classical one, the central poetic tradition of the Romantics.

Robert Lowth was not merely one of the most distinguished theologians of his day, he was also an outstanding Orientalist – in the eighteenth century sense of that word: an expert on the manners, customs, and thought of the Near East, including the ancient Hebrews. His translation of Isaiah (1778) rapidly became a standard work, and his *Short Introduction to English Grammar* (1762) showed a linguistic sophistication that kept it still in use at Harvard in the mid-nineteenth century. After a highly successful Oxford career (he was only 31 when he became Professor of Poetry), he was made Bishop of St Davids in 1776, later the same year Bishop of Oxford, and finally of London in 1777.

The story of *how* he came to write the *Lectures* seems to have been intimately bound up with their revolutionary content. Under the statute governing his appointment, the Professor of Poetry is obliged to give his inaugural lecture on the first Tuesday of the term subsequent to his election. Lowth, however, by some negligence was not elected until 21 May 1741, during the vacation – which was only 13 days long. As a result he was forced to embark on his lectures almost without time to prepare his theme.[26] It seems possible that his choice of biblical poetry and his unconventional approach to it resulted directly from the fact that he did not have the normal length of time to consult conventional authorities. Be that as it may, it is clear from a number of statements in his opening lecture that, at that stage, he had not thought of some of his more epoch-making conclusions.

To Lowth we owe the rediscovery of the Bible as a work of literature within the context of ancient Hebrew life. Hitherto, it had been understood almost exclusively in terms of its allegorical and typological meanings: a timeless compendium of divinely inspired revelation. Old Testament events were read primarily in relation to those they might prefigure in the New, especially in the life of Christ. As Mrs Trimmer was so succinctly to put it, sixty-five years later, in the introduction to her *Help to the Unlearned in the Study of the Holy Scriptures*:

The Histories they (the Scriptures) contain differ from all other histories that were ever written, for they give an account of the *ways of GOD*; and explain *why* GOD *protected and rewarded* some persons and nations, and *why* he *punished* others; also *what led* particular persons mentioned in Scripture to *do* certain things for which they were approved or condemned; whereas writers who compose histories in a common way, without being *inspired of God*, can only form guesses and conjectures concerning God's dealings with mankind, neither can they know what passed in the hearts of those they write about; such knowledge as this, belongs to *GOD* alone, whose ways are *unsearchable and past finding out*, and *to whom all hearts are open, all desires known*!

There can be no argument about divinely inspired history. The Bible was not a historical document so much as the yardstick by which the authenticity of historical documents might be judged. But behind this attitude to inspiration lay a quite different attitude to history itself. It was not a matter of particularities but of generalities: the grand generalities that illustrated Natural Law. History, in essence, was a useful collection of examples for pedagogical purposes.[27] The purpose of sacred history was to provide the types by which God revealed his grand design from the Fall to the eventual redemption of man.

In contrast, Lowth argued that:

He who would perceive the peculiar and interior elegancies of the Hebrew poetry, must imagine himself exactly situated as the persons for whom it was written, or even as the writers themselves; he is to feel them as a Hebrew . . . nor is it enough to be acquainted with the language of this people, their manners, discipline, rites and ceremonies; we must even investigate their inmost sentiments, the manner and connexion of their thoughts; in one word, we must see all things with their eyes, estimate all things by their opinion: we must endeavour as much as possible to read Hebrew as the Hebrews would have read it.[28]

Commonsense[29] as this kind of approach might seem to us today, as we have seen, Lowth's aesthetics involved a new and even revolutionary kind of scholarship. Friedrich Meinecke tracing the rise of the modern idea of history, claims that:

Lowth's book was perhaps the most intellectually important product of the whole pre-Romantic movement in England. It was free of all dilettantism and superficiality of taste and had the indirect result of contributing to the liberation of historical research from the bonds of theology by displaying the purely human and historical content and value of the Bible. It set forth a genuine science of the humanities, and gave it new organs.[30]

In England Lowth's emphasis on the historical context of Hebrew poetry was closely paralleled by similar developments in classical scholarship. We have already mentioned Thomas Blackwell's *Life and Writings of Homer* (1785). In order to understand Homer, argued Blackwell, it was essential to imagine oneself in his audience, as part of a warrior people wishing to hear something of the heroic deeds of their ancestors.[31] Referring to Blackwell, and possibly Wood as well,[32] Lowth writes in Preliminary Dissertation to his translation of *Isaiah*, that 'the method which has been used with good effect in correcting the ancient Greek and Latin authors, ought in all reason to be applied to the Hebrew writings.'[33] Lowth, like Blackwell, insisted that there could be no break between historical and aesthetic scholarship. The clue to the relationship between the prophecy and poetry of the Bible, already noted by, for instance, Dennis, must lie in detailed study of the social setting from which they arose.

It is evident from many parts of the Sacred History, that even from the earliest times of the Hebrew Republic, there existed certain colleges of prophets, in which the candidates for the prophetic office, removed altogether from an intercourse with the world, devoted themselves entirely to the exercises and study of religion.[34]

The Hebrew word 'Nabi', explains Lowth, was used in an ambiguous sense denoting equally 'a Prophet, a Poet, or a Musician, under the influence of divine inspiration'. He cites the case of Solomon, who 'twice makes use of the word, which, in its ordinary sense, means prophecy, strictly so called, to denote the language of poetry'.[35]

From all these testimonies it is sufficiently evident, that the prophetic office had a most strict connexion with the poetic art. They had one common name, one common origin, one common author, the Holy Spirit. Those in particular were called to the exercise of the prophetic office, who were previously conversant with the sacred poetry. It was equally part of their duty to compose verses for the service of the church, and to declare the oracles of God.[36]

Though in places this reads almost like a paraphrase of Dennis,[37] the difference between Dennis's speculative and theoretical argument and Lowth's sense of historical context is illustrated over the relationship between Jesus and the Old Testament prophetic tradition. Dennis saw Jesus as a prophet: 'the method of his Instruction was intirely Poetical: that is, by Fables or Parables, contriv'd, and plac'd, and adapted to work very strongly upon human passions'.[38] Lowth anchors this assertion by pointing out that 'Mashal', one of the words commonly used for a poem in the Old Testament (especially in terms of content) is also the word translated in the New Testament as 'parable'.[39] In other words, he concludes, Jesus's parables are not an innovation, but merely an extension, by the greatest of the biblical 'poets', of the basic mode of Hebrew thought as it had been handed down through the prophetic tradition.[40]

In spite of coming frequently from humble backgrounds – like David, the shepherd boy – the prophets of Israel were not to be seen as rustics, but men whose religious training had included an elaborate grounding in aesthetics – in particular, in the arts of music and verse. The prophets were, in short, the inheritors of a highly sophisticated aesthetic and intellectual tradition. Though Lowth's *Lectures* were to feed directly into the revival of primitivism in English poetry during the latter part of the eighteenth century, he refutes any suggestion that the poet Isaiah or the authors of the Psalms were themselves 'primitives', any more than those they inspired, like Smart, Cowper, Blake, or Wordsworth were. What Lowth implicitly rejects are the stilted conventions of Augustan poetic diction. He praises, instead, the 'simple and unadorned' language of Hebrew verse, that gains its 'almost ineffable sublimity' not by elevated diction, but from the depth and universality of its subject matter. In his humble origins, and in the simplicity and directness of his language, Jesus is similarly also a continuation of the Old Testament poetic tradition. Unlike the modern European poets, the Hebrew ones had never been part of a courtly circle at the centre of power, but had remained, often in opposition to the political establishment of the day, in close touch with the rural and pastoral life of the ordinary people, using in their verse (or 'parables') the homely metaphors of agriculture and everyday life.[41]

Lowth's capacity to bring out, anticipate, and even originate critical principles that were only to come to fruition with Romanticism is everywhere extraordinary. Though previous critics had made play with terms like 'enthusiasm' and 'sublimity' in the context of the Bible, they had remained, as ideas, relatively unfocused. Dennis, for instance, cites the authority of Longinus to show that 'the greatest sublimity is to be deriv'd from Religious Ideas . . .'[42] (something which, incidentally, Longinus never said), but the question of whether this is by definition *all* 'religious ideas', or some more than others is of less interest to him. In contrast, as we have seen, Lowth's idea of the 'sublime' stresses naturalness as against artificiality, the irregular as against the regular, the mysterious as against the comprehensible, in a way that closely anticipates Burke's own *Enquiry into the Sublime and the Beautiful* by several years. For him, as for Burke, it is the ultimate criterion of greatness in art. Foreshadowing Blair and Wordsworth, Lowth goes on to describe the language of poetry as the product of 'enthusiasm', 'springing from mental emotion'.[43] It is hardly surprising that through Lowth's influence the Bible was to become for the Romantics not merely the model of sublimity, but also a source of style and a touchstone of true feeling.

But Lowth's most original scholarly contribution was the rediscovery of Hebrew prosody: the technique of its construction. It had always been clear, of course, that a great deal of the Bible was 'poetic', and earlier critics as far removed from each other as Dennis and Addison had laid great stress on the poetic qualities of the scriptures, but even the Psalms (which were known to be songs) showed perplexingly little evidence of either rhyme or regular metre in the original Hebrew. Even among Jews of Lowth's day the traditional art of Hebrew verse-construction seemed to have been completely lost. Earlier scholars, such as Bishop Hare (1671–1740), had made valiant efforts to discover in the Psalms a system of scansion and a rhyme-scheme, but their results looked distinctly unconvincing. Lowth now demonstrated, with impressively detailed evidence, that Hebrew poetry had never depended upon the normal conventions of European verse at all, but was constructed instead upon a quite different principle which he called 'parallelism':

The Correspondence of one verse, or line, with another, I call *parallelism*. When a proposition is delivered, and a second subjoined to it, or drawn under it, equivalent, or contrasted with it in sense; or similar to it in the form of grammatical construction; these I call parallel lines; and the words or phrases, answering one to another in the corresponding lines, parallel terms.[44]

This 'correspondence of one verse, or line, with another', Lowth argued, was the basic principle on which Hebrew metre was constructed. Its origins lay in the antiphonal chants and choruses we find mentioned in various places in the Old Testament. Lowth cites, for example, I Samuel xviii, 7: when David returned victorious from battle with the Philistines the Hebrew women greeted him with the chant of 'Saul hath smote his thousands,' and were answered by a second chorus with the parallel: 'And David his ten thousands'.[45] This simple, rhythmic, antiphonal structure of statement and counter-statement, though it may have originated spontaneously in song, gave the Hebrew psalmists and prophets a basic pattern of extraordinary flexibility. Its commonest form is what Lowth calls 'synonymous parallelism, when the same sentiment is repeated in different, but equivalent terms', as in Psalm 114:

> When Israel went out from Egypt;
> The house of Jacob from a strange people:
> Judah was as his sacred heritage;
> Israel his dominion.
> The sea saw and fled;
> Jordan turned back:
> The mountains leaped like rams;
> The hills like the sons of the flock.

Lowth himself distinguishes no less than eight different kinds of parallelism. From the simplest forms of repetition or echo that we find in synonymous parallelism, it could provide endless variation, comparison, contrast – as between David and Saul, for instance, in the example noted above, where their respective ratings in the charts were not lost on Saul – through to antithesis and even dialectic. Indeed, parallelism could be said to have shaped the whole structure of Jewish thought. Moreover, form helped to shape content in a way that was almost unknown in European poetry, and this extraordinary coincidence of style and content had another, apparently providential, consequence for European readers of the Bible. As we saw in the last chapter, Hebrew verse could be directly translated into prose without metrical loss.

Lowth's work inaugurated a critical revolution. Not merely did the Bible now give a new authority for the prophetic status of the poet as the transformer of society and the mediator of divine truth, but it was also stylistically taken as a model both of naturalness and sublimity – with the added asssurance that its precious content was almost providentially preserved in the rich prose of the English *Authorized Version*. As Friedrich Meinecke, Isaiah Berlin, and Elinor Shaffer have detailed,[46] Lowth's 'historical' approach was to prove seminal to the German historians and biblical scholars of the second half of the eighteenth century, and to play a key part in the development of the Higher Criticism. Similarly, his ideas may be seen to underline the later development of the hermeneutical tradition from Schleiermacher to Gadamer. Yet, for all the interpretative brilliance of his scholarship, Lowth is not a 'historian' in the modern sense of the word. In the *Lectures* he accepts the biblical narrative at its face value, and rarely questions the textual history of the material he is dealing with, any more than he questions the miracles or the chronology of Genesis. For him, as for his forbears, the Bible was still regarded by Lowth as having 'one common author' – in the person of the Holy Spirit. Lowth has, similarly, no doubts that the books of Jonah and Daniel are 'the bare recital of fact', and the nearest he gets to speculation about authorship is when he discusses whether Moses or Elihu (the late entrant, you will recall, among Job's comforters) actually wrote the Book of Job. We are still a long way from the world of Eichhorn, Lessing and Herder.

This is a point that must be stressed if only because it has not always been appreciated. Murray Roston, in his admirable book *Poet and Prophet: The Bible and The Growth of Romanticism*[47] sets Lowth clearly in his intellectual context, but Lowth's only modern biographer, Brian Hepworth, offers what is, in effect, an extension of Abrams's thesis by seeing the author of the *Sacred Poetry of the Hebrews* as one of the prime agents of secularization. According to him, Lowth's approach to the Bible reveals him as a thoroughgoing 'materialist'[48] while Lowth's stress on the creative capacity of the human mind is that of 'a humanistic theorist, not a Christian'.[49] Apparently to support this view, Hepworth claims that Michaelis, in his 1758 Preface to the Göttingen Latin edition of the *Lectures*, 'saw Lowth not as a churchman *or* even as a professor, but as a poet speaking about poetry'.[50] Distinctions between 'humanists' and 'Christians' in the context of eighteenth-century literary scholarship are, clearly, of little meaning, but the view of Lowth as a materialist and a secularizer needs some discussion.

At first glance his textual criticism and principles of translation might seem to be more modern than traditional, but this impression is misleading. Certainly he is very far being a scriptural literalist. Of *Isaiah* he writes:

Beside the difficulties attending it arising from the nature of the thing in itself; from the language in which it is written; and the condition in which it is come down to us through so many ages; what we have of it being the scanty relics of a language formerly copious, and consequently the true meaning of many words and phrases being obscure and dubious, and perhaps incapable of being clearly ascertained: besides these impediments necessarily inherent in the subject, others have been thrown in the way of our progress . . .[51]

Similarly his notion of translation begins as if it could have been the Preface to the *Good News Bible*, but the difference rapidly becomes apparent:

The first and principal business of a Translator is to give us the plain literal and grammatical sense of his author; the obvious meaning of his words, phrases, and sentences, and to express them in the language into which he translates, as far as may be, in equivalent words, phrases, and sentences . . . This is peculiarly so in subjects of high importance such as the Holy Scriptures, in which so much depends on the phrase and expression; and particularly in the Prophetical books of scripture; where from the letter are often deduced deep and recondite senses, which must owe all their weight and solidity to the just and accurate interpretation of the words of the Prophecy. For whatever senses are supposed to be included in the Prophet's words, Spiritual, Mystical, Allegorical, Analogical, or the like, they must all entirely depend on the Literal Sense.[52]

He himself, Lowth insists, is concerned only with this literal sense; if the reader requires more 'there are many learned Expositors to whom he may have recourse . . .'[53] But for all his disclaimers, Lowth is drawn back, again and again, into what he calls 'mystical' or allegorical interpretations.[54] Both Newton's mystical writings, and those of the Jewish commentator, David Kimchi, are frequently mentioned. Thus the *meaning* of Isaiah is to point to the coming of Jesus:

This seems to me to be the nature and true design of this part of Isaiah's Prophecies; and this view of them seems to afford the best method of resolving difficulties, in which Expositors are frequently engaged, being much divided between what is called the Literal and the Mystical sense, properly; for the mystical or spiritual sense is very often the most literal sense of all.

Such passages – and there are many – do little to support the picture of Lowth as a materialist or secularizer; what they do illustrate is the very traditional side of his scholarship: the textual critic's sense of, and fascination with, the polysemous nature of biblical texts.

They suggest, too, that in the thirty years or so between the *Lectures* and *Isaiah* Lowth was influenced by the Higher Criticism that he himself had helped to fashion. He cites Michaelis's work, and seems more alive to the problem presented by corrupt texts. At the same time, he is, if anything, more aware *also* of the possibilities of poetic meanings that can coexist in a single passage. Thus alongside the rediscovery of the Bible within a historical context runs a no less important rediscovery of the Bible as *poetry*. The debate over the Bible opened up by Lowth is as much aesthetic as historical.

Perhaps the most important area of argument concerned the question of poetic form in the books of prophecy. This was a question on which Lowth himself had been somewhat ambiguous:

In respect to the order, disposition, and symmetry of a perfect poem of the prophetic kind, I do not know of any certain definition which will admit of general application. Naturally free, and of too ardent a spirit to be confined by rule, it is usually guided by the nature of the subject only, and the impulse of divine inspiration.[55]

Though it is perfectly possible to read this in a sense quite compatible with a later Romantic sense of organic form, it is clear from the actual examples Lowth chooses that his ideas of 'regularity' and 'perfection' of form remain by and large neoclassical. Nor had he had reason to revise the caution of his defence of biblical structure by the time he came to publish his translation of the prophet who, by general accord, was given 'first place (after David) among the poets of Israel', Isaiah:

Isaiah greatly excells, too, in all the graces of method, order, connexion, and arrangement; though in asserting this we must not forget the nature of the prophetic impulse, which bears away the mind with irresistible violence, and frequently in rapid transitions from near to remote objects, from human to divine: we must also be careful in remarking the limits of particular predictions, since, as they are now extant, they are often improperly connected, without any marks of discrimination; which injudicious arrangement, on some occasions, creates almost insuperable difficulties.[56]

This pusillanimity in defence of the artistic form of divine inspiration was too much for one of Lowth's sincerest admirers, Thomas Howes, Rector of Thorndon, who, in 1783, published his *Doubts Concerning the Translation and Notes of the Bishop of London to Isaiah, Vindicating Ezechiel, Isaiah, and other Jewish Prophets from Disorder in Arrangement.* Howes out-Lowths Lowth. He has no doubt that the basic principles enunciated by the bishop are correct, but in adopting, however tentatively, the theory that there may be breaks in the text, or mistakes in the ordering, Lowth is being untrue to his own critical canons. Howes brings to biblical criticism contemporary theories of inspiration, natural genius, and poetic grace, thus, in the words of a recent commentator, 'making the Bible the *locus classicus* of the issue of inspiration vs. mechanical composition, artlessness vs. art.'[57] His argument is the more powerful in that it enlists, by implication at any rate, the full authority of the Holy Spirit for the new ideas of organic form. He challenges Lowth's assumption that the natural order for prophecies should be chronological, suggesting two other possible principles of arrangement: that of 'historic order', that in which the prophecies were actually accomplished, and that of 'oratorical order', that which is 'best suited to the purpose of *persuasion and argumentation*'.[58] This last, which Howes describes as the 'still better order', he also calls 'poetic arrangement':

For it has been long conceived, that these prophecies are replete with bold poetic ideas and expressions; the translator (Lowth), with his usual learning and accuracy, has convinced the public, that they are even composed in a similar metre to the other antient poetic works of the Jews: I have only ventured, in pursuance of his example, to advance one step farther in novelty, by shewing, that there are equally good reasons to conceive these prophecies to be put together in a connected method and order, agreeably to such modes of poetic and oratorical arrangement, as were customary in the most antient ages, and this apparently by the respective authors of each prophetic work.[59]

It has been well said by A. O. Lovejoy that 'the history of ideas is the history of the confusion of ideas'. Howes's idea of an 'oratorical order' for the prophets is, in many ways, closer to the notions of rhetoric that we find in Milton or Dennis, than it is to the Preface to the *Lyrical Ballads* or *Biographia Literaria*. Conversely, of course, Lowth's suspicion that there are problems to the text of Isaiah not wholly to be attributed to the agency of the Holy Spirit, and his hypotheses of confusion due either to the frenzy of inspiration or carelessness of an editor, place him closer to the spirit of the Higher Criticism than it does to contemporary aesthetics of the mid-eighteenth century. Yet Howes's argument, that the confused, tortuous, and even apparently rambling structure to some of the prophetic books of the Bible, represented a 'poetic' structure of divinely inspired profundity, analogous to the seemingly confused yet secretly ordered structure of Nature, may be taken as the final tread of the new Jacob's ladder by which the poet had ascended from the role of craftsman and decorator to divine authority and prophetic status. The historical argument that poetry is an older mode than prose, resisted fiercely by such critics as Trapp, who believed that as the superior and more sophisticated form it was logically later than prose, could be, and was, powerfully reinforced by the argument that the Holy Spirit used it.

The influence of these ideas on poetic theory and on the first generation of Romantic poets is not difficult to trace. Though Gregory's English translation of Lowth's *Lectures* was not published until 1787, they had in fact been circulated for a wider English audience in monthly instalments by the anti-Wesleyan *Christian's Magazine* twenty years before in 1767.[60] Moreover Lowth's Isaiah Translation, published in 1778, had contained a very full summary of the *Lectures* together with much new material. Blair had also included an extensive summary of Lowth's work in his *Lectures on Rhetoric and Belles Letters* (1783) – which were to go through many editions before the end of the century.

Already, by the 1780s, two different traditions, both stemming from Lowth's pioneer work, may be discerned. On the one hand, following Michaelis in Germany a new generation of biblical scholars was at work transforming biblical studies on 'Lowthian' principles. In England, however, as we have seen from the examples of Howes and Blair, it was not so much the implications for biblical criticism as poetic theory that aroused attention. Lowth's influence on the poetry of Smart is well-known. By the 1790s the two traditions stemming from Lowth were beginning to come together again. The ideas of Eichhorn, Lessing, and even Herder were beginning to filter into intellectual circles in Britain, chiefly through Unitarian channels, and though there were even home-grown critics and scholars of international standing, such as Alexander Geddes, a Scottish Roman Catholic priest, it proved a false start for the new wave of biblical scholarship.[61] The popular reaction against the French Revolution by 1793 meant that Unitarianism, with its dangerous intellectual and radical associations, was itself suspect. As part of a witch-hunt against suspected Unitarians and radicals, William Frend was expelled from his Fellowship at Cambridge, and Thomas Beddoes from Oxford. The Higher Criticism was not merely felt to be unchristian, it was un-English, unpatriotic, and politically dangerous. For a whole generation it was virtually ignored in Britain, isolated as ever by the appalling quality of the modern language teaching in schools and universities, and engaged in the long wars with Napoleon. It was not until the 1820s that the intellectual climate was again favourable towards the German Historical critics, but when, in 1823, Edward Bouverie Pusey, shortly to become a leading figure in the Oxford Movement, became interested in the new ideas he could find only two men in the University of Oxford capable of reading German.[62] Yet there *were* a few, mostly outside the universities, who could and had studied the Germans. Coleridge was one. Frend had been a Fellow of Coleridge's own college, Jesus, while he was an undergraduate there, and had been a big influence on his intellectual and religious development. It had been Beddoes who persuaded Coleridge to go the University of Göttingen when he was in Germany in 1798 to read Eichhorn and attend his lectures. The influence of Eichhorn on Coleridge's biblical criticism has been well documented.[63] Though we have little evidence of Wordsworth's direct contacts with the German Higher Criticism, there seems little doubt that, at this period of their closest co-operation, he must have learned

something of it from his friend. Similarly, there is reason to believe that
Blake, though he was not frequenting the same Unitarian circles as Coleridge, was also in touch with the new ideas. Internal evidence from *The
Marriage of Heaven and Hell, There is no Natural Religion*, and *All
Religions are One*, seems to suggest an acquaintance with the Higher
Criticism as early as 1788. Certainly he was in touch with people during
the 1790s where the ideas of the German critics were known and discussed. He too knew William Frend. He also belonged to a circle that used to
meet regularly at the house of Joseph Johnson, the radical London
publisher and bookseller, in St Paul's Churchyard. Other members of his
group included William Godwin, Mary Wollstonecraft, Tom Paine,
Joseph Priestley, Richard Price, and Thomas Holcroft.

What we may call the 'second' Lowthian Tradition, that of poetic
theory, is both easier and more difficult to trace. It is easier in the sense
that, as we have seen, the aesthetic principles enunciated by Lowth were
part of a long tradition of debate about the nature and properties of sacred
verse. It is more difficult in that the very diffuseness and widespread
nature of that debate make it less simple to isolate specific authors and
their direct influence. It is probable that Priestly knew Howes's *Critical
Observations* since they included an attack on him. We know that Coleridge used both Marsh's translation of Michaelis's *Introduction to the
New Testament* and Lowth's translation of *Isaiah* in his 1795 Lectures,[64]
and he was almost certainly also directly familiar with the *Lectures on the
Sacred Poetry of the Hebrews*. Wordsworth, apart from his connections
with Coleridge, knew Blair's account of Lowth even if he did not know
the original – which seems unlikely.

It was not Wordsworth or Coleridge, however, who first chose
directly to develop Lowth's poetic theory a stage further. That distinction belongs to Blake. It is clear from his references to the 'poetic
genius' as 'The Spirit of Prophecy' that he was well aware of Lowth's
work by 1788. Two years later, in *The Marriage of Heaven and Hell*,
he elaborated this connection between poetic genius and prophecy into
a scene where the Prophets Isaiah and Ezekiel 'dined' with him:
Ezekiel explaining how 'we of Israel taught that the poetic Genius (as
you call it) was the first principle and all others merely derivative'. But
this is a critical canon that can be turned back on the Bible itself. So
far as I know, no commentator has yet called attention to the fact that
Blake's famous aphorism 'The Old and New Testaments are the Great
Code of Art' (*The Laocoon*, 1820) is *also* a reference to Lowth. In the

New Translation of Isaiah Lowth discusses the problem of scriptural authority in the case of a corrupt text; on Isaiah, his comment that 'the condition of the Hebrew Text is such, as from the nature of the thing . . . might in all reason have been expected . . .' leads to a comparison of his problems, methodologically, with those encountered in translating classical texts, such as Aristotle's *Poetics*. The *Poetics* is, he writes, 'the Great Code of Criticism' – 'the fundamental principles of which are plainly deducible from it; we still have recourse to it for the rules and laws of Epic and Dramatic Poetry, and the imperfection of the copy does not at all impeach the authority of the Legislator'.[66] In *The Laocoon* Blake sets the primary, artistic, authority of the Bible in place of Aristotle's secondary, critical, authority: 'Jesus and his Apostles and Disciples were all Artists . . .' – a point, we recall, made implicitly by Lowth when he described Jesus's parables as being an extension of the poetic tradition of the Old Testament.[66] Blake has completed the Lowthian revolution by re-asserting the primacy of art over neo-classical 'rules', of the Bible over the classics as a model, and shown his support for Howes on the matter of organic form. Every word of Lowth's defence of Aristotle can with even greater propriety be applied to the Scriptures – even to the unimpeached 'authority of the Legislator' – not merely, as Lowth himself intended, textually, but also *aesthetically*. If the poet is also the prophet, then the true model for poetic forms must also be the Bible.

What the aesthetic implications of this might be had already been suggested a few years earlier by Coleridge in his *Biographia Literaria*. In Chapter XIV, the account of the genesis of the *Lyrical Ballads* leads him directly on to a discussion of the nature of poetry in general. Citing Plato, Bishop Taylor and (Thomas) Burnet as examples, Coleridge comments that 'poetry of the highest kind may exist without metre, and even without the contradistinguishing objects of a poem. The first chapter of Isaiah (indeed a very large proportion of the whole book) is poetry in the most emphatic sense'.[67] This apparent endorsement of the principles expounded in the *New Translation of Isaiah* is followed within a few lines by a definition of poetry conceived structurally in terms of what Lowth had termed 'antithetical' parallelism: The power of the poet:

. . . reveals itself in the balance or reconciliation of opposite or discordant qualities: of sameness with difference; of the general with the concrete; the idea, with the image; the individual, with the representative; the sense of novelty and freshness, with old and familiar objects; a more than usual state of emotion, with more than usual order; judgement ever awake and steady self-possession, with enthusiasm and feeling profound or vehement; and while it blends and harmonizes the natural and the artificial, still subordinates art to nature . . .[68]

The verbal and syntactical parallels between this and the famous passage on the scriptures as 'the living educts of the imagination' in the Appendix to *The Statesman's Manual*,[69] written the same year, reinforce our sense of its biblical underpinnings. Lowth's analysis of Hebrew poetry in terms of parallelism had, it seems, made it possible for Coleridge, like Shelley, to think of 'poetry' in terms of mental dialectic characterized by an intensity of thought and feeling rather than by any particular rhetorical arrangement — the Bible providing for both the *locus classicus*. Whatever the differences between Wordsworth and Coleridge over the nature of poetic diction,[70] they are agreed in their sense that formal distinctions between prose and poetry are no longer tenable. With Shelley adopting a similar position in the *Defence of Poetry* only a few years later (with many of the same examples), it would seem that Lowth's rediscovery of Hebrew parallelism had been a key factor in the transition of the main stream of creative writing from verse to prose in the nineteenth century.[71] But there were other possibilities inherent in Coleridge's development of Lowth.

In his essay on 'Poetic Diction', written as an undergraduate for Jowett, the Master of Balliol, in 1865, Gerard Manley Hopkins returns to Wordsworth's theory of poetic diction — in the context both of Lowth's theory of parallelism and of Coleridge's 'antithetical' definition:

The structure of poetry is that of continuous parallelism, ranging from the technical so-called Parallelism of Hebrew Poetry and the antiphons of Church music up to the intricacy of Greek or Italian or English verse. But parallelism is of two kinds necessarily — where the opposition is clearly marked, and where it is transitional rather or chromatic. Only the first kind, that of marked parallelism is concerned with the structure of verse — in rhythm, the recurrence of a certain sequence of rhythm, in alliteration, in assonance and in rhyme. Now the force of this recurrence is to beget a recurrence or parallelism answering to it in the words or thought and, speaking roughly and rather for the tendency than the invariable result, the more marked parallelism in structure whether of elaboration or of emphasis begets more marked parallelism in the words and sense. And moreover parallelism in expression tends to beget or passes into parallelism in thought. This point reached we shall be able to see and account for the peculiarities of poetic diction. To the marked or abrupt kind of parallelism belong metaphor, similie, parable, and so on, where the effect is sought in likeness of things, and anthesis, contrast, and so on, where it is sought in unlikeness. To the chromatic parallelism belong gradation, intensity, climax, tone, expression (as the word is used in music), *chiaroscuro*, perhaps emphasis: while the faculties of Fancy and Imagination might range widely over both kinds, Fancy belonging more especially to the abrupt than to the transitional class.[72]

The paragraph starts with Lowth and ends with Coleridge. The Lowthian argument, that Hebrew poetry is of a fundamentally different kind and structure from European poetry, is now ingeniously turned back upon itself. The principle of parallelism is *not* peculiar to Hebrew verse, Hopkins argues, but is merely a special example of a structure that is in fact common to *all* poetry − and is, indeed, essential to it. The eighteenth-century rediscovery of the structure of biblical verse was not, as Lowth and his successors had imagined, just the discovery of a special case, but served to highlight a hitherto neglected quality latent in all verse, and so effectively to modify poetic theory as a whole. So far from implying that there is no difference between the language of poetry and that of prose, parallelism accentuates the difference because modifications of structure are direct modifications of meaning:

An emphasis of structure stronger than the common construction of sentences gives asks for an emphasis of expression stronger than that of common speech or writing, and that for an emphasis of thought stronger than that of common thought. And it is commonly supposed that poetry has tasked the highest powers of man's mind: this is because, as it asked for greater emphasis of thought and on a greater scale, at each stage it threw out the minds unequal to further ascent. The diction of poetry could not then be the same with that of prose, and again of prose we can see from the other side that its diction ought not to be that of poetry . . .[73]

For Hopkins the rediscovery of the Bible as 'poetry' did not mean the progressive obliteration of formal distinctions between verse and prose so much as a rediscovery of the *meaning* behind the traditional constructs. Because of the nature of human language, the Coleridgean redefinition of poetry in terms of a particular complex state of mind had immediate structural and formal linguistic consequences.

For an illustration to Hopkins's point we need look no further than a sonnet he wrote some seventeen years later:

As kingfishers catch fire, dragonflies dráw fláme;
As tumbled over rim in roundy wells

Stones ring; like each tucked string tells, each hung bell's
Bow swung finds tongue to fling out broad its name;
Each mortal thing does one thing and the same:
Deals out that being indoors each one dwells;
Selves – goes itself; *myself* it speaks and spells;
Crying *What I do is me: for that I came.*

I say móre: the just man justices;
Kéeps grace: thát keeps all his goings graces;
Acts in God's eye what in God's eye he is –
Christ – for Christ plays in ten thousand places,
Lovely in limbs, and lovely in eyes not his
To the Father through the features of men's faces.

In spite of its superficially unconventional appearance, this is a perfectly regular sonnet consisting of an octet of eight lines, divided into two four-line rhyming quatrains (abba, abba) and a six-line sestet (cdcdcd). What will be unfamiliar to those coming to Hopkins for the first time will be a certain originality and neologism of diction ('Selves' and 'justices' as verbs) and an apparent irregularity of line-length. The latter – Hopkins's famous 'sprung rhythm' – is a direct application of the principle of emphasis enunciated in the 1865 essay. In any poem there is a natural tension between the basic rhythm of the verse (which in this case is iambic pentameter: the common ten-syllabic line with five stresses) and the normal rhythm of English speech, which moves rapidly over unstressed syllables and pauses, for emphasis, on the key stressed syllables of each sentence. Hopkins has made this basic fact about English verse into a principle of construction. He counts *only* the stressed syllables. There can be as many unstressed syllables in the line as are necessary for the unforced sense desired. 'Why do I employ sprung rhythm . . . ?' he wrote to Robert Bridges in 1877, 'Because it is the nearest to the rhythm of prose, that is the native and natural rhythm of speech, the least forced, the most rhetorical and emphatic of all possible rhythms, combining, as it seems to me, opposite, and, one would have thought, incompatible excellencies, markedness of rhythm – that is rhythm's self – and naturalness of expression . . .'[74] It is not, he is quick to point out, his invention: Shakespeare, Milton, and Coleridge (whose phraseology he has again been echoing) all used it. What he has done is to state as a principle what previous poets have practised. Thus, for instance, the first line of our sonnet has not ten, but *eleven* syllables, and since his own accenting gives us the final two stresses, we know that the stress-pattern must fall like this:

As kíngfishers catch fíre, drágonflies dráw fláme

For Hopkins, verse accepts, incorporates, and uses the rhythms of prose speech. The antithesis of speech-rhythm and formal metre is but one of a whole series of parallelisms that are central to his poetic strategy. This sonnet is actually *about* parallelism. Each parallel is related to the next so as to form an ascending (or descending) scale of parallel parallels linking structure and meaning.

Underlying and informing the whole poem, of course, is the parallelism inherent in nature itself: the great parallelism of the Elijah story. Nature and God are both separate and intimately connected: meeting perhaps at infinity, but in our experience only to be understood in terms of comparison, resemblance, contrast, and analogy (or verbal parallelism). Thus each sharply individuated link in the Great Chain of Being (that ultimate mediaeval apotheosis of parallelism) reveals both itself and its relationship to the whole. The essential quality of each thing, be it the vivid beauty of kingfishers or dragonflies in sunlight, or the noise of a falling stone in a well, is experienced *externally*. In a dramatic post-Kantian reversal of Thomist philosophy, 'substance' is known by its 'accidents'. What each thing 'does' reveals its particular 'being indoors'. We know a thing not by its essence, but by the way it is perceived. Individuation is defined here in terms of communication; specifically by analogy with music, as a harmony: 'each tucked string tells, each hung bell's/Bow swung finds tongue . . .' The keyword is the Hopkins coinage, 'Selves': used as an Anglo-Saxon verb to mean roughly the same as the Latinate 'to individuate'. The Aristotelian process by which each thing strives more and more fully to become itself is now seen in a most un-Aristotelian way in terms of its interaction with everything else. The mediaeval world-picture has been, as it were, turned inside-out. We are reminded, yet again, of the importance of the concept of individuation to Romantics and Victorians. Just as words and meanings were perceived as progressively desynonymizing, so too, as we have seen, the associated objects of human experience are perceived in ever-sharper clarity as 'not-self', to be appreciated fully only when they are separated from the undifferentiated matrix of primary perception. Part of the intense vigour and freshness of Hopkins's nature poetry is due simply to the fact that it was not until the nineteenth century that this separation of man and nature could be said to be finally complete. It was, in this sense, speaking and spelling '*myself*' almost for the first time to Hopkins' generation. One thinks, for instance, of Ruskin's endless detailed studies of rocks and plants, or Cozens' and Constable's sketches of cloud-shapes. The 'fire' of the kingfisher's flight or the dragonfly's wing is deliberately and self-consciously subjective, dependent on the observer's knowledge of the interactivity of perception in a way that Elijah's or the Pentecostal 'fire' never were – and, for that reason, it is also more consciously objectified: a part of nature, not of divine intervention.

When we come to the sestet, however, this externality of nature is paralleled by the corresponding internality of man. What distinguishes him is not his outward appearance, but his *inwardness* as a vessel of God's grace. The depth and complexity of this inwardness of Christ in man for Hopkins is achieved by a piece of 'emphasis' almost unequalled in English literature. Sense and structure come together in a pun that encapsulates the entire action of the poem: 'Christ plays in ten thousand places . . .' The focal word is, of course, 'plays', and its various layers of overlapping meaning reach out to every part of the poem's imagery. If Christ 'plays' in man as a musician, it is to take up the theme of musical harmony in creation with which the octet was charged: 'each tucked string tells, each hung bell's/Bow swung finds tongue to swing out broad its name . . .' If Christ is taken as 'playing' as an actor, it is to 'act' the just man's part, 'that keeps all his goings graces'. If Christ 'plays' as a child might play a game, it is to express the joy of creation as a Great Dance in which the dragonfly and the kingfisher play their parts – and *deal* out their being as a card-player deals a deck of cards: seen from the back, identical, but from the front, distinct, individuated, and unique. If Christ is taken as 'playing' as a fountain of water, we are reminded of the well[75] wherein stones ring, the fountain in the midst of the garden, and the river of life – not to mention the older, more Catholic conceit where 'Christ's blood streams in the universe . . .' If Christ 'plays' across the face of all nature like the subtle play of light and shade, he is the Light of the World that catches the kingfisher and the dragonfly and reveals their individual inscape.[76] If Christ is to be found in the free 'play' of the mind over its subject, and thus, here, the mind of the poet, we are brought back reflexively to the poem itself as creative artifact. If Christ is thus held to be at 'play' within the pattern of words in language, and is even present within such an outrageous seven-fold pun, it is only a minute example of the involuted complexity of the ten thousand places where he is to be glimpsed, fleetingly as the flash of fire on a bird's wing in sunlight, in the creation of new meaning.

As an illustration of his own poetic principles, Hopkins's poem could hardly be bettered. Though it shares all the freshness and originality of his finest work, it is also, as we have indicated, a profoundly traditional piece. Behind it stands Keble and the whole mediaeval world of correspondences and the parallelisms of the Great Chain of Being so painstakingly reconstructed by the Tractarians; behind it, too, is Coleridge's sense of the 'balance or reconciliation of opposite or discordant qualities', and behind him, Lowth, and the rediscovered parallelism of the Psalms revealing the glory of God in a creation yet transcended by, and separate from, Him.

So, far from constituting a stage in creeping secularization, Lowth's work was to lead both to a revival of biblical influence and a re-vitalization of nineteenth-century poetic theory and aesthetics – leading, as we shall see, to new ways of thinking about language itself. The Bible had indeed proved to be the Great Code of Art.

The Book of Nature

By the eighteenth century the phrase 'the language of nature' had acquired two quite separate connotations. The primary meaning was that of what Boehme had called the 'Adamic' language – the original tongue in which the first human, divinely possessed of speech, had named the animals according to his perfect insight into their real qualities.[77]

The metaphor of the 'book of nature' was, as it were, an extension of this belief. The natural world, though groaning in travail, remained nonetheless after the Fall a visible and concrete reminder to Man of his divine origins – but now as a 'book' written in a lost language whose meaning could only be puzzled out in fragments with prayer and toil. From this idea we find developing the second meaning whereby the phrase 'the language of nature' is applied metaphorically to the 'message' encoded in Creation for the initiated to perceive – originally through mysticism, as in the case of Boehme, but increasingly also by means of progress in the natural sciences. Though originally it was arguable that these two meanings were, in reality, one and the same, since Adam's language was not arbitrary but one of essences, with the decline in belief in the literal truth of the Adamic language, the secondary, metaphorical, meaning had gradually tended to replace the primary one during the seventeenth century. The founders of the Royal Society, Boyle, Hooke,

Locke, Newton, and Wilkins, for instance, were both scientists *and* theologians who made a point of knowing the sacred languages. They were resolutely opposed to the 'Adamism' of Boehme and Fludd, believing that language was not a part of nature, that it described appearances not essences of things, and that it was therefore unable to give 'real knowledge' of Creation.[78] Instead, they were committed to a natural theology that rejected scriptural authority over science because it threatened the independent status of natural philosophy as an additional source of knowledge of God.[79] They desired to read *both* Books.

With the English Romantics this movement from primary to secondary meanings of the 'language of nature' was virtually complete. Moreover the associated idea of the '*liber naturae*', which, as Abrams reminds us, is as old as Augustine, acquired in the wake of Lowth a new hermeneutical significance. As we have seen, the idea of the poet as prophet is not an isolated belief, but rapidly became part of a total re-orientation of traditional concepts of aesthetics, literary structure, and of nature. Yet in spite of its influence on the Higher Criticism, and on political and theological radicals such as Priestley, it would be a mistake to see this critical revolution in purely 'progressive' or secularizing terms.

We have so far tended to stress those aspects of Lowth's work which liberated biblical study from the strait-jacket of typology. Yet, as has been noticed, there remained a strong typological streak even in his late writings, and with the advent of the French Revolution in the 1790s, and its accompanying wave of popular millenarianism, interest in typology tended to grow rather than wane.[80] This is a point easily overlooked by literary critics like Abrams or Hepworth. Typology did not simply disappear overnight with the advent of the Higher Criticism. Indeed, the new historicism took more than a hundred years to gain complete hold. As late as 1860, Kingsley's lectures on *The Roman and the Teuton*, given when he was Regius Professor of History in Cambridge, still show markedly typological elements – as disgruntled colleagues were quick to observe.

One of the most noticeable features of the English 'poetic' theological tradition leading from Lowth to the Romantics is its essential *conservatism*. We have already seen that Lowth's concentration on the literal meaning of the text as a document from a particular concrete historical situation can be seen as less an attempt to abolish the old style of typological and mystical readings, than to put such readings on a sounder scholarly basis – to combat Deist attacks on the authenticity of the Bible in general. Howes's motives for 'vindicating Ezechiel, Isaiah, and other Jewish prophets from Disorder in Arrangement' and his general support for Lowth's approach come from an even more explicit conservatism. His aim is to demonstrate that the accepted biblical chronology was wrong – especially where it assumed that 'prophecies' post-dated the events they apparently referred to.[81] But his determination to prove the Bible a reliable historical guide is directed not so much against Deists as Roman Catholics. Ironically, in view of what was to follow, he sees historical criticism as primarily a weapon in Catholic hands to impugn the Protestant reliance on the Bible[82] – a fact which may go some way to explain the relative tolerance with which Geddes's biblical researches were treated at first by the Catholic authorities.[83]

A similar theological conservatism, paradoxically, motivated one of the most radical of all the biblical scholars of this period: Antoine Fabre d'Olivet in France. Though commonly dismissed as a 'theosophist' and esoteric mystic on the grounds of his conclusions that the Pentateuch was written in a code to be interpreted only by initiates[84] (in essence a position not dissimilar from the Alexandrine tradition of typology) Fabre d'Olivet was in fact an excellent biblical scholar – in touch with the new developments in Anglo-German criticism as well as with the more traditional French Catholic writings and the Jewish interpreters. He was also a good Orientalist, who knew the work of Sir William Jones, and Sir Charles Wilkins in Sanscrit and other Asiatic languages, and Nathaniel Halhead, another distinguished Orientalist and a friend of Jones, who was for a time M.P. for Lymmington. Halhead was also a millenarian and a typologist who believed in the prophecies of Richard Brothers.[85] It is not at all uncommon to find accurate and scholarly linguistics and occultism mixed up at this period.

Taking up a suggestion also to be found in Lowth,[86] that the introduction of the Masoretic punctuation was, in effect, 'a new translation of the Old Testament', Fabre d'Olivet goes on to claim that the pre-Masoretic texts were really of the ancient Egyptian mysteries. His 'version' (the English is his own) of the first two verses of Genesis read as follows:

1. AT-FIRST-IN-PRINCIPLE, he-created, AElohim (he caused to be, he brought forth in principle, HE-The-Gods, the-Being-of-beings), the-selfsameness-of-heavens, and-the-selfsameness-of-earth.

2. And-the-earth was contingent-potentiality in-a-potentiality-of-being: and-darkness (hard-making-power)-was on-the-face of-the deep (fathomless-contingent-potentiality of being); and-the-breath of-HIM-the-Gods (a light-making-power) was-pregnantly-moving upon-the-face of-the-waters (universal passiveness.)[87]

This 'gnostic' version was promptly put on the Index by the Catholic Church, and largely forgotten thereafter. Nevertheless, his accompanying Hebrew grammar, which, instead of following the accepted Latin and Greek models, was based on internal psycholinguistic criteria, has been hailed as the product of one of the most powerful linguistic intellects of any age.[88] It was reading this book that turned the young Benjamin Lee Whorf, who was at the time worried by the conflict between his own fundamentalist background and the findings of evolutionary science, to the study of linguistics. In Fabre d'Olivet Whorf found foreshadowed a methodology flexible enough to respond to the quite different ways of structuring the world used by different languages, and the origins of what is nowadays called the 'phoneme' in his idea of a 'root-sign'.[89] There is a sense, at any rate, in which Fabre d'Olivet has a claim to be considered as one of the founders of modern linguistics.

Yet however innovative his methodology, or occultist his interpretation of the Pentateuch, the motivation behind Fabre d'Olivet's linguistics was the traditional one of reading correctly the *liber naturae*:

The ancient religions and particularly that of the Egyptians, were full of mysteries, and composed of numberless pictures and symbols, sacred work of an uninterrupted chain of divine men, who, reading in the book of Nature and in that of the Divinity, translated into human language, the ineffable language.[90]

The *original* Language of Adam which, as we have seen, was still supposed by many philologists to underlie all recorded languages, is secretly encoded in Nature. To translate it we must read correctly the *other* great book of God, the Bible.

Through this translation which I give of the Sepher, Moses will no longer be the stumbling-block of reason and the dismay of the natural sciences. Those shocking contradictions, those incoherencies, those ridiculous pictures which furnish weapons so terrible for its enemies shall no more be seen in his Cosmogony.[91]

His was, perhaps, the most radical attempt to 'save the appearances' of the biblical text ever attempted.

While the English Romantic poets were none of them motivated by quite this kind of radical conservatism, they had other reasons for holding on to the typological traditions of biblical interpretation. For them, typology was closely connected with an underlying platonism. Kathleen Raine has traced the ways in which the platonic tradition 'lived on as the learning of the poets, like a secret language . . .'[92] 'In England,' she writes, 'it is to the poets rather than to the philosophers . . . that we must look for the continuity of this tradition'.[93] It was largely due to the writings, lectures, and personal influence of Thomas Taylor that the Platonic strand in English poetry was able to provide an effective philosophic counterpoise to the otherwise all-conquering mood of empiricism. He was a friend or acquaintance of Blake, Flaxman, Peacock, Coleridge, Wordsworth, Keats, and Samuel Palmer. Mary Wollstonecraft was for a time his lodger.

As Trevor Levere has shown in his fascinating study of *Coleridge and Early Nineteenth Century Science*, the concept of the 'type' in biology had then not yet become entirely separated from its literary and theological connotations, and the word carried a double meaning when applied to the classification of animals and plants. Thus Coleridge could write in a notebook of animals as '*Types* not Symbols, dim Prophecies not incipient Fulfilments' of Man.[94] Bringing together biology with the neo-platonism of Porphyry, Plotinus, and Iamblichus suggested to him at once the *liber naturae* of:

significant Forms . . . or organizedation, ~~Bodies~~, contemplated as so many Types or Characters impressed on animal bodies, or in which they are, as it were, *cast*. Now Types and Characters variously yet significantly combined form a Language. – The Types of Nature are a Natural *Language* – but a Language is no more conceivable without reference to Intelligence than a ~~system~~ series of determinate actions without reference to a Will, if not immediately yet ultimately. An intelligible, consistent and connected Language no less supposes intelligence for its existence than it requires it for its actual intelligibility.[95]

Levere comments that, 'For Coleridge, the contemplation of animated nature through the idea of types revealed the ascent of powers, purpose, activity of mind and will, and something of the very language of creation, the power of the word, whereby the worlds of nature, mind, and creation coalesced.'[96]

As the notion of a divinely-structured scheme of history or biology slowly retreated during the nineteenth century, the original distinction between 'types' and 'symbols' tended to be blurred, or even lost. A type became a symbol written into Nature by its Author.[97] But, as the above quotation from Coleridge illustrates, there was an important distinction. If a 'symbol' revealed 'the translucence of the Eternal in, and through the Temporal . . .' and 'partakes of the Reality which it renders intelligible',[98] a 'type' only offers a dim foreshadowing, rather than 'an incipient Fulfilment'. So far from being conflatable as synonyms, as they would if the language of typology had been already internalized and psychologized, they still retain even to the end of his life a sharp semantic difference.

Wordsworth is in contact with both worlds, and, like Coleridge, uses the two words as part of the vast vocabulary of Nature. When he had crossed the Alps in Book VI of *The Prelude*, for instance, he describes the natural grandeur in terms of deliberate balanced ambiguity:

> The immeasurable height
> Of woods decaying, never to be decayed,
> The stationary blasts of waterfalls,
> And everywhere along the hollow rent
> Winds thwarting winds, bewildered and forlorn,
> The torrents shooting from the clear blue sky,
> The rocks that muttered close upon our ears –
> Black drizzling crags that spake by the wayside
> As if a voice were in them – the sick sight
> And giddy prospect of the raving stream,
> The unfettered clouds and region of the heavens,
> Tumult and peace, the darkness and the light,
> Were all like workings of one mind, the features
> Of the same face, blossoms upon one tree,
> Characters of the great apocalypse,
> The types and symbols of Eternity,
> Of first, and last, and midst, and without end.   (lines 556–72)

The tone of gratuitous piety that we noted earlier is here present once again, though less obtrusively. The contradictions of Nature, apparently jarring and discordant, are mysteriously reconciled into a harmony and unity comprehending *both* types *and* symbols of eternity. What is at stake here are two concepts of 'eternity'. Traditionally, eternity, the literally unthinkable, has been represented by two conflicting models: on the one hand a sequence of time without end; on the other a simultaneous 'now'. As 'types' these antinomies of Nature point forward to a consummation yet unknown; as 'symbols' they express a totality which (although we may not yet be able to read it fully) is *already* present. The two words give us some clue as to the kind of ellipsis or compression that underlies this extraordinary passage. It is as if every term is given dual reference. The overpowering sense of sublimity in Nature is charged, by a typical Wordsworthian ambiguity, with a corresponding sense that it has been 'arranged' or planted there by God for man to read. If we see in this the role of the poet as prophet, receiving, Moses-like, the inspiration from Sinai the apocalyptic reference becomes more comprehensible. The task of the poet, in Coleridge's terms 'reconciling opposite or discordant qualities' is simultaneously that of the prophet, reading God's signature in his creation, and imaginatively recreating it for the reader.

This brings us back, at last, to the Snowdon scene in Book XIII with which I began the discussion of Lowth. I myself some years ago was guilty of the error of describing it as 'Symbolic',[99] but, of course, it is not – or only in a secular reading; it is also one of the most striking pieces of *typology* in Romantic literature. Only unfamiliarity with the terminology prevents us from seeing at once what Wordsworth is saying, for here he is quite explicit:

> . . . above all
> One function of such mind had Nature there
> Exhibited by putting forth, and that
> With circumstance most awful and sublime:
> That domination which she oftentimes
> Exerts upon the outward face of things,
> So moulds them, and endues, abstracts, combines,
> Or by abrupt and unhabitual influence
> Doth make one object so impress itself
> Upon all others, and pervade them so,
> That even the grossest minds must see and hear,
> And cannot chuse but feel. The power which these
> Acknowledge when thus moved, which Nature thus
> Thrusts forth upon the sense, is the express
> Resemblance – in the fullness of its strength
> Made visible – a genuine counterpart
> And brother of the glorious faculty
> Which higher minds bear with them as their own.

(lines 73–90)

Now it is possible, of course, to interpret what Wordsworth is here describing simply as a psychological experience, for that, at one level, is certainly what it is. Wordsworth is meditating on that shock of discovery by which we can suddenly find mirrored for us in the external world a symbol for an internal or abstract state: here, of the creative unconsciousness, the mind of the poet. It is an experience perhaps parallel to, and not unlike that of Kekulé's 'discovery' of the molecular structure of benzine.[100] But that is only half the story. What he is also describing is the 'typology' of Nature. Just as the Old Testament prophet–poets exercised their dual office by discerning and proclaiming God's judgements in contemporary events, so Wordsworth, the poet–prophet of his own age, is perceiving the language of God in Nature: 'catching', 'creating', 'transforming' it into a symbol within the work of art which his the poem we have before us. The compulsive religiosity that we started by puzzling over is not a gratuitous piece of piety, but a direct reminder of the divine election of the poet for whom 'vows' had been made. The creative imagination is also the prophetic vision.

Yet, of course, there *is* a fundamental difference – and it is a very revealing one. The Hebrew poets we recall, had no word in their vocabulary for anything corresponding to our idea of 'Nature'. For them there was no essential difference between the regular rhythm of the seasons, the fall of Babylon, or the bodily assumption of Elijah in a chariot of fire. All were equally the direct actions of a God who habitually manifested himself through purposeful change. Wordsworth, who had come to maturity with the French Revolution, is no less conscious than the Hebrew poets of living in a world of profound, even cataclysmic changes, but for that very reason, perhaps, he tends to find the evidence of divine meaning and order less in the processes of history than in the great unchanging permanencies of Nature against which they must be set. The fall of Robespierre or the career of Napoleon may indeed exemplify the inexorability of God's judgements, but in so doing, they merely reflect flickeringly and by contrast the truths permanently exemplified in the ordered harmony of man and his natural environment. Though *The Prelude* purports to be a 'history', it contains an opposite movement that is curiously antihistorical. In other words, while Hebrew typology is essentially diachronic, working through history, Wordsworthian typology is in effect, dialectical, repeating within its structure the theological paradox we have already noted between two models of eternity: at once diachronic *and* synchronic.

If before we were justified in detecting the influence of Lowth on Wordsworth's idea of the poet as prophet, now we encounter something that looks suspiciously like that of Howes. The unity in diversity, the mysterious harmony that is revealed through the

apparent randomness and arbitrariness of natural phenomena in the
Simplon Pass is a dramatic reassertion of the way in which the poet,
under the guidance of the Spirit, brings order out of disorder. The list
of abstract pieties, read in this context, takes on a precise and poetically
important meaning: they are no less than the powers of the prophet to
link his own inner harmony with a 'delight/That fails not in the external universe'. They are also a clue towards the structure of *The Prelude*
itself. If its outward structure, with the thirteen books (I refer to the
1805 text) and the crisis over the French Revolution bears as we have
seen a strong resemblance to Augustine's *Confessions*; its inner structure, lacking in any immediately chronological thread, anecdotal and
digressive, bears a stronger similarity to the 'poetic order' detected by
Howes in the Old Testament prophets: the language of the *liber
naturae*.

Though Wordsworth, characteristically, does not use the phrase,
preferring usually to contrast 'nature' and 'books'[101], his follower,
Keble, had no such inhibitions:

> There is a book, who runs may read,
> Which heavenly truth imparts,
> And all the lore its scholars need,
> Pure eyes and Christian hearts.[102]

The 'book', of course, is the 'book of Nature'. Earlier, in a more self-
doubting mood he had confessed:

> Mine eye unworthy seems to read
> One page of Nature's beauteous book;
> It lies before me, fair outspread –
> I only cast a wishful look.[103]

Keble was not given to originality – indeed, solemnly advised his
students against it – and in view of his reputation as a self-confessed
Wordsworthian it would be easy to find in these, and other similar
verses, direct echoes of Wordsworth. But in fact, of course, Keble's
view of nature has none of the Wordsworthian tensional ambiguity.[104]
Nor is his Neo-platonism, with its detailed, almost mediaevally
elaborated system of 'correspondences' particularly close to Wordsworth's theory of the imagination. Nevertheless Keble's image bears
what might be called a 'family resemblance', in that it belongs to a
whole cluster of such literary and linguistic metaphors of the period
describing the relationship between man and his environment not in

terms of law, or even of harmony, but of *communication*. Metaphors
from the music of the spheres or Newtonian mathematics tend to be
replaced by those of publishing and even of speech. This metaphorical
shift is one symptom of the well-documented Romantic phenomenon
of 'internalization'. The objective, external, and universal language of
Adam is now apprehended as an 'internal' language of divine
revelation.

Take, for instance, the following passage from a book by an
American, Sampson Reed, published in 1826 – the year before *The
Christian Year*.

> There is a language, not of words, but of things. When this language shall
> have been made apparent, that which is human will have answered its end; and
> being as it were resolved into its original elements, will lose itself in nature.
> The use of language is the expression of our feelings and desires – the
> manifestation of the mind. But everything which is, is full of the expression
> of that use for which it is designed, as of its own existence. If we did but under-
> stand its language, what could our words add to its meaning? It is because we
> are unwilling to hear, that we find it necessary to say so much; and we drown
> the voice of nature with the discordant jargon of ten thousand dialects . . .
> Everything which surrounds us is full of the utterance of one word, completely
> expressive of its nature. This word is its name: for God, even now, could we
> but see it, is creating all things and giving a name to every work of his love,
> in its perfect adaptation to that for which it is designed.[105]

Though Reed was a Swedenborgian mystic, even without his Wordsworthian title, *Observations on the Growth of the Mind*, we would have
little difficulty in recognizing its family resemblance to, say, the Gerard
Manley Hopkins sonnet examined earlier:

> Each mortal thing does one thing and the same:
> Deals out that being indoors each one dwells;
> Selves – goes itself; *myself* it speaks and spells,
> Crying *What I do is me: for that I came.*

For Reed, and even, it seems, for Hopkins, the analogy is scarcely a
metaphor in the normal sense: language is, rather, perceived as an imperfect human surrogate for a system of communication divinely inherent in
the natural order of things. Now there is nothing particularly new about
this 'imperfect surrogate' argument: it had been used with variations,
religious or secular according to taste by authorities as different in
outlook as Augustine and Locke; what is, or seems to be, different about
the Romantic use of this metaphor is the concept of *language* involved.
Coleridge, as so often, is explicit where others are implicit:

. . . Even so it is in the language of man and of nature. The sound, *sun*, or the figures S, U, N, are pure arbitrary modes of recalling the object, and for visual mere objects not only sufficient, but have infinite advantages from their very nothingness *per se*. But the language of nature is a subordinate *Logos*, that was in the beginning, and was with the thing it represented, and it was the thing represented.[106]

Here the alternative of natural religion to revelation as a source of religious insight is spelled out with a force unequalled since the mediaeval synthesis: 'nature' is nothing less than 'a subordinate *Logos*': the divine Word of God in creation, described in an echo of the opening words of John's Gospel.

The example of the sun to contrast the arbitrary signs of human language with the meaning implicit in the signs of nature may have roots in a passage of Lucretius's *De Rerum Natura*;[107] more immediately the contrast between the mundane appearance and its typological significance within the hierachy of nature is reminiscent of yet another passage from Dennis:

The sun mention'd in ordinary Conversation, gives the idea of a round flat shining body, of about two foot diameter. But the sun occurring to us in Meditation, gives the idea of a vast and glorious Body, and the top of all the visible Creation, and the brightest material image of the Divinity.[108]

We will return to the *logos*; what concerns us here is not the divine language of Nature, but the 'arbitrary' language of man as Coleridge describes it. Coleridge's theory of language seems to have been in a process of constant evolution and development throughout his life; we can nevertheless without much difficulty discern certain clearly-defined stages in that development. From Hartley, he had inherited along with an empiricist theory of mind a corresponding theory of language. Though words might appear to correspond to 'things' they actually correspond to our *apprehension* of 'things' – initially of material objects and their motions, but at greater levels of complexity and abstraction to thoughts – both alike mediated by little vibrations (or 'vibratiuncles') to the 'fibres of the brain' in the form of 'ideas', in the narrow empiricist sense of that word, as the basic building blocks of thought.[109] Thus, though there may not necessarily be a one-for-one correspondence between 'words' and 'ideas', words are composed of 'ideas' in much the same way as complex molecules are composed of simpler atoms in modern chemical theory. On the precise details of this process Hartley is cautiously vague:

And it happens in most Cases, that the decomplex [i.e. highly complex] [110] idea belonging to any sentence, is not compounded merely of the complex Ideas belonging to the Words of it; but that there are also many Variations, some Oppositions, and numberless Additions. [111]

Like most of his age, [112] Hartley is less interested in the nature of language than he is in its epistemological and psychological implications. As a result he tends to take the existence of language *per se* very much for granted. This is even more apparent when he comes to consider the relation of words to ideas: a relationship almost like that of bees to the flowers they pollinate:

> Since Words thus collect Ideas from various Quarters, unite them together, and transfer them both upon other Words, and upon foreign objects, it is evident, that the Use of Words adds much to the number and Complexness of our Ideas, and it is the principal means by which we make our intellectual and moral Improvements. [113]

What appealed to Coleridge about Hartley, of course, was not his empiricist framework but his claim to give a satisfactory and scientifically plausible account of the growth of the mind. Once that was no longer tenable, the accompanying empiricist assumptions about language were exposed. In September 1800 we find Coleridge writing to Godwin:

> I wish you to write a book on the power of words, and the processes by which human feelings form affinities with them – in short, I wish you to *philosophize* Horn Tooke's System, and to solve the great Questions – whether there be reason to hold, that an action bearing all the *semblence* of pre-designing Consciousness may yet be simply organic, & whether a *series* of such actions are possible – and close on the heels of this question would follow the old 'Is Logic the *Essence* of Thinking?' in other words – Is *thinking* impossible without arbitrary signs? & – how far is the word 'arbitrary' a misnomer? Are not words etc parts & germinations of the Plant? And what is the Law of their Growth? – In something of this order I would endeavour to destroy the old antithesis of *Words & Things*, elevating, as it were, words into Things, & living Things too. All the nonsense of vibrations etc you would of course dismiss. [114]

As Coleridge's friends rapidly learned, the statement 'I wish you to write a book on . . .' invariably meant that their correspondent was himself carried away by a new idea for a book. The latter part of this passage is often quoted in isolation as evidence for Coleridge's newfound organic conception of language and his rejection of Hartley. What is omitted by so doing is the opening reference to 'Horn Tooke's System'. Yet, taken as a whole, what the passage suggests is that the rejection of the Hartleian 'nonsense of vibrations' is in some way connected with Coleridge's new-found enthusiasm for Horne Tooke – an impression reinforced by other favourable references to Tooke at this time which contrast sharply with earlier disparaging remarks on his political activities.[115]

The work of John Horne Tooke's that had so transformed Coleridge's opinion of him was entitled *Epea Pteroenta*, or, more colloquially, *The Diversions of Purley*. The Homeric Greek title, *Winged Words*, refers to the power of abbreviations to speed communication: '*Abbreviations* are the *wheels* of language, the *wings* of Mercury. And though we might be dragged along without them, it would be with much difficulty, very heavily and tediously.'[116] Citing, among other authorities, Lowth, Tooke focuses on the very problem of the relationship between words and thought that we had noticed in Hartley. In his *Essay on Human Understanding* Locke had claimed that 'if we could trace them to their sources, we should find, in all languages, the names which stand for things that fall now under our senses to have had their first rise from sensible Ideas'.[117] Tooke takes up Locke's challenge simply by cutting the Gordian knot. Locke's *Essay*, he argues, is not about human thought at all, but human *language*. 'In fact' – a phrase which Tooke redefines by a masterpiece of tactical definition to mean 'etymologically' – there *are* no abstract ideas as Locke (and Hartley) had believed because there are *no* abstract terms. The 'real' meaning of a word is neither more or less than its etymological root – which never changes. Thus, at a stroke, the empiricist process by which complex and abstract ideas are built up from the building blocks of simple ones is rendered unnecessary: we are left only with simple ideas, which it is the task of etymology to expose, and so prevent our deception by the aforementioned 'abbreviations'. Thus:

> CHANCE ('High Arbiter' as Milton calls him) and his twin-brother ACCIDENT, are merely the participles of *Escheoir*, *Cheor*, and *Cadere*. And that is to say – 'it befell me by CHANCE, or by ACCIDENT' – is absurdly saying – 'It befell by falling'.[118]

This reduction of language to the simple units of which, 'in fact', it was etymologically composed had the dual advantage of eliminating some of the more hazy parts of empiricist linguistics, and, at the same time, reducing most parts of speech to nouns. Tooke's 'discovery' and his etymological 'proofs' were to dominate sections of English philology for almost fifty years, and to earn the approval of such men as Noah Webster, Ralph Waldo Emerson,[119] James Mill, Hazlitt, and Archbishop Trench,[120] and the project of creating a true etymological dictionary on Tooke's principles was taken up by a number of lexicographers.[121] Yet, even given this chorus of approbation,[122] it is a little hard to see why Coleridge, of all people, with his strong sense of the complexity of human mental processes should have been so taken by an essentially *reductionist* programme, and found in it a liberation from the doctrines of Hartleian mechanism.

As late as 1809 we find an entry in his notebooks which, though it does not mention Tooke by name, is a classic example of the Tookian method in action – and, once again, the target is Hartley:

. . . it will be my business to set forth an orderly proof, that Atheism is the necessary Consequence or Corollary of the Hartleian Theory of the Will conjoined with his Theory of Thought & Action in general – Words as distinguished from mere pulses of Air in the auditory nerve must correspond to Thoughts, and Thoughts is but the verb – substantive Participle Preterite of *Thing* (So in Latin/Res, a *thing* – reor, I *think* – and observe the passive termination of the verb, which is a verb middle or deponent, i.e. an active-passive – an action upon a passive. *Res* = thing: res in praesenti = thinking, i.e. thinging or thing out of me = a thing in me – it is a thing-thing – *reata*,[123] res preterita, a thought – a thing representative of what was but is not present – thought is the past participle of thing – a thing acts on me but not on me as purely passive, which is the case in all *affection*, affectus, but res agit in co-agentem[124] – in the first I am *thinged*, in the latter I thing or think – Rem reor – reatam rursus reor.[125] If therefore we have no will, what is the meaning of the word? It is a word without a Thought – or else a Thought without a Thing, which is a blank contradiction . . .[126]

It is difficult to gauge the exact tone of these jottings but the suspicion occurs that this parade of Tookian pseudo-erudition is ironic! Even at the time he was first reading Tooke, Coleridge had commented impatiently on his 'charletannery' (*sic*) that 'makes such a mystery & difficulty out of plain palpable things'[127] and his irritation did not diminish with time. In later life he came to reject Tooke entirely.[128] Yet, for all his impatience with Tooke's manner and pretensions, there is no doubt that for a few years around and after 1800 Tooke performed a service of great value to Coleridge. He awakened him, as never before, to the science of etymology.

Tooke believed that he had shown the stable and unchangeable nature of words. Coleridge fell with delight upon his 'proof' and rapidly deduced the opposite: the flux and constant change of language.

Hartley, like his mentor, Locke, had assumed a fixed relationship between words and ideas; in attempting to prune back all words to their
roots, Tooke had shown Coleridge the astonishing diversity and luxury
of the undergrowth that had sprung up, and raised the still more
fascinating question: from where then did all this verbiage grow? As
Coleridge himself developed the metaphor in the already-quoted letter
to Godwin:

> Are not words etc. parts and germinations of the plant? And what is the Law
> of their Growth? – In something of this order I would endeavour to destroy
> the old antithesis of *Words and Things*, elevating, as it were, words into Things,
> and living Things too.[129]

To '*philosophize* Horne Tooke's System' in fact meant nothing less
than standing it on its head.

For once Coleridge was as good as his word – or at least his exhorta-
tion. He did, in some sense, tackle the theme he had proposed to Godwin. In the *Philosophical Lectures* of 1819 we find the fruit of Coleridge's inversion of Tooke:

> let those who exclaim against jargon and barbarous terms and every new and
> original mind that appears before them, . . . recollect that the whole process
> of human intellect is gradually to desynonymize terms, that words, the in-
> struments of communication, are the only signs that a finite being can have of
> its own thought, that in proportion as what was conceived as one and identical
> becomes several, there will necessarily arise a term striving to represent that
> distinction. The whole progress of society might be expressed in a dictionary,
> in which . . . might be expressed from the first and simplest terms which would
> satisfy all the distinction that occurred to the first men, while as they perceived
> that other things and yet other things, which they had grouped in one mass,
> had each their distinctive properties . . . and the whole progress of society
> . . . depends upon . . . the progress of desynonymising, that is, the feeling that
> there is a necessity for two distinct subjects which have hitherto been com-
> prehended in one.[130]

The ironic relationship of this passage to Tooke is, of course, underlin-
ed by the counter-proposal for a dictionary to demonstrate the unfolding process of 'desynonymy' – in other words, for a purpose
diametrically opposed to that of Tooke's. In the unpublished *Logic*,
probably dating from the 1820s, he wrote of the need 'for a dictionary
constructed on the only philosophical principle, which regarding
words as living growths, offlets, and organs of the human soul, seeks
to trace each historically through all the periods of its natural growth
and accidental modifications'.[131] If further evidence of the way

Coleridge had taken, used, and reversed Horne Tooke's backward-looking etymology were needed, we have it in the explanatory footnote to Chapter IV of *Biographia Literaria* where the word 'desynonymise' is first used,[132] where he cites (without acknowledgement) Tooke's idea that 'if' and 'give' were once synonymous.[133] Though the O.E.D. gives the coinage of 'desynonymy' to Coleridge in *Biographia Literaria* in 1817, there was nothing new about the concept of 'synonymy', and in the late eighteenth and early nineteenth centuries there had been a whole spate of works on 'English Synonymy'.[134] What Coleridge has done here, however, is to replace the mechanical metaphors of Hartley by the organic models advocated by the Scots rhetoricians such as Reid[135] and turn the etymological search not towards roots but towards a history of linguistic *development*. We have already mentioned Coleridge's example of the words 'compelled' and 'obliged' which were as late as Charles I's time 'perfectly synonymous' – thus enabling Hobbes to argue there was no such thing as guilt.[136] Similarly as late as the Restoration 'ingenuous' and 'ingenious', like 'property' and 'propriety' were used as synonyms. In seeking to distinguish between 'types' and 'symbols' or to anglicize Kant's distinction between 'reason' and 'understanding' in *Aids to Reflection*, Coleridge is himself serving the growth of our collective consciousness through the continuing progress of desynonymizing.

One could say much more about Coleridge's theories of language. It is a fascinating subject and one that has by no means been fully explored. Yet even from this brief discussion we are in some position to try and see what Coleridge may have meant in the fragment quoted above by the language of nature as a 'subordinate Logos'. The Greek word *logos* as used at the beginning of John's Gospel apparently meant both 'word' and the thought or reason which is expressed in words. Greek philosophers, believing in an essentially rational universe, used the *logos* to denote the rational principle by which it is sustained.[137] But this idea of rational principle has roots in pre-Socratic thought of a rather more dialectical kind. For Heraclitus, God, or the *logos*, is seen as the common connecting element in all extremes: 'They do not apprehend how being at variance it agrees with itself (*literally*, how being brought apart it is brought together with itself): there is a back-stretched connexion, as in the bow and the lyre.' (212)[138] If that balance between opposing forces were *not* maintained, then the unity and coherence of the world would collapse – just as if the tension of a bow-string is lost.[139] This is so close to Coleridge's dialectical concept of the 'imagination', 'reconciling opposite or discordant qualities', that it can hardly be accidental. So, too, does it remind us of the contrasting and counterpoised forces of nature in Wordsworth's description of the Simplon Pass[140] where:

> Tumult and peace, the darkness and the light,
> Were all like the workings of one mind . . .
> The types and symbols of Eternity,
> Of first, and last, and midst, and without end.

Thus not merely does the 'language of nature' speak of an active, creative, and ordering principle – a divine immanence under tension sustaining life throughout the whole chain of being – but there is also the intriguing suggestion that here is the origin of the duality between the diachronic and synchronic 'types and symbols' inherent in the language of nature. So far from merely revealing the great permanencies of its unchanging character popularly associated with Wordsworth, his and Coleridge's 'nature' is in a constantly changing relationship to man as its 'language' evolves and *desynonymizes*.

There are a number of hints that Coleridge at least did in fact come to think of nature in precisely this way. To begin with, it accords very closely with his notion of an 'idea'. By the time of *Biographia Literaria* Coleridge had come to think of an idea in terms directly opposed to Locke – that is, as a platonic 'form' which can only be apprehended symbolically in the material world.[141] Similarly, in *The Statesman's Manual* of the same year, he wrote 'every living principle is actuated by an idea; and every idea is living, productive, partaketh of infinity, and (as Bacon has sublimely observed) containeth an endless power of semination'. The ultimate model for an 'idea', in this sense, is clearly the *logos* itself: perfect and unchanging perhaps in the eyes of God, or in the world of absolute forms, but here dynamic and in a process of constant organic evolution so that it is analogous to the seed that contains within itself the whole history of its past and future growth at any given moment.[142] The opposition between 'words' and 'things' which he was worrying at seventeen years before in his letter to Godwin has been resolved, at least metaphorically, by this nexus of analogies linking language and nature by means of the *logos*. 'For if words are not THINGS, they are LIVING POWERS, by which the things of most importance to mankind are actuated, combined, and humanized.'[143] The echo of Thomas Taylor's attack on those who 'become so mentally imbecile, as to mistake *words* for *things*' in his Introduction to *The Phaedrus* of Plato (1792)[144] indicates the philosophical origins of Coleridge's final position. Yet the big question, of course, still remains to be asked. Languages are systems of communication: they do not communicate themselves, they are *about* something else. Granted that the 'language of nature' is one of progressive desynonymy by which new meanings and subtler shades of distinction are constantly coming into being, what does this have to *tell* us? What *is* this unfolding message?

The immediate answer of the Romantics is not difficult to discover. Wordsworth is at pains to spell out the message throughout his work from the *Lyrical Ballads* through *The Prelude* to *The Excursion*. At its simplest, though by no means its crudest, it can be encapsulated in the famous line from 'The Tables Turned':

> One impulse from a vernal wood
> May teach you more of man;
> Of moral evil and of good,
> Than all the sages can.

It was no doubt his endorsement of this belief that led Keble to give his version in the poem quoted earlier:

> The works of God above, below,
> Within us and around,
> Are pages in that book, to show
> How God himself is found.

Perhaps it was confidence such as this that led Wordsworth to observe publicly that he admired *The Christian Year* so much that he wished he had written it himself – and so improve upon it – and, privately, that Keble's verse was inferior to Watts's and positively 'vicious in diction'.[145] The 'message' of nature, of 'moral evil and of good' is never free from ambiguity for Wordsworth. Moreover, it is an ambiguity that is rooted deep in the perceptual process itself, below the threshold of consciousness. I have already written at some length elsewhere on Wordsworth's notions of perception, in connection with the rainbow, and it would be redundant to repeat it here.[146] One – and perhaps the most striking – example of how the Romantics saw the participation of the perceiver in each act of perception occurs in a short poem of Hopkins, written in 1864:

> It was a hard thing to undo this knot.
> The rainbow shines, but only in the thought

Of him that looks. Yet not in that alone;
For who makes rainbows by invention?
And many standing round a waterfall
See one bow each, yet not the same to all,
But each a hand's breadth further than the next.
The sun on falling waters writes the text
Which yet is in the eye or in the thought.
It was a hard thing to undo this knot.

For nearly all the Romantics, the rainbow had come to stand as a metaphor for man's creative participation in nature. Hopkins takes up this image and combines it with the tradition of 'linguistic' images we have been looking at to make the sunlight upon falling water into his 'text' to be 'read' by the perceiving mind – differently for each beholder, because each has a different standpoint. The biblical symbol of God's unchanging promise to mankind is now to be read as an *exemplum* of the ambiguous and therefore creative nature of perception itself. 'As a man is,' said Blake, 'so will he see'.

Yet if Coleridge's idea of desynonymy is to have any real part in his metaphor of the language of nature, we would also expect that the lasting depth of the process could only be discoverable by hindsight. His examples are, significantly, all taken from the seventeenth century. By a strange irony many of his own attempts at desynonymy proved over-subtle and too complex to have passed into the language. As we have seen, his distinction between 'types' and 'symbols' has not survived; his attempt to anglicize the Kantian polarity of 'Reason' and 'understanding' survives only in relation to Idealist philosophy rather than in standard usage; and the carefully elaborated binaries of *Church and State*, such as 'opposite' and 'contrary' have not passed even into the technical vocabulary of dialectics, whose terms are more often from Germany and France. Certain of his coinages, such as the word 'existential' have, it is true, stood the test of time.[147] But the consummation of Coleridge's own attempts at desynonymizing would seem to be in the distinction between 'Imagination' and 'Fancy' in *Biographia Literaria*.

This distinction has suffered a curious, and possibly unique, fate in the history of semantic separations. On the one hand it has become famous – every student of literature in the English-speaking world finds himself supposed to have heard of it; on the other, it is scarcely ever *used*, and never in common speech. 'Fancy', it is true has become a lower-status word than 'Imagination' in the hundred and seventy

years since the *Biographia*, but there is plenty of evidence, from the
way other Romantics, Blake, Keats, or Shelley employ the words, to
suggest this might have happened anyway. 'Imaginative' is, more often
than not, a high-status word (the exception might be police statements)
but it is notoriously vague. The reason for this may perhaps become
clearer if we recall the actual phraseology of Coleridge's 'desynonymy'
in Chapter XIII of the *Biographia*:

The IMAGINATION then, I consider either as primary, or secondary. The
primary IMAGINATION I hold to be the living Power and prime Agent of
all human Perception, and as a repetition in the finite mind of the eternal act
of creation in the infinite I AM. The secondary Imagination I consider as an
echo of the former, co-existing with the conscious will, yet still as identical with
the primary in the *kind* of its agency, and differing only in *degree*, and in the
mode of its operation. It dissolves, diffuses, dissipates, in order to re-create; or
where this process is rendered impossible, yet still at all events it struggles to
idealize and to unify . . .
  FANCY, on the contrary, has no other counters to play with, but fixities and
definites. The Fancy, is indeed no other than a mode of memory emancipated
from the order of time and space; while it is blended with, and modified by
that empirical phenomenon of the will which we express by the word
CHOICE. But equally with the ordinary memory the Fancy must receive all
its materials ready made from the law of association.[148]

A careful reading suggests that the ostensible distinction between
'imagination' and 'fancy' is not, in fact, central to this account at all.
The paragraph about 'fancy' as a mode of memory (a scissors-and-paste
job of the mind) looks suspiciously like an afterthought tacked on to
show where what amounts to Locke's idea of the 'imagination'[149] fits
into the overall scheme.[150] What the passage really seems to be about,
if we count the second paragraph, is *three* definitions of 'imagination'.
The important distinction, that between the primary and secondary imaginations, is blatantly *not* an act of desynonymy at all. This is such
an odd sleight-of-hand that it is worth looking at more closely.
  The original of this formulation of the two imaginations is normally
taken to be the opening words of the Introduction to Schelling's *Ent-
wurf eines Systems der Naturphilosophie* (1799), but Coleridge is not, as
has sometimes been claimed,[151] here directly plagiarizing his German
source. Schelling reads as follows:

Intelligence is productive in twofold wise, either blindly and unconsciously, or
with freedom and consciousness; unconsciously productive in the perception
of the universe, consciously in the creation of an ideal world.[152]

Coleridge has made a slight, but fundamental alteration to this. For 'intelligence' he has substituted the more Kantian 'imagination' in line with his insistence on the active function of the mind in perception. This parallels Schelling's own use of the terms in his *System des transcendentalen Idealismus* (1800), where '*Einbildungskraft*' ('imagination') is used as a term that includes both the creative and poetic faculty and 'cosmic intuition' (*Anschauung*) – the power by which reality is perceived.[153] Keeping to the egalitarian ideology of the Preface to the *Lyrical Ballads*, Coleridge, like Wordsworth, is here insisting that the poetic and creative faculties of the artist are (despite any appearances to the contrary) of a kind with the basic powers of perception enjoyed by all human beings. The artist is not separated from humanity by the possession of greater powers, he (or she!) exercises those powers by *sharing* them with the rest of mankind. To communicate by art is to share; to read or view a work is to participate. Coleridge's insistence on a *single* term to cover what looks like two discrete mental functions is thus an essential part of his strategy for describing not merely aesthetic experience, but also religious language, and the Scriptures, as 'the living educts of the imagination'.[154] The word for this cross-linking is not, of course, 'desynonymy', but that other forgotten coinage of the *Biographia*: 'esemplastic' – the act of shaping into one[155] – which is Coleridge's attempt to create an English word from the Greek with a parallel root-form to the German '*Einbildungskraft*'. He is in effect here illustrating the self-conscious reflexive powers of the imagination by an act of 'esemplasticism' – showing how the growth of consciousness not merely distinguishes concepts that differ, but also reveals connections hitherto unperceived.

The model for this act of linking apparently disconnected ideas is, once again, the biblical *logos* which, under tension, combines opposite or discordant qualities in a creative unity. For Coleridge, the idea of the 'Word' is itself redolent of the hidden powers of meaning, at once latent, and 'living' through tension with other apparently dissimilar notions. This conflation of two (or, in effect, three) meanings to 'imagination' is central to the development of his mature thought. I have elsewhere described the word as 'bi-focal'.[156] What is at one level operating below the threshold of consciousness in every act of perception, is also the power by which we create our 'internal' worlds. We perceive nature and create fictions by essentially the same process. But the languages of nature and of fiction interact. Thus the fictional

creation of the artist influences and modifies the way in which we
perceive the real world, and viceversa. The biblical story of Elijah has
repercussions on how Wordsworth came to see the Lake District – just
as *The Prelude* modifies both our perceptions of the Lake District *and*
the way we read the story of Elijah.[157] The scriptures are the
paradigm example of the way in which any major work of art modifies
and recreates not merely our way of thinking but also our sense-
impressions. The subordinate *logos* of nature is a repetition in the finite
human mind of God's eternal act of creation. 'The great book . . . of
Nature', wrote Coleridge, in 1817 'has been the music of gentle and
pious minds in all ages, it is the *poetry* of all human nature, to read it
likewise in a figurative sense, and to find therein correspondencies and
symbols of the spiritual world.'[158] Its language, like all language, has
its origins in poetic experience.

We are here very close to what Abrams has designated 'apocalypse
by cognition'.[159] Behind the continual Romantic reiteration of the
'poetic' as a metaphor for religious experience lies what we have seen
is the very ancient association of poetry with divinity, but here the
'peculiar language of heaven' has been translated into a typology of
psychological and spiritual states. As in Dante, poetry is a kind of
imaginative psychopomp leading the soul towards a mystical and
otherwise inexpressible bliss, or 'apocalypse', in which the partaker is
caught up in the divine vision. But just as Schiller's 'third
kingdom'[160] of aesthetic liberation (a direct allusion to Joachim of
Fiore's 'third kingdom' of freedom, community, joy and intellect)[161] is
not merely an internal state, but is also a social one, so Coleridge's
poetic 'apocalypse' is at once individual and communal. The difference
is that Coleridge's mature theory of language and his later Trinitarian
Anglicanism (as always in his thought, all elements are connected) no
longer involves seeing this transformation as part of a future ideal state,
but, in true New Testament style, proclaims that it is *already* here. In
one of the late, and still unpublished, notebooks, now in the British
Library, he illustrates this point by an image of organicism from
nature, drawn this time not from the vegetable world, but from human
anatomy:

The small Artery in the Finger or the thread-like Vein in the Foot witteth not
of the Blood in the Chambers of the Flesh, and but a small portion thereof doth
it need or can it contain – Yet by the never-resting Energy of the Heart, ever
expanding to acquire, and contracting to communicate, is the distant vein fed,

and its needful portion renewed, and the feeding Artery receives an aiding impulse in the performance of its humble ministry.[162]

Faith is the blood which activates and nourishes the Church as the 'body' of Christ. It renews both itself and the whole organism by *circulating*; if it is not continually being passed on throughout the members of the body it simply congeals. Stagnation is death. Conversely, however corrupt or diseased the body may be, while the pulse still beats the divine life-blood is still able to perform its healing and renovating task.[163]

By what one supposes can only be coincidence, an almost identical image appears in Feuerbach's *Essence of Christianity* some twelve years later:

As the action of the arteries drives the blood into the extremities, and the action of the veins brings it back again, as life in general consists in a perpetual systole and diastole; so it is in religion. In the religious systole man propels his own nature from himself, he throws himself outward; in the religious diastole he receives the rejected nature into his heart again.[164]

Yet the contrast could hardly be more dramatic. Where Coleridge's image is of divinely-instigated community, and of *communication*, Feuerbach's is essentially one of *solipsism*. The interaction with the environment by which, at every level, we define ourselves as human, is at a spiritual level one of mistaking the echo for a voice – or, in the words of Coleridge's famous description of Wordsworth, one of receiving 'the light reflected as a light bestowed'.[165] The Feuerbachian language of nature partakes of the same solipsistic closed-circle of meaning that runs like a counterpoint to the biblical and Romantic tradition throughout the nineteenth century, and finds expression in the twentieth in, for instance, the linguistic ideas of Merleau-Ponty or Roland Barthes.[166]

Contemporaries were well aware of the magnitude and significance of the shift in sensibility that had occurred with Romanticism. F. D. Maurice, arguably the most important Anglican theologian of the century, and a lifelong Coleridgean, wrote in 1838:

From about the middle of the last century, we may trace the commencement of a poetry which had a much more direct and substantive reference to the outward universe than that of earlier periods. The doings of men, as well as the songs in which they were celebrated, had become artificial and conventional: those whom domestic habits had inspired with a dislike of the hollowness of general society, or whom their early cultivation had taught to desire something more living and permanent than the modes of a particular generation, took refuge in nature.[167]

More personal and dramatic was Hopkins' opinion of Wordsworth:

There have been in all history a few, a very few men, whom common repute, even when it did not trust them, has treated as having had something happen to them that does not happen to other men, as having *seen something*, whatever that really was.

Plato is the most famous of these . . . human nature in these men saw something, got a shock; wavers in opinion, looking back, whether there was anything in it or no; but is in a tremble ever since. Now what Wordsworthians mean is, what would seem to be the growing mind of the English speaking world and may perhaps come to be that of the world at large/is that in Wordsworth when he wrote that [*Immortality*] ode human nature got another of those shocks, and the tremble from it is spreading. This opinion I do strongly share; I am, ever since I knew the ode, in that tremble. You know what happened to crazy Blake, himself a most poetically electrical subject both active and passive, at his first hearing: when the reader came to 'The pansy at my feet' he fell into a hysterical excitement.[168]

Hopkins, like Maurice, was a Coleridgean, and had had the added advantage as a college friend of H. N. Coleridge, of having stayed in the Coleridge household and having had access to the unpublished letters and notebooks of his friend's famous uncle. He was familiar with the theory of desynonymy, which, as we have seen, was closely parallel to his own ideas.

Coleridge's theory of language, with its stress on the evolving collective consciousness of the culture and the accompanying process of desynonymizing words comes at a moment when the semantic shift from inner to outer in nature, and from outer to inner in consciousness, that we noted in the last chapter, was just becoming observable. It constitutes one of the principal themes of his *Philosophical Lectures*. Consider, for instance, this passage:

In the commencement of literature man remained for a time in that unity with nature which gladly concedes to nature the life, thought, and even purposes of man, and on the other hand gives to man himself a disposition to regard himself as part of nature. Soon however he must have begun to detach himself; his dreams, the very delusions of his senses which he became acquainted with by experience, must have forced him to make a distinction between the object perceived and the percipient.[169]

The basic model, of course, is similar to that of Vico, and though there is no external evidence that he had read either Vico or Herder until a few years later,[170] that resemblance alone must make it likely. He had, however, read Schiller.[171] Where he differs decisively from Vico, Herder, Schiller, and other putative predecessors is, of course, that he also knew Wordsworth. The result is the second volume of *Biographia Literaria*: the most sustained attempt so far to understand the revolution in sensibility created by Wordsworth in the English language. There is a sense in which the *Philosophical Lectures* of 1819 are an extended footnote to that profound intuition – an attempt, as it were, to sketch the historical background to what he dimly perceives as being a watershed in human mental development. If we have come to identify that change in consciousness at the beginning of the nineteenth century with Wordsworth more than with any other single figure, I believe that we must give much of the credit for the realization of the nature of that change to Coleridge.

We can, I suggest, distinguish in the development of Coleridge's thinking about language at least three phases. In the first, following Locke and Hartley, he was willing to accept a fairly simple and essentially a-historical view of the logical relationship between words and things. In the second, which we would associate with the influence of Horne Tooke, he became aware of the illogical complexities of etymology, and saw words primarily in relation to their supposed semantic roots rather than to external objects. In the third, he came to see language as a process of continual semantic change and evolution, with words related not so much to things as changes in human consciousness itself.[172]

We can, moreover, connect each of these phases with stages in the development of Romanticism – and, in particular, with the evolution of meaning in the word 'nature'. In the first phase, which we might associate with Locke's attempts to empiricize Newton, 'nature' is thought of largely in terms of the scientific or theological laws governing the material world – an extreme example would be the first book of Pope's *Essay on Man*. Hartley's *Observations* are, in effect, an attempt to extend this notion of 'mechanical' laws to cover the workings of the mind and the progress of the race. In the second, we find an awareness of nature in terms of history and therefore of origins. Wordsworth's interest in childhood, especially in his conception of the child as the 'best philosopher' in the *Immortality Ode*, and his primitivism in such matters as poetic diction would correspond to this stage. The third, while it retains a sense of historical origins incorporates them into the process and evolution of human consciousness – recognizing the perceptual shifts inherent in such a process. In literary terms it anticipates some aspects of the nineteenth-century novel, and poems like *In Memoriam* – and even, arguably, Darwin.

That, however, was in the future. If our quest here has been the more limited one of tracing the development of the metaphor and its meanings to the Romantics primarily through the well-documented prism of Coleridge's mind, we have in so doing been able to see something of its centrality in the development of Romantic ideas of language on a wider scale. It is to Coleridge and Wordsworth, for instance, that we must turn if we wish to understand the pervasiveness of the metaphor from Keble through to Tennyson and Hopkins and beyond. Though the evidence is less complete, it is also clear that just as the French linguisticians, such as de Brosses or Condillac,[173] who influenced Tooke and the British empirical linguistic tradition, were themselves heavily indebted to Locke, so a French Romantic like Fabre d'Olivet, whose interest in language was primarily religious, stands as much within the poetic and theological tradition of the English Romantics as he does within his native one. Similarly, it is in Coleridge that we also find hints of the fundamental ambiguity that was eventually to lead towards a tensional theory of metaphorical language as a whole long after the particular metaphor had lapsed as a paradigm of religious language in the nineteenth century. His semi-mystical platonic vision that could make him write confidently of the time when 'the other great Bible of God, the Book of Nature, shall become transparent to us, when we regard the forms of matter as words, as symbols, valuable only as being the expression, an unrolled but yet a glorious fragment of the wisdom of the Supreme Being'[174] is incomplete without the counterintuition: 'We understand nature just as if, at a distance, we looked at the image of a person in a looking-glass, plainly and fervently discoursing, yet what he uttered we could decipher only by the motion of his lips or by his mien.'[175] It was, as we have seen, an ambiguity always present in the idea of the *logos*.

4

The paradoxes of disconfirmation

Elijah and Dante: The Word *and the 'Voice'*

Let us return to the story of Elijah – this time not through New Testament, Patristic, or Romantic spectacles, but, initially, through fourteenth-century ones.

In Canto XXXII, of the *Purgatorio* Dante, awakening from the pageant of revelation, likens himself to the disciples Peter, James, and John, after the Transfiguration:

> Quali a veder de' fioretti del melo
> che del suo pome li angeli fa ghiotti
> e perpetüe nozze fa nel cielo,
> Pietro e Giovanni e Iacopo condotti
> e vinti ritornaro alla parola
> dalla qual furon maggior sonni rotti,
> e videro scemata loro scola
> così di Moïsè come d' Elia,
> ed al maestro sue cangiata stola;
> tal torna' io . . .
>
> (XXXII: 73–82)

As, when brought to see some of the blossoms of the apple-tree that makes the angels greedy for its fruit and makes perpetual marriage-feast in heaven,[1] Peter and James and John were overpowered and came to themselves again at the word by which deeper slumbers were broken and saw their company diminished by both Moses and Elias and their Master's raiment changed, so I came to myself . . .[2]

The question that had broken Dante's trance, however, was not that of Matthew xvii, 7 ('Arise and be not afraid') – the word of Christ that had raised the dead – but is an echo of the Elijah story in I Kings xix 'What doest thou here?':

Surgi: che fai?   (XXXII: 72)

To gather the full significance of this more severe question we must turn back some five Cantos, and follow through one of the most remarkable and dramatic disconfirmations in European literature. In Canto XXVII Virgil's last words to Dante as he is about to enter the Earthly Paradise are in the form of a blessing:

> Come la scala tutta sotto noi
>   fu corsa e fummo in su 'l grado superno,
>   in me ficcò Virgilio li occhi suoi,
> e disse: 'Il temporal foco e l'etterno
>   veduto hai, figlio; e se' venuto in parte
>   dov' io per me più oltre non discerno.
> Tratto t' ho qui con ingegno e con arte;
>   lo tuo piacere omai prendi per duce:
>   fuor se' dell'erte vie, fuor se' dell'arte.
> Vedi lo sol che in fronte ti riluce;
>   vedi l'erbetta, i fiori e li arbuscelli,
>   che qui la terra sol da sè produce.
> Mentre che vegnan lieti li occhi belli
>   che, lacrimando, a te venir mi fenno,
>   seder ti puoi e puoi andar tra elli.
> Non aspettar mio dir più nè mio cenno:
>   libero, dritto e sano è tuo arbitrio,
>   e fallo fora non fare a suo senno:
> per ch' io te sovra te corono e mitrio.   (XXVII: 124–42)

When all the stair was sped beneath us and we were on the topmost step Virgil fixed his eyes on me and said: 'The temporal fire and the eternal thou hast seen, my son, and art come to a part where of myself I discern no further. I have brought thee here with understanding and with skill. Take henceforth thy pleasure for guide. Thou hast come forth from the steep and the narrow ways. See the sun that shines on thy brow; see the grass, the flowers and trees which the ground here brings forth of itself alone; till the fair eyes come rejoicing which weeping made me come to thee thou mayst sit or go among them. No longer expect word or sign from me. Free, upright and whole is thy will and it were a fault not to act on its bidding; therefore over thyself I crown and mitre thee.'

This is at once the climax and the finale of Virgil's tutelage of Dante. With Virgil as his guide he has seen and come safely past the eternal fire of Hell and the temporal fire of Purgatory. Now, purged, enlightened, and mature, Dante's hitherto corrupted will is for the first time truly free; for him duty and desire have at last become one and the same thing. He is free to want only what he ought. To attain this Augustinian freedom to be able to love God and do as he wishes, he has been led by Virgil who, for Dante, personified the greatest of human wisdom and artistic craftsmanship. The gifts that have brought him this far, Virgil tells Dante, are *ingegno* and *arte* – translated by Sinclair as 'understanding' and 'skill'. Virgil's distinction is between the intellectual insight ('understanding' or 'wisdom'), and the necessary technical skill or craft to give that insight effective expression. Now, here at the entrance to the Earthly Paradise, understanding and skill are not to be discarded as no longer valuable or appropriate, but on the contrary acquire a *new* meaning and value subsumed for the first time under *pleasure*. Human reason has brought Dante through Hell and Purgatory; now, in a sudden unexpected twist, it is dissociated from all that it has mastered and reason itself is seen as an attribute of pleasure – from henceforth the higher good (rather than vice versa, as it is for us for whom reason is only intermittently pleasurable). For Dante, the consummation of reason is freedom. In token of this new-found self-lordship, Virgil now invests him with crown and mitre; the symbols of Empire and Papacy, temporal and spiritual authority are suddenly transformed into symbols of what look like their direct opposites: independence and freedom.

It is a direct concomitant of this freedom that Dante in the poem does not at this point turn to look backwards and survey his achievement, but only forwards to the longed-for meeting with Beatrice that Virgil tells him is now very close. So irresistibly does the movement of the poem echo Dante's expectations and carry us forward that in the intervening 350 lines until the actual encounter with Beatrice, Virgil is mentioned briefly only twice. Though he remains with Dante until the moment of meeting in Canto XXX, these words of blessing and investiture in Canto XXVII are Virgil's last. From this point onwards he is silent. When, in the Masque of Revelation in Canto XXX, Dante recognizes that the veiled figure on the triumphal car is indeed Beatrice, it is with the words *Manibus o date lilia plenis* still ringing in his ears – a direct quotation from *The Aeneid*. Virgil's own words are being uttered by the 'messengers of eternal life'. In a moment of unexpected nervousness he turns again to Virgil for confirmation and encouragment, to find his guide and friend has vanished:

> Tosto che nella vista mi percosse
> l'alta virtù che già m'avea trafitto
> prima ch' io fuor di puerizia fosse,
> volsimi alla sinistra col rispitto
> col quale il fantolin corre alla mamma
> quando ha paura o quando elli è afflitto,

per dicere a Virgilio: 'Men che dramma
di sangue m'è rimaso che non tremi:
conosco i segni dell'antica fiamma';
ma Virgilio n'avea lasciati scemi
di sè, Virgilio dolcissimo patre,
Virgilio a cui per mia salute die'mi;
nè quantunque perdeo l'antica matre
valse alle guance nette di rugiada,
che, lacrimando, non tornasser atre.

(XXX: 40-54)

*As soon as the lofty virtue smote on my sight which already had pierced me before
I was out of my boyhood, I turned to the left with the confidence of a little child
that runs to his mother when he is afraid or in distress, to say to Virgil: 'Not a
drop of blood is left in me that does not tremble; I know the marks of the ancient
flame.' But Virgil had left us bereft of him, Virgil sweetest father, Virgil to whom
I gave myself for salvation, nor did all the ancient mother lost avail my cheeks
washed with dew that they should not be stained again with tears.*

At the moment of the long looked-for meeting, the dramatic consummation of all that he has undergone and the event for which Virgil's
blessing was only the preparation, Dante is suddenly desolated by grief
at the loss of his friend and 'father' who was so much a part of himself.
Nothing that has gone before has prepared us, either, for the
devastating sense of loss that dominates the actual moment of meeting
Beatrice, or for the shattering disconfirmation of all his expectations
and self-respect that follows. Beatrice's first words strike the more
brutally because they are at a tangent:

Dante, perchè Virgilio se ne vada,
non pianger anco, non piangere ancora;
che pianger ti conven per altra spada.

(XXX: 55-7)

*Dante, because Virgil leaves thee weep not, weep not yet, for thou must weep for
another sword.*

Worse, much worse, is to follow:

Guardaci ben! Ben son, ben son Beatrice.
Come degnasti d'accedere al monte?
non sapei tu che qui è l'uom felice?

(XXX: 73-5)

*Look at me well; I am, I am indeed Beatrice. How durst thou approach the moun-
tain? Didst thou not know that here man is happy?*

There follows Beatrice's famous rebuke to Dante where she charges him with infidelity, and in a public act of humiliation reduces him first to tears, and finally to a faint. The passage is a long one, and it would need full quotation of the rest of the Canto and half of Canto XXXI to do justice to Beatrice's sustained systematic destruction of every shred of his self-respect. Following on the disappearance of Virgil, the attack is the more overwhelming since it falls from a quite unexpected angle – on Dante's past conduct. We have been led to expect a comment on Virgil, and even a direct reproof for Dante's grief at his loss would have been confirmation that this was indeed the issue at stake. Instead, the question of Virgil's vanishing is studiously ignored.

Sinclair's comment on this traumatic overthrow of expectations is as follows:

So moving is the human drama of his grief at the loss of Virgil that the moral symbolism is absorbed and concealed in it; but Beatrice's rebuke proves at once that it is not forgotten . . . The passage is an example, singular even for Dante, of the *fusing* power of his imagination, his power to tell a great story with complete objectivity and to make it at the same time the symbol and the vehicle of his own inner life and thought.[3]

Rightly, it seems to me, he notes that Dante is stressing here the sheer *disconcertingness* of Revelation. The natural reason of man is utterly confounded by the overpowering 'otherness' of the transcendent. It is the re-enactment of an experience testified to by countless saints and mystics. Yet to cite this as an example of 'the *fusing* power of his imagination', thus linking it with Coleridge's idea of the 'esemplastic' power of the imagination to 'shape into one' opposite or discordant elements, runs the risk of avoiding with a half-truth the actual complexity of what Dante has here achieved in the relationship of the personal and the symbolic.

We may be able to see this more clearly if we look for a moment at another example. There are not many instances of disconfirmation on this scale in literature, but, as we might expect, Shakespeare has one: Hal's rejection of Falstaff:

> I know thee not, old man: fall to thy prayers;
> How ill white hairs become a fool and jester!
> I have long dream'd of such a kind of man,
> So surfeit-swell'd, so old, and so profane;
> But, being awaked, I do despise my dream.
> Make less thy body hence, and more thy grace;
> Leave gormandizing; know the grave doth gape

> For thee thrice wider than for other men.
> Reply not to me with a fool-born jest:
> Presume not that I am the thing I was;
> For God doth know, so shall the word perceive,
> That I have turn'd away my former self;
> So will I those that kept me company.
> When thou dost hear I am as I have been,
> Approach me, and thou shalt be as thou wast,
> The tutor and the feeder of my riots:
> Till then, I banish thee, on pain of death . . .
>
> (*Henry IV* Part 2, V, v, 46–63)

This is both like and unlike Dante and Beatrice. The difference is that Falstaff has been riding for a fall all along. It is unthinkable that the new king who is to be paragon of chivalry and honour can any longer associate with such a overthrower of degree. We know he will be rejected – and all that has gone before is coloured by the irony of that knowledge. And yet, when it comes, it *is* betrayal: at a personal level a betrayal of the very worst kind, and in realizing that it had to be we are not allowed to lose sight of this. Shakespeare makes us feel the same event from two entirely opposite aspects, and makes no attempt to reconcile the tension between them. The symbolism of kingship, the role of office, and the personal are here seen to contradict one another. The drama, the disturbing power of this scene, lies in the fact that we find this tension unacceptable and yet unresolvable.

The similarity I want to point to between Dante and Shakespeare lies in the creation of precisely this tension. The necessity of Falstaff's rejection is contrasted with the personal viciousness of the smooth and pious way Hal actually does it. Dante is innocent. He is awestruck by Beatrice; the symbolic necessity that 'reason' be humbled before 'revelation' is made deliberately more harsh by the striking *personalness* of it all. Beatrice's rebuke gains weight not merely by the tangential nature of her response in *not* speaking to his immediate condition at the discovery of Virgil's disappearance, but also by challenging him at a different level. The real incongruity is that the 'otherness' of revelation manifests itself in this encounter as intensely private and personal. This is the only point in the poem where Beatrice addresses Dante by name. We are accustomed to thinking of 'emotion' as somehow antithetical to 'reason', yet here the superseding of reason by revelation is presented not as the incorporation of one good into another that is higher than itself (as Sinclair's model of 'fusion' would imply), but as an intense private grief for the passing of a friend in Virgil, and consequently a sharpened sense of personal *betrayal* by Beatrice in her attack on Dante for 'faithlessness' at this juncture – an attack so personally humiliating that even her choir, we are told, raises an eloquent if oblique protest.

> ch' i' 'ntesi nelle doci tempre
> lor compatire a me, più che se detto
> avesser: 'Donna, perchè sì lo stempre?' (XXX: 94–6)

. . . I heard in the sweet harmonies their compassion on me, more than if they had said: 'Lady, why dost thou so shame him?'

Sinclair's 'Coleridgean' model of 'fusion' between the allegory and personal narrative is not necessarily wide of the mark; Coleridge's idea of the imagination was formulated in response to the need to describe just such a tension between different (and incompatible) levels of discourse; but if we adopt it, we need to keep constantly in mind that this fusion is inseparable from tension. The appropriate model is in fact supplied by Dante himself in the next Canto. Revived by the ever-useful Matilda, Dante is brought through the waters of Lethe to the same bank as Beatrice. Here he is rewarded by a curious vision. Beatrice is mounted in a triumph-car drawn by a griffin in what has been variously called the 'Masque of the Church', of 'Revelation', or of 'the Holy Sacrament'. Until now the griffin has been but one wonder among many: as relatively ordinary a mythical beast as one with the head of an eagle and the body of a lion can hope to pass for. From his new vantage-point Dante now sees it no longer directly, but for the first time reflected in the emerald eyes of Beatrice herself:

> . . . e poi
> al petto del grifon seco menarmi,
> ove Beatrice stava volta a noi,
> disser: 'Fa che le viste non risparmi:
> posto t'avem dinanzi alli smeraldi
> ond'Amor già ti trasse le sue armi.'
> Mille disiri più che fiamma caldi
> strinsermi li occhi alli occhi rilucenti,
> che pur sopra 'l grifone stavan saldi.
> Come in lo specchio sol, non altrimenti
> la doppia fiera dentro vi raggiava,
> or con altri, or con altri reggimenti.
> Pensa, lettor, s' io mi maravigliava,

> quando vedea la cosa in sè star queta,
> e nell' idolo suo trasmutava.

(XXXI: 112–26)

. . . then they brought me with them to the breast of the Griffin, where Beatrice stood turned to us, and they said: 'See thou do not withhold thy gaze; we have set thee before the emeralds from which love once shot his darts at thee.'

A thousand desires hotter than flame held my eyes on the shining eyes, which remained still fixed on the Griffin, and even like the sun in a mirror the two-fold beast shone within them, now with the one, now with the other nature. Think, reader, if I marvelled when I saw the thing still in itself and in its image changing.

He sees reflected something very odd indeed: the griffin is not a composite creature at all, it is 'two-fold'. It has, it seems, when viewed obliquely through Beatrice's eyes *two* totally different forms, and this double image is in a constant process of transition from one manifestation to the other. Seen thus, the griffin is two different and incompatible things at the same time. Viewed directly by Dante however it remains a fusion – a composite creature as before; only through the eyes of Beatrice can we see that fusion as a tension of opposites.

The normal 'explanation' given of this curious phenomenon is that Beatrice's eyes are (at an allegorical level) the mirror of revelation, showing Dante what he cannot yet see directly: the double nature of Christ as incarnate love, both immanent and wholly human, and, simultaneously, transcendent and divine. Yet this assumption, made by nearly all the traditional sources on Dante, that the griffin is 'symbolical of Christ'[4] is sharply challenged by at least two recent critics. Colin Hardie points out that there is no known example of a griffin (or gryphon, to use the alternative spelling of some translators) used in this way before Dante:

The primary meaning of the gryphon, before Dante put it in his own new context, is that of a guardian of treasure (of a tomb or of a church, or as the legs of a chair, of an enthroned person) and a winged courser of the Chariot of the Sun or of Alexander the Great, and it often has a negative aspect, as avaricious or devilish, hostile to mankind.[5]

He concludes that the griffin stands for the two sides of Dante's own restored nature: animal and spiritual. Peter Dronke supports Hardie's negative conclusion:

When one turns to the gryphon, the scholars are so unanimous about its being an emblem of Christ that for many years I assumed this must be a traditional Christian usage – like the eagle for St John or the dove for the Holy Ghost – but one which I had strangely failed to observe. After long and strenuous gryphon-hunting, however, I must fully confirm the negative conclusion of Dr Colin Hardie: there is no single instance in Christian tradition of a gryphon associated with Christ before Dante – or rather, before Dante's commentators. Various well-known modern Dante commentaries, and an impressive new encyclopaedia of Christian iconography, claim that the gryphon as Christ can be found in Isidore of Seville; even a chapter reference to Isidore – a spurious one – is often given for this erroneous assertion. It is an heirloom that several generations of scholars have handed down to one another – a tissue of fabrication as priceless as the Emperor's clothes.[6]

For any work as symbolically complex as the *Divine Comedy* an exhaustive tabulation of symbolism is out of the question. In his Epistle to Cangrande Dante himself had outlined a four-fold system of biblical exegesis: the literal, allegorical, moral, and analogical. Such systems were a commonplace of the period.[7] Whether or not Hardie's own theory is more satisfactory than the earlier, unfounded, tradition, there is no doubt that the symbol of the griffin is both more complex and polyvalent than has normally been assumed. Whatever else may be its theological significance, it seems to me that this image of simultaneous fusion and contradiction has an immediate dramatic relevance to the action of the story at this point, and highlights the double nature of Dante's encounter with Beatrice.

The care with which we seem to be prepared for the idea supports this hypothesis. There is a sense in which Dante seems to be trying to describe a paradox at the centre of a great deal of 'religious' experience – and of the language of that experience. What happens in his meeting with Beatrice is only the climax of series of events that we can see beginning at Virgil's blessing as they enter the Earthly Paradise. Its most noticeable feature is that at each stage all that he has learned so far leaves him quite *unprepared* for what happens next.

The Earthly Paradise represents the best documented of all human dreams. It is Eden – the most well-remembered of the places we shall never visit. The metaphor of innocence is a garden, and culturally we are conditioned by that metaphor to think about both gardens and innocence in a very special and connected way. That other dark forest where Dante first met Virgil was the reverse image of this garden: the black parody that even in its denial of the reality of the dream, affirms its appeal. Yet what strikes us now, even as Dante comes to recognize the familiarity of where he has come to, is the very opposite – its sheer unexpectedness:

> Coi pie ristetti e con li occhi passai
> di là dal fiumicello, per mirare

la gran varïazion di freschi mai;
e là m'apparve, sì com'elli appare
subitamente cosa che disvia
per maraviglia tutto altro pensare,
una donna soletta che si gìa
cantando e scegliendo fior da fiore
ond'era pinta tutta la sua via.

(XXVIII: 34–42)

With feet I stopped and with eyes passed over beyond the steamlet to look at the great variety of fresh-flowering boughs, and there appeared to me there, as appears of a sudden a thing that for wonder drives away every other thought, a lady all alone, who went singing and culling flower from flower with which all her way was painted.

Who is this lady whom later we learn, almost casually, is called Matilda? Virgil's counterpart – the type of the active Christian life, and, as such, a fit herald of Beatrice herself? A historical personage? Perhaps Matilda of Canossa, Countess of Tuscany, as some early commentators thought; perhaps the German, Mechtildis von Hackenborn, a saintly nun who died in 1298? We can work out her allegorical role with some hesitation, we can try to fit some shadowy historical personage to her character, yet neither of these answers (supposing they were demonstrable), nor similar exegesis at this level really answer our question. Again, as in Dante's later meeting with Beatrice herself, we are led to expect in the narrative an event of primary symbolic or allegorical importance, and when we get there what dominates our attention instead is the personal. The simple fact is that Matilda is not at all what Dante (or the reader) *expects* at this point, and her gently ironic first words, 'You are new here,' suggest, among other things, her awareness of his surprise. They set the tone for what follows. Dante has been crowned and mitred, initiated through reason into freedom, 'Lord over himself'; his first subsequent encounter in the new Eden is with a young woman very much not a part of our traditional Edenic folk-lore who fails to fit into any immediately obvious allegorical slot, and who neatly catches his first question and replies with a brief geography lecture. The irony, once again, lies in the change of level. Matilda's appearance is unexpected, and her apparent foreknowledge of him implies the miraculous, yet when he asks (in effect) 'What's going on here?' – expecting a miraculous answer about the nature of the garden, what he receives is a talk on physics and topography. The effect is to stress not his spiritual limitations, but the finiteness of his

ordinary terrestrial knowledge. The result is like that of Marlowe's
Mephistophilis who evades Faustus's quest for the miraculous by
answering his questions always within the known framework of the
science of the time. The miraculous does not contradict the laws of
science; it occurs at a different level of experience. Dante's progress is
as disconcerting as that of a bad horseman trying to trot: he rises and
falls at the wrong places. Each time he attempts to switch to the right
level of question he is promptly met at a different one. The lecture on
physical geography gives way to an elaborate allegorical masque: The
Pageant of the Church:

> Poco più 'oltre, sette alberi d'oro
> falsava nel parere il lungo tratto
> del mezzo ch'era ancor tra noi e lorì;
> ma quand' i' fui sì presso di lor fatto
> che l' obietto comun, che 'l senso inganna,
> non perdea per distanza alcun suo atto,
> la virtù ch'a ragion discorso ammanna,
> sì com'elli eran candelabri apprese,
> e nelle voci del cantare 'osanna'.
> Di sopra fiammeggiava il bello arnese
> più chiaro assai che luna per sereno
> di mezza notte nel suo mezzo mese.
> Io mi rivolsi d'ammirazion pieno
> al buon Virgilio, ed esso mi rispose
> con vista carca di stupor non meno.

(XXIX: 43–57)

*A little way on, a false appearance of seven trees of gold was caused by the long
space still intervening between us and them; but when I had come so near that the
ambiguous shape which deceives the sense did not lose by distance any of its features,
the faculty which provides for the discourse of reason made them out as they were,
candlesticks, and in the voices of the singing 'Hosanna'. Above flamed the splendid
array, far brighter than the moon in the clear midnight sky of her mid-month. I
turned round full of wonder to the good Virgil and he answered me with a look no
less charged with amazement*

Virgil is as amazed as Dante; reason now flounders, completely out of
its depth. To find a masque – that most conventional and courtly of
dramatic forms – as the vehicle by which Beatrice is mediated to
Dante is yet another disturbing incongruity. We expect in Eden
'naturalness'; what we find is a stylized literary convention. This, if
anything, might prepare us for the humiliation of reason that is to
follow. Yet when it comes, as we have seen, the distancing formality
of the masque is dropped, and Beatrice's attack is delivered and felt at

a primarily personal level. Once again Dante's switch-back technique has left us confused and uncertain how to respond.

How unexpected and disconfirming this technique is we can see simply by cross-reference to other literary attempts to show us Eden. *Paradise Lost*, for instance, suggests a pastoral idyll as 'natural' and miraculous in its unfallen perfection as that of Dante. Milton's problems in portraying the daily routine of an unfallen Adam and Eve are not the same as those of Dante in search of Beatrice, but the problem of how far such a world would conform to our expectations is the same for both. Milton, like Dante, feels the mythic 'familiarity' of Eden, and unlike Dante, tries to stress the unfallenness of his world by an atmosphere of timeless normality. The result is the weakest section of *Paradise Lost*: a sententiously philosophized round of picturesque trivia, and a great deal of unnecessary gardening – more coy and artificial than the games of Marie Antoinette and her court shepherdesses at Versailles because, after all, Adam and Eve can hardly be aware of the pastoral convention, or understand it against the background of another kind of formality: that of the Court. The pastoral convention depends on a tension between different sets of expectations, and it is precisely this tension that Milton cannot allow:

> Under a tuft of shade that on a green
> Stood whispering soft, by a fresh fountain side
> They sat them down; and, after no more toil
> Of their sweet gardening labour than sufficed
> To recommend cool zephyr, and made ease
> More easy, wholesome thirst and appetite
> More grateful, to their supper-fruits they fell,
> Nectarine fruits, which the compliant boughs
> Yielded them sidelong as they sat reclined
> On the soft downy bank damasked with flowers:
>
> (Book IV 325–34)

Milton's Paradise is fundamentally *cosy*. He seems to believe in this pastoral *literally* – as if what is merely a convention among fallen men is in some sense the Platonic reflection of the ideal reality in which unfallen man would be 'naturally' at home. In contrast, Dante's Earthly Paradise is no place for cosily being at home; its bliss is not that of a convention, but a challenge:

> Guardaci ben! Ben son, ben son Beatrice.
> Come degnasti d'accedere al monte?
> Non sapei tu che qui è l'uom felice?   (XXX: 73–6)

Look at me well; I am, I am indeed Beatrice. How durst thou approach the mountain? Didst thou not know that here man is happy?

It is very tempting to describe Dante's treatment of what is, admittedly, a slightly different situation from that of Milton as displaying a surer 'instinct' than the later English poet, but as a critical concept 'poetic instinct' is too easy a way out here. The difference between an Eden that, even if it contains some novelties, still confirms our basic presuppositions, and one that constantly denies them, is a reflection of a fundamental difference between the two poets. Dante's play on the tension between the familiar and the quite unexpected in the Earthly Paradise reveals not a surer literary instinct than Milton, but a surer *theology*.

What is the meaning of Beatrice's mysterious question:

> Didst thou not know that here man is happy?

Once again, it seems, we are on the switchback. Beatrice's question catches Dante at the wrong level of response. His personal grief at the loss of Virgil is flung into juxtaposition with the symbolic and theological assertion of man's bliss here in Eden: if he feels unhappy, it is *his* fault, she implies. If he were perfect, he could only be happy. What are we to make of this? Given the *a priori* basis of our idea of 'Paradise' she must, of course, be right: it's part of our definition of the word. But that is no guarantee of the truth of the particular version he has created. If we simply accept that Beatrice's challenge reveals the apparent 'harshness' of divine love seen in human terms we have to accept too that Dante the poet has failed to justify his own theology. Beatrice doesn't 'seem' to be unfair to Dante: she *is* unfair to him — and even her entourage feel it. The whole technique of these Cantos with their abrupt and confusing shifts of level is part of a mechanism that systematically seeks to prevent Dante receiving any confirmation of his perceptions. It is a situation familiar to the psychiatrist:

> Modes of confirmation or disconfirmation vary . . . The crux seems to be that it is a response by the other that is *relevant* to the evocative action, in according recognition to the evocative act, and accepting its significance at least for the evoker, if not for the respondent. A confirmatory reaction by the other is a direct response, in the sense of being at least 'to the point', or 'on the same beam' or 'wave-length' as the first person's initiatory or evocatory action. This means that a partially confirmatory response need not be in agreement, or gratifying, or satisfying. Rejection can be confirmatory if it is a direct response that gives recognition to the evoking action and grants it its own significance and validity.[8]

When patients in a mental-hospital are denied such 'recognition' we are rightly indignant. 'Disconfirmation' is not simply the denial or rejection of a particular belief or intellectual position, it involves the discovery or disclosure that a whole way of seeing and feeling to which one is personally committed (such as in a view of oneself, the kind of 'personal knowledge' described by Michael Polanyi,[9] or what Newman calls 'real assent') is undermined tangentially or shown in such a changed perspective that it is made to appear partial, inadequate, or, indeed, irrelevant. It involves the revelation of a difference *in kind*. Dante believes (and has good grounds for believing) that he is, through reason, lord and master over himself. What he is then confronted with by Beatrice is the discovery not that this is *untrue*, but that this is at an altogether different level from what she is demanding of him, and that only when it is seen as quite irrelevant does it acquire any relevance again – and then it is an utterly different relevance. Dante is the man of perfected reason; Beatrice accuses him of faithlessness. He is caught in what is sometimes called 'double-bind'. The situation is so set up that he can respond with his whole self neither at a personal level, nor at the level of the theological allegory. However he responds, he is wrong.

How are we to explain this contradiction, let alone try to justify the earlier assertion that he was a better theologian in his poetry than Milton? The answer, it seems to me, is to be found in the griffin, and its two-fold nature. The vision of the griffin is directly juxtaposed with Beatrice's disconfirmation of Dante, and it seems by implication to be in some sense a part of it. Only when Dante finally comes to Beatrice, having crossed the river of Lethe, can he see through her eyes that the hybrid is not a unity, but two different and ever-merging wholes. To human eyes it is neither beast nor bird; to Beatrice it is *both* beast *and* bird – human *and* divine. The paradox of this vision needs to be laboured if only because for so many critics and even scholars the idea of 'divine vision' or even of 'revelation' implies a way of neatly evading awkward ambiguities and tensions. Milton's *Paradise Lost*, to take our most recent example yet again, represents one of the greatest sustained attempts to iron out theological ambiguity in the name of divine truth – as Blake was only one of many to notice. What Dante shows us here is the opposite view. Seen through Dante's eyes the griffin is a paradox; seen through the eyes of Beatrice the paradox is transformed into an absolute contradiction. Only much later, in the beatific vision of the *Paradiso* will this revelation itself be disconfirmed by a greater vision of unity. But that is at an altogether inaccessible level of experience for Dante at this stage; here, it seems, he has first of all to cope with a new and very complex revelation: that all he has so far learned to see and understand as valuable with Virgil is both as important as he knows it to be, *and*, at the same time, utterly worthless. His affection for Virgil himself is both noble and culpable. These antitheses may seem from a human point of view to modify each other, or to be 'explicable' as a dialectic, but through the divine vision we see that this is in fact not so. What seems to man's experience like a contradiction *is in reality an even greater contradiction.* Thus Dante both is, and is not free; he does, and does not understand; Beatrice is both just, and unjust to him. As Aquinas eventually saw, the study of theology is both man's supreme intellectual good, and of no value at all in face of revelation. The language of disconfirmation is, it seems, that of complete ambiguity.

'Ambiguity' is a fashionable word, and it must nowadays be used with care. It looks at first sight as if we can represent this language of complete contradiction visually by the kind of simple 'either/or' ambiguity that we find in certain well-known puzzle-pictures:

E. H. Gombrich reminds us in connection with figures like this that 'an ambiguity, as such, cannot be perceived'.[10] 'To perceive', means,

in this context, to form a complete and reasonable plausible image
– even at the risk of excluding other plausible, but contradictory images. We can never 'see' directly something as ambiguous; we can only
infer that it is so by a process of making first one reading and then
another until all possible configurations are satisfied. In this case we
can see *either* a vase, *or* two faces in silhouette; we cannot, however
hard we try by switching rapidly from one interpretation to the other,
'see' both at the same time. A parallel situation seems to occur with verbal ambiguity. In his now classic *Seven Types of Ambiguity*, William
Empson points out that a word can never be read with two meanings
at the same time. He takes the example of the words 'rose' and 'rows':

. . . it is hard to believe that they are pronounced the same. Homonyms with
less powerful systems of association, like the verb 'rows' and the 'roes' of fishes,
lend themselves easily to puns and seem in some degree attracted towards the
two more powerful systems; but to insist that the first two are the same sound,
to pass suddenly from one to the other, destroys both of them, and leaves a sort
of bewilderment in the mind.[11]

Initially Empson is making the same point as Gombrich: that one
'reading' of an ambiguity effectively *excludes* any other. But he also
makes a second point of some importance to our argument: that this
exclusion is not necessarily as absolute as the bare logic of the perceptual mechanism might suggest. The mind can and often does 'carry
over' one reading and try to relate it to the other possible alternatives
– and the degree to which it can make sense of such a transfer may
be the criterion of success. The effect of such overlapping of meanings
is to increase the 'charge' of the passage – the sensation of multi-
layered meaning where the layers are not fully separable but in some
sense dependent on one other. In making sense of a visual ambiguity,
or in grasping a verbal pun, there has to be a real effort of distinction
whereby one *selects* (albeit unconsciously) one reading from other possible alternatives – even while remaining aware that there *are* other
possible alternatives.

It begins to appear that the ambiguity Dante is calling our attention
to in the griffin is *not* the simple case of exclusion which it seemed at
first sight to resemble. There is no 'carry over' between the vase and
the two faces. Let us look at a second possibility which is found in a
cartoon by the American artist Saul Steinberg:

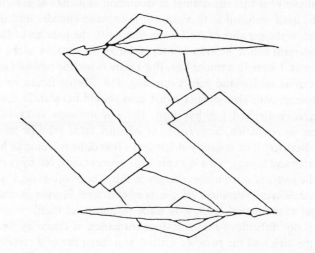

Only one of these can be the 'real' hand, the other must be the 'image'; yet since there is nothing to indicate which is which we find that each interpretation stumbles over its equally possible opposite. Gombrich cites this drawing and comments:

> If proof were needed of the kinship between the language of art and the language of words, it could be found in this drawing. For the perplexing effect of this self-reference is very similar to the paradoxes beloved of philosophers: the Cretan who says that all Cretans lie, or the simple blackboard with only one statement on it which runs, 'The only statement on the blackboard is untrue.' If it is true it is untrue and if untrue true.[12]

Though Dante is not quite trying his own version of the Cretan paradox in Canto XXX, what he is doing involves something essentially similar. How *are* we to take Beatrice's challenge: 'Didst thou not know that here man is happy'? What she is apparently asserting is a dogmatic standard so harsh that it only makes sense at a symbolic level: our opinion of Dante as a man would be the less if he *were* unconcernedly happy to lose Virgil in meeting Beatrice. One feels like replying to Beatrice 'What kind of a man do you want, who can be happy at the loss of a friend'? But this again, of course, is to misunderstand what Beatrice is doing. The similarity to the Cretan paradox lies not in what is said at this point, but in what Dante is – or discovers himself to be. The fallacy in the Cretan paradox (as Bertrand Russell has shown)[13] is that the definer or definition of a class of objects cannot be itself included in that class. It *must* stand outside. And this, of course, is the paradox of the Incarnation itself: the paradox of Dante's predicament before Beatrice is a repetition of the paradox of the Incarnation as it were in a minor key. But Dante is not the two-fold griffin, and cannot understand yet its meaning. He is being forced to accept the role of both class-definer (what man should be) and, at the same time, an individual faithless man. If he is unhappy at exchanging reason for revelation, he is failing to measure up to what he might be with Beatrice; if he is happy at losing his friend, he is failing in human affection and loyalty. This is an old Christian paradox, but by juxtaposing the levels of discourse as sharply as this, Dante is making his point with deliberate brutality. At the symbolic level Reason is made to resign; at the logical level, it is made to contradict itself.

It is not difficult to read this disconfirmation of Dante by Beatrice, and the vision of the two-fold griffin, as a metaphor of a certain kind of religious experience where the same event must be seen in two very different ways *at the same time* if either is to be understood at all. Looking back, we find that we have been prepared for the peculiar 'double-focus' of this metaphor by Dante's dream of Leah in Canto XXVII:

> ... giovane e bella in sogno mi parea
> donna vedere andar per una landa
> cogliendo fiori; e cantando dicea:
> 'Sappia qualunque il mio nome dimanda
> ch' i' mi son Lia, e vo movendo intorno
> le belle mani a farmi una ghirlanda.
> Per piacermi allo specchio qui m'adorno;
> ma mia suora Rachel mai non si smaga
> dal suo miraglio, e siede tutto giorno.
> Ell' è de' suoi belli occhi veder vaga
> com' io dell' adornarmi con le mani;
> lei lo vedere, e me l'ovrare appaga.'

(97–108)

... I seemed to see in a dream a lady young and beautiful going through a meadow gathering flowers and singing: 'Know, whoever asks my name, that I am Leah, and I go plying my fair hands here and there to make me a garland; to please me at the glass I here adorn myself, but my sister Rachel never leaves her mirror and sits all day. She is fain to see her own fair eyes as I to adorn me with my hands. She with seeing, and I with doing am satisfied.'

The language is strikingly similar to that describing Matilda in the next

Canto, and the episode has been seen as intended to make us associate Matilda, when we meet her, with Leah, and Beatrice with Rachel. The use of these two sisters as types of the active and the contemplative life was part of an old and familiar tradition to Dante's readers. J. S. Carroll writes: 'St. Gregory the Great, when the office of the Papacy was forced upon him, bewailed the loss of his Rachel, the quiet life of contemplation in his monastery':

> The beauty of the contemplative life I have loved as Rachel, barren indeed but clear-eyed and fair which, although by its quiet it bears less, yet sees the light more clearly. Leah is wedded to me in the night, the active life namely, fruitful but blear-eyed, seeing less though bringing forth abundantly.[14]

Yet, as so often, Dante is doing something more than employing a stock image. As we have seen, his expectations built partly on this dream are thrown into complete confusion when he actually meets Matilda. In the dream it would appear that – as St Gregory found – the two modes of religious experience are antitheses between which some kind of 'either-or' choice must be made. This, we recall, was also Jacob's own impression when the Bible tells us he began to work for his uncle Laban, and, passing over Leah, the elder and less attractive daughter, he asks for his younger cousin Rachel as a wife.[15] What follows is the first example of the famous bed-trick. Having worked seven years for Rachel, Jacob is tricked into bedding the wrong sister, and though he is afterwards given Rachel as well, he has to earn her by another seven years' service. By way of explanation, Laban tells Jacob that it is not customary to give the younger sister in marriage before the elder. Not unnaturally, Jacob continues to prefer Rachel to Leah, and so God, we are told, ensures that Rachel shall remain barren while Leah proves only too fecund. The story has certain oddities worth pausing over. Contrary to all expectations Jacob does not have to choose between the two sisters; on the contrary, if he wants one he *must* accept both. The beautiful contemplative Rachel will only be his if he will first take the plainer 'active' sister. Dante's own disconfirmation of expectations in the meeting with Matilda is thus directly referred back to Jacob's own even more drastic disconfirmation. No only *can* he have his cake and eat it: he *must*. The fertile Leah is 'wedded in the night' by mistake for the barren Rachel. There is an old Talmudic version of the story that makes the interrelation of the sisters even more grotesquely dramatic: Rachel, it is said, lay under Jacob's bed on the wedding night, and whenever the infatuated bridegroom asked Leah 'Do you love me?' answered for her from under the bed, 'Yes!'[16]

Leah/Matilda are the world of creativity, yet what gives meaning to their art lies beyond them in the unutterable vision of Rachel/Beatrice. They are antitheses, but not alternatives: only *through* art can art be transcended. There is no short cut. Matilda and Beatrice stand for opposite worlds, yet as maid and mistress each is inescapably dependent upon the other. What we have here in this relationship is in effect a repetition in microcosm of the whole action of the *Commedia* up to this point. Dante has come through Hell and Purgatory to Beatrice through the 'ingegno' and 'arte' of Virgil, the pagan poet. Now, as in the theological field the structure is suddenly inverted and thrown into confusion, so it is in the aesthetic. Jacob had no intention that Leah should be his way to Rachel – nor did he intend to get her with child in the process; yet without Leah's sons he would not have been the founder of Israel. The confusion, the element of mistaken identity, persists at every level of the narratives: Dante's confusion when he first encounters Matilda instead of Beatrice in the Earthly Paradise is apparently not fortuitous, but, it seems, an essential aspect of the creative process itself. Seen as it were from 'the other side', artistic creation is come upon as a discovery, a disconfirmation, whose role is perplexing and obscure. It is interesting to notice in this connection that in describing Leah Dante makes one very important change from the Bible and Gregory. In both these sources Rachel has clear and beautiful eyes, while Leah is plainer with dull or 'blear' eyes. The artist, if not blind like Tiresias, is dim-sighted. Not so Dante's Leah, who is beautiful in her own right, and who like her sister gazes in the mirror of revelation – though garlanded with the flowers of nature. When we discover Matilda similarly garlanded in the next Canto the dazzling radiance of her eyes is deliberately stressed by Dante who compares them with those of Venus herself. The ugly duckling has become a swan.

Thus art is seen by Dante not as a crude and inadequate translation of the glory of God into sensual terms: a trying to speak the unspeakable. The divine glory *cannot* be separated from the Incarnation. Art is seen as a symbol in almost Coleridgean terms: the translucence of the eternal in and through the temporal, not merely partaking in the nature of what it represents, but a *necessary* part of it: a way of awakening man to the radical difference and otherness of what, in some sense, he already knows. The disconfirming experience of creativity is both a divine gift, *and*, at the same time, an inherent property of language itself. So long as Jacob despises Leah, Rachel is barren; only when Jacob is finally reconciled to his first wife, does his second bear a child.

As such an analysis suggests, the whole episode of Dante's humiliation before Beatrice is a richly woven fabric of biblical allusions – of which the Elijah story is only one strand among many. Yet its presence is fundamental. The two Old Testament figures in the Transfiguration, Moses and Elijah, are both traditionally types of Christ.[17] Moses led Israel out of bondage, and received the tablets of the Law on Sinai/Horeb; Elijah ascended the same mountain looking for a similar experience – and found something totally unexpected in its place. In the *Divine Comedy* the substitution of the Old Testament challenge, 'What doest thou here?', for the New Testament reassurance, 'Be not afraid,' highlights the unspoken parallel between Elijah and Dante. Like Elijah, Dante has come at great cost – through Hell, no less! – to what he knows to be the 'mountain of the Lord', the mountain of Purgatory, only to have all his expectations similarly overthrown. He came believing that he knew what was about to happen, and found he did not. He came prepared for an encounter with the supernatural; what he finds, for the first time, is the truly 'natural' – the unfallen Earthly Paradise.

Yet, of course, there are differences, and the differences are as important as the parallels. Elijah, knowing only the old dispensation, came to Horeb in despair;[18] Dante, having experienced the new, comes in hope. For Elijah it is his perception of the external world, the world of what we would now call 'nature', that is radically disconfirmed; for Dante, it is his internal world, his sense of *self*, that is undermined. Dante's story is thus not a re-enactment of the Elijah story, it is a particular development of it.

It was a development of incalculable importance for succeeding centuries. The meeting of Dante and Beatrice in the Earthly Paradise is presented as a paradigm *both* of religious language *and* of artistic creativity as a whole – or, to be still more precise, the paradox of failure at the heart of the former becomes the paradigm by which we may come to understand the latter. We only begin to understand Virgil after we have met Beatrice. This suggestion is reinforced by the way in which the question that arouses Dante from his trance, in the passage with which we began (*Purgatorio* XXXII: 77–8) is described in terms of 'the word by which deeper slumbers were broken . . .' That 'Word' is, of course, the word of Christ that had already raised from the dead Jairus's daughter (Luke viii, 54), the widow's son (Luke vii. 14), and most spectacularly of all, Lazarus (John xi. 43). It is the *logos* of John i, whose type in the Old Testament is assumed to be Elijah's 'still small voice'. That identification takes us back to the tension of opposites which, as we have seen, was always present in the idea of the *logos* from the very beginning. It is central, for instance, to St John of the Cross's meditation on the Elijah story:

'Oh delicate touch of the Word, delicate, yea wonderously delicate, to me, which, having overthrown the mountains and broken the stones in Mount Horeb with the shadow of Thy power and strength that went before Thee, didst reveal Thyself to the Prophet with the whisper of gentle air.[19]

The *logos* is at once 'tumult and peace' – the fact that Wordsworth's description of the Simplon Pass, with its 'voice' that speaks through the antinomies of nature as 'characters of the great Apocalypse/The types and symbols of Eternity' (*Prelude* (1805) 570–1) should seem to echo so closely the Mediaeval and Renaissance typological tradition is yet another illustration of how persistent that tradition is in Romantic and Victorian poetics. Lowth's identification of the poetic with the prophetic tradition was to give a new aesthetic impetus to typology at the very moment when it was ceasing to provide a principle of historic interpretation. The process of internalization that we associate with Romanticism finds its opposite in the parallel process of *psychomachia*: that is, the portrayal of critical events and conflicts of the soul as external occurrences. Typological events repeat in the world of time the paradigmatic 'events' (if that is an appropriate word) of eternity; such typology becomes analogous to spiritual or psychological patterns in the mind of the reader, so that typological fictions will tend to appear as a psychomachia.[20] As we have seen, the difference between this and 'symbolism' is a fine but persistently drawn line. Thus the description of Elijah's original experience on Horeb (I Kings xix) can be understood as a psychomachia.[21] It is not 'symbolic' in at least Coleridge's finely-honed sense because it only points forward towards a fuller revelation; it does not partake of, or encapsulate, that revelation itself. Dante's fictional use of that typological tradition is, however, by the same token, clearly symbolic.

We have already discussed Keble's use of that same typological tradition.[22] It was left to an American, John Greenleaf Whittier, however, to bring together two very different strands in Keble's thought:

Drop Thy still dews of quietness,
   Till all our strivings cease;
Take from our souls the strain and stress
And let our ordered lives confess
   The beauty of Thy peace.

Breathe through the hearts of our desire
   Thy coolness and Thy balm;
Let sense be dumb, let flesh retire;
Speak through the earthquake, wind and fire,
   O still small voice of calm!

The New England Quaker's sense of the 'inner light' in every man draws him to identify the 'soothing' aspects of the gospel, so prominent in Keble's thought, with the now-familiar tradition of the *logos* as the still small voice. In so doing, he touches once more on the *aesthetic* tradition that, as we have seen, has always been essential to it. Keble's notion of the health-giving and cathartic properties of poetry is related back specifically to the 'word': poetry is a communication at once artifact and *logos*, human and divine. The duality of the *logos* and its aesthetic counterpart in the duality of the poetic image, symbolized by Dante in the image of the griffin, persists right into the poetic theory of the eighteenth and nineteenth centuries. Poetry is felt to be 'the natural language of religion' because it reveals the *logos* in human terms.

But there is a second aspect to Dante's use of the Elijah story that was to have an even greater significance in romantic and Victorian experience – and that is its typology of disconfirmation. Undoubtedly the most famous expression of influence is in Blake's illustration of the meeting of Dante and Beatrice. Dante himself stands at the extreme right of the picture. His head is slightly bowed as if humbly accepting Beatrice's rebuke, but his eyes are still fixed on her face – so making possible the vision of the griffin's dual nature. The platform decorations of the car on which Beatrice is standing are suggestive of an altar. By her wheel are the three virgins mentioned in Canto XXIX. Hope, in green, raises her hands to heaven; Charity, in red, is surrounded by tiny children, apparently incorporated into her golden hair; while Faith is running forward, pointing to an open book (presumably the Bible) and to Dante, as if in intercession against the charge of faithlessness. The 'four living creatures' grouped around Beatrice are each crowned with green leaves, and plumed with six wings full of eyes – Dante's conflation of images from Ezekiel and Revelation representing the four

Evangelists. In all this, even down to the colours of the griffin, Blake has followed Dante very accurately (far more so than, for instance, Flaxman, who had illustrated this same scene shortly before, and whose work had influenced Blake). Where Blake differs from Dante is therefore the more significant.

Her car is explicitly modelled on the chariot from Ezekiel (Ezekiel i, 4–28). Its wheels are a swirling vortex of reflections of the eyes in the wings of the four creatures and of the three virgins' faces. Though the four creatures may suggest such an addition by association, it is nowhere to be found in Dante. For him, Beatrice at this point seems to represent the sacrament – she is, for Dante, the God-bearing image. For the Protestant and nonconformist Blake, however, her meaning seems to be rather different. Her place within the chariot of Ezekiel gives her less a sacramental than a *prophetic* significance. It is Ezekiel who, in Blake's *Marriage of Heaven and Hell*, appears to have been reading Lowth:

We of Israel taught that the Poetic Genius (as you now call it) was the first principle and all the others merely derivative, which was the cause of our despising the Priests and Philosophers of other countries, and prophecying that all Gods would at last be proved to originate in ours & be the tributaries of the Poetic Genius.

(Plates 12–13)

For Blake, Dante's bi-fold vision of the griffin is not merely an encounter with the spirit of prophecy, but more specifically with Poetic Genius. He seems also to have known something of the cabbalistic significance of the chariot in Jewish Merkabah ('Chariot') mysticism[23] – where it is both specially holy and dangerous: so much so that some rabbis sought to withdraw the Book of Ezekiel from general circulation.[24] Maimonides, in the Fourth Book of the *Guide to the Perplexed*, similarly argued that Ezekiel's vision *ought* not to be expounded because it was too holy.[25] Since by almost universal consent, (including that of Dante and Blake) the four creatures were assumed to be types of the four Evangelists, the statement that 'the spirit of the living creatures was in the wheels' (Ezekiel i, 20) was taken by long tradition to mean that the wheels are words – or even, specifically, a manifestation of *the* 'Word' or *logos*.[26] The association of words, or the Word, with the vision of the chariot is clearly central to Blake's idea of the prophetic role of the poet:

Bring me my Bow of burning gold:
Bring me my Arrows of desire:

Bring me my Spear: O clouds unfold!
Bring me my chariot of fire!

I will not cease from Mental Fight,
Nor shall my Sword sleep in my hand:
Till we have built Jerusalem,
In England's green & pleasant land.[27]

Would to God that all the Lord's people were Prophets.

(Numbers xi, 29)

Most commentators link the chariot in this poem with 'the chariot of fire' that took Elijah in a whirlwind up to heaven (II Kings iii, 11), but, of course, the 'chariot' of Ezekiel[28] is *also* manifested with fire and a whirlwind (Ezekiel i, 4), and it seems clear that Blake is following Dante in associating the encounter with Beatrice with Elijah on Horeb. Elijah was, for Blake, the 'spirit of Prophecy' (*Milton* 24: 71) who 'comprehends all the Prophetic Characters'.[29] In *The Ghost of Abel*, Blake addresses Byron with the famous challenge from I Kings xix, echoed by Dante: 'What doest thou here, Elijah?' In *A Vision of the Last Judgement* Blake also clarifies his own personal 'chariot' symbolism: 'If the spectator could Enter into these images in his Imagination, approaching them on the Fiery Chariot of his Contemplative Thought . . . then he would arise from his Grave . . .'[30] The Word 'by which deeper slumbers were broken' is now the spirit of poetry to be seized by everyman in his imagination.

Central to this nexus of biblical images, types, and motifs is the necessity for disconfirmation and failure as a condition of growth. The vision of dialectic embodied in the two-fold griffin is essentially the same as that which had preoccupied Blake more than thirty years before he painted his picture, in *The Marriage of Heaven and Hell*:

Without Contraries is no progression. Attraction and Repulsion, Reason and Energy, Love and Hate are necessary to Human Existence.

(Plate 3)

It is a fundamentally *uncomfortable* vision. The hearing of the Word, the encounter with the fiery chariot, the meeting with Beatrice, the experience of the prophetic nature of poetry are profoundly disturbing, unsettling, and even destructive. They constitute a turning-point in consciousness.

Convention and realism: The shaking of the foundations

We now turn to another incident of dramatic disconfirmation in a cave – this time from the early twentieth century:

There are some exquisite echoes in India; there is the whisper round the dome at Bijapur; there are the long solid sentences that voyage through the air at Mandu, and return unbroken to their creator. The echo in a Marabar cave is not like these, it is entirely devoid of distinction. Whatever is said, the same monotonous noise replies, and quivers up and down the walls until it is absorbed into the roof. 'Boum' is the sound as far as the human alphabet can express it, or 'bou-oum' or 'ou-boum', – utterly dull. Hope, politeness, the blowing of a nose, the squeak of a boot, all produce 'boum' . . . Coming at a moment when she happened to be fatigued, it had managed to murmer, 'Pathos, piety, courage – they exist, but are identical, and so is filth. Everything exists, nothing has value.' If one had spoken vileness in that place, or quoted lofty poetry, the comment would have been the same – 'ou-boum'. If one had spoken with the tongues of angels and pleaded for all the unhappiness and misunderstanding in the world, past, present, and to come . . . it would amount to the same . . . Devils are of the North, and poems can be written about them, but no one could romanticize the Marabar because it robbed infinity and eternity of their vastness, the only quality that accommodates them to mankind.[31]

The implication that Mrs Moore's experience in the Marabar cave is to be read as a paradigm example of a 'negative' religious experience is reinforced both by the Elijah-like situation, with its unexpected encounter with the murmur of the echoing 'voice', and the oblique Pauline quotation from the New Testament.[32] Coming at a moment when she is peculiarly vulnerable, when she is tired, overwrought, and claustrophobic, Mrs Moore is suddenly offered in the dull echo an extreme image of mankind's relationship to the universe. Pathos, courage, piety, and filth are all reduced to the hollow 'boum', in which even the uniqueness of the human voice is muffled into impersonality. The lifeless unresponsive echo provides a terrifying Feuerbachian metaphor of man's desperate attempt to project his values upon the cosmos in search of an answering resonance. Forster's image can be seen as the culmination of a hundred years of progressive disenchantment with Nature.

Yet there are dangers in describing the mood of an age in terms of certain key images. Though we have, for instance, concentrated on a particular story from the Elijah cycle as the 'origin' of our traditional idea of Nature we can have no idea if this is really so. What we can say is that it is one of the earliest (very probably *the* earliest) written statements we have of this complexly experienced relationship, and that the story has resonated through European literature down to our own time. It initiated a particular rebirth of images. What was struggling to inarticulate and painful symbolic birth in the story of the Old Testament prophet's failure was the beginning of the long semantic drama of desynonymy that was to separate 'wind' from 'spirit', natural fire from Pentecostal, and the shaking of the earth from the shaking of the foundations. In that account we can see the world of primal participation, in which neither the concept of the 'natural', nor consequently, the concept of the 'divine' could exist, in the act of giving way to a world where science and religion were possible for the first time. An idea of Nature that was at once an expression of God, but yet subject to regular and objective laws, could begin to emerge. In this millennia-long tradition of imagery Carlyle's 'natural supernaturalism', for instance, must be seen not as the beginning of a new or 'modern' way of experiencing the environment (significantly, the word 'environment' is another of Carlyle's coinages) so much as the final stage of an attitude that can be traced back to that anonymous story about a dispirited prophet hiding in a cave on a lonely mountain. Carlyle's attempt to re-infuse the world of the natural sciences with a sense of mystery and numinous awe was a last, late-Romantic, effort to retain something of that balanced bi-focal vision that had for so long held the natural and supernatural in a particular and highly fruitful tension in European culture. So powerful was the image that it persisted even after the failure (for Carlyle) of the religious belief that had given birth to it, providing yet another example of the continuing power of a particular 'poetic' image to reshape human consciousness.

But the relationship of such a shift in image-paradigms to the age which produced it is neither straightforward nor simple. Dante's *Divine Comedy* is in one very obvious sense 'of its age', yet, in so far as it is profoundly original, it is clearly in another sense a major force of change within it. Similarly, it is true, for instance, that the failure of the Romantic idea of Nature as a source of joy and inspiration is a commonplace of Victorian aesthetics. The beneficent 'foster-mother' of Wordsworth's *Immortality Ode* through whose agency in Book IV of *The Prelude* he is chosen as a 'dedicated spirit', had, by the time of Tennyson's *In Memoriam*, become a blind evolutionary force, 'red in tooth and claw', in turns indifferent or malevolent. Though the optimistically desired future 'crowning race' might number among its achievements the capacity to read 'Nature like an open book',[33] such was all too evidently not the lot of his own nineteenth century – a view echoed with topical precision by Hardy's *Darkling Thrush* at the century's close. Indeed, it is tempting to say that what was buried by Hardy that last December afternoon of the nineteenth century with such *fin-de-siècle* pessimism was not just a particular metaphorical conceit that had outlived its usefulness for him, but the entire centuries-long view of the relationship between man and Nature that we have been looking at; that Forster's empty echo in the Marabar caves is the summation of this shift in defining images. The problem with such a view, of course, is that no period – least of all the nineteenth century – is actually so monolithically consistent. While one can argue, with good evidence, that Tennyson's popularity makes him a key figure in understanding his period, it is worth remembering that Hopkins's synthesis of biblical parallelism and his own feeling for the inscape of nature came to poetic fruition more than quarter of a century *after* the publication of *In Memoriam*.

In his book, *Images of Crisis*, George Landow has called attention to a series of such organizing images, or 'paradigms', that he sees as having haunted western imaginations since the middle of the eighteenth century. Though his thesis has its ostensible roots in structuralist and post-structuralist criticism, it soon becomes clear that his real debt is to Kuhn's *Structure of Scientific Revolutions*.[34] Just as a scientific paradigm, in Kuhn's special sense, has 'the function of sealing off certain areas of dispute and thus allowing scientists to go about their main endeavour', so cultural paradigms such as the shipwreck, argues Landow, 'impose a sense of order upon the formlessness and sheer multiplicity of existence in this world'.[35] The crises of a culture in transition express themselves through the transformation of previously dominant cultural paradigms.

This argument, we note, bears some similarity to Farrer's 'rebirth of images'. The difference lies in the specifically Kuhnian input: the idea that a 'paradigm' has the function of sealing off some areas of dispute in order to clear the way for the exploration of others. Unfortunately, though the thesis is illustrated exhaustively with a wealth of detail from both visual and literary sources, Landow never manages to explain satisfactorily what exactly were the 'areas of dispute' sealed off from discussion by, say, the shipwreck paradigm, so that he ends up with something that looks in practice more like one of Coleridge's 'organising images'.[36] Yet there may be a sense in which Landow's unsubstantiated intuition may be correct. There is little need to seek for any hidden 'explanation' for the iconography of crisis in the nineteenth century. Few, if any, societies have undergone such rapid and even cataclysmic change; few societies have been more aware of the fact, or searched harder for appropriate imagery and models by which to come to terms with the experience of a quite new order of change. Victorian society was both self-conscious and highly self-critical. What was, perhaps, obscured by such urgent cultural debates as Carlyle's 'the Condition of England Question' were fundamental changes also going on in the nature of the aesthetic conventions that were purveying those very images of crisis.

As we have seen the idea of Nature itself – that first desynonymy of the material and the spiritual – emerges from the failure of the old participatory world-picture. Nor is this story a one far-off event. The history of the subsequent literary idea of nature can be seen in terms of a series of essentially similar disconfirmations, each of which, opened the way to a 'rediscovery' of, or a 'return' to nature in reaction to a growth of artifice or convention that inhibited spontaneous 'natural' perception. The tired Augustan conventions against which Wordsworth reacted were themselves the product of an earlier revolt against stilted complexity and laboured wit:

> First follow Nature, and your judgement frame
> By her just standard, which is still the same;
> Unerring Nature, still divinely bright,
> One clear, unchanged, and universal light,
> Life, force, and beauty must to all impart
> At once the source, and end, and test of art.[37]

Moreover Pope, too, is aware of a historical dimension to his rediscovery of Nature. Virgil himself, rejecting the tradition of Homer and turning directly to Nature, had according to Pope, made just such a rediscovery:

> Nature and Homer were, he found, the same.

For Pope, of course, 'Nature' has very different connotations from Wordsworth.[38] Just as Newton had discovered the motions of the universe to be a matter of mathematically predictable laws, so the 'laws' of art were themselves expressions of the unitary (and divinely created) Natural Law. Pope's Virgil did not discover Nature through Homer, but Homer through Nature. The rediscovery of Nature thus enabled him to rediscover his own aesthetic tradition, and therefore his own poetic identity. But if both Pope and Wordsworth (not to mention Virgil and Homer) believed in what Whitehead called 'The unchanging permanencies of nature'[39] as a direct source of poetic inspiration, however differently in practice they interpreted the notion, what is *also* clear, by their own proclaimed 'rediscovery' of it, is that in literary experience at any rate those 'permanencies' were only occasionally and intermittently perceived with any vigour and freshness. The stuff of the European poetic tradition is not a matter of unchanging permancies, but of the shock of the new. The original participatory poetic vision, is only rediscovered, with a shock of 'recognition' as something both new and yet unconsciously familiar, through the now conscious artifice of poetry. The growth of poetry and the extension of language and consciousness, is thus directly related to preceding experiences of failure. The great moment of the *Purgatorio* is not when Dante, inheritor of the great poetic tradition of Virgil, is crowned and mitred Lord over himself, but when, faced by the *actual* presence of Beatrice, rather than his expectation of it, he is totally humiliated and his expectations are disconfirmed. Moreover, though he does not then realize it, so keenly is he looking forward to that meeting, what he is actually offered in the Earthly Paradise, after Virgil's poetic tutelage, is just such a rare and fleeting rediscovery of Nature. In a sense, we may read symbolically into that 'rediscovery' the end of the Middle Ages and the dawn of another great but fleeting moment of perception of Nature – the Renaissance.

Though Pope claims Virgil as his most powerful example of Nature informing Art, his thesis, in line with standard neo-classical aesthetic theory, is presented as universal rather than particular. Nor is there any conscious or explicit link suggested between the experience of failure and artistic creativity or the birth of the new. Such ideas had little place in the conventional stasis of Augustan aesthetics, based on assumptions not of organic development but of decline from a past golden age. In the post-Lowthian revival of Hebraism, however, the dialectical pattern of the Bible became central to Romantic theories of inspiration. When the nineteenth century sought for the 'soothing' and healing powers of the gospel, or the 'still small voice of calm', it was because its deepest spiritual experiences were of a very different kind. The paradigm 'inner' event of the age was that of breakdown and recovery. It lies at the heart of Coleridge's *Ancient Mariner*, Wordsworth's *Prelude*, Tennyson's *In Memoriam*, and, in a slightly more concealed way, Hopkins's *Wreck of the Deutschland*.[40] At the same time there is a corresponding shift in ways of reading the Bible. Though typological interpretations persist alongside historical ones, the Bible as a whole tends to be seen less and less in terms of a story whose outcome is already known and settled, and more and more as a record of growth and spiritual development. The famous structure of *The Prelude*, with its 'spots of time' which sum up and provide renewal for the growth of Wordsworth's mind, is, of course, an essentially *biblical* pattern. For the nineteenth century, the affirmation that the Bible was 'poetic' went hand in hand with its rediscovery as the *locus classicus* of the process of growth through disconfirmation, breakdown, and recovery that for so many characterized their own age.

Moreover this pattern is by no means confined to poets, or even to literature in a broader sense. If it is common to Carlyle's *Sartor Resartus*, Kingsley's *Alton Locke*, and to many of Dickens's novels, it is also recorded in the biographies of numerous Victorians. Take the famous case of John Stuart Mill. In his *Autobiography* he describes how he started learning Greek, arithmetic, and history at the age of 3; Latin at 8; logic, philosophy, and 'a complete course of political economy' at 13.[41] To the modern reader what seems improbable is Mill's claim at the end of a detailed description of this precocious system of infant-stimulation that this was no more than might be attempted by any child of 'average capacity,'[42] but, given the fact that he was in a one-to-one teaching situation with his father, his regime was, comparatively, not much more arduous than that expected of many well-educated eighteenth-century children. Lowth himself, with his contemporaries Collins, Young, Spence, and the Warton brothers, Joseph and Thomas, had been subjected at Winchester to a course of study in the classics nearly as massive in quantity a hundred years before.[43] What was more unusual, as Mill says himself, was the particular content of his education, with its heavy emphasis on contemporary philosophy and political economy. At the age of 20, in 1826, he entered a severe and prolonged 'crisis': what would nowadays probably be called a 'breakdown'. There followed two years of profound, even clinical, depression that did not resolve itself until the autumn of 1828 when he began reading the poetry of Wordsworth.

As Mill makes clear, however, it was not the power of Nature in

Wordsworth that had such a healing effect upon him but his power of 'human feeling'. Though *The Prelude* was not to be published for another 22 years, it seems obvious, reading between the lines, that there were sufficient hints in Wordsworth's poetry at this time for Mill to recognize the symptoms of a very similar breakdown to his own. As a result of his disastrous love-affair with Annette Vallon, and the eclipse of his hopes for a new dawn for mankind in the French Revolution, Wordsworth had in 1793 come to a crisis in his personal life. Without an adequately internalized base for his own values, all human knowledge and endeavour had become meaningless:

> . . . endlessly perplexed
> With impulse, motive, right and wrong, the ground
> Of moral obligation, what the rule
> And what the sanction, till, demanding *proof*,
> And seeking it in everything, I lost
> All feeling of conviction . . .
>
> (*Prelude*, (1805) Bk X, 894–9)

Looking back, both Wordsworth and Mill are aware that their personal, 'inner', growth can in some very profound way be dated from their respective crises. As Wordsworth himself tells us earlier in *The Prelude*, though he had received an adequate, or even, by the standards of the day, a good academic education, first at Hawkshead Grammar School and then at Cambridge, this learning contributed little or nothing to his own inner development. It was the influence of his sister Dorothy, who had had very little formal education, and Coleridge, who had actually run away from Cambridge to enlist as a dragoon, that eventually restored him.[44] Mill, on the other hand, had never been to school, but had been educated at home by his father.

What is interesting about the testimony of Wordsworth and Mill is that, from their polar opposite backgrounds and educations, when they come to tell the story of their own growth, they do so not in terms of either formal academic learning, or of public successes (they were, after all, both very eminent Victorians), but in terms of their *failures*. At first glance one might suppose this perceived gap between formal education and personal growth was an accident of their unusual upbringings, but a wider survey of their contemporaries suggests that the pattern is widespread enough to be remarkable.[45] As the nineteenth century recognized in its response to Wordsworth, it is not the moments of ecstatic experience, harmony with creation, or feelings of brotherhood with man that are seen in retrospect as leading to growth; but rather experiences of isolation, doubt, loss, guilt and failure:

> The thought of our past years in me doth breed
> Perpetual benediction: not indeed
> For that which is most worthy to be blest;
> Delight and liberty, the simple creed
> Of childhood, whether busy or at rest,
> With new-fledged hope still fluttering in his breast –
>   Not for these I raise
>   The song of thanks and praise;
> But for those obstinate questionings
> Of sense and outward things,
> Fallings from us, vanishings;
> Blank misgivings of a Creature
> Moving about in worlds not realised,
> High instincts before which our mortal Nature
> Did tremble like a guilty thing surprised;
>
>   (*Immortality Ode*, 135–49)

What is seen to emerge with Wordsworth and the Romantics is nothing less than a revolutionary psychological and internalized approach to human growth and development.[46]

This is the more remarkable in that it is largely at odds with official educational theory of the period. The world of Bell and Lancaster, like that of Charlie Hexam's ragged school in *Our Mutual Friend*, is one of unrelieved cramming. Nor was the more humane and liberal ideal of moral and spiritual nurture associated with the name of Thomas Arnold any more 'Wordsworthian' in this particular respect. When, in 1828, the Provost of Oriel wrote to the Trustees of Rugby School that, if they were to make the 33-year-old tutor of his college their new head-master, he would 'change the face of education through all the public schools of England', he wrote perhaps more truly than he knew. Mark Pattison has, for instance, described the shattering effect of the new 'Rugby men' on the torpid and unreformed Oxford of the 1830s and 40s.[47] Gracefully conscious of their scholastic and moral superiority over both fellow students and their teachers, within a generation they terrified the academic world into desperate imitation.[48] Though Arnold did not invent the concept,[49] Rugby in the 1830s and 1840s was the high-watermark of the peculiarly English educational ideal of 'gentlemanliness' that, ever since A. P. Stanley's biography of him, has become inerradicably associated with Arnold's name. Arnold was no in-tellectual crammer; he had simple and essentially *religious* priorities. In his own words, these were: 'first, religious and moral principle; secondly, gentlemanly conduct; thirdly, intellectual ability'. There is no hint, however, here, or in Arnold's numerous sermons to Rugby school, or, indeed, in the nineteenth-century public school ethos as a whole, that failure could be seen as a precondition of growth. The paradox is even more striking in the case of Kingsley, whose own life repeated just such a pattern of 'crisis' and recovery,[50] and who makes this 'Wordsworthian' theme central to both his adult fiction and the *Water Babies*, and yet, who, when he was asked to address the boys of Wellington, the newly-founded public school, slips at once into the appropriate terminology of Christian manliness, declaring that learning consists 'first and foremost, in the art of observing'.[51] We are pulled with a jerk from the linguistic world of Wordsworth to that of *Scouting for Boys*. Nor is Kingsley an isolated example. Mark Girouard has shown in *The Return to Camelot* how pervasive the idea of 'manliness' was during the Victorian period, and how far, in particular, its rhetoric affected almost every aspect of upper-class educational theory.[52] The biblical and Romantic pattern of failure and regeneration becomes, as it were, in the nineteenth century a subversive undercurrent – a literary motif at once widespread and at the same time tacitly denied or ignored; commonest in 'low-status' literature (fantasy and writings for children, for example)[53] more blurred or less prominent in the mainstream tradition of prose.

Yet its existence had a profound effect on the development of Victorian aesthetics. Precluded from the debate, initially at any rate, by more urgent images of social crisis, were fundamental changes in the nature of both verse and prose, that provide, in effect, a kind of 'hidden agenda' to any debates over nineteenth-century poetic theory or imagery. Though it was far from clear to most contemporaries, the real crisis of nineteenth-century aesthetics was one of *genre*. To put it simply, sometime in the early nineteenth century the main stream of creative writing went over from verse to prose. For Ezra Pound the key figure is Stendhal:

... from the beginning of literature up to A.D. 1750 poetry was the superior art, and was so considered to be, and if we read books written before that date we find the number of interesting books in verse at least equal to the number of prose books still readable; and the poetry contains the quintessence. When we want to know what people were like before 1750, when we want to know they had blood and bones like ourselves, we go to the poetry of the period.

But ... one morning, Monsieur Stendhal, not thinking of Homer, or Villon, or Catullus, but having a very keen sense of actuality, noticed that 'poetry', *la poésie*, as the term was then understood, the stuff written by his French contempararies, or sonorously rolled at him from the French stage, was a damn nuisance. And he remarked that poetry, with its bagwigs and its bobwigs, and its padded calves and its periwigs, its 'fustian à la Louis XIV', was greatly inferior to prose for conveying a clear idea of the diverse states of our consciousness ('les mouvements du coeur').

And at that moment the serious art of writing 'went over to prose', and for some time the important developments of language as a means of expression were the developments of prose.[54]

Though Pound finds his key moment in France, there is plenty of evidence to suggest something very similar had already happened in England between 1820 and 1830 with the death or silence of all the great Romantic poets. Keats had died in 1821, Shelley in 1822, Byron in 1824, Blake in 1827, Coleridge in 1834, and though the apparently indestructible Wordsworth survived until 1850, his major life's work, the body of poetry that was to modify so profoundly the consciousness of the English-speaking world, had been completed long before 1820.[55] In England, Thomas Love Peacock (1785–1866), an almost exact contemporary of Stendhal (1783–1842), had noticed the fact a decade before his French counterpart in a strangely ironic and prophetic essay, *The Four Ages of Poetry* (1820).[56] Ostensibly with the aim of attacking the Lake Poets ('that egregious confraternity of rhymesters') Peacock gives a new twist to the familiar eighteenth-century argument that poetry is a more ancient and fundamental form than prose. This is illustrated, he says, by the way in which poetry has progressively ceased to be the prime vehicle for conveying either facts or ideas:

As the sciences of morals and of mind advance towards perfection, as they become more and more enlarged and comprehensive in their views, as reason gains the ascendancy in them over imagination and feeling, poetry can no longer accompany them in their progress, but drops into the background, and leaves them to advance alone.

Thus the empire of thought is withdrawn from poetry, as the empire of facts had been before.[57]

Though this is, in fact, only a restatement of an argument that goes back to Vico,[58] and which had become commonplace by the beginning of the nineteenth century,[59] Peacock's ironic use of it is altogether different in that it is argued not from a proto-sociological position, but from a literary standpoint. His argument is, in effect a complete inversion of the German historical method. Whereas historians such as Niebuhr, for instance, had stressed the 'poetic' nature of early historical accounts of Rome in order to show their primitiveness as *history*, Peacock, specifically alluding to Vico, does so to show the primitiveness of *poetry*. He thus provides his own tongue-in-cheek gloss on the 'extensive' tradition of poetics stemming from Dennis. Since poets were 'regarded as portions and emanations of divinity; building cities with a song, and leading brutes with a symphony; which are only metaphors for the faculty of leading multitudes by the nose . . .'[60] their claim to primacy is *ipso facto* a claim to obsolescence. The truths of poetry must, Peacock insists, be judged by the same standards as any other kind of truth – and if we do so, poetry will be found inadequate:

Poetry was the mental rattle that awakened the attention of intellect in the infancy of civil society; but for the maturity of mind to make a serious business of the play-things of its childhood, is as absurd as for a full-grown man to rub his gums with coral, and to be charmed to sleep by the jingle of silver bells.[61]

In fact, of course, Peacock did *not* believe this. He was himself a minor, if unsuccessful poet, and we know from his novels that he did not believe in the kind of 'moral' and 'intellectual' progress that he is wickedly assuming here. *The Four Ages* is, in effect, a *defence* of poetry – on the lines of the anonymous eighteenth-century pamphlet, variously attributed to Pope and Swift, *The Art of Sinking in Poetry*. Just as Swift in *A Modest Proposal* or *An Argument Against Abolishing Christianity* had blandly advocated cannibalism and atheism in order to show how (in a sense) they were already built into the fabric of his society, so Peacock casually details the growing irrelevance of poetry precisely because he fears that is what really *is* happening. *The Four Ages* provoked, as Peacock intended it should,[62] his friend Shelley into reply: a reply that has become more famous than the challenge – *The Defence of Poetry*. But Shelley's 'defence' is, in its way, as alarming as Peacock's 'attack'. The logical conclusion of the 'extensive' tradition of eighteenth-century poetics was to obliterate the formal distinction between prose and verse, so that the great minds of all ages, from Plato to Bacon, may be enlisted as 'poets', while conversely Dante, Shakespeare and Milton may appear as 'philosophers of the very loftiest power'. Indeed, claims Shelley, 'all the authors of revolutions in opinion are necessarily poets as they are inventors'.[63] Shelley's 'defence' is to sever the last link between 'poetry' and 'verse'.

Yet Peacock's model, ironic as it appears to have been in intention, was uncannily prophetic of the future development of literary sensibility. Though his contemporaries included some of the greatest novelists and essayists in English literature – Scott and Jane Austen, Hazlitt, Lamb and De Quincey, for instance – it remains true nevertheless that poetry was still assumed to be the central literary art form of the age. Scott is an interesting case in point. Though most of his not inconsiderable income came from his novels, he was thought of by his contemporaries primarily as a poet – the author of *The Lay of the Last Minstrel* (1805), *Marmion* (1808) and the *Lady of the Lake* (1810). It is, of course, easy to be knowledgeable about literary trends with the aid of hindsight. What we see as the richness of the age in prose would simply not have been apparent to those who automatically thought of poetry as the dominant form and of Samuel Rogers as the greatest poet of the age. Yet the question of status is also connected with subject matter. Poetry was where it was assumed that the major aesthetic, religious, and philosophic debates of the day were to be encountered. Prose merely reflected social reality. Peacock himself, remembered and read now as an exquisitely subtle prose-writer and author of some of the most witty satires in the language, had also published long poems (quite unknown today) such as *Rododaphne*. Even while he proved more sensitive than his contemporaries to the shifting balance, he was still in no doubt that prose was the inferior form.

The career of Coleridge is even more significant. His actual poetic phase spans less than six out of his sixty years. To many contemporaries, as to many Victorians, he was principally a prose-writer. As such he is a disturbingly perfect example of Peacock's satirical thesis. It is in his prose that we find the 'serious' aesthetic, religious, and philosophic discussions; his verse, written almost all before the age of 30, seemed to many occasional, fantastic, and escapist. It is Coleridge the author of *Church and State* that Mill compares with Bentham as one of the great 'seminal minds' of the age, not Coleridge the poet.[64] If Shelley's *Defence* seems, with hindsight, to have sold the pass, it was perhaps an acknowledgement that the poets were already outflanked. Tennyson and Browning are great poets, but they are not as central to the Victorian age as, say, Dickens or George Eliot. When we wish to understand the Romantics, we read the poets; when we wish to understand the Victorians we read first of all the prose. Moreover it is perhaps no accident that the 'extensive' idea of the poetic as a quality of all linguistic activity, should have been pressed most fervently by the

Anglo-Germans Bunsen and Müller, just at the point when prose was being seen for the first time as the dominant literary art-form. The convention of Victorian prose realism could be taken as the natural heir to the social realism of Wordsworth and the philosophic and creative power claimed by Shelley.

Such has been its unconscious conditioning power on nineteenth and twentieth-century biblical critics that it is easy to assume for prose realism a monolithic cultural and philosophic coherence that it did not actually possess. Recent studies of Dickens, for instance, have stressed the degree to which his writing relied on an older emblematic and even typological tradition of the fantastic and the grotesque.[65] If we accept David Lodge's definition of 'realism' as 'the representation of experience in a manner which approximates closely to description of similar experience in a non-literary text of the same culture'[66] then it is easy to see why for so many critics the norm of prose realism is to be found in George Eliot's novels. We have already seen how, in *Scenes of Clerical Life*, 'fact' and 'fiction' are conventionally interchangeable. Philosophically, as a disciple of Feuerbach and Comte, she is a committed materialist in a sense that Dickens never was, and few other novelists approached. Her novels are rooted in a natural supernaturalism more thoroughgoing than anything in Carlyle. As a result artistic form is dependent on philosophic content in a way that is peculiarly vulnerable. In the course of a discussion of Mary Shelley's secularization of the creation myth in *Frankenstein*, George Levine makes a pregnant aside:

As George Eliot turned to Feuerbach to allow her to transform Christianity into a humanism with all the emotional power of religion, so the novel itself, as a genre, put its faith in a material world of fact that, as Matthew Arnold pointed out, had failed us.[67]

This is a paradox he returns to explore more extensively in his book *The Realistic Imagination*. His interest in Mary Shelley is, we discover, not so much a fascination with the bizarre and Gothic side of the nineteenth-century imagination as a critical and philosophic preoccupation with the shifting conventions of "realism" itself.

'My concern', he writes, 'is not with a definition of 'realism', but with a study of its elusiveness.'[68] This elusive quarry is not to define any tactical or specialist sense of the word (such as the late-century 'realisms' of Zola or Gissing) but with the kind of general umbrella proposed by David Lodge. It is a literary ideal Levine sees as broadly common to Jane Austen, Scott, Thackeray, George Eliot, Trollope, Hardy, and even Conrad. Yet, from the first, it was an ideal that contained within itself the seeds of its own destruction. 'Despite its appearance of solidity', Levine suggests, 'realism implies a fundamental uneasiness about self, society, and art.'[69] As we have seen, it is no accident that such a theoretical concept should have emerged at the very point when the twin linguistic processes of internalization and individuation should have made the idea of an objective common reality highly problematic.[70] As Levine puts it:

> It was not a solidly self-satisfied vision based on a misguided objectivity and faith in representation, but a highly self-conscious attempt to explore or create a new reality. Its massive self-confidence implied a radical doubt.[71]

The novelist's process of coming to terms in words with the world 'as it is' was ultimately as chimerical as the parallel attempt (so brilliantly exposed by Gombrich[72]) of the visual arts to paint an unequivocal and objective reality. The collapse of visual realism at the end of the nineteenth century was closely paralleled by a similar collapse of literary confidence in a common perception of the individual in his relationship to nature and to society. What at one level had made itself felt in Jane Austen or Scott as no more than an ambivalence about established authority, gradually intruded itself as the century progressed as an increasingly sharp moral conflict between the individual and the external world in such very different novelists as Eliot, Thackeray, and Trollope, and finally in the late nineteenth-century cosmic pessimism of Hardy, and in Conrad's feeling that ultimately reality was incompatible with the human mind itself. 'The Victorian realists had put their faith in "fact", and the fact had failed them.'[73]

As always, a changing view of nature implies a corresponding shift in aesthetics. Mrs Moore's experience in the Marabar cave was, in this sense, perhaps much more than the final destruction of an optimistic or meaningful view of nature; it suggests also a collapse of the common 'world of fact' as the nineteenth century had tried to create it in its fictional worlds. Mrs Radcliffe and Conan Doyle, writing at the two ends of the century had this at least in common; both believed staunchly in the world of fact. However mysterious and arbitrary events in *The Mysteries of Udolpho* or the Sherlock Holmes stories might appear, there is always a full and entirely rational explanation forthcoming in the end. By contrast, in *A Passage to India*, we never do find out exactly what had happened to Adela Quested in the cave. The legal question

of 'fact' – whether Aziz is or is not 'guilty' – is never explictly
resolved. The central fact of the novel's plot remains at least formally
ambiguous. All the human schemata, hypotheses, and constructs to
discover the nature of our enviroment – all our detective-work to find
out 'what happened' – is met by the same empty, relentless, stifling
echo: 'boum'. Everything exists – meaning is what you make of it.

We encounter here the full oddity of a paradox that has dogged the
whole history of our idea of nature. The traditional 'dualistic' view of
nature implicit in the Elijah story and explicit in Dante, however difficult or odd it might appear, served in some not-easily discernible way
to uphold the world of fact. We are reminded of John Wisdom's observation that certain 'way out', extreme, paradoxical or bafflingly contradictory statements seem to exert a very peculiar logical influence
over our schemes of normality.[74] He cites the traditional
philosopher's example of the table which appears solid and serviceable,
and yet which is also, we are now reliably informed, a mere regulated
pattern of rapidly rotating particles of energy. The assertion that the
table can be *both* may be difficult to accept at first sight, yet the reason
for holding such an apparently contradictory belief is that only in this
way can we explain certain peculiarities in the behaviour of matter.
Nor should we think of the solidity as a quality puzzlingly detached
from the molecular structure. We have grown accustomed to different
scales of description each with its own perspective and level of focus.
Against all apparent probability, we find that in practice such beliefs
can and do serve as affirmations of order. The paradox is essentially
conservative, in that it is not designed to create difficulties but to reaf-
firm an order that transcends particular peculiarities. Similarly, we
may observe that historically the story of Elijah, with its emphasis on
God as *outside* and, in some undefinable sense, over against nature has
always served to affirm the reality of nature. The material world of earthquakes, fire, and wind, however we may perceive it, is nevertheless
actually *there*, tangible and even dangerous; it is not a veil or illusion,
nor the plaything of arbitrary magical forces. In contrast, the 'Marabar
revelation' – the symbolic embodiment of the Feuerbachian
humanism of George Eliot or Matthew Arnold – eventually undermines that very sense of order alike in nature and aesthetics. Though
it has taken nearly a century for the implications to become apparent
in the work of Barthes, Foucault, and Derrida, the end result is a loss
of that vital balance between text and reader that had been the basis

of traditional hermeneutics. If all is in the reader, all is relative, all is equal. A laundry-list is no different from literature. All principles of interpretation are equally valid or invalid – including that one.

Yet, once again, in the collapse of one system, or paradigm, the ever-present potential of breakthrough becomes, momentarily at any rate, an actuality. So long as prose realism was, consciously or unconsciously, felt to be the natural inheritor of the Romantic poetic tradition, and a hitherto unrivalled vehicle for describing a common and scientifically verifiable 'objective' world of fact, there was little possibility of perceiving that it, too, was a literary convention. The so-called 'world of fact' was not a direct means of perceiving things-in-themselves but, like other previous paradigms, a way of organizing appearances that served certain useful purposes. From its collapse was to emerge not another all-embracing system substituting its own claim to 'truth' for that of the preceeding convention, but a recognition and exploration of convention itself. The novels of James Joyce, Franz Kafka, Virginia Woolf, Nathalie Sarraute, Alain Robbe-Grillet, Günter Grass, John Fowles, or Thomas Pynchon all depend not on particular artistic conventions, but on exploring points of intersection between different conventions – the moments when the existing conventions become inadequate or fail. Similarly, it has become a commonplace to observe that twentieth-century poetry has made a central theme of its own aesthetic discontinuities: 'These fragments', wrote T. S. Eliot 'have I shored against my ruin.' *The Waste Land* is well-known. It has, perhaps, been less often noted that the central structure of Eliot's *Four Quartets*, which are based upon what he calls 'moments of grace', is that of what Wordsworth called 'spots of time' – the essentially biblical pattern of historical moments of breakdown and regeneration.

At this point, it is, perhaps, worth recalling the actual passage of Matthew Arnold that Levine made so central to his argument:

The future of poetry is immense, because in poetry where it is worthy of its high destinies, our race, as time goes on, will find an ever surer and surer stay. There is not a creed which is not shaken, not an accredited dogma which is not shown to be questionable, not a received tradition which does not threaten to dissolve. Our religion has materialized itself in the fact, and in the supposed fact; it has attached its emotion to the fact, and now the fact is failing it. But for poetry the idea is everything; the rest is a world of illusion, of divine illusion. Poetry attaches its emotions to the idea; the idea *is* the fact. The strongest part of our religion today is its unconscious poetry.[75]

'Poetry', as we have seen, for Arnold is not a matter of form *or* of content, but of approach. It is a matter of 'so dealing with things as to awaken in us a wonderfully full, new, and intimate sense of them, and of our relations with them':

... it interprets by expressing, with magical felicity, the physiognomy and movement of the outward world, and it interprets by expressing, with inspired conviction, the ideas and laws of the inward world of man's moral and spiritual nature.[76]

If this captures with some sensitivity that constant need for rejuvenation and renewal which, as we have seen, has always been an essential quality of the history of European poetry, it is also typical of Arnold to combine this with a denial of the power of poetry to convey fact. For him, poetry is not about fact, but *feeling*. Arnold the reluctant materialist has no place in his system for what Coleridge had called 'facts of mind'. Nor does Kant's demolition of empiricism ever seem to have impinged on his consciousness. The worlds of matter and mind remain separated for ever by an unbridgeable gulf. Facts had failed us not because they had been discovered to be culturally variable, and subject to the relativities of human perception, but because they remained stubbornly independent of our ways of seeing them. Christianity had claimed to be founded upon a historical fact: the supreme miracle of the resurrection – but 'miracles do not happen'. They are *Aberglaube*; the resurrection is 'poetry' not 'fact'. Significantly, Levine's quotation from Arnold alters the final pronoun. 'Facts' have not failed 'us': 'fact is failing *it*' – that is, 'Religion'. Thus Arnold is not, in this passage, pointing out the failure of prose realism to establish a satisfactory common world of material fact, but acknowledging sadly that the poetry of religious belief has finally foundered on the rock of scientific materialism.

Though this does not alter what seems to me to be the essential truth of Levine's case, it *does* alter substantially Arnold's role in it. He is not some proto-modernist, proclaiming the imminent collapse of the dominant literary convention, but a poet, struggling to articulate what he *feels* rather than knows to be an irreducible difference between poetry and prose realism which has been lost or overlooked in the attempt to hail prose as the appropriate poetic medium of the Victorian age. *Something* of value had been left out of account in the new synthesis:

More and more mankind will discover that we have to turn to poetry to interpret life for us, to console us, to sustain us. Without poetry, our science will appear incomplete; and most of what now passes with us for religion and philosophy will be replaced by poetry.[77]

It would be easy here to say simply that Arnold was wrong: that the hope that one day science, religion, and philosophy would all appear incomplete without poetry was mere whistling in the dark. Yet, before we do so, we should perhaps consider again Arnold's elusive and curiously convoluted attempts to define what he means by 'poetry'. It is as if the word is constantly trying to bear a greater weight than he will consciously (or, at least, rationally) permit it to carry. Each attempt to deny to it cognitive content leaves us at the end with the impression that *something* – and perhaps more than he intended – has survived in the residue beyond mere emotion. We recall the similar way in which Arnold's definitions of God always seem, as on an asymptotic curve, to be approaching Feuerbachian atheism, but always leave us still with a lurking uncertainty as to whether the 'not-ourselves which makes for righteousness' might not enjoy a transcendence sufficient to make it suspiciously like the God of Abraham, of Isaac, and of Jacob after all. It would be easy to assume that this seeming unwillingness to be more precise is the typical final manoeuvre of a piously brought-up Victorian who has lost his faith but lacks the intellectual courage of a George Eliot to come out and say so. Yet there may be something more complex at work in Arnold's tortuous ambiguities. We recall also the surprising connections between Arnold and Vico – and that Vico's 'human' science of history always retained a shadowy presence, an 'immanent will' or divine thread running through it and shaping it in ways not fully understood by its protagonists. Once again, this *may* be no more than a redundant gesture in the direction of an older, God-centred, view of history that Vico was too intellectually timid (or prudent) to dispense with altogether. The Feuerbachian interpretation of Vico would be difficult to disprove. It is the logical conclusion if one accepts that his idea of the 'poetic' is wholly a description of a primitive and archaic state of mind. And yet, as we saw in Chapter 2, such an account of Vico leaves out the no less important point that his notion of the 'poetic' is linked with the quite central idea of man as a creative being, who only understands by *making* things. Human creativity is, to paraphrase Coleridge, a repetition in the finite mind of the eternal act of creation by a God whose very nature is to create. Similarly, one suspects that the reason why Arnold cannot finally embrace a Feuerbachian humanism and continues to assert a *meaning* in poetry that does not seem to be justified by a poetics based on feeling alone, is that all human creativity, for him, remains a fundamentally 'poetic' activity. What we see in Arnold is, as it were, a profoundly traditional poetic sensibility uneasily coupled with a Victorian rationalist mentality. He was only too conscious of the ways in which 'fact' was failing 'religion'. At the level of historical enquiry the appeal to a miracle which supposedly lay at the root of Christianity had been met by Hume, Feuerbach, and Strauss; 'history', as it had come to be defined, could not be cognizant of the radically unrepeatable event. At a linguistic level he was also aware that the language of descriptive prose was itself inadequate to discuss religion. The 'religion' so circumscribed was not the thing he was 'poetically' conscious of. The distinction is precisely that Vichian one between creativity and alienation: religion cannot satisfactorily be described from the outside in terms of facts; it does not belong to the world of objectivity but to that of participation.

The change in the meaning of the word 'fact' seemed with peculiar irony to illustrate this point. Arnold almost invariably uses the word in its normal nineteenth-century sense, which is also our modern one, as the term for something that is 'demonstrably the case' in what he conceives of as an objective and scientific sense. Yet its original meaning in the sixteenth century (the O.E.D. lists its first use in 1539), reflecting its Latin root, *factum*, was 'a thing done, or performed', making it cognate with 'feat' – a use that had persisted alongside the later meaning until the beginning of the nineteenth century. So far from denoting objectivity, this original meaning was essentially participatory. A 'fact' was something *made* by human agency. Commenting on this reversal of meanings, Alasdair MacIntyre writes:

> The notion of 'fact' with respect to human beings is thus transformed in the transition from the Aristotelian to the mechanist view. On the former view human action, because it is to be explained teleologically, not only can, but must be, characterised with reference to the hierarchy of goods which provide the ends of human action. On the latter view human action not only can, but must be, characterised without any reference to such goods. On the former view the facts about human action include the facts about what is valuable to human beings (and *not* just the facts about what they think to be valuable); on the latter view there are no facts about what is valuable. 'Fact' becomes value-free, 'is' becomes a stranger to 'ought' and explanation, as well as evaluation.[78]

By Arnold's time the word was well on the way towards the curious process of disintegration that we observed surrounding the incident in the Marabar caves – and its legal aftermath. With the progressive evacuation of meaning, the shrinking residue, so far from exhibiting an ever-denser objective hardness and clarity, recedes into the ultimate impenetrability of Kantian 'things-in-themselves'. It is as if the actual word undergoes the process Arnold attributes to the concept. The root meaning, of something 'done' or 'made', carried with that implicit suggestion of creativity the shadowy potential of that other shaping spirit – the 'not-ourselves' haunting every creative act. With the last spark of human participation finally extinguished the word itself begins to lose credibility. 'What is a *fact*?' becomes a legitimate topic of philosophic debate as it begins its Snark-like disappearance from view.

Though he might not have foreseen its twentieth-century progress, Arnold, with his classical education, was well enough aware of the dramatic shift in meaning already shown by the word, and even seems to be playing on it in the course of the argument quoted earlier:

Our religion has materialized itself in the fact, and in the supposed fact; it has attached its emotion to the fact, and now the fact is failing it. But for poetry the idea is everything; the rest is a world of illusion, of divine illusion. Poetry attaches its emotions to the idea; the idea *is* the fact.

Something of his dilemma can be seen in that unexpected twist of the last sentence. I remarked earlier that Arnold's description of poetry seemed to deny it all cognitive content. Clearly, if we take the word 'cognitive' in its full latinate sense this is untrue: poetry *does* provide, even by his definition, 'knowledge' of a kind. What it does not do, however, is provide the kind of 'knowledge' of things in the externalized scientific sense that, increasingly, was the only sense in which the nineteenth century was prepared to interpret the word 'fact'. Clearly, whatever other kinds of knowledge we go to them for, we do not go to the *Iliad*, the *Divine Comedy*, or *Paradise Lost*, for an accurate scientific world-picture. That there might be other kinds of 'facts' (like Coleridge's 'facts of mind') is something that Arnold seems frequently to be quite oblivious of. Here, however, in a sudden semantic twist, Arnold makes the connection in such a way as to leave us uncertain. Is he saying that the 'idea' of poetry is *itself* a 'fact' to be reckoned with in his normal objective sense of the word? – an undeniable but not very startling point; or is he saying that the central 'idea' of poetry, as distinct from science, is inseparable from the fact that it is something made and participated in by us? – for Arnold, a much more significant admission. Empson has taught us to suspect in such cases of radical ambiguity a correspondingly radical uncertainty in the writer's mind.[79]

If that hypothesis is correct, Arnold's uncertainty is not peculiar to himself, but is, as it were, a litmus for his age. The apparent certainties of literary realism were in a process of dissolution from its inception.

It is one of the supreme ironies of nineteenth-century biblical criticism, including Arnold's own, that it was to be seduced by the norms of a particular narrative convention as representing 'reality' at the very moment when its inadequacies were beginning to reveal that it, too, was no more than one convention among others. In spite of – or, perhaps, because of – their scholarly excellence in the narrowly specialist sense, the revitalized schools of theology in England and Germany were to be more influenced by the apparent certainties of contemporary literary criticism than by the hesitant, but more profound, expressions of uncertainty. In so doing they set in motion once more the age-old dialectic of disconfirmation.

The immediate result, as Hans Frei notes, was that:

> Commentators, especially those influenced by historical criticism, virtually to a man, failed to understand what they had seen when they had recognised the realistic character of biblical narratives, because every time they acknowledged it they thought this was identical with affirming not only the history-likeness but also a degree of historical likelihood in the stories.
> . . . in effect, the realistic or history-like quality of biblical narratives, acknowledged by all, instead of being examined for the bearing it had in its own right on meaning and interpretation was immediately transposed into the quite different issue of whether or not the realistic narrative was historical.[80]

But even Frei, however, though well aware of the distinction between realistic narrative and history, seems less conscious of the way in which *both* depend upon the conventional nexus of ideas associated with the nineteenth-century notion of 'nature'.

His own parallels between narrative and the conventions of realistic prose fiction are, as he shows, in reaction to the traditional German disregard of fictional narrative as an acceptable art form.[81] As a result he is much less clear about the degree to which, as we have seen in discussing Northrop Frye's similar distinction in relation to George Eliot's *Scenes of Clerical Life*,[82] prose realism is itself a highly problematic convention. These problems moreover, are compounded by the tendency in both Frei and Frye to assume an essentialist view of 'history' and 'historical fact'. At the other extreme, a critic like Robert Alter, in *The Art of Biblical Narrative*, is prepared to assume for the Old Testament narratives a direct correspondence with prose fiction.[83] The real question, however, is not whether, or how far, the biblical narratives can be approximated to realistic prose narrative, which may or may not correspond in turn to historical fact, but rather what does it *mean* to compare biblical narrative with prose fiction, and what do we *mean* in this instance by 'historical fact', bearing in mind that realistic prose fiction was a nineteenth-century attempt to create a common and seemingly objective perspective on a world already prone to subjective fragmentation, and that the corresponding notion of 'history' was no less culturally biased along certain positivist and materialist lines? Frei does not seem fully aware that what he calls the 'eclipse of biblical narrative' is in fact part of a much wider collapse of confidence in traditional notions of both narrative and history.

If fact had failed religion, the question of whether poetry could sustain it was an altogether more complex matter; what was obvious at any rate was that prose realism was not going to save it.

5
Metaphor and reality

Even such a brief and necessarily incomplete survey as that of the last three chapters suggests something of the complexity of the idea of the 'poetic' in the past few hundred years. Merely the fact that it can, and has been, invoked by representatives of such essentially different exegetical traditions as Nineham and Ricoeur indicates the range of the diverse positions it can be used to support. Moreover such divergences are not a matter of twentieth-century confusions of an originally simple idea: they continue ambiguities that were *always* present. We only have to look at the contrasts between Vico and Dennis, Coleridge and Arnold, to see how the 'poetic' has always contained opposite connotations of primitiveness and sophistication, falsification and insight, picture-language and symbolic truth.

What bearing, then, does this complex web of apparently contradictory notions have on the problems with which we began? — the seeming inability of modern translators of all persuasions to cope with a difficult passage of the Old Testament. That inability, we discovered, stemmed in part at any rate from the inadequacy of current conceptual models for dealing with cultural change and the emergence of the 'new'. This failure has had profound and traumatic consequences for biblical interpretation and translation. Indeed, it is hardly over-stating the case to say that in the last three hundred years it has become *the* central problem of biblical criticism. It is no accident that the process of discovering the Bible as 'poetic' should have coincided historically with the breakdown of the older typological models of exegesis, and the beginnings of the modern crisis of hermeneutics — a crisis that, for purposes of convenience and coherence, we have focused in the discussion of a single problematic biblical story: that of Elijah on Horeb. What bearing can a concept from literary criticism have on this crisis?

To understand this question, we need first of all to stand it on its head. The contemporary crisis in hermeneutics affects a much wider field than biblical criticism. If, on the one hand, we have Dennis Nineham claiming that 'there is nothing properly described as "*the* meaning" of the Bible',[1] we have Terry Eagleton, on the other, concluding that there is no such thing as literary theory either:

> It is an illusion first in the sense that literary theory . . . is really no more than a branch of social ideologies, utterly without any unity or identity which would adequately distinguish it from philosophy, linguistics, psychiatry, cultural and sociological thought; and secondly in the sense that the hope it has of distinguishing itself – clinging to an object named literature – is misplaced.[2]

This is not the place to discuss Eagleton's general thesis. He might or might not be disposed to argue with the comment that each of the above disciplines could doubtless be deconstructed into a similar combination of the others; any discipline is in part an arbitrary construct – a tool rather than a platonic form. But that is beside his point, which is that as the study of literature has become increasingly, even desperately, eclectic in its ideas and methods, so it has also suffered an internal crisis of confidence over what its proper constituency should be. Yet there is no doubt historically where that constituency began. As Eagleton himself points out earlier in the same essay, English, as a literary discipline, developed in the nineteenth century out of what he calls 'the failure of religion'. He does not take the further step of adding that, as we have seen in the last three chapters, literary theory was in the first place a direct offshoot of biblical criticism. Its origins (like, incidentally, those of linguistics, psychiatry, and a great deal of philosophy) lie in the application to secular works of techniques and ways of thinking originally developed to deal with classical and biblical texts – and, as we have seen, for instance, in the evolution of the idea of the sublime, it is impossible to draw a sharp distinction between the two sources. What is abundantly clear, however, is that the separation of traditional literary concepts from their biblical roots by the *Gletscherwall* of the Humboldtian university reforms of the early nineteenth century, was in the long run as damaging to literary theory as it was to biblical studies. To discuss biblical hermeneutics in the light of poetic theory is not to apply an alien concept, but to restore a wholeness of approach that has been disastrously fragmented over the past hundred and fifty years.

There are two corollaries to this. The first is the very simple one that theology, like many amputees, has become painfully aware of the ache in its missing limb. The last few years have witnessed a spate of books attempting to link some aspect of literary critical theory with biblical or religious studies.[3] In more general terms, it is clear that some theologians – Hans Frei, for instance, or Robert W. Funk – are explicitly looking to literary theory as offering a way out of the current hermeneutical stalemate. Whether such expectations are justified is another question, but there can be no doubt as to the relevance to theology of developments in poetic and critical theory over the past three hundred years.

Contrariwise, the relevance of biblical criticism to literary theory can, in historical terms, scarcely be overestimated. Eagleton's polemical statement that literary studies developed in England out of the 'failure of religion' contains rather more than the predictable half-truth. It is, at any rate, *one* of the reasons why the study of English literature was to acquire in the early part of this century moral and even semi-evangelical overtones that never afflicted literary studies in continental Europe. It was part of a spirit that T. E. Hulme was to castigate scornfully as 'romanticism'. What it turns out he meant by this unusual use of the term is specifically a certain brand of humanist optimism 'that man, the individual, is an infinite reservoir of possibilities':

Just as in the case of the other instincts, Nature has her revenge. The instincts that find their right and proper outlet in religion must come out in some other way. You don't believe in a God, so you begin to believe that man is a God. You don't believe in Heaven, so you begin to believe in a heaven on earth. In other words you get romanticism. The concepts that are right and proper in their own sphere are spread over, and so mess up, falsify and blur the clear outlines of human experience. It is like pouring a pot of treacle over the dinner table. Romanticism then, and this is the best definition I can give of it, is spilt religion.[4]

Hulme's 'romanticism', like Eagleton's proclamation of the death-of-literature, is not unaffected by the desire to shock, but it does highlight an important truth: that literary critics, even when disowning their begetter, theology, have never quite lost their sense that they are somehow still in the salvation business.[5] Eagleton's own writing has we notice a moral urgency, even a stridency, that would look odd for, say, a music critic.

Yet this inherited, but largely unacknowledged, genetic tendency is hardly the whole story. As we saw earlier, language is not itself value-free. To use an appropriate piece of Kantian terminology, language can be seen as inherently 'religious' in a *regulative* sense, but not in a *constitutive* one. That is, it raises what another theologian has called

questions of 'ultimate significance', without, of course, implying
answers – which are a matter of whatever philosophy or theology any
particular person or group happens to be influenced by. We should be
naive, however, in not recognizing that English, for instance, is saturated
with Protestant Christian, or, in some cases post-Christian, values and
connotations. It is, one imagines, a difficult language in which to practise
Buddhism. Nevertheless, it is not *impossible* to be a Buddhist, a Taoist, or
even a member of the Aetherius Society in excellent English. Indeed, we
recall that it is the introduction of alien concepts, for which no adequate
equivalent exists, that has the greatest effect upon the development of a
language.[6] Similarly, at a meta-linguistic level, however we choose to
define literature – or even if we deny its existence – criticism and
critical theory show a marked tendency to concentrate on those works
and themes of long-term interest to substantial sections of the human
race. If literary criticism shows an inclination to be more moralizing
than, say, music criticism, it is also partly because literature itself is more
obviously and overtly concerned with ideas of morality in the first place[7]

If we look at the idea of the 'poetic' in terms of its eighteenth-century
ancestry, however, it is easy to see why the modern preoccupation with
the question, 'What is literature?', did not arise. While debates about the
status of contemporary works were as fierce, or fiercer, than any
twentieth-century ones, classical and biblical texts were accepted as
given. Though there might be a growing penumbra of sub-biblical
literature that was considered worthy of study to a greater or lesser
degree, forgeries to be investigated, new discoveries to be assessed, or problems of authorship to be decided – the unity of the *Pentateuch*, for
instance, or Philo to be distinguished from pseudo-Philo – the existence
of the main corpus could not be in doubt; nor could the importance of
studying it. 'The Reformation, after all,' writes Edmund Carey, 'was
primarily a dispute between translators.'[8] Though the Bible may now be
read 'as any other book', modern debates have not altered this central
hermeneutical quest. Christianity has always been, right from its inception, peculiarly, even introvertedly, interested in the manifold
possibilities of meaning implicit in its own writings. As Ricoeur asks:

Why has Christian preaching chosen to be hermeneutic by binding itself to the
rereading of the Old Testament? Essentially to make the event itself appear, not
as an irrational irruption, but as the fulfillment of an antecedent meaning which
remained in suspense... This signifying relation attests that the kerygma, by this
detour through the reinterpretation of an ancient Scripture, enters into a network
of intelligibility. The event becomes advent.[9]

It has always been a hermeneutical religion. There has always persisted that sense of 'antecedent meaning' waiting in suspense to be called forth by the event. The process of historical interpretation occasioned by the study of every text is not a fortuitous accident, a custom that has grown up over the years for contingent reasons, but is somehow central to historical Christianity. Thus the current debate over theories of translation, for example, is not a temporary modern phenomenon – a sign of spiritual or intellectual 'crisis' – but a particular manifestation of the normal hermeneutical activity of the Church. Similarly, the contemporary crisis in literary criticism over the nature of a text, and the relationship between the reader and what is read is, seen historically, no more than an extension of that activity into an unprepared secular world.

So long as all biblical interpretation was primarily typological, there could be no distinction between the figurative and the literal or historical. It is only with the rise of natural science in the seventeenth century, with its concomitant of the biblical literalism of such scientific divines as Craig, Wilkins, and Ussher, that we find also the need for *another* way of describing qualities in the text that were felt to be of permanent value. The separation of the 'poetic' as a literary quality, to be distinguished from the actual metrical forms of poetry, begins historically to emerge as a direct response to this perceived need to account for certain statements and narratives as being 'true' in some *other* sense than the literal, scientific, or historical, on the one hand, or the allegorical and typological on the other. The process is reflected in the accompanying desynonymy of 'history' and 'narrative'. Until sometime towards the end of the seventeenth century the two words meant virtually the same thing – both implying merely a story of some length. Those which purported to relate events which had actually happened were frequently prefixed by the term 'true'.[10] By the nineteenth century, partly as a result of the work of such great German historians as Ranke, the word 'history' had acquired its modern meaning, while 'narrative' and 'story' were tending increasingly to become technical terms within the general category of fiction. The word 'poetic', with its connotations of creativity and of an alternative kind of 'truth' from the unembellished recitation of events as they were perceived to have occurred, was, as we have seen, now increasingly used to validate the serious, or 'true-to-life', content of fiction or fictionalized narratives.

If Vico is more overtly concerned with applying this idea to classical rather than to biblical texts, Dennis pre-dates him with his specifically biblical emphasis. Herder and his German successors were able to draw on both English and Italian antecedents in developing and reifying this concept of the 'poetic' as a critical tool, but it should not be forgotten how much Herder himself remains directly rooted in biblical criticism. Both *The Spirit of Hebrew Poetry* and the *Essay on the Origin of Language* are grounded specifically in this need to describe that creative quality quintessentially to be found in poetry, yet which informs so much of human linguistic activity besides. That attempts to describe and define such an important quality should be ambiguous, at variance with each other, or even conflict, should not strike us as surprising; what is, perhaps, surprising is not the disagreement, but the areas of implied, tacit, or even explicit consensus. It is to this debate, with both its areas of agreement and controversy, that we must now turn if we are to assess its implications for the present state of biblical hermeneutics.

We have observed how *neither* what we have called the 'extensive' nor the 'intensive' meanings of the word 'poetic', have proved satisfactory. Both were, in effect, essentialist models, based on *a priori* notions either of the creative function of language, or of its supposedly primitive, non-cognitive, and emotive qualities. Though they appear as logical opposites, historically they have displayed a curious tendency to collapse into each other – especially in the context of those emotivist philosophies that have tended to view both language and values as being, at bottom, merely expressions of feeling.[11] The problem with all such essentialist models is that by stipulatively claiming to provide for all possible eventualities, they actually exclude the possibility of the really new and unpredictable. It was a line of argument Blake was familiar with:

From a perception of only 3 senses or 3 elements none could deduce a fourth or fifth.[12]

As none travelling over known lands can find out the unknown, so from already acquired knowledge Man could not acquire more; therefore an universal Poetic Genius exists.[13]

For Blake, as for his contemporary Romantic poets, the 'Poetic Genius', however unpredictable it might be in advance, was historical in the sense that, with hindsight, it revealed an ever-unfolding growth and development of human consciousness. So, too, for Coleridge:

'For if words are not THINGS, they are LIVING POWERS, by which the things of most importance to mankind are actuated, combined, and harmonized.'[14]

But if the 'Poetic Genius' is to be identified with the *logos* as a human manifestation of the 'living word' of God, it is important not to read that metaphor of 'life' in any *organic* sense. As Dorothy Emmet has nicely observed, there is a fundamental difference between organism and psyche.[15] The growth of an organism is continuous, depending on a constant environment without sharp changes or shocks; human growth – the growth of the mind – depends upon the ability to assimilate variety, discontinuity, and disconfirmation. When poetic language is described in terms of 'life' it is in that latter peculiar and disturbing sense. Its occasion is the moment of rawness when the familiar, known, and predictable collapses: when there emerges that for which there is no adequate equivalent or 'translation'. In proclaiming that 'The Jewish and Christian Testaments are An original derivation from the Poetic Genius'[16] Blake is similarly making explicit what was always implicit in the eighteenth-century rediscovery of the Bible as the source of the poetic sublime. Where Lowth had seen the Hebrew scriptures in their temporal and social context, Blake – having absorbed Lowth – is adding the immediate and necessary corollary that the 'true and lively word' spoken by the prophets transends context and speaks across the ages to his own time.

His idea of the 'Poetic Genius' shows how Blake had found in Lowth the seeds of a devastating critique of empiricist epistemology. Knowledge did not develop by the steady accretion of 'ideas', building from simple to complex association, but by discontinuities, disconfirmations, and sudden imaginative leaps and flashes of insight. Above all, what we mean by 'knowledge' is itself defined by the overall imaginative structure – by the suppositions we make and the questions we ask. The mind does not build from fragments, but works in wholes: 'More! More is the cry of a mistaken soul; less than ALL cannot satisfy Man.'[17]

The Romantic view of the scriptures in terms of growth and change was to transform the whole development of English poetry. But in Germany it did little to answer the nagging questions of historical fact that were being asked by the new generation of historical critics. To describe the biblical narratives in terms of a derivation of the 'Poetic Genius', or as 'living educts of the imagination' does not answer awkward questions about Joshua causing the sun to stand still or the raising of Lazarus. Such 'literary' responses did little to help nineteenth-century readers with what has become one of the oddest and seemingly most intractable problems of biblical narrative: that it *looks* realistic, but on investigation appears to stand in some oblique and not-easily-defined relationship to what is now generally conceived as 'history'. We recall Northrop Frye's engaging admission that 'the linguistic idiom of the bible does not really coincide' with any of the various phases he traces in the history of language. Nor does the solution suggested in different ways by Frye, Frei, and Alter, that biblical narrative be treated as realistic fiction, come any closer to providing an answer to the problem. As we saw in the last chapter, the idea that prose realism is in itself a natural and unproblematic medium providing a common approach to reality has also proved to be a chimera. We are left with the uncomfortable fact that biblical narrative can, in the twentieth century, *neither* be treated as history *nor* as realistic ('fact-like') fiction. It is at this point that we turn again to the concept of the 'poetic'.

Twentieth-century usages of the word have, by and large, taken it to imply a dissolving of reality in subjectivity – a connotation common to both modern-day positivists *and* to the contemporary exponents of the tradition stretching back through Heidegger to Vico, who assume the word to describe a primal and undifferentiated state of being in which subjective and objective are still indistinguishable parts of a common matrix. Ricoeur, we recall, sees the poetic as (in his distinctly unpoetic phraseology) 'restoring to us that participation in our belonging-to an order of things which precedes our capacity to oppose ourselves to things taken as objects opposed to a subject.'[18] The former view assumes a common objective reality in the present which the 'poetic' undermines or subverts by its blatant subjectivity, while the latter assume a common subjective reality in the past from which we stand alienated by the fragmented world of objective things. The former naively assumes the premises of nineteenth-century realism in a way that (as we have seen) is highly questionable; the latter, more subtly but equally questionably, assumes a kind of mirror-image of that 'realism' in a primal participation that is, by definition, now lost to us. Significantly, neither view connects the 'poetic' with creation of reality in the present. Yet, as we saw earlier, that is a theme central to the Romantic aesthetic tradition stemming from the Kantian rejection of empiricism.[19] For Blake, Wordsworth, and Coleridge, the imaginative 'leap' necessary to all perception was 'poetic' and essentially of a kind with the creative and originating power of the artist. For them, the 'poetic' was concerned not with a retreat from reality, but with helping to constitute it.

Two recent books illustrate, perhaps unwittingly, the implications of this point. The first concerns what is normally taken to be a dramatic fiction: A. D. Nuttall's *A New Mimesis: Shakespeare and the Representation of Reality*.[20] In this book Nuttall remarks on the underlying tension in Shakespeare's plays between what he calls the 'formalist' qualities (displayed in their ideological and theoretical structure) and the 'real' or mimetic (the degree to which they are 'true-to-life'). In *Henry IV*, for example, we have at the formal level an extended discussion of kingship – the conflicts of order and disorder, degree and anarchy, represented by the characters of Henry himself, Hal, and Falstaff. At the realistic level, however, Nuttall points out that there is, as it were, *another* story being told that is much more subversive and less reassuring: that Hal's formal role makes his behaviour *as a person*, in Falstaff's words at a famous crux in the text, 'madd'. 'Hal', writes Nuttall, 'is inside out. Instead of concealing his human features beneath a stiff, impersonal mask, he wears the golden mask of kingship beneath an ordinary, smiling human face.'[21] By any normal criteria such behaviour must rank as insane. The qualities of Tudor monarchist ideology, which any historical understanding of the play must recognize as central to its formal structure, are actively criticized and even subverted by what Nuttall sees as mimetic and poetic qualities in the dramatic representation.

My second example is Robert Alter's *The Art of Biblical Narrative*, published two years before Nuttall's book, in 1981. Alter observes how the author of the David stories stands in basically the same relationship to Israelite history as Shakespeare, in his history plays, stands to English history.[22] The accuracy of this parallel is suggestively illustrated, in a way he could not have foreseen, by his analysis of the narratives of David and Saul. What he discovers is a pattern closely akin to that identified by Nuttall as 'Shakespearian'; a double-motion between a theologically-determined scheme of cause-and -effect, and its constant subversion by a much more complex sense of character:

... causation in human affairs is itself brought into a paradoxical double focus by the narrative techniques of the Bible. The biblical writers obviously exhibit, on the one hand, a profound belief in a strong, clearly demarcated pattern of causation in history and individual lives, and many of the framing devices, the motif-structures, the symmetries and recurrences in their narratives reflect this belief. God directs, history complies; a person sins, a person suffers; Israel backslides, Israel falls. The very perception, on the other hand, of godlike depths, unsoundable capacities for good or evil, in human nature, also leads these writers to render their protagonists in ways that destabilize any monolithic system of causation, some of them complementary or mutually reinforcing, others even mutually contradictory.

. . . the underlying biblical conception of character as often unpredictable, in some ways impenetrable, constantly emerging from and slipping back into a penumbra of ambiguity, in fact has greater affinity with dominant modern notions than do habits of conceiving character typical of the Greek epics.[23]

In the story of David and Bathsheba, where their first-born child dies (II Samuel xii, 19–24), David's behaviour takes his own servants (and the reader) by surprise. When the child is dying he refuses all sustenance, fasting and sleeping on the ground. When it dies, however, David refuses to mourn in the conventional manner (which his previous behaviour had foreshadowed) but gets up, bathes, puts on fresh clothes, and has a meal. At his servants' unconcealed surprise he comments bitterly '. . . now that he is dead, why should I fast? Can I bring him back again? I am going to him but he will not come back to me.'[24] 'As readers', comments Alter, 'we are quite as surprised as the servants by David's actions, then his words, for there is very little in the narrative before this point that could have prepared us for this sudden, yet utterly convincing revelation of the sorrowing David, so bleakly aware of his own inevitable mortality as he mourns his dead son.'[25] Where Alter differs sharply from Nuttall is in the conceptual framework he applies to his observation. For him, this way of representing the world is a matter of conscious literary convention. 'The conception of biblical narrative as prose fiction which I have been proposing,' he writes, consciously or unconsciously echoing Eichhorn and Frei, 'entails an emphasis on deliberate artistry'.[26] In contrast, Nuttall, writing about what is unquestionably the deliberate artistry of Shakespeare, is interested in the pressure of the need for mimetic 'reality' on the schematized historical narrative. What Alter calls 'fiction' in the writing of biblical history, Nuttall sees as 'mimesis' in Shakespeare; what one sees as conscious invention, the other sees as reality.

At first sight Alter's terminology appears to have the greater common-sense plausibility. Yet a moment's reflection may suggest that the case is not so simple as it might appear. His model seems to rest on the familiar essentialist assumption that there is a *thing* called 'history' – a particular unequivocal sequence of events that in theory could (if only we had enough evidence) be known as it 'really happened' – and that the midrashic process of interpretation acts as a fictionalizing agent on that raw material of history. His position is that of Matthew Arnold. Nuttall's definition of 'mimesis', moreover, could be taken to support Alter's: 'its essence,' he writes, 'is the reconciliation of form with veridical or probable representation . . . mimesis is mimesis *of* something, or it is not mimesis. It exists in tense relation with that which is other than itself.'[27] Yet, in fact, there is a fundamental difference. In an earlier book, *A Common Sky*,[28] Nuttall's explicit preoccupation was with literary solipsism: the fear that if, as Locke had claimed, all we can know of things are their appearances, all knowledge is relative, subjective, and finally incommunicable. It represents a secret horror that has haunted literary representations of reality ever since Sterne, and whose footsteps, like those of a never-quite-banished childhood bogeyman, have stalked with muffled tread behind so many critical and historical debates since the early eighteenth century.[29] For Nuttall, as for Levine, the relationship between mimesis and 'that which is other than itself' – that thing we loosely call 'reality' – is of its very nature 'tense'. It is, as it were, under constant threat, and in a process of constant renewal. Now this tension is quite foreign to Alter's idea of 'fiction'; for him, the categories of 'history' and 'fiction' seem to be self-evidently distinct. His model of fiction is, in effect, a mode of explanation of problems in history.

Nuttall comes to the problem from the other side. For him it is not the subjective or imaginative side of Shakespearean narrative that is in doubt; nor is it the formalist; it is the relationship between that fictional construct and 'a common sky' – that tangible and universally recognizable element of common experience that is constantly and actively present in all fiction, modifying, and even undermining its 'official' programme in order to achieve *mimesis*. This is by no means a defence of nineteenth-century realism. '*Mimesis*' in Nuttall's sense would equally be present in the stylized and conventional forms of Jacobethan poetic drama, the nineteenth-century realistic novel, or twentieth-century fantasy.

Nuttall is fully prepared to concede that all knowledge is subject to specific cultural and historical perspectives. 'All representation of reality,' he writes, 'is conventionally ordered; it is never possible in a finite work to exhaust reality.'[30] His choice of the word *mimesis* to describe the relationship between the culturally-bound perspectives of the observer and what he is concerned to affirm as an independent reality (without inverted commas) is itself revealing. That word is, of course, Aristotle's term for 'imitation' in the *Poetics*. Nuttall's redeployment of the word in the quite different context of post-Kantian perceptual theory follows Blake and the other Romantics in acknowledging 'imitation' in this sense as being a creative and 'poetic' activity. *Mimesis* is no longer a matter of 'holding the mirror up to nature'; it is itself a matter of *creation*.[31]

'Reality' in this Romantic, almost phenomenological, sense, is not something scientifically quantifiable, independent of perception or unconditioned by the web of social, philosophic, and metaphysical assumptions that lie often below the threshold of consciousness but which help to constitute our particular 'perspective'. Scientific quantification is as much a human construct as an epic poem. This does not, equally, imply total subjectivity. We do not, as Hopkins observed, 'make rainbows by invention'. Without a common reality the notions of subjectivity and objectivity, truth or falsehood, fact or fiction, have no meaning.[32] We share a common world – not least in our common discovery of limitations. If our perceptions are culturally conditioned, they do not exist in a solipsistic vacuum. People are born and die – between which limiting experiences they have others of God or nature and of each other, and are, in part, determined by those delimitations which they attempt to express in language that, in turn, has to be interpreted by others in the light of their own experiences. Shakespeare's plays and the Bible may only be entered by each one of us by a personal act of 'translation'; they may be in themselves problematic and polysemous, but that does not imply they can mean anything we like – or have no meaning. E. H. Carr, writing of the study of history, once commented that 'the fact that a mountain looks different when seen from different angles does not mean either that it has no shape, or an infinity of shapes.' When Romantic poets and critics thought of the 'poetic' as helping to constitute reality, they were concerned with the mode of relationship between the perceiver and the perceived, primarily in so far as it was verbal, but, by extension, and analogy, with other non-verbal forms of perceptual schemata as well. Our ideas of 'history', whether of the Old Testament theocentric variety, the New Testament and typological, Shakespearean, or post-Ranke models are among the most important of these schemata, but our ideas of religion, philosophy, and nature are also constituents of the closely-woven pattern.

The original distinction between 'fiction' and 'realism' is thus, as we suspected, a matter of conceptual framework and perspective, not of content. They are, in effect, as Alter and Nuttall use them no more than two words for the *same* essentially 'poetic' process. But the difference in conceptual framework *is* a real and important one. The positions of Alter, Frei, and Frye, which assume the creation of deliberate 'fictions' in biblical narrative, are subtly but fundamentally opposed to that of Nuttall, who sees *mimesis* in terms of the creative gravitational pull, conscious or unconscious, of reality on an otherwise formal and philosophically schematized literary structure.

So far we have tended to think of the problem of historicity in biblical narrative in terms of two models. The first is that of the deliberate creation of 'fact-likeness' or verisimilitude – what George Eliot's readers (mistakenly) imagined they were getting in *Scenes of Clerical Life*. The second is that of Shakespeare in the History Plays, where he is bound by his sources to use the names of the real historical personages and to portray their relationships, in outline at least, as they were assumed to have been, but where he is free nevertheless to adjust the order of events, invent dialogue, compress time, and conflate incidents to satisfy either the formal or mimetic needs of his dramatic art. When Alter, for instance, compares the method of the Old Testament writers to that of the creation of prose 'fiction', which model is he invoking?

The answer does not matter, for the alternatives are false ones. Just as George Eliot's belief in the creation, by means of fiction, of a common world of prose 'realism' turned out to be, both in theory and in practice, a chimera, so the notion that Shakespeare created a fictional art out of the raw material of Holinshed's history is also unsustainable. 'History', whether secular or religious, for the sixteenth century was, we recall, essentially figurative and typological. What Shakespeare was creating in his plays *was* 'history'. He was providing the figures and types that had meaning from the raw material of events which, of themselves, without the interpretative schemata, had little significance. It is not the contrast between fact and fiction, but between chaos and form that is the appropriate one. He was not creating fiction but *meaning* – polysemous and many-sided, demanding in turn fluid responses and interpretation on the part of his audience.

Alter's own example of the story of David and Bathsheba's child illustrates admirably the dangers of a common-sense a-historical distinction between 'fact' and 'fiction'. Is it an instance of 'fictionalizing', *mimesis*, or actual 'history'? At a formal level the story construes the death of the child as divine punishment for David's adultery and the contrived death of Uriah, Bathsheba's former husband (II Samuel xii, 13–14); it takes David's actions and comment to cast doubt on this arbitrary 'justice' that demands the death of his innocent son. The implications reach right outside the moral schemata of the time. Only with the breakdown of the traditional principle of the extended family and the sense of group rather than individual identity does the idea of the sins of the fathers being visited on the children begin to seem inadequate. David's action suggests two things – both of which remain unstated. The first is that because God's justice is *moral* rather than arbitrary in the most straightforwardly dramatic sense (the death-sentence had orginally been pronounced by David himself in response to Nathan's allegory of the rich man and his poor neighbour) the only possible response is repentance. The second is that when the child dies, and it is seen that God is not to be pleaded with or bought off, David does not indulge in the expected mourning, but simply makes his oblique comment about God's will and human mortality. His bid has failed. The strange mixture of arbitrariness and dramatic justice leaves the reader oddly disturbed. Thus it is with a frisson neither exclusively literary nor historical that we realise on reflection that there *is* a strange typological half-echo to David's bitter reflections. As John points out, over an episode even more arbitrary and mysterious, God did not spare his son either. If one is so-minded, one can even trace a dim reverberation of David's agonized prayer and then calm acceptance of mortality in the garden of Gethsemane. But not even Eichhorn has suggested that the story of David antedates the gospels, or that the central drama of John's Gospel was composed to answer David's oblique suggestions of arbitrariness. Biblical realism, even at its most subversive, is never quite free of symbolic and typological overtones.

Yet as Erich Auerbach has pointed out, a great deal of biblical narrative is *not* 'realistic' in the normal sense at all. It lacks the multiplicity of 'foreground' detail that gives verisimilitude to, for instance, Homeric narratives. Instead, as we have seen here or in the Elijah story, it is concentrated, enigmatic, and suggestive of profound but withheld meaning. Comparing Homer with the Old Testament Auerbach writes:

The two styles, in their opposition, represent basic types: on the one hand fully externalized description, uniform illumination, uninterrupted connection, free expression, all events in the foreground, displaying unmistakable meanings, few elements of historical development and of psychological perspective; on the other hand, certain parts brought into high relief, others left obscure, abruptness, suggestive influence of the unexpressed, 'background' quality, multiplicity of meanings and the need for interpretation, universal-historical claims, development of the concept of the historically becoming, and preoccupation with the problematic.[33]

What is being described here are *two* very different concepts of 'realism' or *mimesis*, both of which have played their parts in the development of Western literature. Though it might appear at first glance that the quality most prominent in the modern novel, its sense of complexity, richness of meaning and interpretation – what Bakhtin (perhaps the greatest contemporary theorist of the novel) has called 'heteroglossia'[34] – is most obvious in the former, Homeric, tradition, it is arguably the biblical tradition that is the more complex and variedly 'heteroglot'. This fundamental division over what can be said to constitute 'realism' itself is reflected in differing twentieth-century conceptions of the novel and its portrayal of the world. As we have seen, Nuttall's conception of 'realism', though superficially similar to that of George Eliot, is in fact fundamentally opposed to it. In contemporary theory of the novel, Lukács, similarly, writes in the materialist and Homeric tradition, discovering the origins of the novel in the Greek epic form,[35] while Bakhtin, on the other hand, sees the 'realism' of the novel bound up with its multiplicity of voices and viewpoints:

Literary language is not represented in the novel [as it is in other genres] as a unitary, completely finished off, indubitably adequate language – it is represented precisely as a living mix of varied and opposing voices.[36]

Just as the English Romantics were to stress the creative role of the perceiver in every act of perception, so Bakhtin stresses the creative role of the reader in the meaning of every text. Communication in language depends on recipient as well as author. It is to Bakhtin that we owe the idea that *all* reading is 'translation':

The language of the novel is a *system* of languages that mutually and ideologically interanimate each other. It is impossible to describe and analyse it as a single unitary language.[37]

Michael Holquist, while noting the parallels between Auerbach and Bakhtin, concludes nevertheless that the fundamental difference between them can be seen in that for Bakhtin:

. . . the Bible could never represent the novel in contrast with epic, since *both*, Bible and epic, would share a presumption of authority, a claim to absolute language, utterly foreign to the novel's joyous awareness of the inadequacies of its own language.[38]

Yet an author's views must be understood in their intellectual context. The presumption to authority and to absolute language which Bakhtin, from a Russian Orthodox background, living under constant Soviet totalitarian control, finds so powerful an element in the Bible, is less apparent to Auerbach (or, indeed, to Alter) writing within a Jewish tradition of constant debate and theological questioning. The Bible is by no means a unitary document in style, genre, or philosophy, and the very qualities of the novel which Bakhtin specifically contrasts with history-writing are those which Auerbach and Alter discover in many of the writings of the Old Testament:

... histories differ from novels in that they insist on a homology between the sequence of their own telling, the form they impose to create a coherent explanation in the form of a narrative on the one hand, and the sequence of *what* they tell on the other ... The novel, by contrast, dramatizes the gaps between what is told and the telling of it, constantly experimenting with social, discursive and narrative asymmetries ...[39]

That element of the subversive double-movement of narrative which Alter finds so typical of the Bible is totally missing in Bakhtin's account of it. Similarly his conception of poetics is likewise one of centralization and authority:

Aristotelian poetics, the poetics of Augustine, the poetics of the mediaeval church, of 'the one language of truth,' the Cartesian poetics of neoclassicism, the abstract grammatical universalism of Leibniz (the idea of a 'universal grammar'), Humboldt's insistence on the concrete — all these, whatever their differences in nuance, give expression to the same centripetal forces in sociolinguistic and ideological life; they serve one and the same project of centralizing and unifying the European languages.[40]

In contrast to what he sees as this powerful historical pressure towards centralization and closure of meaning, Bakhtin's concept of heteroglossia in the novel demands that we 'radically reconsider' traditional ideas of poetic discourse as they now exist.[41]

It is at this point that we begin to realize how aberrant, by continental European standards, the English Romantic conception of the 'poetic' we have been considering so far may appear. Thus German romantic criticism, because, as we have seen, of the low status of prose realism in Germany, always tends to see the 'poetic' less in terms of realism and variety than of grandly generalized philosophic truth. Friedrich Schlegel, for instance, following a line of thought suggested by Herder,[42] had characterized what he called the *Roman* as a philosophic form, essentially poetry in prose, which embraced everything from criticism to theory of art, history, and science. He was insistent that the novel could not be a separate genre,[43] but was a branch of poetics:

I would have . . . *a theory of the novel* which would be a theory in the original sense of the word; a spiritual viewing of the subject with calm and serene feeling, as it is proper to view in solemn joy the meaningful play of divine images. Such a theory of the novel would have to be itself a novel which would reflect imaginatively every eternal tone of the imagination and would again confound the chaos of the world of the knights.[44] The things of the past would live in it in new forms; Dante's sacred shadow would arise from the lower world, Laura would hover heavenly before us, Shakespeare would converse intimately with Cervantes, and there Sancho would jest with Don Quixote again.[45]

The extraordinary thing about this statement is that though his four examples, Dante, Petrarch, Shakespeare and Cervantes are notably – even incomparably – writers of immense heteroglot variety of form, Schlegel's 'poeticizing' of them has seemingly ironed out what would be to many their most salient common feature. Epic, lyric, drama, and novel are blurred into a single medium, and the products of some of the most passionate and chaotic imaginations in human history are characterized by their 'calm and serene feeling'. What looks at first sight like an anticipation of Bakhtin's analysis is, in fact, nothing of the kind; moreover from an English perspective it seems strikingly 'classic' rather than 'Romantic' in tone. Thus whereas Bakhtin's tradition may be described as classic or neo-classical (at least in this sense), the English Romantic tradition is passionate, biblical, and marked by a sense of the sheer confused variety of things; whereas Bakhtin's tradition is ideologically authoritarian (at least in effect) the Romantic and biblical line represented by Blake or Coleridge is much more open and even anarchic; whereas Bakhtin's is basically formalist, the English Romantic biblical tradition is basically 'realist' in Nuttall's particular sense of the word. Now it is possible to argue that this is, yet again, merely a matter of terminology, but, as we see from the debate over the nature of biblical narrative that runs like a central thread throughout this whole discussion, there is a genuine hermeneutical point at stake. If illustration were needed of Bakhtin's point about the reader's participation, we have it here. The Bible has been understood in very different ways by different times and places. In spite of Bakhtin's specifically discounting the Bible as a proto-novelistic form, we have a multitude of witnesses to testify that for them it possesses the very qualities of heteroglossia and questioning openness of form that he finds of such central importance in the emergence of the novel. We recall not merely Blake's idea of the 'Poetic Genius', but also Thomas Howes's conviction that the apparently confused yet secretly ordered structure of the Bible represented an 'oratorical order' analogous to the hidden complexities of Nature itself. Howes is, one suspects, a proto-heteroglot. What fascinates him about the Bible is the richness and polyphony of its many voices, not the authority of its message. For the Protestant exegete the 'authority' could be taken for granted; it was the problematic and metaphorical nature of its message that was of overriding interest.

But a comparison of Howes' 'oratorical order' in the Bible and Bakhtin's conception of heteroglossia reveals a much more important structural quality of biblical dicourse. For Bakhtin, *all* human discourse is not merely polyphonic, but *marginal*: it 'lives, as it were, on the boundary of its own context and another, alien context.'[46] At one level this is a recognition that every time a word is used, it is, if ever so slightly, recontextualized, pulled in a different direction, and given a different inflexion and resonance:[47]

The word, directed towards its object, enters a dialogically agitated and tension-filled environment of alien words, value-judgements and accents, weaves in and out of complex interrelationships, merges with some, recoils from others, intersects with yet a third group; and all this may crucially shape discourse, may leave a trace in all its semantic layers, may complicate its expression and influence its entire stylistic profile.[48]

Yet the Bible, we recall, is not just a monoglot recontextualization of words and ideas, it is a *translated* text, not merely for modern English-speakers (or Europeans) but in its very origins. It is a palimpsest of languages and contexts meeting and overlapping one another. Thus, though the Old Testament is written almost entirely in Hebrew, substantial parts of it incorporate translation or paraphrase of other Near Eastern texts – Mesopotamian, Egyptian, Canaanite, and others. By New Testament times Hebrew had, however, fallen out of use as a vernacular language, and in synagogues had to be 'explained' by *Targums* (Aramaic paraphrases), or, in Greek-speaking areas, by the *Septuagint*. Though Jesus presumably spoke in the Palestinian Jewish vernacular of his time (Aramaic), the Gospel tradition survives only as a Greek translation – in the popular form of the language of a classic and centralizing high-culture. The early Christians, after perhaps only the first generation, lost almost all contact with the Semitic biblical languages (Hebrew and Aramaic), and for them the 'Old Testament' was henceforth either the *Septuagint* or, later, the Old Latin and then the *Vulgate* versions.[49] We have already observed the impact of the translation of the Hebrew scriptures into Greek.[50] If we are prepared to accept Caird's argument that Hebrew was, in fact, the traditional language of the Canaanites, and (more controversially) that Aramaic was originally the Israelite vernacular,[51] we have yet more evidence for the way in which the Bible not only illustrates Bakhtin's thesis, but actually provides one of the supreme examples of the way in which discourse arises and takes its meanings from the intersecting of contextual and linguistic boundaries.

Such boundaries, of course, occur not merely on a macro-scale between languages and cultures, but also, in a micro-scale *within* languages – in the structure of metaphor itself. With the emergence of the idea of the 'poetic' in the eighteenth century we find also a rehabilitation of the classical notion of metaphor as its appropriate centre of activity. Though the study of metaphor had traditionally been a part of the discipline of rhetoric from the time of Aristotle onwards (it had been defined as a trope of resemblance) the virtual demise of the classical study of rhetoric by the nineteenth century undermined any further study of metaphor in that context.[52] From the break-up of the Aristotelian meaning of 'poetics', which included, for instance, his dramatic ideas of tragedy and catharsis (still surviving, for example, in Dryden's use of the word 'poesie'), we find that the new more intense and value-laden word 'poetic' is increasingly seen as belonging essentially to the realm of metaphor. As so often, Lowth is a key figure in this process. His interest in the power of Hebrew metaphor (its concreteness often very difficult to render accurately in English) encouraged a tendency to re-interpret the idea of 'prophecy' as a matter of altering or modifying the metaphorical structure of the language involved – a notion directly anticipating Farrer's description of the Apocalypse in terms of a rebirth of images.

We can crudely schematize much of the ensuing debate by distinguishing between three discrete levels of linguistic activity, each with its appropriate analytic discipline or disciplines. At the most basic level we have words themselves – the proper study of linguistics and etymology; at the most complex we find 'story', what is being intentionally said, whether intended as fictional, historical, or discursive – the proper field of a whole range of disciplines including theology, philosophy, literary criticism, and the various branches of history. Between these two extremes, and in some sense joining them as by a bridge, we now have to insert metaphor – by common assumption the proper realm of the poetic – but whose exact theoretical function is disputed and unclear. Moreover, just as we cannot draw a clear boundary between the various analytic disciplines at each level, so we cannot draw exact boundaries between each of these interacting levels themselves. Metaphor, for instance, clearly affects the meaning of a story or argument; the etymology of words affects both individual metaphors and the 'surface' level of story; particular stories can change the connotations of both words and metaphors – and so on. One only has to think of the repetition of the 'borrowed robes' imagery in *Macbeth*, the ironic uses of the word 'nature' by Hardy, or what *Animal Farm* has done to the word 'equality' to take the point. Each level has, as it were, a gravitational pull on the movements of the other two. Thus we can have 'poetic' narratives on the one hand, or 'poetic' etymologies on the other – implying in each case a certain metaphorical predominance in the meaning. Indeed, much of the historical dispute over the meaning of the word 'poetic' can in fact be accounted for by how the particular interpreters see the role of metaphor. Both Mill and Arnold, for instance, tend to see biblical narrative primarily in terms of metaphors of emotion, while conversely for the Anglo-German philologists Bunsen and Müller language is itself a structure of poetic and religious metaphor.

In 1786 we find a Reverend William Jones (not to be confused with his contemporary, Sir William Jones) arguing in a lecture on 'The Figurative Language of Scripture' that what made the Bible prophetic was the metaphorical and figurative nature of its expression:

It being the professed design of the Scripture to teach us such things as we neither see nor know of ourselves, its style and manner must be such as are no where else to be found. It must abound with figurative expressions; it cannot proceed without them: and if we descend to an actual examination of particulars, we find it assisting and leading our faculties forward; by an application of all visible objects to a figurative use; from the glorious orb which shines in the firmament to a grain of seed which is buried in the earth. In this sort of language did our blessed Saviour instruct his hearers; always referring them to such objects as were familiar to their senses, that they might see the propriety and feel the force of his doctrine. This method he observed, not in compliance with any customary speech peculiar to the Eastern people, but consulting the exigence of human nature, which is everywhere the same.

Though Jones has read Lowth[53] and is in accord with Lowth over the

Bible's peculiar abundance of complex figurative allusions and per-
sonifications, the main thrust of his argument is traditional and
typological. Jesus's identification of John the Baptist with Elijah for
instance is evidence that the scriptures were intended as universal
allegory.[54] His case rests specifically on the uniformitarian assumption
that human nature 'is everywhere the same' and that the Bible is
therefore to be read as a timeless work of spiritual wisdom, without
reference to its particular time or geographical context. With this specific
rejection of Lowth's Orientalism, and with his manifestly anti-historical
bias, Jones may be considered deeply conservative, yet, simply by focusing attention at such length on the imagery of the Bible he is raising questions about the nature and function of metaphor that point forwards to
Romantic modes of analysis. Though this notion of a universal symbolism goes back as far as Augustine, his particular phraseology suggests
a more immediate philosophic source in the systems of Locke and
Hartley. The language of signs, writes Jones, is 'the language of the
mind; which understands and reasons from the ideas, or images of things,
imprinted upon the imagination.'[55] Though Locke's idea of the *tabula
rasa* is still clearly the dominating model in Jones's mind, there is in his
notion of an inherent progression in biblical imagery, 'leading our
faculties forward', more than a suggestion of Hartley's necessitarian and
psychologized version of Locke by which the growth of the mind, and
consequently of spiritual capacities, is an essential consequence of the
Law of Association.[56] This Janus-like feel is reinforced by Jones's attitude
towards the traditional theme of the 'language of nature'. The original
Adamic language is, for him, not one of words, but rather of signs to be
read from the visible works of creation:

Words are changeable; language has been confounded; and men in different parts
of the world are unintelligible to one another as barbarians; but the visible works
of nature are not subject to any such confusion; they speak to us now the same
sense as they spoke to Adam in paradise; when he was the pupil of heaven, and
their language will last as long as the world shall remain, without being
corrupted.[57]

In view of such sentiments, it comes as no surprise to find that Jones
delivered the following year (1787) 'A Lecture on the Natural Evidences
of Christianity'. Its aim is the now familiar one to bring 'the volume of
Nature in aid to the volume of scripture', and to this end he invokes the
traditional names of Bacon, Boyle and Newton.[58] As one might expect,
the themes of the lectures are closely interwoven:

To those who understand it, all nature speaks the same language with revelation; what the one teaches in words the other confirms with signs . . . If Christ is called the *true bread*, the *true light*, or the *true vine*, and the talents or gifts of God's grace are the *true riches*, etc., then the objects of sense, without this their spirit and signification, are in themselves mere image and delusion; and the whole life of man in this world is but a shadow.[59]

Though this clearly declares its origins in the mediaeval system of 'correspondences', in the context of the eighteenth-century revival of biblicalism and mediaevalism in reaction to the deistic tendencies of the Enlightenment, this is, in itself, a manifestation of what would shortly be thought of as a 'Romantic' sensibility. We recall the massive systematiza- tion of these ideas a generation later by Keble and his fellow- Tractarians.[60] What is perhaps even more germane is that Jones con- ceives of the *liber naturae* in terms of 'signs'. The homely and domestic metaphors of the Bible, in which Lowth had discovered such sublimity, are seen as double-edged in a way that illuminates the tenor as much as the vehicle. The metaphor that Christ is the 'light of the world' changes not merely the way in which we are to understand Christ, but also the way we understand *light*. The conclusion is not unexpected: this language of signs is essentially that of 'poetry'.[61]

We have already mentioned how Newman, the heir to Keble's sacramental sense of the visible world, also turned increasingly towards analogy, metaphor and symbol as the appropriate vehicles for the living ideas of a community.[62] Philosophic systems may change, from fashion, the logic of scientific discovery, or for other reasons – necessary or con- tingent – but the great formative and focal images of art and religion live on. For Newman, the Church lived not through its theology, but in its symbols and sacraments. 'Christ lives, to our imaginations, by His visi- ble symbols'[63] – not simply sacraments, but by the whole complex web of visual iconography and literary metaphor which has grown from the Bible and the associated traditions of the Church. It is to these things, which appeal not merely to our intellects, but to our imaginations, that we can give 'real' as opposed to 'notional' assent. As did Jones and Col- eridge, therefore, Newman draws a sharp distinction between theology and the scriptures. The latter have that concreteness and inwardness that engender real assent, in contrast to the generalized and abstract nature of theological propositions – just 'as true poetry is a spontaneous outpour- ing of thought, whereas no one becomes a poet merely by the canons of criticism.'[64] As 'poetry' the scriptures appeal not just to the intellect, but also to the imagination. Not for the first time we hear the echo of Coleridge behind Newman's formulations: for him too, the scriptures are 'the living educts of the imagination'.

Newman sees the vital psychological importance of so much that Arnold was prepared to dismiss as *Aberglaube*, while at the same time placing it in a post-Kantian critical context. The starting-point for his concept of religious language, was a work that had also been a major formative influence on Coleridge: Butler's *Analogy of Religion* (1736). Certainty, Butler had argued, is not a part of the human condition. We rarely, if ever, act upon certainties but on accumulations of probability. Newman had read and been influenced by not only Butler but Hume, and knew well the uncertain foundations of all human knowledge. We possess, he concluded, what he calls an 'illative' sense, by which we are enabled to make an imaginative leap from scattered and disparate parts to an intuition of the whole, and by which we convert inferences and probabilities into what amount to practical certainties – and which we treat as such. Though there is no evidence that Newman had read Blake, the parallels with the latter's 'Poetic Genius' are obvious. The workings of the 'illative sense' apply not just to questions of *religious* certainty (which, he argued, was strictly of a kind with any other) but affect every part of our lives from the simplest and most basic forms of sense perception through to the most complex of metaphysical propositions. As Hume had so devastatingly demonstrated, the empiricist theory of mind had, paradoxically, undermined *all* objective certainty: even our domestic lives and everyday actions involve the most complicated pieces of inference and assent from the most questionable and shaky evidence. Yet, for practical purposes, we routinely call this unconscious illative process 'certainty', and trust it with our lives. Thus, argues Newman, it is not the case that religious assent demands a peculiar *kind* of existential leap, it merely represents the most extreme, and therefore the most clearly visible example of a process that is constantly going on in every part of our lives without us being aware of it. From being a doubtful and borderline area of experience, religious belief is suddenly transformed into *the* paradigmatic example of the whole problem of epistemology: the question of how we can *know* anything. Seen thus, it becomes the touchstone by which we understand the rest of our experience.

The strength of the *Grammar of Assent* is that it places religious experience in relation to all other kinds of human experience – both epistemologically and psychologically. The illative sense, for instance, provides a close psychological parallel with the role of the imagination in perception, creating complete 'pictures' from partial and incomplete sense-data. The difference is that whereas Coleridge's primary imagination must, by definition, be below the threshold of consciousness, Newman's illative sense (though it may also on occasions be unconscious) is normally part of a process involving judgement and will. Though Newman does not employ the model, one might perhaps describe human perception in terms of a continuum: at one extreme would be located the basic unconscious illative creations of sense-perception; at the other would be the conscious aesthetic creativity of Coleridge's secondary imagination – and beyond the aesthetic (to slip into the appropriate Kierkegaardian terminology) would be the religious: the power of assent. The mere fact that one can integrate, however loosely, the models of Coleridge, Kierkegaard, and Newman suggests how broad is the field of common ground between them – even though we have no evidence that the Dane knew the writings of either Englishman.[65] The stress in each case is not on the truth or falsehood of propositions, but on the *wholeness* of human experience. We do not perceive in terms of propositions; our schemata come from the life of the whole personality, and beyond that, of the cultural and linguistic community.

It was this basic conviction that led Newman more and more towards discussions of metaphor and symbol, and their role in our apprehension of the world. In particular he was always keenly aware of a paradox right at the heart of his notion of real assent. On the one hand was his deeply held conviction, born of personal experience, that 'assent' in his sense was inseparable from the Church as a living community of belief with its own metaphorical and symbolic structure; on the other was the no less personally intuitive observation that, whereas notional assent can be easily shared and communicated, *real* assent 'is proper to the individual, and as such, thwarts rather than promotes the intercourse of man with man'.[66] It is a necessary part of the inwardness of real assent that it is *both* so deeply personal as to be almost incommunicable, *and* simultaneously the product not just of an individual but of a linguistic and symbolic community. To the theologian the paradox may seem an odd one, but to the poet it is immediately familiar. We recall Keble's idea of the poet as a man speaking to men, but *necessarily* under tension, and by disguise, hiding his own feelings even as he arouses them in others.

As we suggested in the first chapter, Newman's image of religious assent in terms of a 'Grammar' is significant. He stands almost as the last in a line of poet–theologians, extending back via Keble, Wordsworth, Coleridge and Blake to Lowth, who sought to understand the complexities of religious language – and through that perhaps of all language – in the paradoxes and tensions of metaphor and symbol. It was not until the twentieth century that critical interest would again be focused to the same degree on this problem – and then the impetus would be from continental Europe and the United States.

Mid-twentieth-century English discussions of religious language have tended to be dominated by the more unhelpful aspects of what was then popularly known as 'Oxford philosophy': a loose compendium of linguistic-analytic ideas ranging from the early Wittgenstein to those of A. J. Ayer, the weakness of whose often arrogantly a-historical approach was devastatingly diagnosed at the time by Owen Barfield:

> ... the linguistic analyst who attempts to tackle the problem of meaning without looking at its history, appears in much the same pitiful perspective as the earlier eighteenth century biologists who attempted to tackle the variety of natural species as though there were no such thing as evolution.[67]

Perhaps the nadir was reached with John Wilson's *Language and Christian Belief*. In what was apparently an attempt to reply to the crude positivist argument that denied any normal meaning to religious propositions, Wilson argued that religious language was in effect a form of technical vocabulary constituting a separate and different 'language-game' from ordinary speech, and subject to its own independent set of rules[68]. In its extreme form this argument could be used to claim that it was a game only open to initiates – 'religious people' – the rest being simply excluded by ignorance of the rules. As Newman would have been quick to observe,[69] the obvious objection is that the terms of a technical vocabulary differ from ordinary language in that they have been 'stripped of that depth and breadth of associations which constitute their poetry, their rhetoric, and their historical life'.[70] They are, in short, words deliberately fabricated for a limited pre-set purpose: as, for instance, the words 'volt', 'watt' and 'amp' were designated as units of measurement for a mysterious natural force we call 'electricity'. To try and classify religious language as a 'technical' vocabulary in this sense is simply to confuse the unit of measurement with the phenomenon to be measured.[71]

Apart from the minority 'poetic' tradition already discussed – C. S. Lewis, Charles Williams and Owen Barfield among the 'Inklings', and Austin Farrer – the first signs of a return to philosophic discussions of the figurative nature of religious language came with Ian Ramsey's two books, *Religious Language* (1957) and *Models and Mystery* (1964). For him there was a distinction between the 'picture' models of a technical language where, as we have seen, there is a one-for-one correspondence between the model and the object signified, and what he calls the 'disclosure' models to be found in literature, the more creative kinds of scientific thinking, or religious experience. In these latter cases the analogical model reveals or illuminates in a 'moment of truth' some relationship hitherto concealed. Though the distinction had other applications, the main area of debate remained firmly centered around the truth-content (or otherwise) of propositional statements such as the Creeds, and it seemed (however unwittingly) to lend support to the notion that it was in the fields of theological polemic and the use of analogy that the real problems of religious language were to be found. Nor did he ever really shake himself free of the notion of 'language-games'. The effects of this assumption on works like John Macquarrie's *God-talk* (1967) have already been noted. It was left to Americans such as Max Black, Monroe Beardsley, and Douglas Berggren, to take up the more central questions of the role of metaphor in religious language in relation to poetry and narrative, and, above all, to Paul Ricoeur to provide a link between the ideas of the English- and French-speaking worlds.

Ricoeur's own magisterial study, *The Rule of Metaphor*, is a major piece of twentieth-century syncretistic scholarship, at once historical and polemical. As he himself is the first to acknowledge, his own theory of metaphor is largely derived from two short but highly influential articles published by Douglas Berggren in 1962 to which we have already made reference: *The Use and Abuse of Metaphor*. Drawing on a revival of interest in the nature of metaphor sparked off partly by Croce and Collingwood's re-examination of Vico, Berggren puts forward a tensional theory that both builds on and modifies the thinking of a whole group of linguistic philosophers of the late 1950s and early 60s.[72] His basic position is astonishingly reminiscent of Jones two centuries earlier. The two-sided nature of a metaphor, he argues, means that through the literal absurdity of their conjunction *both* referents are seen in a new way. 'To construe life as a play or a dream is not only to organize or interpret life in different ways, but also to give plays or dreams a significance they might otherwise not have.'[73]

Yet at the same time, if the initial differences between the two referents were not simultaneously preserved, even while the referents are also being transformed into closer alignment, the metaphorical character of the construing process would be lost. *The possibility or comprehension of metaphorical construing requires, therefore, a peculiar and rather sophisticated intellectual ability which W. Bedell Stanford metaphorically labels 'stereo-scopic vision': the ability to entertain two different points of view at the same time.* That is to say, the perspectives prior to and subsequent to the transformation of the metaphor's principle and subsidiary subjects must both be conjointly maintained. It is precisely this transformation of both referents, moreover, interacting with their normal meanings, which makes it *ultimately impossible to reduce completely the cognitive import of any vital metaphor to any set of univocal, literal, or non-tensional statements. For a special meaning, and in some cases even a new sort of reality, is achieved which cannot survive except at the intersection of the two perspectives which produced it.*[74]

(my italics)

There is, Berggren argues, a whole area of human experience which can only be represented by the tensional language of metaphor. Yet it is significant that though Ricoeur adopts Berggren's (and Max Black's) tensional theory, he shows remarkably little interest in the actual metaphor which Berggren himself makes the organizing image of his whole argument: that of 'stereoscopic' or 'bi-focal' vision, taken from W. Bedell Stanford's *Greek Metaphor: Studies in Theory and Practice.*[75] In what sense, for instance, can we say that Elijah's experience on Horeb demands a stereoscopic vision, which asserts a new sort of reality peculiar to the intersection of the two perspectives which produced it?

In taking Stanford's image of stereoscopy as the model for his tensional theory of metaphor, Berggren, we notice, is selecting his paradigm from the very fringes of normal experience. It is clear from the way he uses it that he is *not* thinking of stereoscopic vision as we normally experience it. In ordinary bi-focal vision the images received by each eye vary only by the distance separating them – which is rarely more than a couple of inches. These images augment each other by providing nearly, but not quite, identical information. It is the minute difference, the very slight shift in viewpoint that enables us to see in depth. But this is not, apparently, what Berggren has in mind. If we describe a man as a mouse, however we consider it, the area of overlap is very small indeed. Metaphors are literally absurd. Men are self-evidently not mice; life is not a play, nor is it a dream, and we only retain the power of the metaphor to make us look at men and mice, life and plays, in a new way, as having anything in common, while we retain a firm grasp of their difference. Without that tension they would be dead metaphors and would relapse into cliché, or even, as we saw earlier, into a new literalness. But in normal bi-focal vision the relationship of the two images, as we have seen, does *not* constitute an absurdity. There is no question of a contradiction between the images. The occasions when our two eyes provide two different sets of information are extremely rare, and happen only under quite exceptional circumstances. We may know, for instance, the devices sometimes used for testing children's eyes where each eyepiece offers a different image, and the child has to integrate the two by manipulating knobs. The optician tells the child to 'put the soldier into his sentry-box', or 'make the man go into the house'. Alternatively, we may be familiar with the kind of 3-D picture where one views a blurred image through special spectacles with different-coloured lenses to make the figures stand out from the page. If Berggren's metaphor of stereoscopy is to be appropriate to his purpose of holding two different viewpoints at the same time, it must relate to examples as extreme as these. Yet are even these satisfactory? Devices of this kind may produce two separate images, but there is no contradiction, no palpable absurdity, no tension between the soldier and his sentry-box. Significantly, Berggren does not try to explore his own key-image at all; he seems to take it for granted that we will know what he means.

And, strangely enough, I think we do. It will not have escaped notice that we have already examined in some depth the perfect, indeed, *paradigm* illustration of what he wishes to say, and has such difficulty in expressing, about metaphor. Dante's vision of the griffin, first as an incongruous unity in his own eyes, and then as a two-fold contradiction in the eyes of Beatrice, is precisely the model Berggren has been looking for to explain what he means by stereoscopy. Moreover, with this model of incongruity and two-fold unity in mind we can see much more clearly how well his idea of stereoscopy seems to suit the phenomenon of metaphor as a whole. It is as if Berggren senses that this model of con- tradiction is at the centre of what he wants to say about all the other examples where contradiction does not occur – or is less visibly acute. Like Dante, he seems impelled to try and explore the normal in terms of certain highly abnormal experiences, as though it were through these that we come to understand normal experience for the first time – as if, like Blake, he had come to see double-vision as an essential prerequisite for understanding the 'single-vision and Newton's sleep'.[76]

As Gombrich has reminded us in *Art and Illusion*, our powers of see- ing depend upon an unconscious process of what he calls 'making and matching' between our initial expectations, on the one hand, and the actual visual data received, on the other. The more the visual data conform to our initial expectations, the *less* in real terms do we 'see'; the greater the difference, the more we have to struggle with interpretation, and the *more* we actually see. All vision is to a greater or lesser degree dependent on this learning-gap – which is why, for instance, at the very simplest physiological level it is very difficult for us to look steadily at a motionless object for more than a few seconds together. Similarly, as we have seen, by an analogous process, a language gains more through its resistance to translated material than it does through receptivity. It is the new formulation, the fresh phrase, the startling conjunction from which we learn – and, as we have seen, the experience of disconfirmation is a paradigm biblical event. It was suggested in the first Chapter that the reason why it was not possible to use unambiguous language in translating the Bible was that the Bible was not about things that were unambiguous. We are now, perhaps, in a position to extend that observation and suggest that such a language of disconfirmation and ambiguity is not merely a concomitant of religious experience, but is actually characteristic of, and historically central to, man's experience of God. Elijah on Horeb, Moses and the Burning Bush, the Incarnation itself present events so baffling as to imply quite new ways of seeing the world.

Similarly for Dante, it is the image of the griffin which seems to articulate and illuminate the encounter with Beatrice. It was for him the type of those rare experiences where the groundwork of assumptions, on which our perception of the world and our sense of self rests, is suddenly called in question, and disconfirmed. Religious language for him, it seems, began here where the single vision was challenged by another so radically different that it could neither be accommodated nor rejected in the former's terms: where only a particular kind of metaphor of stereoscopy would answer to the contradiction suddenly revealed in the very ground of his experience – and even in sense-perception itself.

It will not have escaped notice, moreover, how closely this idea of the paradigmatic nature of way-out experiences accords with Newman's sense of the function of religious language. J. R. Watson, in a recent book,[77] has drawn attention to the quality of what he calls 'liminality' in Wordsworth: the sense of being on a margin or threshold of something further. He quotes a remark of Philip Wheelwright (also one of Berggren's influences): 'Man lives always on the verge, always on the borderland of something more . . . The essential structure of human life is radically, irreducibly, liminal.'[78] The state of liminality, anthropologically[79] speaking, he points out, involves losing an old and accepted identity in order to achieve in the future a new and more significant status. There is, Watson suggests, an analogy between this and Wordsworth's sense of man's radically changed relationship with his environment. Having lost the old primal participation with the natural world, humanity is now liminal: at once precariously marginal, and at the same time potentially on the threshold of a much more significant relationship with nature. Religious language, in this sense, can be seen as the language of liminality.

But as Berggren makes clear in the second of his articles, the stereoscopic quality that he sees as essential to metaphorical vision is as present in science as it is in poetry. The scientific metaphor functions in precisely the same way as the poetic one: by serving to construct new modes of reality. Though he does not mention Wordsworth by name, one of Berggren's prime targets is the Wordsworthian distinction between science and poetry – which, as we have seen, has perpetuated itself into the twentieth century in the form of the idea of separate language-games:[80]

While it is possible to develop a literal or univocal language for spatial reality, and while an equally univocal language for non-spatial reality is also at least theoretically conceivable, their philosophically necessary interconnections or correlations can be formulated only in terms of vital metaphors. In other words, just as the coordinative definitions and theoretical entities of mathematical physics must be irresolvably tensional, so any conceivable substitute for Descartes' pineal gland, Platonic participation, Christ, Sancho Panza, or Cinderella's glass slipper must preserve an equally tensional status.[81]

However univocal the actual terms of any particular scientific description may appear, our apprehension of the universe as human beings is inescapably bi-focal: 'it is the only possible solution to the dilemma of monism versus dualism'.[82] We participate in our physical, social, and historical environments by means of metaphors which are in a constant state of modification and change. As Vico, Farrer, Frye, and Barfield have all demonstrated in different ways, there have been historically fundamental and irreversible shifts in the metaphors by which we perceive ourselves and the world since Old Testament times – of which our images of, say, nature constitute only one strand: though an important one. Romanticism is but the latest and perhaps best-documented, because the most self-conscious, of these.

But, if this is so, the distinction between 'metaphorical' and 'literal' use of language which has been present, explicitly or implicitly, behind so many of the discussions of the changing nature of linguistic practice, needs to be significantly modified. Frye's distinction between 'hieratic', 'metonymic', and 'demotic' usages assumes, for instance, that it is *possible* to have both metaphorical and literal descriptions of the world – however late and sophisticated a linguistic development the latter may turn out to be. Barfield, though he is no less interested in the process by which individual words acquire literal meanings, appears to be sceptical over the broader question of how far literal and unambiguous descriptions of the world are *ever* possible. Berggren, though as we have just seen he allows for literal descriptions of spacial reality, seems to suggest that such descriptions are in some way dependent upon an underlying metaphorical structure. For him and for Ricoeur, though the nature of our descriptions of reality have changed radically over the past three thousand years, and are still changing, they are all utimately metaphorical. The distinction between hieratic, metonymic, and demotic or scientific descriptions is a valuable and important one so long as we remember that all three stages stand in a relationship to a reality that is perceived bi-focally and metaphorically in the sense we have been looking at. The literal language of scientific description (to be distinguished from the scientific language that is *overtly* metaphorical) rests upon assumptions that are, in their own way, as bi-focal and tensional as the language of Homer or Ezekiel. And indeed, if we think about it, this must be so as long as we continue to conceive of language in terms of change. As Nuttall reminds us, reality is never exhausted by our descriptions of it. A genuinely literal non-tensional descriptive language would *ipso facto* exclude the possibility of the new, and would, therefore, be purporting to offer a total, adequate and comprehensive description of reality. It would, in effect, be a return to the language of God and of Angels – the language of essentials spoken by Adam.

There are other echoes of the past in the current debate. If we accept, as do Berggren and Ricoeur, Monroe Beardsley's description of a metaphor as 'a poem in miniature',[83] we appear to be coming very close to the position of the Anglo-German philologists, Bunsen and Müller, and their 'extensive' claim that *all* language is fundamentally poetic and religious. Historically there are links through Heidegger with the nineteenth-century German philological tradition. While we can concede there is a sense in which this may be argued, it is only if we add that any such 'poetic' content is, as it were, *regulative* only; metaphor does not of itself hold the key to all mythologies. Clearly this is largely a semantic problem. Since for Ricoeur the 'poetic' carries connotations of primitive and undifferentiated modes of being, such a description of metaphor suggests that by its nature it belongs to the most fundamental and deep-seated part of our being. But the problem with any such formulation is that it can make it much more difficult to distinguish, as for instance Austin Farrer wished to do, between the 'poetic' form of the Apocalypse and the prose of the Johannine Epistles. Any use of the word 'poetic' that does not allow for the *non*-poetic is unhelpful. As we noted earlier, descriptive prose, though it may give no more adequate an account of reality than any other linguistic mode, is very far from being dead. On balance, it would seem convenient not to use the words 'poem' or 'poetic' for what Frye would call the 'demotic' – the language of non-figurative description, however tensive and bi-focal the underpinnings of such apparently neutral accounts may ultimately turn out to be. Just as Ricoeur's attempt to classify *all* the various genres of biblical writing as 'poetic' (in his primal sense of the word) has had the effect of diminishing their inherent variety and heteroglossia, so the application of any term of this kind to *all* language can only have the effect of obscuring one of its most important characteristics: its multiplicity, polyvalence, and capacity to provide contrast. The word 'poetic' is in this usage metaphorical, but if it is used in a way that loses the sense of difference between the two referents it loses its metaphorical capacity and force. It must be reserved (as it traditionally has been by poets) for what Barfield describes as 'a felt change of consciousness'.[84] 'The poetic', he insists, 'can only manifest itself as *fresh meaning*.'[85] It is here that the modern debate echoes and coincides most closely with the nineteenth-century German philological tradition. For Humboldt 'all understanding is at the same time a not-understanding'. Though each nation may be said, in general terms, to speak the same language, every individual has a personal linguistic code. 'No one when he uses a word has in mind exactly the same thing as another.'[86] The consequences of this for our understanding of language itself are momentous. The creative energy of words is inseparable from their particularity and fleetingness.

Language conceived in its true essence is something continuously and in every moment transitory. Even its perpetuation by means of a script is never more than an incomplete mummified preservation, which always requires for full actualization that one animate it by living speech. Language itself is not a finished product, an *Ergon*, but a creative activity; it is *Energeia*.[87]

As Barfield himself recognizes, one of the prime sources of 'fresh meaning' in any language is translation, but in his desire to distinguish between really new ideas or concepts and the quaintness of expression sometimes achieved by clumsy translation or dialect forms, he describes this power as 'semi-accidental'. Yet how far in this does it really differ from any other new idea? If we accept that any act of reading (or even hearing) involves a participatory act of 'translation' in response, then any unfamiliar expression or turn of phrase has to be dealt with much the same way. We ourselves will normally exercise a degree of censorship to distinguish between unfamiliarity that is relevant, useful, or interesting, and that which is not. Such classifications will depend more on our mental state of alertness or receptivity than on any inherent scale of relevance in the terms themselves. We must presume, for instance, that the translators of the *Good News Bible*, operating on Nida's principle of dynamic equivalence, found the 'voice of thin silence' heard by Elijah a source of semi-accidental quaintness of no real significance to the English-language reader. Contrariwise, fleeting oddities of expression have sometimes been the trigger for great poetry. We can trace examples of this serendipity at work in every great poet.[88] As Lowth was only the first of many to point out, the process is even more clearly observable in Hebrew, not merely because of the domestic and vernacular nature of so much Old Testament imagery, but also because of the structure of the Hebrew language itself.[89]

There is, however, a further level of metaphorical significance to our discussion. The idea of the 'poetic' which we have been following with such assiduity is *itself*, of course, a metaphor. The Bible is not literally a 'poem': it embraces a whole gamut of literary forms.[90] But describing it as 'poetic' has had a profound effect not only on the way in which we read the Bible, but also on the way in which we regard a poem. It is no accident, for instance, that in the wake of Dennis, and Lowth's work on Hebrew poetics, there was a whole crop of poetic prose works of prophetic import – ranging from MacPherson's notorious Ossian to Blake's *Marriage of Heaven and Hell*. Similarly, though there was nothing new in seeing biblical events as part of a sustained and organized narrative – that, after all, was what typology was all about – in treating miracles as 'acted parables', or metaphors, there had not hitherto been much discussion of the nature of metaphor itself. Yet that is precisely what Jones, for instance, is attempting. If the Bible is 'poetic', analyses of poetics are clearly in order.

It seems clear, for example, that what attracted Ricoeur in Berggren's tensional theory of metaphor was the possibility that metaphor created new meaning: that 'new sort of reality' which comes into being 'at the intersection of the two perspectives which produced it'. It was this desire to account for the creation of the new which lies behind Ricoeur's opposition to the classical Aristotelian idea that metaphor is basically a form of 'redescription' or 'substitution'.[91] As we saw in the case of Nida's translation theory, substitution implicitly denies the entry of new information into the descriptive process. It was the closed 'substitutionary' nature of structuralist poetics that finally led Ricoeur to reject it, and the covert positivist epistemology that he saw as supporting it.[92] Instead, he comes back to the text as a kind of free-standing entity that is 'given'. 'The kind of hermeneutics I now favour,' Ricoeur writes, 'starts from the recognition of the objective meaning of the text as distinct from the subjective intention of the author.'[93] Agreed. Yet for those readers approaching the problem from the perspective of the poetic, that formulation, framed in terms of the 'subjectivity' of authorial intention versus the 'objectivity' of the autonomous text, still seems to suggest a degree of question-begging.

We recall his apparent failure in *Toward a Hermeneutic of Revelation* to admit a tensional definition of the poetic that would distinguish between 'fact-likeness' and 'factuality'.[94] Both, it seems, were assumed to bear the same relation to reality as realistic fiction (in the nineteenth-century sense). Berggren's tensional model of metaphor is reserved for the rather different function of reconciling the conflict between speculative and poetic discourse.[95] The result is to reinforce the notion that while a text may be metaphorical within its own world of discourse, it is sealed off from interaction with the external world. We seem to be encountering here what is either a radical inconsistency in Ricoeur's thought, or a radical change of direction. The closed-circle of meaning implied by the root of the word 'hermeneutic' is somehow at odds with his insistence on openness and the possibility of the new. In *The Symbolism of Evil* (1967) Ricoeur wrote:

Such is the circle: hermeneutics proceeds from a prior understanding of the very thing that it tries to understand by interpreting it. But thanks to that circle in hermeneutics, I can still today communicate with the sacred by making explicit the prior understanding that gives life to the interpretation. Thus hermeneutics, an acquisition of 'modernity', is one of the modes by which that 'modernity' transcends itself, insofar as it is forgetfulness of the sacred. I believe that being can still speak to me − no longer, of course, under the precritical form of immediate belief, but as the second immediacy aimed at by hermeneutics.[96]

The idea is not a new one, though Ricoeur's application of it has some original features. Behind it lies an analogy with language itself. As we have seen in the cases of other words of a similar class, 'language' is itself a metaphor in the last stages of becoming literal. The root-word, that for 'tongue',[97] carried with it connotations of both the physical organ and of 'words'; until the two meanings were desynonymized the tongue could not achieve its literal meaning simply as a part of the human anatomy. But more significant here is the implicit use of the idea of language to describe metaphorically the even more abstract notion of hermeneutics. What we are seeing is, in effect, a new desynonymy at work, but as yet incomplete.[98]

Thus Ricoeur's image of hermeneutics as constituting a 'closed-circle' echoes one of the more intriguing points in the linguistic theory of his friend Maurice Merleau-Ponty. As the latter put it in a review of *Les Voix de Silence*, by André Malraux:

What we have learned from Saussure is that, taken singly, signs do not signify anything, and that each one of them does not so much express a meaning as mark a divergence of meaning between itself and other signs . . . language is made of differences without terms; or more exactly . . . the terms of language are engendered only by the differences which appear among them. This is a difficult idea, because common sense tells us that if term A and term B do not have any meaning at all, it is hard to see how there could be a difference of meaning between them; one would have to know the language in order to learn it. But the objection is of the same kind as Zeno's paradoxes; and as they are overcome by the act of movement, it is overcome by the act of speech. And this sort of circle, according to which language, in the presence of those who are learning it, precedes itself, teaches itself, and suggests its own deciphering, is perhaps the marvel which defines language.[99]

By breaking into the closed-circle of language we perform the logically impossible. For Merleau-Ponty language is 'oblique and autonomous . . . its ability to signify a thought or a thing is only a secondary power' derived from its 'inner life'.[100]

The two central planks of this argument, first that the world consists not of things, but of relationships, and, second, that language is prior to meaning, are both statements that are absurd – on ground of logic and common sense alike. Nuttall puts what he calls the 'psychological' objection to this basic tenet of structuralism:

> . . . if identity invariably depends on context, so that the nature of a context will depend on the context of that context, and so on, where is the point of entry? How does one begin to learn if one must know everything before one knows anything?[101]

This is, of course, the point that Merleau-Ponty anticipates and attempts to meet by reference to Zeno's paradoxes. How far is Nuttall's objection an exercise in logic-chopping that is overcome by *praxis*? Zeno of Elea, you will recall, is famous chiefly for his attack on the Pythagoreans by means of a series of logical paradoxes proving that plurality, motion, and space are alike impossible according to their principles.[102] The best-known of these is probably that of 'Achilles and the Tortoise' where Zeno argues with brilliant perversity that Achilles can never overtake his opponent in the race because by the time he has reached the point where the tortoise was, the tortoise will have moved on, by the time he has reached the tortoise's new position, it will still have moved (if ever so slightly) further, and so on.[103] That the argument was impossible, Zeno, of course, knew as well as anyone. It is a Swiftian exercise in specious logic: by taking his opponents' arguments and pressing them to absurdity he demonstrates the consequences of their position. What Merleau-Ponty is doing, however, in spite of his claim, *is precisely the opposite of this*. He is arguing a logical absurdity and claiming that the *common-sense* objections are the equivalent of Zeno's paradoxes. In fact it is he who is raising the Zeno-like paradox: that given the closed nature of language argued by Saussure, no one ought to be able to speak at all. The difference is whereas Zeno was *defending* common sense, Merleau-Ponty is attacking it.

Setting aside the Machiavellian possibility that Merleau-Ponty is playing Zeno to the Pythagorean Saussure, and demolishing his argument by logically extending it, we notice that it is in other ways subtly familiar in flavour. Take, for instance, the following:

> Language is much more like a sort of being than a means, and that is why it can present something to us so well. . . Its opaqueness, its obstinate reference to itself, and its turning and folding back upon itself are precisely what makes it a mental power; for it in turn becomes something like a universe, and it is

capable of lodging things themselves in this universe – after it has transformed them into their meaning.[104]

The argument is, in effect, an elaborate and extended series of similes relating to its own structure and function, and this highlights a quality present throughout the essay: a kind of continual 'as if . . .' clause. Any discussion of the nature of language has to be by means of metaphor; the literal and logical absurdity of Merleau-Ponty's argument may be read as an essential part of the metaphorical process by which we are enabled to examine something that we cannot look at directly: language itself. His own imagery, moreover, seems to support precisely this reading. He does not argue, for instance, that language is unrelated to reality, but that our linguistic approach to reality is oblique, and achieved by treating it *as if* it is already known:

Language speaks peremptorily when it gives up trying to express the thing in itself. As algebra brings unknown magnitudes under consideration, speech differentiates significations no one of which is known separately; and it is by treating them as known . . . that language ends up by imposing the most precise identification upon us in a flash.[105]

Merleau-Ponty has been a major influence on the development of French structuralist and post-structuralist thought. As we have seen, he has also influenced his friend Ricoeur. In the passage from *The Symbolism of Evil* on the closed-circle of hermeneutics quoted earlier, we can see how Merleau-Ponty's idea of language provides the analogy by which Ricoeur suggests we can solve the problem noted in Chapter 2: how can we re-enter a poetic way of thinking if the 'poetic' is to be defined as belonging to an earlier, and now irrecoverable, world of primal participation? The argument sounds suspiciously like a re-run of Zeno. Just as we can only enter the closed circle of language by a logical impossibility, so also the logical impossibility of recapturing the 'precritical form of immediate belief' can only be achieved by the further impossibility of hermeneutics. *Credo quia absurdum.* Paradox can become a habit. We must conclude, it seems, that either *the Rule of Metaphor* represents a radical shift from the earlier position of *The Symbolism of Evil*, or that Ricoeur's theory of metaphor conflicts with his theory of language. To take this 1967 statement literally would be not merely to embrace the very dubiously-argued paradox already discussed, but would also be to endorse what looks like a sealed system of meaning as well. Such a hermeneutic would, in effect, incorporate the very principle of redescription and systematic substitution he is ostensibly so opposed to.

There is, however, another alternative. The notion that language presents a closed and self-referential world is, of course, much older than Saussure. Novalis, for instance, (in an undated 'Monologue') was only echoing the widespread Romantic rejection of Lockeian linguistics when he insisted that language did not directly refer to things, but 'is concerned only with itself'.[106] But this assertion is, for him, immediately connected with the Vichian distinction between things that are 'given' (and which can therefore only be known from without) and those which we create for ourselves (and thus know from within): not merely art, history, and the 'science' of society, but the structure of communication on which the human sciences are built − language and mathematics themselves:

> If it were only possible to make people understand that it is the same with language as it is with mathematical formulae − they constitute a world in itself − their play is self-sufficient, they express nothing but their own marvellous nature, and this is the very reason why they are so expressive, why they are the mirror to the strange play of relationships among things. Only their freedom makes them members of nature, only in their free movements does the world-soul express itself and make of them a delicate measure and a ground-plan of things . . . and though I believe that with these words I have delineated the nature and office of poetry as clearly as I can, all the same I know that no one can understand it . . .[107]

Here the 'closed-circle' is to be transcended not by appeals to Zeno's paradoxes, but by a doctrine of poetry that sees its connection with reality in terms of its own fundamentally metaphorical structure.

Similarly, if in the case of Merleau-Ponty and Ricoeur we accept the model of the closed circle as what it (literally) is, a metaphor, and read it in Berggren's sense of the way-out or literally absurd statement, the problem vanishes. It is only so long as we retain a sense of the literal impossibility of the 'closed-circle' image that it carries effective meaning. To take the statement literally implies the wilder absurdities of structuralism; to read it metaphorically, in the sense we have been discussing, suggests a new sense of the logical tensions discovered right at the heart of language itself.

It would not be difficult, for example, to take the last-quoted Merleau-Ponty passage in Kantian terms as a gloss on the ever-present dialectic between the unknowability of things-in-themselves and the

precarious status of our linguistic descriptions of them. The leap by
which we may be said to see or know 'in a flash' has echoes indeed of
Blake and the 'Poetic Genius' (not to mention Ian Ramsey). Nor is this
argument, read thus, inconsistent with Newman's *Grammar of Assent*.
The question of whether Merleau-Ponty himself would have accepted
these implications is interesting but, of course, as his own principle of
the autonomy of the text insists, entirely irrelevant. What is important
is that he, like so many of the earlier figures we have been discussing,
conveys in his writing a sense of the inexhaustible richness and complexity of a reality that can only be known in terms of the 'poetic':

> Since perception itself is never complete, since our perspectives give us a world
> to express and think about which envelopes and exceeds those perspectives, a
> world which announces itself in lightning signs as a spoken word or an arabes-
> que, why should the expression of the world be subjected to the prose of the
> *senses* or of the concept? It must be poetry; that is, it must completely awaken
> and recall our sheer power of expressing beyond things already said or seen.[108]

One wonders whether Merleau-Ponty, the Marxist, would have been
happy with an English translation that in that last phrase manages to
catch a fleeting echo of the Pauline definition of Faith from the King
James Bible. The speculation may be by definition irrelevant, but the
substantive point is not, for whatever the intention, the *effect* is to place
his view of the 'poetic' within an English and biblical tradition
stretching back through the New Testament to the pre-Socratic
philosophers which sees human language in terms of the *logos*: in the
tension and paradox of metaphor.

As a metaphor, moreover, the idea of hermeneutics as a closed circle
is revealing and useful not merely for the study of language, but for
the study of history itself. John Burrow, writing as a professional
historian of ideas, applies it to the process of language-learning as a
metaphor for our understanding of the past. 'We break into the
hermeneutical circle,' he writes, 'as we learn a natural language, learning to understand the parts by the whole and building an understanding of the whole by the parts.' But this analogy, he continues, has certain implications:

> ... although we can characterise the method in very general and perhaps un-
> necessarily pretentious terms as hermeneutic, there are no recipes. We may get
> guidance, tuition, and above all example, from those who know the language,
> and we may learn by rote some of the rules of grammar, but ultimately, to come
> to inhabit a language, we must learn as we say, to play it by ear . . .[109]

Once again we note the bi-focal nature of the analogy – here both subtle and with far-reaching implications. It is by no means self-evidently absurd to describe our understanding of the past as learning a natural language – though the word 'natural' in this context reminds us that the analogy is with an organic and historical system in the process of continual change, and specifically excludes Esperanto, Newspeak, or technical vocabularies. Yet the comparison also reminds us of the differences. To describe the practice of intellectual history as an attempt to 'listen to the conversations of the past' reminds us that learning any language involves submitting ourselves to *its* rules, *its* particular way of describing experience, *its* unique metaphorical structure. We learn almost nothing from approaching a language with a set of pre-conceived criteria by which it must be judged: especially if our object is to find out what it has to say. Burrow is, in effect, advocating what Popper has called 'methodological nominalism'.[110] He is refusing to try and answer the portentous question 'What is language?' (or 'What is intellectual history?') but simply saying '*listen*'. In this respect the analogy with language is doubly significant. We do not ask of languages, as we do of 'facts', are they true or false? We listen to what is being said within the given framework of possibilities afforded by that particular linguistic convention. Burrow is conscious, moreover, of the two-sidedness of his analogy:

But the analogy with translation draws our attention to another consideration. You cannot translate *from* a language without also translation *into* one. This points, I think, to the limitation in the representation of intellectual history as a recreation or re-experiencing of past thoughts. In writing it or speaking about it we have to ask and for whom do we translate? The answer, presumably, is oneself and one's readers or pupils: more generally, ourselves. But who are 'ourselves'? Inhabitants of the late twentieth century? The late twentieth century, even in England, is a fairly culturally bewildering place (and incidentally a hard case for any holistic theory of culture) . . . In choosing the language into which to render the past, one in a sense chooses both one's past and one's present, declaring not only what one finds interesting in the former and how, but whom one wishes to address in the latter.[111]

This is not, I think, an argument for seeing translations into modern English in terms of language-games. As we saw in Chapter 2, natural language does not easily submit to such demarcations. Bakhtin's concept of heteroglossia, the concurrent existence of many different styles or modes of discourse that are under tension from one another, mutually interacting and modifying, is a much more appropriate model not merely for the novel, but for the state of our language. The Bible Society's assumption that present-day English represents a popular scientific and materialistic culture, ill-at-ease with ambiguities or mystery, needs only to be confronted with the size of the 'Occult' section in any bookshop; Grayston's assertion that modern English is an enfeebled thing unable to cope with the depth and richness of Old Testament Hebrew similarly sounds not unlike Milton bewailing that he had seen the end of culture. To take one very obvious example (which, because it is so obvious is easily missed): the language of Shakespeare and the Authorized Version of the Bible is not a dead language in the late twentieth century, either in Britain, America, or Australasia – and certainly not in the English-speaking areas of Africa or Asia. It is archaic, but still present to us as a current linguistic idiom: *in use* every day in churches and theatres, taught and discussed in schools, seminaries, and universities, broadcast in some form almost every day on radio and television. It is not the language of ordinary colloquial speech, but then, *it never was*. Shakespeare wrote mostly in blank verse or in a highly elaborated, artificial, and densely punning prose – both of which were the products of a complex and stylized literary convention; his vocabulary is full of neologisms, and is greater in size than that of any other English-speaking person there has ever been. Similarly, the King James Bible was always consciously archaic, and is written by deliberate intent in an English that was never that of ordinary speech. Both literary codes were affected by, have left, and still leave, a lasting impression on ordinary speech-rhythms and vocabulary. They do not constitute separate language-games, but are a part of that immensely complicated and polyvalent flux of styles that we call 'English' – that also includes pidgin English, commercial English, dialect, slang, and a host of others.

Thus, returning to Burrow's pregnant phrase, the way in which we 'break into the hermeneutical circle' of the past brings into a specific focus the whole complex range of problems that group themselves around the question of how far our metaphorical constructs, thrown out, as it were, in the face of reality, can reshape for us from the fragmentary evidence of the past that intelligible whole we conceptualize as 'history'. His image reminds us that what the nineteenth century supposed to be a yawning gulf between history and typology may not be as wide as some Victorian commentators supposed. Mrs Humphry Ward, Matthew Arnold's niece, and author of what is probably the finest novel of the period to deal with the impact of the Higher Criticism, described in 1888 how her young clergyman hero, Robert Elsmere, began to try and break into that 'closed-circle':

Hitherto he had been under the guidance of men of his own day, of the nineteenth century historian, who refashions the past on the lines of his own mind, who gives it rationality, coherence, and, as it were, modernness, so that the main impression he produces on us, so long as we look at that past through him only is on the whole an impression of *continuity*, of *resemblance*.

Whereas, on the contrary, the first impression left on a man by the attempt to plunge into the materials of history for himself is almost always an extraordinarily sharp impression of *difference* of *contrast*. Ultimately, of course, he sees that these men and women whose letters and biographies, whose creeds and general conceptions he is investigating, are in truth his ancestors, bone of his bone, flesh of his flesh. But at first the student who goes back, say, in the history of Europe, behind the Renaissance or behind the Crusades into the actual deposits of the past, is often struck with a kind of *vertige*. The men and women whom he has dragged forth into the light of his own mind are to him like some strange puppet-show. They are called by names he knows – kings, bishops, judges, poets, priests, men of letters – but what a gulf between him and them! What motives, what beliefs, what embryonic processes of thought and morals, what bizarre combinations of ignorance and knowledge, of the highest sanctity with the lowest credulity or falsehood; what extraordinary prepossessions, born with a man and tainting his whole way of seeing and thinking from childhood to the grave! Amid all the intellectual dislocation of the spectacle, indeed, he perceives certain Greeks and certain Latins who represent a forward strain, who belong as it seems to a world of their own, a world ahead of them. To them he stretches out his hand: '*You*', he says to them, 'though your priests spoke to you not of Christ, but of Zeus and Artemis, *you* are really my kindred!' But intellectually they stand alone. Around them, after them, for long ages the world 'spake as a child, felt as a child, understood as a child.'

Then he sees what it is that makes the difference, digs the gulf. '*Science*', the mind cries, '*ordered knowledge*'. And so for the first time the modern recognises what the accumulations of his forefathers have done for him. He takes the torch which man has been so long and patiently fashioning to his hand, and turns it on the past, and at every step the sight grows stranger, and yet more moving, more pathetic. The darkness into which he penetrates does but make him grasp his own guiding light the more closely. And yet, bit by bit, it has been prepared for him by these groping half conscious generations, and the scrutiny which began in repulsion and laughter ends in a marvelling gratitude.[112]

Though the tone of patronizing confidence is unlike that of Nineham and other similar twentieth-century commentators, the *argument* is not that different. Certainly it does represent a genuine attempt to listen to the conversations of the past, but it is in the frame of mind of a Piaget listening to a five-year-old's chatter to see how it corresponds with his schematized theory of child development. There is little sense that, apart from that minority of classical writers who 'represent a forward strain', there is anything worth listening to for its own sake. But it is one of Mrs Ward's many qualities that she is well aware of the degree to which history is an interpretative activity. The dominating image is that of 'enlightenment': the figures of the past are 'dragged forth' into the 'light' of the historian's own mind; 'science', that is here the 'ordered knowledge' of scientific history, provides a 'torch' by which he may 'penetrate' the darkness of the past. The sequence of images is significant. The historian – and Elsmere in particular – is in intention almost a Christ-like figure, whose task is to lighten the world (and spread 'sweetness and light' in her uncle's sense), but there is a Promethean strain that gradually intrudes (especially with the 'forward-looking' Greeks) until the final effect is that of Conrad's Marlowe sailing towards the heart of darkness up the Congos of the past. Intertwined with this chain of images is another, of growth from childhood to maturity, echoing in its evolutionary tones Tennyson's view of Hallam in *In Memoriam*: we reach out to our contemporaries of the past who belong to a world of their own, and whom only later generations will appreciate. The Hebrew prophets, we notice, are conspicuously absent from this evolutionary elite. The Bible, Mrs Ward tell us a few pages later, is of interest not to the historian of 'fact' but of 'testimony':

Testimony like every other human product has *developed*. Man's power of apprehending and recording what he sees and hears has grown from less to more, from weaker to stronger, like any other of his faculties, just as the reasoning powers of the cave-dweller have developed into the reasoning powers of a Kant . . .

To plunge into the Christian period without having first cleared the mind as to what is meant in history and literature by 'the critical method', which in history may be defined as the 'science of what is credible', and in literature as 'the science of what is rational,' is to invite fiasco. The theologian in such a state sees no obstacle to accepting an arbitrary list of documents with all the strange stuff they may contain, and declaring them to be sound historical material, while he applies to all the strange stuff of a similar kind surrounding them the most rigorous principles of modern science. Or he has to make believe that the reasoning processes exhibited in the speeches of the Acts, in certain passages of St. Paul's Epistles, or in the Old Testament quotations in the Gospels, have a validity for the mind of the nineteenth century, when in truth they are the imperfect, half-childish products of the mind of first century, of quite insignificant or indirect value to the historian of fact, of enormous value to the historian of *testimony* and its varieties.[113]

It is important to be reminded that, just as there is more than one audience for whom the historian may translate, so there is more than one
history to be translated. Mrs Ward's 'history of testimony' is, in effect,
part of a much larger Victorian history: the 'history of progress'. Richard
Jenkyns's *The Victorians and Ancient Greece*,[114] Mark Girouard's *The
Return to Camelot*, and, above all, John Burrow's own *A Liberal
Descent*,[115] have all illustrated how far Victorian historiography was
dominated by certain semi-conscious or even unconscious images and
motifs. Burrow's illustration of William Theed's sculpture of Queen Vic-
toria and Prince Albert in Saxon dress must be put alongside Girouard's
many versions of the Prince as a mediaeval knight in full armour, and
Emil Wolff's sculpture of him as a Greek warrior.[116] There is no reason
to assume that our own histories are any the less dominated by such semi-
submersible paradigms – whether we consider Winston Churchill's
Second World War, E. P. Thompson's *Making of the English Working
Class*, or a computer-aided study of historical demography.

The specific conflict between 'scientific history' and miracles which
was to prove such a stumbling-block to the faith of progressively-minded
Victorians, must be seen in this context. As we have seen, a culture with
no concept of nature has no concept of the miraculous. A 'miracle' in the
sense of Hume's *Essay on Miracles* – a break in the laws of natural science
– which was to destroy the orthodox belief of Elsmere, is a product of the
scientific revolution of the seventeenth century just as surely as was
biblical literalism. As Lionel Snell has argued, the legacy of that particular metaphorical ordering of perception has been a mental set that
conditions its participants *not* to see inexplicable events as powerfully as
certain other societies have conditioned their acceptance.[117] But a century which has seen the phenomenal growth of tourism around Lourdes;
the recovery of Solzhenitzyn from cancer; or the spoon-bending activities
of Uri Geller and Professor John Taylor is not short of events with potentially miraculous interpretations. Any language-system, except the
Adamic language of pure essences, will encounter events that cannot be
adequately described within the terms of its particular schemata. What
marks a dynamic and living linguistic culture from an atrophied one is
its capacity to translate the new and unschematized. We cannot (by
definition) approach or explain miracles; they are simply the most
dramatic examples of the way in which way-out or boundary-breaking
events act as definers of a reality that is larger than our metaphors of
it.

The metaphors which we choose or are conditioned to use in defining reality, therefore, are, and have been historically, of vital significance. In the discussion of the quotation from *Robert Elsmere* we noted how prominent were images of 'light' and 'enlightenment' in understanding the past. There was, of course, an excellent semantic reason for this. Mrs Ward was a good enough classicist to know that the derivation of the Greek word for 'truth', *alétheia*, is from 'unconcealment' or that which is 'not-hidden'. In discovering the truth we illuminate and thus see that which was previously dark and obscure. But as Heidegger has pointed out, in one of his most insightful discussions of poetic imagery, the relationship between 'unconcealment' or 'openness' and 'light' is not quite what common sense might suggest:

> In the history of language the German word *Lichtung* is a translation derived from the French *clairière*. It is formed in accordance with the older words *Waldung* [foresting] and *Feldung* [fielding].
> The forest clearing [or opening] is experienced in contrast to dense forest, called *Dickung* in our older language. The substantive *Lichtung* goes back to the verb *lichten*. The adjective *licht* is the same word as "open". To open something means to make it light, free and open, e.g., to make the forest free of trees at one place. The free space thus originating is the clearing. What is light in the sense of being free and open has nothing in common with the adjective "light" which means "bright", neither linguistically nor factually . . . light never first creates openness. Rather light presupposes openness.[118]

As in the English word 'light', the German verb *lichten* contains the double meaning (from roots in both Sanskrit and Greek) of having little weight and of luminosity, and Heidegger is conscious of both meanings.[119] But the association of 'light' with 'openness' has, Heidegger argues, other roots in Greek as well:

> In the same way as speculative dialectical thinking, originary intuition and its evidence remain dependent upon openness . . . *Evidentia* is the word which Cicero uses to translate the Greek *enargeia*, that is, to transform it into the Roman. *Enargeia*, which has the same root as *argentum* (silver), means that which in itself and of itself radiates and brings itself to light. In the Greek language, one is not speaking about the action of seeing, about *videre*, but about that which gleams and radiates. But it can radiate only if openness has already been granted. The beam of light does not first create the opening, openness, it only traverses it.[120]

Hence, too, the significance of that chain of imagery of 'opening', 'breaking-open', and 'break-through', that have run like a *leitmotif* throughout this study both in connection with the structure of biblical narrative and in the subsequent Western experience of Nature – to the point where we can speak of an 'opening' to a narrative or a 'breakthrough' in the search for the solution to a problem, and scarcely be conscious of the metaphor or its implications. But (as Heidegger has also observed) that essentially negative derivation of *alétheia* means in addition that another, opposite, notion, that of *léthé*, 'concealment' or as it is better known from Classical mythology) 'forgetfulness', is an inescapable part of the semantic genesis of the word. Hence Plato could write of 'truth' as something 'remembered' (i.e. 'un-forgotten') rather than something found. Nevertheless, the association with light is not altogether left out: the platonic root of our word 'idea' is *eidos* – 'to see'.[121]

It was, perhaps, Heidegger's early experience as a seminarian in Freiburg and his subsequent rejection of a religious vocation, as much as his formal philosophical training, that led him so often to develop his semantic arguments from Greek rather than Hebrew roots.[122] Certainly the imagery of light and darkness, openness and closure, belongs as much to the biblical tradition as the Classical. Nor have they lost their philosophical significance today – as the growing interest in Heidegger's work testifies. For our purposes, however, it is the parallel contemporary debate over openness and closure in the structure of language itself that assumes a new significance in the context of Heidegger's analysis. Just as the Greek word for 'truth' contains an inherent semantic tension between 'openness' and 'concealment', so it seems that over and over again in the last three hundred years discussions of language have had recourse to models that imply an underlying and perhaps unresolvable conflict. It is present, as we have seen, in Heidegger himself, who never seems to have quite resolved the tension between asserting the autonomy of language and its capacity to relate to the world of things. Neither the Empiricist notion that words corresponded simply to things, nor the counter-assertion that it refers only to itself, serve satisfactorily to explain the phenomenon of the New.[123] The process of 'making' inherent in the root of *poesis* and its many extensions and cognates only helps to illuminate this problem if we recognize that it is (and always has been) itself a *tensional* concept. To make the New is the prerogative of the *logos*.

We began this book with a practical problem: the failure of one popular modern English translation of the Bible to cope adequately with its basic material. We have seen how this turned out to be symptomatic of a much wider malaise in modern biblical translation stemming, in part at any rate, from the way in which contemporary biblical criticism has become separated from its own historical roots in the eighteenth and nineteenth centuries – and from the parallel and cognate discipline of literary criticism (which has also suffered from the imposed 'glacier-wall' of partition). In the process we have discovered how certain theoretical problems, that of cultural relativity, for instance, and the emergence of the new, are in turn related to a confused and often inchoate, but amazingly dynamic, group of ideas centering around the notion of the 'poetic'. For all its contradictions and unresolved problems, it is an idea that has shown an astonishing vitality since its origins in the early part of the eighteenth century, to the extent that no modern discussion of the Bible seems able to do without it. In that sense, if in no other, it appears to be an idea whose time has come. If this is so, then the foregoing discussion may be some aid to greater clarity in its use.

Moreover, if, on the one hand, the metaphor of the 'poetic' has shown us things hitherto unperceived about the Bible, its structure and mode of expression, on the other, it has enabled us also to see poetry in a different light. Similarly *both* history and typology may be seen as essentially metaphorical approaches to a reality which is both finite and inexhaustible.[124] It is possible to explore the story of Elijah on Horeb – to continue our paradigm image – in both historical and typological terms. The former takes us into the long progressive desynonymy of the 'natural' and the 'supernatural', the history of science, theology, and etymology; the latter through a chain of imagery and iconography that includes Dante, St John of the Cross, and Blake. Our problem is not so much that the original event is inaccessible to us (as it is) but that, in another sense, it is apparently accessible in too many ways. We can seem to approach it by a multitude of routes. It is, rather, that at its centre lies an event of such complexity and mystery that it resists translation into any of our preconceived categories or disciplines (as it resisted Elijah's own). As such, it may be taken as emblematic of other events and acted metaphors which occur throughout the Bible and which defy classification. The greatest problem with 'miracles' is, perhaps, that we attempt to classify them as such. What we have seen here (and it is only a fragment of the story) is a conflict between open and closed systems of hermeneutics: those which claim to possess the Word, and those which are capable of being translated by it.

Notes

Place of publication is London, unless otherwise specified.

INTRODUCTION

1 See Charles E. McClelland, *State, Society, and University in Germany 1700–1914*, Cambridge University Press 1980, pp. 115–6; D. F. S. Scott, *Wilhelm von Humboldt and the Idea of a University*, Durham University, 1960, pp. 3–4; Paul R. Sweet, *Wilhelm von Humboldt: A Biography*, 2 vols. Columbus, Ohio State University Press, 1978–80, II, p. 57.

2 The story of F. A. Wolf at Göttingen, though possibly apocryphal, typifies attitudes of the day. In 1777 Wolf 'insisted on being inscribed in the matriculation-book as "Student of Philology". The prorector, Baldinger, an M.D. of some celebrity, laughed at the absurdity, and informed him there was no such faculty. Medicine, Law, Arts, and Theology were the four faculties; if he wanted (God forbid he should!) to become a schoolmaster, the way was to enter as student of theology. Wolf, with his habitual obstinacy, refused to see the force of this. He meant to study philology, and did not intend to study theology; why should he be called what he was not? The prorector gave up the point, and Wolf was actually inscribed as "Student of Philology", the first instance, not only at Göttingen, but at any university. The matriculation was an epoch in German education.' (Mark Pattison, 'F. A. Wolf' in *Essays*, ed. Nettleship, vol. I, 1889, p. 343)

3 See F. W. J. von Schelling, *On University Studies*, tr. E. S. Morgan, Athens, Ohio, 1966. For the writings of Schelling, Fichte, Schleiermacher, Steffens and Humboldt on universities see E. Anrich (ed.) *Die Idee der deutschen Universität: Die fünf Grundschriften aus der Zeit ihrer Neubegründung durch klassischen Idealismus und romantischen Realismus*, Darmstadt, 1960.

4 Written in 1888. *Religionsgeschichtliche Untersuchugen*, Bonn, 1911, repr. Hildesheim, 1972. p.x. Cited by Edwin A. Judge, 'Antike und Christentum': 'Towards a Definition of the Field', *Aufstieg und Niedergang der Römischen Welt*, eds. Hildegard Temporini and Wolfgang Haase, II, 23.i. Berlin, de Gruyter, 1979, pp. 8–9.

5 It is interesting to note that, for instance, in the case of Mark Pattison's recommendations on the reform of Oxford, those curriculum changes which served the ideal of *Wissenschaft* tended to be more influential than his more radical interdisciplinary proposals. See 'Report of H.M. Commissioners appointed to inquire into the State, Discipline, Studies, and Revenues of the University and Colleges of Oxford', *Parliamentary Papers*, XXII, 1852; *Suggestions on Academical Organization with Especial Reference to Oxford*, Edinburgh 1868; and John Sparrow, *Mark Pattison and the Idea of a University*, Cambridge University Press, 1967.

6 See Prickett, *Romanticism and Religion: The Tradition of Coleridge and Wordsworth in the Victorian Church*, Cambridge University Press, 1976.

7 Hans W. Frei, *The Eclipse of Biblical Narrative: A Study in Eighteenth and Nineteenth Century Hermeneutics*, New Haven, Yale University Press, 1974; and Robert W. Funk, *Language, Hermeneutics, and the Word of God: The Problem of Language in the New Testament and Contemporary Theology*, N.Y., Harper and Row, 1966. For an account of some other (mostly Jewish) attempts to use literary models in understanding biblical narrative see Robert Alter, *The Art of Biblical Narrative*, Allen and Unwin, 1981, ch. I.

8 *Coleridge and Wordsworth: The Poetry of Growth*, Cambridge University Press, 1970.

9 *Romanticism and Religion*.

CHAPTER 1

1 S. T. Coleridge, *Confessions of an Inquiring Spirit*, 2nd edn, 1849, p. 9.

2 Coleridge, *Confessions*, p. 13.

3 Letter to the Editor of *Theology*, May 1978.

4 Erich Auerbach, *Mimesis*, Princeton University Press, 1953, Ch. I, pp. 3 ff.

5 That the story is self-evidently 'mythological' in this restricted literary sense of carrying a particular weight of meaning, does not, of course, imply anything about its historical factuality. The Tangshan earthquake of July 1976, the year of Mao's death, in China, for instance, was preceded by a display of natural phenomena almost identical to those described here, and, according to a witness, Dr Jocelyn Chey, was followed by an absolutely unearthly stillness without any sound of living creature or movement of the elements.

6 G. B. Caird, *The Language and Imagery of the Bible*, Duckworth, 1980, p. 2.

7 I am grateful to Professor Sten Stenson for this translation. See also Aharon Wiener: 'The Hebrew words "*kol dammanah dakkah*" are usually taken to mean "gentle breeze" or "quiet voice", occasionally also "shrill whistling". They are accordingly interpreted either as a spiritualisation of

Elijah's image of God, as a lesser theophany, in which the Divine is hardly perceptible, or as an expression of the demonic aspect of God. However the literal translation of the text, "small voice of silence", expresses as a *coincidentia oppositorum* the *mysterium tremendum et fascinans* of Elijah's theophany.' 'The Talmud', he adds, 'regards the "*kol dammanah dakkah*" as "soundless stillness".' (*The Prophet Elijah in the Development of Judaism*, Routledge, 1978, p. 14.)

8 Alan Richardson (ed.), *A Theological Word Book of the Bible*, S.C.M. Press, 1950, pp. 234 ff.

9 Ward Allen (ed.), *Translating for King James*, Allen Lane, The Penguin Press, 1970, p. 89.

10 A. W. Pollard, *Records of the English Bible*, Oxford University Press, 1911, p. 308. The Catholic translators of the period were no less tolerant of ambiguity and fully prepared to cite the Greek as well as the Vulgate. I Peter ii, 2, they rendered by 'As infants even now borne, reasonable, milke without guile desire ye', commenting, 'We do so place *reasonable*, of purpose, that it may be indifferent both to infants going before, as in our Latin text: or to milke that followeth after, as in other Latin copies and in the Greeke . . .' (Ward Allen, *Translating for King James* ibid.)

11 The fifteenth-century German translator, Nicholas von Wyle, had been even more uncompromising, insisting that even errors should be faithfully transcribed. See George Steiner, *After Babel: Aspects of Language and Translation*, Oxford University Press, 1976, p. 262.

12 Kenneth Grayston, 'Confessions of a Biblical Translator', *New Universities Quarterly*, vol. 33, no. 3, Summer 1979, p. 288.

13 Ibid., p. 287.

14 Ibid., p. 286.

15 See H. Wheeler Robinson, *Inspiration and Revelation in the Old Testament*, Oxford University Press, 1962, p. 34.

16 The most stimulating discussion of this changing relationship for me is to be found in Owen Barfield's *Saving the Appearances*, New York, Harcourt Brace, 1957, culminating in a discussion of this passage on p. 114. Whether Israel's withdrawal from primal participation in the natural world was fundamentally similar to that of the evolution of other societies, or, as Barfield convincingly argues, fundamentally different, is not important to my argument at this point, though, of course, it does have a very profound influence on how we interpret the Elijah story.

17 See, for instance, Claus Westermann, 'The Interpretation of the Old Testament', tr. Dietrich Ritschl, *Essays on Old Testament Hermeneutics*, ed. Westermann, (English tr. ed. J. L. Mays, Richmond, Va., John Knox Press, 1966), p. 44; or Martin Buber, *The Prophetic Faith*, N.Y., Harper Torchbooks, 1960, p. 46.

18 Illustrating how this is one of a group of polemical stories against Baal-worship, Leah Bronner writes: 'Ugaritic sources indicate that Baal was not only the god of rain, vegetation, and fertility, but also controlled fire and lightning.' The great drought (I Kings, xvii-xviii) was thus one attack on

Baal's efficacy; so also were 'the various Biblical passages where Elijah enlisted the aid of fire to prove that God rules over all these forces, aimed to undermine a popular belief that Baal had dominion over this element'. (*The Stories of Elijah and Elisha*, Leiden, E. J. Brill, 1968, pp. 55 and 62.) See also, Wiener, *The Prophet Elijah*, p. 7.

19 A point that appealed greatly to Augustine. See *De Civitate Dei*, xvii. 22; *Enn. II in Ps.*, c. 5; *En. II in Ps. 30*, s. 2, c. 7.

20 *New English Bible*. I have followed this translation here because the repeated phrase 'as the scriptures say . . .' emphasizes the midrashic element more forcefully than the 'it is written' of the Authorized Version – a point again stressing a shift of cultural interests.

21 II Kings ii, 11.

22 For the parallel identification of Jesus with Melchizedek see Hebrews v, 1–10; vii, 1–17.

23 Malachi iv, 4–5. Wiener, *The Prophet Elijah*, pp. 32–4.

24 A. C. Charity, *Events and their Afterlife: The Dialectics of Christian Typology in the Bible and Dante*, Cambridge University Press, 1966, p. 126.

25 The weight of scholarly opinion seems to be in favour of accepting this as a genuine saying of Jesus. See Charity, ibid., p. 125.

26 ' "What is Torah?" asks one rabbi in a passage from the Babylonian Talmud (Kiddushin 496) and Torah, remember, stands here, as it often does, as a collective designation for the whole of the Jewish Scriptures, and not merely the Pentateuch. And the answer comes "It is the interpretation of the Torah", *midrash Torah* in the Hebrew. This midrash technique and process, this mode of Jewish interpretation, plays such a vital part in the making of Scripture, that we can understand it against the background of the power at work in the putting together of a biblical text, in the transmission of that text, and in subsequent post-canonical interpretations of that text. It is the germ, the seed of Scripture, and understanding it will help us in our reading of both Old and New Testaments, since with its aid we can see the text with the eyes of the midrashist, who was at one and the same time maker and interpreter, and used his skill to build up his text from traditional material, and – after it had been constructed – to read something new out of the text for each succeeding generation.' Michael Wadsworth, 'Making and Interpreting Scripture', *Ways of Reading the Bible*, ed. Wadsworth, Brighton, Harvester Press/New York, Barnes and Noble, 1981, p. 8.

27 In typology, Origen, for instance, distinguishes between three levels of understanding, corresponding to the 'flesh', the 'soul', and the 'spirit' of man, in an ascending order of insight (John Wilkinson, *Interpretation and Community*, Macmillan, 1963, ch. VI). See also Henri de Lubac, *Exégèse médiévale: les quatre sens de l'Ecriture*, Paris, F. Aubier, Editions Montaigne, 1959–64 (4 vols.). In contrast the Antiochene school taught that there were four levels, of which one permitted the reader to discount the apparent literal meaning altogether (Wilkinson., ch. VII). With Augustine

this kind of immensely detailed exegesis was to find perhaps its greatest exponent and theoretician. He provided not merely detailed commentaries on great swathes of biblical texts, but a completely coherent theoretical base for his system. As Peter Brown explains: 'For Augustine and his hearers, the Bible was literally the "word" of God. It was regarded as a single communication, a single message in an intricate code, and not as an exceedingly heterogeneous collection of separate books. Above all, it was a communication that was intrinsically so far above the pitch of human minds, that to be made available to our senses at all, this "Word" had to be communicated by means of an intricate game of "signs" (very much as a modern therapist makes contact with the inner world of a child in terms of significant patterns emerging in play with sand, water and bricks): "Wisdom's way of teaching chooses to hint at how divine things should be thought of by certain images and analogies available to the senses." ' (Peter Brown, *Augustine of Hippo*, Faber, 1967, pp. 252–3.)

28 Peter Brown, *Augustine*, p. 253. There was a further theological reason why this obscure communication should have been necessary in the first place. It was the result of a specific dislocation of the human consciousness – namely, of the Fall (ibid., p. 261). After the Fall, Adam and Eve had ceased to possess direct intuitive knowledge, and were forced to fall back upon the clumsy artifice of words for communication. But God had, in the Bible, irradiated the murky depths of fallen language with gleams and flashes from another realm so that, with effort and careful attention, something of the divine meaning of existence could still be distinguished, if only through a glass darkly.

29 For example Augustine, *Quaest. Gen.*, 168, and *En. in Ps.* 110, i; Ambrose, *Expositio in Lucan*, iv, 15 (probably from Origen); Jeremiah, *In Isaiam*, xvi, 58, 3–4; Cassian, *Conf.*, x., 6; Maximus of Turin, *S.* 35, sect. 3.

30 'Living Flame of Love', Stanza II, 16. *The Complete Works of St John of the Cross*, tr. and ed. E. Allison Peers, Burns and Oates, 1964, vol. III.

31 Even if, as Hans Frei has claimed, that typology is fundamentally different in function. (*The Eclipse of Biblical Narrative*, ch. I.)

32 Mrs Sarah Trimmer, *Help to the Unlearned in the Study of the Holy Scriptures*, 1806, p. 196.

33 Frei, *The Eclipse of Biblical Narrative*, ch. 10 stresses the a-typicality of Herder as biblical critic, but here the judgement is noticeably conventional.

34 J. G. Herder, *The Spirit of Hebrew Poetry*, (Dessau, 1782/3), tr. James Marsh, Burlington, Vermont, 1833, ii, 40.

35 J. Keble *The Christian Year*, 43rd edn, 1851, p. 80.

36 For Keble the entire natural world was charged with a system of divinely appointed 'correspondences' drawn from mediaeval mystical thought. In *Tract Eighty Nine* he tells us, for instance, that the sky represents 'a canopy spread over the tents and dwellings of the saints'; birds are tokens

of 'Powers in heaven above who watch over our proceedings in this lower world'; and waters flowing into the sea are 'people gathered into the Church of Christ'. The smell of flowers is the 'odour of sanctity'; trees and weeds are 'false principles'; the tamarisk, 'the double mind'; the palm 'eternal purity'. 'The Sun, the greatest light, is our Lord; the Moon, the lesser light, the Church.' 'He appointed the moon for certain seasons, and the Sun knoweth his going down.' See Prickett, *Romanticism and Religion*, p. 106; B. W. Martin, *John Keble, Priest, Professor, Poet*, Croom Helm, 1976; and also Lytton Strachey, 'Life of Cardinal Manning', *Eminent Victorians*, Chatto, 1918, pp. 19–20.

37 T. Carlyle, *Sartor Resartus*, 1834; see also M. H. Abrams, *Natural Supernaturalism*, N.Y., Norton, 1973.

38 An idea that goes back at least to Joseph Butler's *The Analogy of Religion*, 1736.

39 J. Robinson, *The First Book of Kings*, Cambridge University Press, 1972, p. 221. See also John Gray, *I and II Kings: A Commentary*, S.C.M. Press, revised edn, 1970, p. 140.

40 See, for instance, Dennis Nineham, *The Use and Abuse of the Bible*, Macmillan, 1976, ch. III.

41 *Faith and the Mystery of God*, S.C.M. Press, 1982, pp. 6–7.

42 Nineham, *Use and Abuse of the Bible*, p. 70.

43 Ibid., pp. 64–5.

44 Ibid., p. 187.

45 Ibid., p. 190.

46 *A Rebirth of Images*, Dacre Press, 1944.

47 John Bowden, in a discussion with Stephen Medcalf in the Meeting House, University of Sussex, 1975.

48 Caird, *Language and Imagery of the Bible*, p. 193.

49 Ibid., p. 9.

50 H. Prado and J. B. Villalpando *In Ezechielem Explanationes*, 3 vols., Rome, 1596–1605. See Joseph Gutmann, *The Temple of Solomon*, Missoula, Montana, Scholars Press, 1976; Helen Rosenau, *Vision of the Temple*, Oresko Books, 1979; A. Businck, *Der Tempel von Jerusalem von Salomo*, Leiden, 1980.

51 See for instance, 'Belshassar's Feast' (mezzotint 1832), 'Joshua Commanding the Sun to Stand Still upon Gideon', (oil 1816; mezzotint 1827) or 'The Crucifixion' (mezzotint 1834).

52 See Quentin Bell, *On Human Finery*, Hogarth Press, 1976, pp. 76–89.

53 Steiner, *After Babel*, p. 17.

54 See, for instance, Roger Scruton, *Kant*, Oxford University Press, 1982, pp. 46–7.

55 Northrop Frye, *The Great Code: The Bible and Literature*, Routledge, 1982, p. xv.

56 Nineham, *Use and Abuse of the Bible*, pp. 260–61.

57 'It is not only the last part of this statement that is relevant to the Bible . . . practically everything Professor Trilling says here is relevant and impor-

tant for our enquiry.' Ibid., p. 261. That literary criticism owed in the first place many of its principles to biblical criticism is not considered.

58 Ibid., p. 262

59 Caird, *Language and Imagery of the Bible*, p. 165.

60 See Richard E. Palmer, *Hermeneutics: Interpretation Theory in Schleiermacher, Dilthey, Heidegger, and Gadamer*, Northwestern University Press, 1969, ch. 6.

61 Paul Ricoeur, *The Rule of Metaphor*, tr. Robert Czerny, with Kathleen McLaughlin and John Costello, S. J., University of Toronto Press, 1977, p. 220.

62 Nor is Caird's view historically true of Christendom. Note G. W. H. Lampe's comment, specifically in relation to typology, that: 'Those elements in the Church's traditional liturgical forms which today so often seem to be most in need of revision or deletion in order to make what is said and done appear relevant to the ordinary man of the twentieth century ... are precisely those which would have given the service a familiar and homely touch in the ears of his ancestor.' ('The Reasonableness of Typology', *Essays in Typology*, G. W. H. Lampe and K. J. Woollcombe, S.C.M. Press, 1957, p. 12.)

63 For an extended discussion of allegorical and figurative modes of interpretation in biblical texts, see John Wilkinson, *Interpretation and Community*, Macmillan, 1963.

64 Birger Gerhardsson, 'The Good Samaritan – The Good Shepherd', *Coniectanea Neotestamentica*, XVI, Lund, C.W.K., Gleerup, 1958.

65 Matthew xxi, 33–41; Luke xx, 9–16; Mark xii, 1–10.

66 See, for instance, Gareth Knight, *A History of White Magic*, Mowbrays, 1978, p. 24.

67 Ward Allen, *Translating for King James*, p. 47.

68 Frank Kermode, *The Genesis of Secrecy: On the Interpretation of Narrative*, Harvard University Press, 1979, p. 18.

69 W. K. Wimsatt, Jr and M. C. Beardsley, 'The Intentional Fallacy'. First published in the *Sewanee Review*, reprinted in *Essays in Modern Criticism*, ed. Ray B. West, N.Y., Holt, Rinehart and Winston, 1952.

70 *Henry IV* Part 2, Act III, Sc. i, 46–50; *Midsummer Night's Dream*, Act V, Sc. i, 12–18.

71 W. Blake, *The Marriage of Heaven and Hell* (1793), in *Complete Writings*, ed. Geoffrey Keynes, Oxford University Press, 1966. p. 150.

72 K. R. Popper, *The Open Society and its Enemies*, 4th edn, Routledge, 1962, vol. I, p. 31.

73 See Palmer's distinction between the tradition of Schleiermacher and Dilthey, and the followers of Heidegger – Bultmann, Ebeling, Fuchs, and Gadamer – who lay greater stress on the historian as himself conditioned by the historical process. Palmer, *Hermeneutics*, p. 46.

74 'De iusto discrimine theologiae biblicae et dogmaticae regundisque recte utriusque finibus', Frei, *The Eclipse of Biblical Narrative*, p. 165.

75 As his letters to Bentley show, Newton was, of course, very far from being a methodological essentialist, but there is no doubt that this was how

he was popularly interpreted.

76 *Aids to Reflection*, ed. T. Fenby, Edinburgh, Grant, 1905, p. 363; see also Prickett, *Coleridge and Wordsworth*, p. 196, and *Romanticism and Religion*, pp. 78–90.

77 Steiner, *After Babel*, p. 136.

78 Roland Barthes, 'The Death of the Author', *Image-Music-Text*, tr. Stephen Heath, N.Y., Hill and Wang, 1977, p. 146.

79 Ibid., p. 147.

80 'The Struggle with the Angel', ibid., p. 135.

81 'Intellectual History: The Poverty of Methodology' (unpublished paper), pp. 8–9 ff.

82 Edmund Leach, *Genesis as Myth and Other Essays*, Cape, 1969.

83 *The True Interpreter: A History of Translation Theory and Practice in the West*, Oxford, Blackwell, 1979, pp. 1–2, 34.

84 John Dryden, *Of Dramatic Poesy and Other Critical Essays*, ed. G. Watson, 2 vols., Everyman, 1962, I, 268–9.

85 Steiner, *After Babel*, p. 253.

86 'In Praise of Metaphrase', *Comparative Criticism*, ed. E. S. Shaffer, vol. 6, Cambridge University Press, 1984.

87 Kelly, *The True Interpreter*, pp. 1–2.

88 Eugene A. Nida, 'Principles of Translation as Exemplified by Bible Translating', *On Translation*, ed. Reuben A. Brower, Harvard Studies in Comparative Literature No. 23, Cambridge, Mass., Harvard University Press, 1959, p. 19.

89 For accounts of this distinction and its application see Eugene A. Nida, *Towards a Science of Translating*, Leiden, E. J. Brill, 1964; and Nida and C. Taber, *The Theory and Practice of Translation*, Brill, 1969. See also Susan Basnett-McGuire, *Translation Studies*, Methuen, 1980 pp. 26–8.

90 Nida, *On Translation*, p. 15.

91 Ibid., p. 19.

92 Caird, *Language and Imagery of the Bible*, pp. 28, 77–78.

93 Itself often more of a paraphrase, 'sense for sense' rather than 'word for word', as in the Vulgate version of Elijah story under discussion. See H. F. D. Sparks, *The Cambridge History of the Bible*, eds. P. R. Ackroyd and C. F. Evans, vol. I, Cambridge University Press, 1970, p. 525.

94 Steiner, *After Babel*, p. 349.

95 Ibid., p. 414.

96 Wiles, *Faith and the Mystery of God*, p. 5.

CHAPTER 2

1 e.g. *Nichomachean Ethics*, Book I, (1094 b).

2 See, for instance, Brown, *Augustine*, p. 261.

3 J. Locke *Essay Concerning Human Understanding*, ed. J. W. Yolton, Everyman, 1961, Book III, ch. x, Sect. 34.

4 Longinus, *On the Sublime*, tr. A. O. Prickard, Oxford University Press, 1906, Sect. IX, p. 18.

5 Ep. 22. 30. Cited by H. F. D. Sparks, *Cambridge History of the Bible*, vol. I, p. 524.

6 Ep. 49. 4. Sparks, ibid.

7 Gerald Bonner, ibid., p. 542.

8 Boileau, *Réflections critiques sur quelques passages du rhéteur Longin*, X (1710). See D. A. Russell (ed.), *'Longinus' On the Sublime*, Oxford University Press, 1964, pp. xlii ff.

9 Preface to Isaac Watts, *Horae Lyricae*, (1709), 6th edn, 1731, pp. xii–xiii.

10 Dugald Stewart, *Philosophical Essays*, Edinburgh, 1810. Essay II, 'On the Sublime', p. 367.

11 Albertus Pighius *Hierarchiae Ecclesiasticae Assertio* (Cologne, 1538) fo. lxxxx, sect. B., tr. Jewel, *Works*, Parker Society, Cambridge 1841–53 iv., p. 759. Cited by H. C. Porter, 'The Nose of Wax: Scripture and the Spirit from Erasmus to Milton', *Transactions of the Royal Historical Society*, 5th Series, vol. 14, 1964, p. 155.

12 It goes back at least as far as Alain of Lille (1120–1202), see Porter, *The Nose of Wax*.

13 *The Critical Works of John Dennis*, ed. E. N. Hooker, Baltimore, Johns Hopkins Press, 1939, vol. I, p. 358.

14 Ibid., p. 364.

15 Ibid., p. 335.

16 Ibid., p. 336.

17 Ibid., p. 364.

18 Ibid., p. 364.

19 Watts, *Horae Lyricace*, p. xiv.

20 *An Historical Account of the Lives and Writings of our most Considerable English Poets*, 1720, p. 257; see also David B. Morris, *The Religious Sublime: Christian Poetry and Critical Tradition in Eighteenth Century England*, Kentucky University Press, 1972, pp. 47–78.

21 Joseph Trapp, *Lectures on Poetry* (1742), tr. William Bowyes (asst. William Clarke), reprinted Menston, Scolar Press, 1973, pp. 27, 156–7. Trapp was Professor of Poetry 1708–18. The *Lectures* were first published in 3 volumes, in 1711, 1715, and 1719. Second edn 1722; third, 1736.

22 James Thomson, *Eighteenth Century Critical Essays*, ed. Scott Elledge, Cornell University Press, 1961, vol. I, p. 406.

23 Robert Lowth, *Lectures on the Sacred Poetry of the Hebrews*, tr. G. Gregory, 1787, vol. II, p. 18.

24 Dennis, *Grounds of Criticism*, p. 331.

25 Lowth, *Sacred Poetry of the Hebrews*, vol. I, pp. 71–2.

26 Hugh Blair, *Lectures on Rhetoric and Belles Lettres* (1783), 2 vols., Edinburgh, 1820, vol. II, pp. 270–1.

27 Ibid., II, 212–13.

28 William Wordsworth, 'Preface to *Lyrical Ballads*', ed. R. L. Brett and A. R. Jones, revised impression, Methuen, 1965, p. 253.

29 Morris, *The Religious Sublime*.

30 Dennis, *Grounds of Criticism*, pp. 267–9; Morris, ibid., pp. 64–5.

31 Morris, *The Religious Sublime*, p. 49.

32 S. T. Coleridge, *Biographia Literaria*, ed. J. Shawcross, 2 vols., Oxford University Press, 1907, ch. XVII.

33 S. T. Coleridge, *The Statesman's Manual*, in *Lay Sermons*, ed. R. J. White, Routledge, 1972, pp. 28–9. See also Prickett, *Romanticism and Religion*, p. 18.

34 See Roger Scruton, *Kant*, ch. 6; Donald W. Crawford, *Kant's Aesthetic Theory*, University of Wisconsin Press, 1974.

35 Coleridge, *Lay Sermons*, p. 80.

36 For a further discussion of this point, see Prickett, *Romanticism and Religion*, pp. 18–22.

37 Coleridge, *Biographia Literaria*, ch. XIV, vol. II, p. 12.

38 Ibid., II, p. 11.

39 Ibid., I, 202; for a detailed discussion of the background to this point, see Prickett, *Romanticism and Religion*, pp. 19–22.

40 Coleridge, *Confessions*, p. 13.

41 J. T. Coleridge, *Memoir of the Rev. John Keble*, 1869, p. 199. For a more lengthy discussion of Keble's poetic theories see Prickett, *Romanticism and Religion*, pp. 91–119.

42 John Keble, *Lectures on Poetry*, tr. E. K. Francis, Oxford University Press, 1912, vol. I, p. 36.

43 *Occasional Papers and Reviews*, 1877, p. 6; cited by M. H. Abrams, *The Mirror and the Lamp*, N.Y., Oxford University Press, 1953 (reprinted Norton, N.Y. 1958) p. 145.

44 Keble, *Lectures*, I, p. 38.

45 Ibid., I, p. 88.

46 The proto-Freudian implications of this theory have not been missed. Abrams, for instance, points out that Keble 'conceives literature as disguised wish-fulfilment, serving the artist as a way back from incipient neurosis.' (*Mirror and The Lamp*, p. 157).

47 Keble, *Lectures*, I, p. 53.

48 Keble, *Lectures*, II, 477.

49 Keble, *Lectures*, II, 481.

50 *The Letters of John Keats*, ed. M. Buxton Forman, 4th edn, Oxford University Press, p. 67 (Letter to Benjamin Bailey, 22 November 1817).

51 Keble, *Lectures*, II, 479–80.

52 Keble, *Lectures*, II, 481.

53 Keble, *Lectures*, II, 480.

54 Prickett, *Romanticism and Religion*, pp. 117–19.

55 F. W. Robertson, *Lectures on the Influence of Poetry and Wordsworth*, (1852), reprinted 1906, p. 68.

56 *Auszug aus Dr R. Lowth's . . . Vorlesungen über die heilige Dichtkunst der Hebräeer, mit Herders und (Sir William) Jones Grundsätzen verbunden . . .*

Nebst einigen vermischten Anhängen entworfen von C. B. Schmidt. Danzig, 1793.

57 Herder, *The Spirit of Hebrew Poetry*, p. 13.
58 See Friedrich Meinecke, *Historism: The Rise of a New Historical Outlook*, tr. J. E. Anderson, Routledge, 1972, p. 206.
59 Published in England in 1735; translated into German by Johann Heinrich Voss in 1766.
60 1763; translated into German, 1769.
61 Privately printed in 1769; republished and enlarged after his death in 1775.
62 Meinecke, *Historism*, p. 209.
63 See Isaiah Berlin, 'Herder and the Enlightenment,' *Vico and Herder: Two Studies in the History of Ideas*, Hogarth Press, 1976; Steiner, *After Babel*, pp. 73–85 ff.
64 *The New Science of Giambattista Vico*, revised translation of the third edn (1744) by Thomas Goddard Bergin and Max Harrold Frisch. Ithaca, N.Y., Cornell University Press, 1968, p. 21.
65 For a discussion of these, see pp. 70–1.
66 Vico, *New Science*, p. 21.
67 Berlin, *Vico and Herder*, p. 42.
68 Ibid., p. 336.
69 Ibid., p. 77.
70 Ibid., p. 127.
71 Ibid., p. 120.
72 Ibid., p. 112.
73 Ibid., p. 111.
74 Benedetto Croce, *The Philosophy of Giambattista Vico* tr. R. G. Collingwood (1913), reissued N.Y., Russell and Russell, 1964, p. 48.
75 Thomas Arnold, Matthew's father, was profoundly influenced by his reading of Vico. Berlin, *Vico and Herder*, p. 94.
76 The *New Science* was reviewed in the Leipzig *Acta Eruditorum* in 1727. 'Italian Influence on Aesthetic Theory in Germany', *Studies in the Genesis of Romantic Theory in the Eighteenth Century*, by J. G. Robertson (1923), reissued N.Y., Russell and Russel, 1962, pp. 287–8.
77 Berlin, *Vico and Herder*, p. 168.
78 Herder, *Spirit of Hebrew Poetry*, II, p. 7.
79 Peter Meinhold, *Luthers Sprachphilosophie*, Berlin, 1958, pp. 32–6 and 42–4.
80 See Hans Aarsleff, 'Leibniz on Locke on Language', *From Locke to Saussure: Essays on the Study of Language and Intellectual History*, Minneapolis, University of Minnesota Press, 1982, pp. 58–60. An interesting variant on this theme was James Parsons' argument that Irish and Welsh are the oldest European languages, from which all others are descended, being the remains of 'Japhetan' – the original antediluvian language. *The Remains of Japhet* (1767) reprint Menston, Scolar Press, 1968, x–xii.
81 Aarsleff, *From Locke to Saussure*, p. 60. He cites Boehme: 'For as Adam

spoke for the first time, he gave names to all the creatures according to their qualities and inherent effects. And it is truly the language of nature, but not every man knows it, for it is a secret, a mystery, which by the grace of God has been granted to me by the spirit that has taken delight in me.' *Aurora, oder Morgenröthe im Aufgang*, ch. 20, para. 91 in *Sämtliche Schriften* (Faksimile-Neudruck der Ausgabe von 1730, ed Will-Erich Peuckert), vol. I, Stuttgart, 1955, p. 296.

82 *Mysterium Magnum*, ch. 19. para. 22. (Aarsleff, *From Locke to Saussure*, p. 60).

83 Because 'the gap between spontaneous mimetic speech-sounds and the wonder of mature language seemed too great . . . the theory of a divine act of special bestowal was never far from Herder's thoughts.' Steiner, *After Babel*, p. 78.

84 Johann Peter Süssmilch, *Versuch eines Beweises, dass die erste Sprache ihren Ursprung nicht vom Menschen, sondern allein vom Schöpfer erhalten habe*, 1766.

85 Johann Gottfried Herder, 'Essay on the Origin of Language' (1772), in *Herder on Social and Political Culture*, tr. and ed. by F. M. Barnard, Cambridge University Press, 1969, pp. 125–6. For a chronological survey of theories about the origin of language see Arno Borst, *Der Turmbau von Babel. Geschichte der Meinungen über Ursprung und Vielfalt der Sprachen und Völker*, 4 vols. in 6. Stuttgart, 1957–63.

86 'The Tradition of Condillac: The Problem of the Origin of Language in the Eighteenth Century and the Debate in the Berlin Academy before Herder', Aarsleff, *From Locke to Saussure*, pp. 146–199.

87 Herder, *Essay*, p. 131. Here, perhaps, too Herder was influenced by yet another English-language writer, the Scottish peer, Lord Monboddo, the first three volumes of whose *Origin and Progress of Language* he encouraged E. A. Schmid to translate in to German, and for which he composed an approving preface. Monboddo, though unfashionable and much ridiculed in Britain, was a good scholar, and a correspondent of Sir William Jones. (*Des Lord Monboddo Werk von dem Ursprunge und Fortgange der Sprache übersetzt von E. A. Schmid. Mit einer Vorrede des Herrn Generalsuperintendenten Herder*. Riga, 1784–5.) See W. A. Krebs 'The Study of Language in Scotland 1760–1810', unpublished Ph.D. Thesis, University of Leeds, 1977, pp. 277 ff.

88 Herder, *Essay*, Introduction, p. 20.

89 Herder, *Essay*, p. 169.

90 Coleridge, *Biographia Literaria*, vol. I. p. 202.

91 See Wilhelm von Humboldt, *Uber die Verschiedenheit des menschlichen Sprachbaues und ihren Einfluss auf die geistige Entwickelung des Menschengeschlechts* (1836) translated into English as: *Linguistic Variability and Intellectual Development* tr. G. C. Buck and F. A. Raven, Miami Linguistics Series no. 9, Coral Gables, Fla, University of Miami Press, 1971. Note also Aarsleff's argument that Humboldt's ideas of language owe very little to Herder – of whom he had a low opinion. *From Locke*

to Saussure, 'Introduction', p. 15.

92 Schmidt, *Anszug aus Dr R. Lowth's* . . .

93 'The *Sanscrit* language, whatever may be its antiquity, is of a wonderful structure; more perfect than the *Greek*, more copious than the *Latin*, and more exquisitely refined than either, yet bearing to both of them a stronger affinity, both in the roots of verbs and in the forms of grammar, than could possibly have been produced by accident; so strong indeed, that no philologer could examine them all three, without believing them to have sprung from some common source, which, perhaps no longer exists: there is a similar reason, though not quite so forcible, for supposing that both the *Gothick* and the *Celtick*, though blended with a very different idiom, had the same origin with the *Sanscrit*; and the old *Persian* might be added to the same family, if this were the place for discussing any question concerning the antiquities of Persia.' 'Third Anniversary Discourse, on the Hindus', 2 February (1786), *Works of Sir William Jones*, vol. III, with a life of the author by Lord Teignmouth, 1807, p. 34.

94 Friedrich von Schlegel, *Uber die Sprache und Weisheit der Indier*, Heidelberg, 1808. Quoted by Steiner, *After Babel*, p. 79.

95 Sir William Jones, *Asiatic Researches*, vol. III, 1799.

96 F. Bopp, 'Analytical Comparison of the Sanskrit, Greek, Latin, and Teutonic languages, shewing the original identity of their grammatical structure', partial translation of 'Uber das Konjugationsystem der Sanskritsprache' (1816), *Annals of Oriental Literature*, vols. I–III, 1820–1; A. W. Schlegel, 'Aus dem Indischen: Ramayana' (1820), *Sämtliche Werke*, ed. E. Böcking, vol. III, Leipzig, 1846; Schlegel, *Über die Sprache und Weisheit der Indier*; Jacob Grimm, *Deutsche Grammatik*, 4 vols., Göttingen, 1822–37. See also Sweet, *Humboldt*, pp. 392–428, and see J. W. Burrow, 'The Uses of Philology in Victorian England', *Ideas and Institutions of Victorian Britain*, ed. Robert Robson, Bell, 1967, p. 185.

97 General accounts are to be found in J. O. H. Jesperson, *Language, its Nature, Development and Origin*, Allen and Unwin, 1922, and H. Pederson, *Linguistic Science in the Nineteenth Century*, tr. J. W. Spargo, Cambridge, Mass., Harvard University Press, 1931. Aarsleff's view of the essentially aberrant nature of this tradition should also be noted: 'Bréal vs. Schleicher: Reorientation in Linguistics during the Latter Half of the Nineteenth Century'. *From Locke to Saussure*, pp. 293–320.

98 For a further account of this group see Duncan Forbes, *The Liberal Anglican Idea of History*, Cambridge University Press, 1952, and Prickett, *Romanticism and Religion*.

99 See below Ch. 3 pp. 135–8 ff.

100 Burrow, 'Uses of Philology', pp. 192–3.

101 J. W. Donaldson, *The New Cratylus*, 1839, p. 54.

102 F. W. Farrar, *Essay on the Origin of Language*, 1860, pp. 15, 140.

103 Burrow, 'Uses of Philology', p. 191.

104 F. W. Farrar, *Chapters on Language*, 1865, p. 49; cited by Burrow, 'Uses of Philology'.

105 'Athenäum Fragments' 249, tr. Peter Firchow. *German Aesthetic and Literary Criticism: The Romantic Ironists and Goethe*, ed. Kathleen M. Wheeler, Cambridge University Press, 1984, p. 49.

106 'Ideas' 46, ibid., p. 56.

107 See, for instance, the Tieck–Solger correspondence, ibid., pp. 154–8.

108 *Letters of Matthew Arnold 1848–88*, ed. G. W. R. Russell, N.Y., Macmillan, 1900, vol. I, p. 442. It was evidently a congenial theme to many of the period with pro-German and Hellenistic instincts. Kingsley makes use of it in *Alton Locke*. In *Culture and Anarchy* (1869) Arnold noted loftily that: 'Science has now made visible to everybody the great and pregnant elements of difference which lie in race, and in how signal a manner they make the genius and history of an Indo-European people vary from those of a Semitic people. Hellenism is of Indo-European growth, Hebraism is of Semitic growth; and we English, a nation of Indo-European stock, seem to belong naturally to the movement of Hellenism.' (*Complete Prose Works*, ed. R. H. Super, University of Michigan Press, vol. V, 1965, p. 173.) It is true, he adds hastily, that the Anglo-Saxons are also noted for 'the strength and prominence of the moral fibre, which, notwithstanding immense elements of difference, knits in some special sort the genius and history of us English, and our American descendants across the Atlantic, to the genius and history of the Hebrew people.' (Ibid., p. 174). Yet Arnold, like his fellow 'ethno-philologists', totally ignores the real problem lurking behind this confident assumption of the powers of Indo-European religious genius.

As Richard Jenkyns has pointed out, the total death of a religion is one of the rarest events in history. 'Once any new system of belief has commended itself to a considerable body of people it is seldom altogether eradicated; Zoroastrianism, founded more than two and a half thousand years ago, has survived for the past millennium or so with less than 150,000 adherents . . . Religions do not die; they become cataleptic. . . . To this general rule there is one enormous exception. The growth of Christianity completely destroyed the great Indo-European pantheons, Norse, German and Greco-Roman. Some time in about the sixth century A.D. the last man died who believed in the existence of Juno and Venus and Apollo, and in the succeeding centuries Asgard and Niflheim went the way of Olympus. (*The Victorians and Ancient Greece*, Oxford, Blackwell, 1980, pp. 174–5.)

109 C. K. J. von Bunsen, *God in History, or the Progress of Man's Faith in the Moral Order of the World*, 3 vols., 1868, vol. III, p. 305.

110 C. K. J. von Bunsen, *Outlines of the Philosophy of Universal History Applied to Language and Religion*, 2 vols., tr. S. Winkworth, vol. II, p. 78.

111 Ibid., vol. II, p. 77.

112 Bunsen, *Outlines*, vol. II, p. 78.

113 'So in the passage of the Red Sea, the description may be interpreted with the latitude of poetry . . .' Rowland Williams, 'Baron Bunsen's Biblical Researches,' *Essays and Reviews*, 1861.

114 F. M. Müller, *Natural Religion*, 1889; *Physical Religion*, 1891; *An-*

thropological Religion, 1892; and *Theosophy, as Psychological Religion,* 1893. For his work on Indian and comparative religion see G. W. Trompf, *Fredrick Max Mueller as a Theorist of Comparative Religion,* Bombay, Shakuntala Publishing House, 1978.

115 See Owen Barfield, *Poetic Diction,* new edn, Faber, 1952, pp. 65–85 ff. and Aarsleff, 'Breal vs. Schleicher', *From Locke to Saussure,* p. 298.

116 Burrow, 'Uses of Philology', p. 200.

117 *Life,* vol. I, p. 203.

118 Müller, *Natural Religion,* p. 198.

119 Burrow, 'Uses of Philology', pp. 202–3.

120 See, for instance, Müller's pupil A. H. Sayce, who held the Chair of Assyriology in Oxford 1891–1919: 'language itself is poetry, symbolizing the impalpable things of the spirit under the veil of metaphor'. *Principles of Comparative Philology* (1874–5), 4th edn, 1892, p. 34.

121 Edmund Burke, *A Philosophical Enquiry into the Origin of our Ideas of the Sublime and the Beautiful,* 1757, facsimile of 2nd edn, 1759, Menston, Scolar Press, 1970, pp. 114–22 ff.

122 Ibid., pp. 210–18 ff.

123 Ibid., p. 340.

124 'Alle Entzückungen und Visionen sind, meinem Urtheil nach, blosse Einkleidung, blosse poetische Dichtungen', *Einleitung in das Alte Testament,* 3 vols., Leipzig, 1780–3, vol. III, p. 188, cited by E. S. Shaffer, *'Kubla Khan' and 'The Fall of Jerusalem': The Mythological School in Biblical Criticism and Secular Literature 1770–1880,* Cambridge University Press, 1975, p. 88.

125 'Diesem einfachen Stoff prophetische Würde zu geben, bedient sich Jeremia der Dichtung eines Unterredung mit Jehova.' Cited by Shaffer, *'Kubla Khan',* p. 324.

126 J. S. Mill, *Autobiography,* 1873, ch. V.

127 'What is Poetry?' *Mill's Essays on Literature and Society,* ed. J. B. Schnee-wind, N.Y., Collier-Macmillan, 1965, p. 103.

128 Some of Wordsworth's actual words are: 'The remotest discoveries of the Chemist, the Botanist, and Mineralogist, will be as proper objects of the Poet's art as any upon which it can be employed, if the time should ever come when these things shall be familiar to us, and the relations under which they are contemplated by the followers of these respective Sciences shall be manifestly and palpably material to us as enjoying and suffering beings.' Preface to the *Lyrical Ballads,* p. 260.

129 J. S. Mill, 'What is Poetry?' pp. 103–4.

130 It is interesting to note the similarity between this idea of 'Two Truths' and Coleridge's contrast between the opposing worlds of 'I AM' and 'it is'. See Thomas McFarland, *Coleridge and the Pantheist Tradition,* Oxford, Clarendon Press, 1969, ch. I.

131 J. S. Mill, 'What is Poetry?' p. 106.

132 Ibid., p. 116.

133 Matthew Arnold, *Literature and Dogma,* Popular edn, 1895, p. 80.

134 *God and the Bible, The Complete Prose Works of Matthew Arnold*, vol. VII, 1970, p. 155.
135 See, for instance, Ludwig Feuerbach: 'feeling is the essential organ of religion', *The Essence of Christianity*, tr. George Eliot, N.Y., Harper Torchbooks, 1957, p. 9.
136 See Prickett, *Coleridge and Wordsworth*, ch. IV.
137 Arnold, *God and the Bible*, p. 156.
138 Ibid., p. 370.
139 See his definition of poetry in 'Maurice de Guerin' as a tension between 'natural magic' and 'moral profundity' *Essays in Criticism: First Series* (1865).
140 Cf. *Literature and Dogma*, p. 15: 'Religion . . . is ethics heightened, enkindled, lit up feeling; the passage from morality to religion is made when morality is applied to emotion'.
141 Arnold, *God and the Bible*, p. 378.
142 See Prickett, *Coleridge and Wordsworth*, pp. 7–8; and A. D. Nuttall, *A Common Sky*, Chatto, 1974, ch. I.
143 Arnold, *Dover Beach*, lines 30–4.
144 Blake, *Marriage of Heaven and Hell*, plate 3, *Complete Writings* p. 150.
145 *The Month*, 96 (1900) p. 573; reprinted in George Tyrell, *The Faith of the Millions*, 2nd series, 1901, p. 60; cited by Nicholas Sagovsky, *Between Two Worlds: George Tyrrell's Relationship with the Thought of Matthew Arnold*, Cambridge University Press, 1983, p. 25.
146 Ibid., p. 31.
147 Ibid., p. 56.
148 G. Tyrrell, *Through Scylla and Charybdis; or The Old Theology and the New*, 1907.
149 Letter to the Abbé Verand, 15 January 1905, Sagovsky. *Between Two Worlds*, p. 56.
150 J. H. Newman, *Essays Critical and Historical*, 1846, vol. I, p. 10; see also Prickett, *Romanticism and Religion*, p. 194.
151 J. H. Newman, *Essay on the Development of Christian Doctrine* (1845), Sheed and Ward, 1960, p. 22.
152 J. H. Newman, *A Grammar of Assent* (1870), ed. C. F. Harrold, new edn, Longman, 1957, p. 238.
153 Ibid., p. 285.
154 In a debate on Newman's idea of 'conscience', Freiburg, 1975.
155 The fullest exposition of this point is in *The Idea of a University*, but see also Wilfred Ward, *Life of John Henry Cardinal Newman*, Longman, 1912, vol. I, ch. XII; and John Coulson, *Newman and the Common Tradition*, Clarendon, 1970, p. 174.
156 Quotation is from Wittgenstein, *Philosophical Investigations*, Oxford, Blackwell, 1953, Part II, section XI; for a fuller discussion of this point see Prickett, *Romanticism and Religion*, pp. 194–9.
157 Newman, *Grammar of Assent*, p. 203.
158 Newman, *Essays Critical and Historical*, vol. II, p. 442.

159 Kelly, *The True Interpreter*, p. 3.
160 Martin Heidegger, 'Language', *Poetry, Language, Thought*, tr. Albert Hofstadter, N.Y., Harper and Row, 1971, p. 190.
161 Ibid., pp. 101, 197.
162 Ibid., p. 194.
163 Martin Heidegger, 'Hölderlin and Essence of Poetry' tr. Douglas Scott, *Existence and Being*, Vision Press, 1949, pp. 306–7.
164 'Typological Interpretation of the Old Testament', tr. John Bright, *Essays on Old Testament Hermeneutics*, ed. Claus Westermann (English tr. ed. James Luther Mays), Richmond, Va, John Knox Press, 1966, pp. 17–19.
165 Heidegger, *Poetry, Language, Thought*, p. 299; see also Robert W. Funk, *Language, Hermeneutics, and the Word of God*, p. 20.
166 P. Ricoeur, *Freud and Philosophy*, tr. D. Savage, New Haven, Yale University Press, 1970, p. 3.
167 Paul Ricoeur, 'Towards a Hermeneutic of the Idea of Revelation', *Essays on Biblical Revelation*, tr. David Pellauer, ed. Lewis S. Mudge, Philadelphia, Fortress Press, 1980, p. 101.
168 Ibid., pp. 102, 103.
169 Northrop Frye, *The Great Code: The Bible and Literature*. Routledge, 1982, p. 6.
170 Ibid., p. 7.
171 Ibid., p. 8.
172 Ibid., p. 12.
173 Ibid., p. 13.
174 Cf. Joan Oates, 'The Emergence of Cities in the Near East', *The Cambridge Encyclopaedia of Archaeology*, ed. A. Sherratt, Cambridge University Press, 1980, pp. 116 ff.
175 For an account of these see G. R. G. Mure, *Aristotle*, N.Y., Oxford University Press, 1966, pp. 178–84.
176 Frye, *The Great Code*, p. 29.
177 For Macquarrie's debt to Heidegger, see his *Principles of Christian Theology*, S.C.M. Press, 1974.
178 J. Macquarrie, *God-Talk*, S.C.M. Press, 1967, pp. 33–4.
179 'A Deliberate Mistake?', *Christ, Faith, and History*, eds. S. W. Sykes and J. P. Clayton, Cambridge University Press, 1972, p. 13.
180 Macquarrie, *God-Talk*, pp. 101–2.
181 Aaron's rod (Exodus vii, 8–12) is possibly an exception; but the fact that magicians could do the same trick (albeit less effectively!) makes it suspect – not least in Pharaoh's sceptical judgement.
182 D. Berggren, *Review of Metaphysics*, December 1962, pp. 237–58; and March 1963, pp. 450–72.
183 Study 8: 'Metaphor and philosophical discourse', pp. 257–313.
184 'There is No Natural Religion', *Complete Writings*, ed. G. Keynes, Oxford University Press, 1966, p. 97.
185 Ricoeur, *Essays on Biblical Interpretation*, pp. 101–2.
186 Frei, *The Eclipse of Biblical Narrative*, p. 187.
187 Frye, *The Great Code*, p. 40.

188 Ibid., p. 42.
189 E.g. 'Janet is living still. Her black hair is grey and her step is no longer buoyant . . .' George Eliot, *Scenes of Clerical Life*, ed. David Lodge, Penguin, 1973, p. 412.
190 See Marghanita Laski, *George Eliot and her World*, Thames and Hudson, 1973, pp. 55–8.
191 It is interesting to read Coleridge's rejection of Eichhorn's similar identification of the 'poetic' with the 'fictional'. See Prickett, *Romanticism and Religion* p. 66; and E. S. Shaffer, '*Kubla Khan*', pp. 88–9.
192 Lewis S. Mudge, 'Paul Ricoeur on Biblical Interpretation', *Essays on Biblical Interpretation*, pp. 25–6.
193 Ibid., pp. 73–89.
194 Lecture VII: 'Prophecy and Poetry'; *The Glass of Vision*, Dacre Press, 1948, pp. 113–31.
195 'Poetic Truth', *Reflective Faith*, ed. Charles C. Conti, S.P.C.K., 1972.
196 Farrer, *A Rebirth of Images*, pp. 22–5.
197 Ibid., p. 6.
198 Ibid., p. 14.
199 Ibid., p. 306.
200 C. S. Lewis, 'Is Theology Poetry?', *Screwtape Proposes a Toast*, Collins (Fontana), 1965.
201 *Fern-Seed and Elephants, and Other Essays on Christianity*, ed. Walter Hooper, Collins (Fontana), 1975, pp. 107–8.
202 See Farrer, *Reflective Faith*, Editor's Preface, p. ix. 'Greats' are the final honour School of *Literae Humaniores* at Oxford University.
203 Lewis, *Fern-seed and Elephants*, pp. 106–7.
204 See Heidegger, 'Hölderlin and the Essence of Poetry'; 'What are Poets for?' 'Language', and '. . . Poetically Man Dwells . . .', *Poetry, Language, Thought*.
205 Frei, *The Eclipse of Biblical Narrative*, p. 142.
206 Wheeler, *German Aesthetic and Literary Criticism*, p. 64.
207 Ibid., p. 120.
208 *Wilhelm von Humboldts Gesammelte Schriften*, eds. Albert Leitzmann et al., 17 vols., Prussian Academy of Sciences, Berlin 1903–36, vol. XIV, 310–20. Cited by Sweet, *Wilhelm von Humboldt*, vol. I, p. 207.
209 *German Aesthetic and Literary Criticism*, p. 92.
210 Frei, *Eclipse of Biblical Narrative*, pp. 213–14.
211 I am indebted to Professor Hans Kuhn for clarifying for me some of the relationship between these two words and their literary associations.
212 Frei, *The Eclipse of Biblical Narrative*, p. 151.
213 See Prickett, *Romanticism and Religion*, ch. 9.
214 For the ambiguities inherent in traditional debates between naturalistic and historical approaches to 'primitive' religious, see Victor Turner's Forward to Mircea Eliade's *Australian Religions: An Introduction*, Ithaca, Cornell University Press, 1973, pp. xiv ff.
215 See above, p. 70

216 Nevertheless such statements as the 'poetic function conceals a dimension of revelation . . . capable of entering into resonance with one or the other of the aspects of biblical revelation' (Ricoeur, *Essays*, p. 102) can certainly bear such interpretation.

217 S. T. Coleridge, *Shakespeare Criticism*, ed. T. M. Raysor, 2nd edn, Everyman, 1960, vol. I, pp. 174–5.

218 See Prickett, *Coleridge and Wordsworth*, pp. 118–19.

219 Existing works of poetry, according to him, already 'form an ideal order among themselves, which is modified by the introduction of the new (the really new) work of art among them . . . To conform merely would be for the new work not really to conform at all; it would not be new, and would therefore not not be a work of art.' 'Tradition and the Individual Talent', *Selected Essays*, 3rd edn, Faber, 1951, p. 12.

220 'The Nature of Meaning,' *Seven*, Vol. II, 1981, p. 38.

221 *Saving the Appearances*, pp. 182–3.

222 *Metaphor and Symbol*, eds. Basil Cottle and L. C. Knights (Bristol, Butterfield, 1960) reprinted in *The Rediscovery of Meaning*, Middletown, Conn., Wesleyan University Press, 1977.

223 Not all metaphors of value, however, show either the complete transformation of 'scruple' or the neat binary fission that has left us with the 'literal' word 'wind' and its 'metaphor' 'spirit'. Take the apparently similar development of the word 'heart'. Here the literal meaning only emerged from the figurative ones after anatomy had finally become a science. But unlike Barfield's example, the word also retained its inner symbolic meaning as the centre of life and being. When we say that someone's 'heart is not in' a particular task we can either paraphrase it with an inner meaning (he lacks motivation) or an outer one ('he is not working properly'), neither of which is the literal anatomical sense. Yet neither paraphrase conveys exactly what we are trying to say. What the 'heart' does, as neither of the paraphrases can do, is to suggest meanings that are *both* material *and* figurative at the same time. It has retained something of its primal meaning. When the Hebrew was commanded to 'Love the Lord thy God with all thy heart, and with all thy soul, and with all thy strength, and with all thy mind', by a typical parallelism the first word of the sequence, 'heart', encapsulates the following three, 'soul', 'strength', and 'mind'. To take another example, when Horatio says at the death of Hamlet, 'Now cracks a noble heart', he is referring *both* to the actual physical death of the prince, and consequently to the extinction of the personality of the man he loved, *and* to the tragedy surrounding his death by treachery and poison. Hamlet has indeed nothing left to live for: Gertrude and Ophelia are dead, his father is avenged, and Claudius, Laertes, Rosencrantz and Guildenstern have been caught and killed in their own plots. Death is seen by Horatio simultaneously at two levels of significance. What is odd, and therefore interesting in this case, is that the normal metaphorical process whereby a material phenomenon is given an 'inner' meaning is unexpectedly inverted. Hamlet's death is from a poisoned

sword-wound – a straightforward physical cause – but in describing it in terms of a broken heart Horatio is using the language of an existential experience. The outer event is described by a metaphor from the inner world. The physical event, death, is seen as part of the psychological one, rather than vice versa. This sudden metaphorical inversion echoes yet again what has been a major theme of the whole play: Hamlet's quest for an inner meaning or sense of value to make his life worth living. Horatio's words are an integral part of the discourse of the whole play-world.

224 Steiner, *After Babel*, pp. 185–6; Richard Jenkyns, *The Victorians and Ancient Greece*, pp. 163–74.

225 Steiner, *After Babel*, p. 186.

226 Barfield's own work, *History in English Words*, Faber, 1962, is a classic in this field.

227 French Romanticism, for instance, follows that of England and Germany by a full generation. That of Italy occurs even later, at the very end of the nineteenth century.

228 See, for instance, Berggren, 'Use and Abuse of Metaphor'.

229 Michael Roberts, Preface to *The Faber Book of Modern Verse*, Faber, 1947.

230 Interestingly enough, the apparently obvious corollary, 'to collect' or 'concentrate', is not recorded by the O.E.D. until the late 18th century (1782) and must, therefore, be ruled out here.

231 See A. D. Nuttall, *Overheard by God*, Methuen, 1981.

232 One wonders, also, if there is a subliminal reference here to a new-born baby's reflex capacity to grasp things.

233 S. T. Coleridge, *Philosophical Lectures*, ed. Kathleen Coburn, Routledge, 1949, Lecture V, p. 174.

234 See Prickett, *Coleridge and Wordsworth*, pp. 103–6; Richard E. Brantley, *Wordsworth's 'Natural Methodism'*, Yale University Press, 1975; and *Locke, Wesley, and the Method of English Romanticism*, Gainesville, University of Florida Press, 1984.

CHAPTER 3

1 Abrams, *Natural Supernaturalism*. p. 13.

2 Ibid.

3 Ibid., p. 68.

4 J. Lindsay, *William Blake*, Constable, 1978, p. xiv. For the contemporary secular political debate see *Burke, Paine, Godwin, and the Revolution Controversy*, ed. Marilyn Butler, Cambridge University Press, 1984.

5 E. J. Hobsbawm, *Primitive Rebels: Studies in Archaic Forms of Social Movement in the Nineteenth and Twentieth Centuries*, Manchester University Press, 1959; E. P. Thompson, *The Making of the English Working Class*, Gollancz, 1963; see also J. F. C. Harrison's critique of this position in *The Second Coming: Popular Millenarianism 1780–1850*, Routledge, 1979.

6 Abrams, *Natural Supernaturalism*, pp. 88–9.
7 Ibid., pp. 89–90.
8 See, for instance, Tennyson or Hardy.
9 See A. D. Nuttall's discussion of precisely this point in *Overheard by God*, ch. I.
10 See Prickett, *Coleridge and Wordsworth*, pp. 37–42.
11 Percy Reprints, ed. H. F. B. Brett-Smith, No. 3, Oxford, Blackwell, 1921, p. 56.
12 Abrams, *Natural Supernaturalism*, p. 90.
13 Quoted by Lady Holland, *Memoir of the Life of the Rev. Sydney Smith*, 1855, vol. I, pp. 61. One might not expect the Whig *Edinburgh Review* to favour the church sometimes known as 'the Tory party at prayer,' but other pro-Anglican sources offer similar pictures. George Crabbe, the poet, and himself a country clergyman in Suffolk, describes the parson in *The Village*, (1783) thus:

> A jovial youth, who thinks his Sunday's task,
> As much as GOD or Man can fairly ask;
> The rest he gives to Loves and Labours light,
> To Fields the morning and to Feasts the night;
> None better skill'd the noisy Pack to guide,
> To urge their chace, to cheer them or to chide;
> A Sportsman keen, he shouts through half the day,
> And skill'd at Whist, devotes the night to play;
> Then, while such honours bloom around his head,
> Shall he sit sadly by the sick Man's bed,
> To raise the hope he feels not, or with zeal
> To combat fears that ev'n the pious feel?
>
> (lines 306–17)

14 See Robert Currie, Alan Gilbert, and Lee Hursley, (eds.) *Churches and Churchgoers: Patterns of Church in the British Isles since 1700*, Oxford University Press, 1977.
15 Thomas Mozley, *Reminiscences*, 2 vols., 1882, vol. I, p. 184.
16 Ibid. vol. II, pp. 384–5.
17 Mary Moorman, *William Wordsworth: The Later Years*, Oxford University Press, 1965, pp. 104–5.
18 Blake, *Complete Writings*, p. 97.
19 Ibid., p. 98.
20 Shelley, *Defence of Poetry*, p. 6. See also Prickett, 'Peacock's *Four Ages* Recycled', *British Journal of Aesthetics*, Spring, 1982.
21 Ibid., p. 27.
22 Ibid., p. 88.
23 Thomas Percy, *Reliques of Ancient English Poetry*, 4th edn, 3 vols., 1794.
24 Dennis, *Critical Works*, pp. 364 and 370.
25 Richard E. Brantley, *Wordsworth's 'Natural Methodism'*.

26 Note by Translator, (G. Gregory) to 1847 ed. of *Lectures*. Term began on the first Wednesday after Trinity Sunday (May 27th) and the first lecture was due the following Tuesday.

27 Meinecke, *Historism*, p. lviii.

28 Lowth, *Lectures*, vol. I, pp. 113, 114.

29 But before we take the commonsense too much for granted it is worth noticing the almost identical words of a modern writer (seemingly unaware of Lowth) whose argument that 'We must endeavor to see the Scriptures through their eyes . . .' is part of a plea for a *return* to typological modes of interpretation. L. S. Thornton, *The Apostolic Ministry* cited by G. W. H. Lampe, '*The Reasonableness of Typology*', from *Essays on Typology*, eds. G. W. H. Lampe and K. J. Woollcombe, S.C.M. Press, 1957, p. 18.

30 Meinecke, *Historism*, p. 206. As a historian of ideas working specifically here on Herder and the rise of the modern notion of 'history', Meinecke has his own perspective on Lowth, but his assessment of the influence of the *Lectures* on the subsequent development of German thought is the more significant in consequence.

31 Ibid., pp. 203–4.

32 Wood's, *On The Original Genius and Writings of Homer* was first published 1775, 30 years after Lowth's *Lectures*, but 3 years before the translation of *Isaiah*.

33 Robert Lowth, *Isaiah: A New Translation* (1778), 5th edn, Edinburgh, 1807, vol. I, p. lxxx.

34 Lowth, *Sacred Poetry of the Hebrews*, vol. II, p. 12.

35 Ibid., vol. II, p. 12.

36 Ibid., vol. II, p. 18.

37 See, for instance, Dennis, *Critical Works*, p. 370: 'For the Prophets were Poets by the institution of their Order, and Poetry was one of the Prophetick Functions . . .'

38 Ibid., p. 371.

39 Lowth, *Lectures*, vol. I, pp. 76–8.

40 Ibid., vol. I, p. 224.

41 Ibid., vol. I, pp. 123 and 311.

42 Dennis, *Critical Works*, p. 358.

43 Lowth, *Lectures*, vol. I, p. 336.

44 Ibid., vol. II, p. 32. For a modern discussion of Lowth's work from a technical point of view, see James L. Kugel, *The Idea of Biblical Poetry; Parallelism and its History*, New Haven, Yale University Press, 1981.

45 Ibid., vol. II, p. 53.

46 Meinecke, *Historism*; Berlin, *Vico and Herder*; Shaffer, *Kubla Khan*.

47 M. Roston, *Poet and Prophet: The Bible and the Growth of Romanticism*, Faber, 1965.

48 Brian Hepworth, *Robert Lowth*, Boston, Twayne, 1978, p. 36.

49 Ibid., p. 97.

50 Ibid., p. 39.

51 Lowth, *Isaiah*, vol. I, p. lxx.

52 Ibid., I, p. lxviii.

53 Ibid., I, p. xcviii.

54 e.g. Lowth, *Isaiah*, vol. II, p. 232: 'According to the allegorical interpretation they may have a further view: this part of the prophecy may run
parallel with the former, and relate to the future advent of Christ; to the
conversion of the Jews, and their restitution to their land; to the extension
and purification of the Christian Faith; events predicted in the Holy Scriptures, as preparatory to it.'

55 Lowth, *Lectures*, vol. II, p. 69.

56 Ibid., vol. II, pp. 85–6.

57 Leslie Tannenbaum, *Biblical Tradition in Blake's Early Prophecies: the
Great Code of Art*, Princeton University Press, 1982, p. 29.

58 Thomas Howes, *Critical Observations on Books, Antient and Modern*, 4
vols. (1776–1813), reprinted New York, Garland, 1972, vol. II, p. 139.

59 Ibid., vol. II, pp. 442–3.

60 Tannenbaum, *Biblical Tradition*, p. 10.

61 R. C. Fuller, *Alexander Geddes*, Sheffield, Almond Press, 1983.

62 David Newsom, *The Parting of Friends*, Murray, 1966. p. 78. There were,
of course, more in Cambridge. Herbert Marsh, who had translated
Michaelis's *Introduction to the New Testament* into English with original
notes of his own (1793–1801) became Lady Margaret Professor of Divinity
in 1807, and had introduced German Scholarship there; Julius Hare, a
Fellow of Trinity in the 1820s, before becoming Archdeacon of
Hurstmonceaux, was one of the finest German scholars in England – his
private library contained more than 2,000 volumes in German.

63 Shaffer, *'Kubla Khan'*, chs. 1 and 2.

64 S. T. Coleridge, *Lectures on Politics and Religion* (1795), eds. Lewis Patton
and Peter Mann, Bollingen Series LXXV, Routledge/Princeton University Press, 1971, p. 153.

65 Lowth, *Lectures*, vol. I, p. 224.

66 Lowth, *Lectures*, vol. I, p. lxviii.

67 Coleridge, *Biographia Literaria*, vol. II, p. 11.

68 Ibid., vol. II, p. 12.

69 See pp. 43–5 above.

70 Coleridge, *Biographia Literaria*, ch. XVII.

71 See Chapter 4 below pp. 182–6.

72 *A Hopkins Reader*, ed. John Pick, Oxford University Press, 1953, p. 80.

73 Ibid., pp. 80–1.

74 Ibid., p. 86.

75 See for instance stanza 4 of *The Wreck of the Deutschland*:

>   I steady as water in a well, to a poise, to a pane,
>   But roped with, always, all the way down from the tall
>   Fells or flanks of the voel, a vein
>   Of the gospel proffer, a pressure, a principle, Christ's gift

A 'voel' is a Welsh word meaning 'hill'. The elaborate simile links the water-level in the bottom of the well with the entire system of the catchment-area and the resulting underground water-table. Christ is thus seen as the hydraulic pressure system invisibly underlying the whole landscape.

76 Another Hopkins coinage. The word is formed by analogy with 'land-scape' to mean the 'inner landscape' of each individual thing, and hence its own principle of individuation. This sonnet is about the theology of inscape.

77 See Aarsleff, *From Locke to Saussure*, p. 25: 'languages even now, in spite of their multiplicity and seeming chaos, contain elements of the original perfect language created by Adam when he named the animals in his prelapsarian state. In the Adamic doctrine the relation between signifier and signified is not arbitrary; the linguistic sign is not double but unitary. Still retaining the divine nature of their common origin, languages were in fundamental accord with nature, indeed they were themselves part of creation and nature. They were divine and natural, not human and conventional.'

78 Wilkins, for instance, though he was in no doubt that the 'first Language was *con-created* with our first Parents, they immediately understanding the voice of God speaking to them in the Garden' (*Essay Towards a Real Character and a Philosophical Language*, 1668, p. 2) and believed Adam had 'in the process of time, upon his experience of their great necessity and usefulness' invented letters and, therefore, writing, (p. 11) is nevertheless highly critical of the Hebrew script, and thinks both it and the language capable of improvement (p. 14). By the middle of the next century, James Harris, in *Hermes, or a Philosophical Inquiry concerning Universal Grammar* (1751) could be much blunter: 'HENCE . . . we may perceive a Reason, *why there never was a Language, nor indeed can possibly be framed one, to express the Properties and real Essence of things,* as a Mirrour exhibits their Figures and their Colours . . . ALL LANGUAGE IS FOUNDED IN COMPACT, and not in Nature; for so are all Symbols, of which words are a certain species.' (5th edn, 1794, pp. 336–7.)

79 Aarsleff, *From Locke to Saussure*, p. 242.

80 See J. F. C. Harrison, *The Second Coming*.

81 Howes, *Critical Observations on Books*, vol. II, p. 112.

82 Ibid., II, 129–30.

83 See R. C. Fuller, 'Dr Alexander Geddes: A Forerunner of Biblical Criticism', unpublished Ph.D. thesis, Cambridge University, 1968. p. 31 ff.

84 See Léon Cellier, *Fabre d'Olivet: Contribution a l'étude des aspects religieux du Romantisme*, Paris, Nizet, 1953, pp. 10–12.

85 Richard Brothers (1757–1824) was a half-pay naval officer, who in 1792, began to prophesy against the threatened war with France, saying it was the one 'alluded to by St. John, in the nineteenth chapter of Revelation, which God called a war against himself'. In 1794 he published *A Revealed*

Knowledge of the Prophecies and Times *predicting the conquest of England and the* destruction of the Empire. The Government, alarmed by fears for public morale, had him arrested in March 1795. Examined by the Privy Council, he was declared insane and incarcerated in an asylum in Islington for the next eleven years. He continued to receive visits from disciples and revolutionary sympathizers, and to publish, including a *Description of* (the New) *Jerusalem* (1801). See Morton D. Paley, 'William Blake, the prince of the Hebrews, and the woman clothed with the sun', in Morton D. Paley and Michael Phillips (eds.), *William Blake: Essays in Honour of Sir Geoffrey Keynes*, Oxford, Clarendon Press, 1973.

86 Lowth, *Isaiah*, I, p. lxxi.
87 Antoine Fabre d'Olivet, *The Hebraic Tongue Restored: and the Meaning of the Hebrew Words Re-established and Proved by their Radical Analysis*, tr. N. L. Redfield, Putnam, N.Y., 1921, part II, p. 27.
88 Benjamin Lee Whorf, 'A Linguistic Consideration of Thinking in Primitive Communities', *Language, Thought and Reality*, ed. J. B. Carroll, Cambridge, Mass., M.I.T. Press, 1956. p. 75.
89 J. B. Carroll, Introduction, Ibid., pp. 7–9.
90 Fabre d'Olivet, *The Hebraic Tongue Restored*, Part II, pp. 7–8.
91 Ibid., part II, p. 21.
92 Kathleen Raine, 'Thomas Taylor in England,' in *Thomas Taylor the Platonist*, (eds.) Kathleen Raine and George Mills Harper, Bollingen Foundation/Princeton University Press, 1969, p. 6.
93 Ibid., p. 7.
94 Notebook 25 pp. 87 ff. Trevor H. Levere, *Poetry Realised in Nature: Samuel Taylor Coleridge and Early Nineteenth Century Science*, Cambridge University Press, 1981, p. 214.
95 Notebook 56, pp. 9–10 ff; Levere, Ibid., p. 215.
96 Ibid.
97 For the continuing importance of typology in Victorian art, see George P. Landow, *Victorian Types, Victorian Shadows: Biblical Typology in Victorian Literature, Art and Thought*, Routledge, 1980.
98 See Ch. 2, p. 44.
99 Prickett, *Coleridge and Wordsworth*, pp. 37–42.
100 He saw in a flash the ring-structure of the molecule that had been eluding him on awakening from a dream of snakes biting their tails.
101 See, for instance, 'Expostulation and Reply', 'The Tables Turned', or *The Prelude*, Book V.
102 John Keble, *Christian Year*, 43rd edn, 1851, Septuagesima Sunday, p. 80.
103 Ibid., p. 22.
104 See Prickett, *Romanticism and Religion*, ch. IV.
105 Sampson Reed, *Observations on the Growth of the Mind*, (Boston, 1826), reprinted Florida, 1970, pp. 46–7.
106 Fragment 'On Genius and Public Taste', *Shakespeare Criticism*, p. 185.
107 'The wheel of the sun cannot be much larger nor its glow less than is perceived by our senses . . .' *De Rerum Natura*, tr. W. H. D. Rose, Loeb

Classical Library, N.Y. 1928, 5, 564–5; cited by David Morris, *The Religious Sublime*, p. 50.

108 Dennis, *Critical Works*, p. 339. Blake, too, seems to be recalling Dennis in his *Vision of the Last Judgement*: ' "What," it will be Questioned, "When the Sun rises, do you not see a round disk of fire somewhat like a Guinea?" O no, no, I see an Innumerable company of the Heavenly host crying "Holy, Holy, Holy is the Lord God Almighty." I question not my Corporeal or Vegetative Eye any more than I would Question a Window concerning a Sight: I look thro it & not with it.' (*Complete Writings*, p. 617.)

109 See Prickett, *Coleridge and Wordsworth*, ch. II.

110 The usage is unique to Hartley – see O.E.D.

111 David Hartley, *Observations on Man, his Frame, his Duties and his Expectations*, 1749, vol. I, p. 79.

112 I am indebted for the speculative background to this conclusion to W. A. Krebs, 'The Study of Language in Scotland, 1760–1810'.

113 Hartley, *Observations*, vol. I, p. 297.

114 Letter to William Godwin, 22 September, 1800, *Collected Letters of Samuel Taylor Coleridge*, ed. E. L. Griggs, Oxford University Press 1956, vol. I, pp. 352–3.

115 See, for instance, *Collected Letters*, I, 494 and 559–60.

116 John Horne Tooke, *The Diversions of Purley*, 2 vols., (1798–1805), reprinted Menston, Scolar Press, 1968. vol. I. p. 25.

117 John Locke, *An Essay*, II, p. 10.

118 Tooke, *Diversions*, II, pp. 19–20.

119 Note for instance this passage, following Webster, from his essay *Nature* (1836): 'Every word which is used to express a moral or intellectual fact, if traced to its root, is found to be borrowed from a material appearance. *Right* means *straight*; *wrong* means *twisted*. *Spirit* means primarily *wind*; *transgression* the *crossing of a line*; *supercilious* the *raising of the eyebrows*. We say the *heart* to express emotion, the *head* to denote thought, and *thought* and *emotion* are words borrowed from sensible things, now appropriate to spiritual nature. Most of the processes by which this transformation is made is hidden from us in the remote time when language was formed . . .' Ralph Waldo Emerson: *Selected Prose and Poetry*. ed. R. L. Cook, N.Y. Holt, Rinehart and Winston, 1950, p. 15.

120 Krebs, 'Study of Language in Scotland 1760–1810', p. 85; Hans Aarsleff, *The Study of Language in England, 1780–1860*, Princeton University Press, 1967, pp. 73 ff.

121 See, for instance, Charles Richardson, *Illustrations of English Philology*, 1815, p. 18, '. . . if the Dictionary of John Horne Tooke had been completed, the united labours of Samuel Johnson and Henry J. Todd might have been spared to warm the baths of Alexandria.'

122 Not that Tooke had it all his own way. See, for instance, John Fearn's *Anti-Tooke, or an Analysis of the Principles and Structures of Language* (1824–7), reprinted, with Introduction by Brigitte Asbach-Schnitker and

Preface by Herbert E. Brekle, Friedrich Frommann Verlag, Stuttgart-Bad Cannstatt, 1972; also B. Asbach-Schnitker, *A Linguistic Commentary on John Fearn's 'Anti-Tooke'* (1824–7), Tübingen, Niemeyer, 1973.

123 'Thought', or having been thinged.
124 The thing acts upon the co-agent.
125 I think or thing – I think it again when I have thought it.
126 S. T. Coleridge, *Notebooks*, ed. Kathleen Coburn, Routledge, 1957, vol. III, 3587.
127 Coleridge, *Collected Letters*, I, p. 309.
128 S. T. Coleridge, *Table Talk*, ed. H. N. Coleridge, 1852, p. 66.
129 Coleridge, *Collected Letters*, I, p. 352–3.
130 Coleridge, *Philosophical Lectures*, Lecture V, pp. 173–4.
131 S. T. Coleridge, *Logic*, ed. J. R. de J. Jackson, Routledge/Princeton University Press, 1981, p. 126.
132 'In all societies there exists an instinct of growth, a certain collective unconscious good sense working progressively to desynonymize those words originally of the same meaning.' *Biographia Literaria*, ed. Shawcross, Oxford University Press, vol. 1, p. 61.
133 Tooke, *Diversions*, I, p. 102.
134 See, for instance, John Trusler, *The Difference Between Words Esteemed Synonymous in the English Language, and the Proper Choice of them Determined*, 2 vols., 1766, and Hester Piozzi, *British Synonymy*, 2 vols., Dublin, 1794. Coleridge himself cites W. Taylor's, *British Synonymes Discriminated* (1813), *Biographia Literaria*, vol. I, p. 63.
135 'Language is like a tree, which grows from a small seed, grows imperceptibly, till the fowls of the air lodge in its branches, and the beasts of the earth rest under its shadow. The seed of language is the natural signs of our thoughts, which nature has taught all men to use, and all men to understand. But its growth is the effect of all who do or ever did use it. One man pushes out a branch, another a leaf, one smooths a rough part, another lops off an excrescence. Grammarians have, without doubt, contributed much to its regularity and beauty; and philosophers, by increasing our knowledge, have added many a fair branch to it; but it would have been a tree without the aid of either.' Thomas Reid, *Works*, ed. Sir W. Hamilton, 8th edn, Edinburgh, 1895, Vol. I, p. 70. In a letter to James Gregory, 26 August, 1787.
136 Coleridge, *Biographia Literaria*, 174. See also part II, ch. I of Tooke's *Diversions* on the 'Rights of Man' where he argues that 'right' means, etymologically, what was 'ordered and commanded' (pp. 11–14).
137 Richardson, *Theological Word Book*, p. 285. As his careful phraseology implies, Richardson's account represents an attempt at a consensual overview of highly controversial terrain. Whether the Johannine *logos* was as rational as he argues is debatable, and Paul Friedländer, for example, claims for Plato four hundred years earlier a strikingly personified and dynamic version. With Plato, he argues, the *logos* 'becomes a living thing, pre-existing, as it were before particular verbal expressions and to be

realized by the speaker. It makes demands; at times it leads us to the goal by apparently wrong ways; it runs away; it must not be deserted; it accuses us like a human being and laughs at us; it tramples upon us and treats us as it pleases; wherever it is carried like a breath of wind, one must follow.' (*Plato: An Introduction*, tr. Hans Meyerhoff, Routledge, 1958, pp. 108–9). Though modern scholars might dispute this portrait of the Platonic *logos*, written in 1928, it captures an aspect of German Romanticism that would have been highly congenial to Coleridge – see, for instance, Humboldt's notion of language as *Energeia*, p. 227–8 below.

138 G. S. Kirk and J. E. Raven, *The Presocratic Philosophers*, Cambridge University Press, 1957, pp. 192–3. I am indebted to Mrs Helen Irwin for this reference.

139 Ibid., p. 194.

140 See above. p. 128.

141 'An IDEA, in the highest sense of that word, cannot be conveyed but by a symbol.' Coleridge, *Biographia Literaria*, Vol. I, p. 100.

142 For a further discussion of this point see Prickett, *Coleridge and Wordsworth*, pp. 197–8.

143 Coleridge, *Aids to Reflection*, p. xvii.

144 T. Taylor, Introduction to Plato, *The Phaedrus*, 1792, p. 5.

145 Georgina Battiscombe, *John Keble*, Constable, 1963, p. 104; Moorman, *Wordsworth*, pp. 479–80.

146 Prickett, *Coleridge and Wordsworth*, Introduction.

147 Coleridge, *Philosophical Lectures*, p. 48.

148 Coleridge, *Biographia Literaria*, vol. I, p. 202.

149 Locke, of course, though he talks of 'imaginary combinations' of ideas does not use the word 'imagination' anywhere in the *Essay*. For him the 'imaginary' is synonymous with 'fantasical or chimerical' creations, 'which are made up of such collections of ideas as were really never united', such as a centaur. *An Essay*, Book II, ch. 30.

150 This is also, of course, roughly the meaning of 'phantasia' in Aristotle's *De Anima*.

151 In, for instance, Norman Fruman's *Coleridge: the Damaged Archangel*, Allen and Unwin, 1972, pp. 179–84.

152 Coleridge, *Biographia Literaria*, vol. I, p. 272.

153 See G. N. G. Orsini, *Coleridge and German Idealism*, Carbondale and Edwardsville, Southern Illinois University Press, 1969, pp. 222–5.

154 See above, p. 44; Appendix to *The Statesman's Manual*.

155 Coleridge, *Biographia Literaria*, ch. X, vol. I, p. 107.

156 *Romanticism and Religion*, p. 19.

157 Norman Nicholson's play, *The Old Man of the Mountains*, Faber, 1946, a re-telling of the Elijah story in a Lake District setting, is interesting in this connection.

158 Coleridge, *The Statesman's Manual*, Appendix C, p. 70. See J. Robert Barth's discussion of this passage in *The Symbolic Imagination: Coleridge and the Romantic Tradition*, Princeton University Press, 1977, pp. 6 ff.

I am here, as so often elsewhere, deeply indebted to this subtle and suggestive study.

159 Abrams, *Natural Supernaturalism*, ch. VI. Though Abrams seeks to differentiate between what he calls 'apocalypses by imagination' and by 'cognition' the distinction often seems arbitrary, and here is very difficult to support.

160 To be contrasted with what he calls 'the kingdom of forces' and 'the kingdom of laws'.

161 Abrams, *Natural Supernaturalism* p. 351.

162 Coleridge, *Notebooks*, Notebook no. 37 (B.M. *ms.* 47,532) p. 60.

163 For a further account of this passage in its context, see Prickett, *Romanticism and Religion*, p. 50.

164 Ludwig Feuerbach, *The Essence of Christianity*, tr. George Eliot, Harper Torchbooks, 1957, p. 31.

165 'To William Wordsworth' (1807), line 19.

166 See above, pp. 26–7, and below, pp. 229–32.

167 F. D. Maurice, *The Kingdom of Christ*, 4th edn, 1891, vol. I, pp. 77–8.

168 *The Correspondence of G. M. Hopkins and R. W. Dixon*, ed. Abbott, Oxford University Press, 1935, pp. 147–8.

169 Coleridge, *Philosophical Lectures*, pp. 343–4.

170 Ibid., p. 399, n. 8.

171 'So long as Man in his first physical condition accepts the world of sense merely passively, merely perceives, he is still completely identified with it, and just because he himself is simply world, there is no world yet for him. Not until he sets it outside himself or *contemplates* it, in his aesthetic status, does his personality become distinct from it, and a world appears to him, because he has ceased to identify himself with it.' Friedrich Schiller, *On the Aesthetic Education of Man* (1795), tr. R. Snell, Routledge, 1954, p. 119.

172 'Words are things. They are the mightly instruments by which thoughts are excited and by which alone they can be [*expressed*] in a memorable form. And delightful it is to listen to the common people, hear them in the streets, overhear them when they are conversing with each other, and particularly at any moment when they are interested or animated, and you may count on your fingers word after word the history of which you can trace and find. How familiar words are with them and how appropriately used which but a century ago were placed as pedantic and fit only for the schools.' Coleridge, *Philosophical Lectures*, p. 201.

173 Charles de Brosses, *Traité de la formation méchanique des langues et des principes physiques de l'étymologie*, 2 vols., Paris, 1765; Etienne Bonnot de Condillac, *Essay on the Origin of Human Knowledge: A Supplement to Mr Locke's 'Essay on Human Understanding'*, 1756.

174 Coleridge, *Philosophical Lectures*, p. 367.

175 S. T. Coleridge, *Anima Poetae*, ed. E. H. Coleridge, 1895, p. 232.

272 *Notes to pp. 149–70*

CHAPTER 4

1 'As the apple-tree among the trees of the wood, so is my beloved among the sons.' Song of Sol. ii, 3.
2 *The Divine Comedy of Dante Alighieri*, tr. John D. Sinclair, N.Y., Oxford University Press, 1939, vol. II, pp. 422–3.
3 Dante, *Divine Comedy*, p. 412.
4 See, for instance, Paget Toynbee, *A Dictionary of Proper Names and Notable Matters in the Works of Dante*, Oxford, Clarendon Press, 1898.
5 Colin Hardie, 'The Symbol of the Gryphon in *Purgatorio* xxix.108 and following Cantos', *Centenary Essays on Dante*, by members of the Oxford Dante Society, Oxford, Clarendon Press, 1965, pp. 128–9.
6 Peter Dronke, 'The Procession in Dante's *Purgatorio*', *Deutsches Dante-Jahrbuch 1978–9*. I am indebted to Drina Oldroyd for this reference in her unpublished paper 'Hunting the Griffin in Dante's *Purgatorio*' delivered to the Australasian Language and Literature Association, Melbourne, 1985.
7 'la doctrine du "quadruple sens", que dès l'aube du moyen-âge avait été au principe de l'exégèse, s'y maintient jusqu'à la fin.' de Lubac, *Exégèse médiévale* p. 118. Others, such as Joachim of Fiore, had evolved more or less idiosyncratic systems of even greater complexity.
8 R. D. Laing, *The Self and Others*, Tavistock Press, 1961, p. 89.
9 M. Polanyi, *Personal Knowledge: Towards a Post-Critical Philosophy*, Routledge, 1958.
10 E. H. Gombrich, *Art and Illusion*, Phaidon, 1960, p. 4.
11 William Empson, *Seven Types of Ambiguity*, Peregrine (Penguin Books), 1961, p. 64.
12 Gombrich, *Art and Illusion*, pp. 200–1.
13 Bertrand Russell, *The Principles of Mathematics*, Allen and Unwin, 1903, ch. X, and Appendix B.
14 J. S. Carroll, *Exiles of Eternity*, Hodder, 1903, p. 361.
15 Genesis, xxix.
16 I am indebted for this story to Professor Judah Stampfer.
17 For Joachim of Fiore, Moses is the herald of the first *tempus*, Elijah of the second, and John the Baptist of the third. It will be Elijah, however, who also ushers in the fourth and final Coming. See Marjorie Reeves and Beatrice Hirsch-Reich, *The 'Figurae' of Joachim of Fiore*, Oxford, Clarendon Press, 1972, pp. 196–7.
18 'The extermination of Jahwism which he sees staring him in the face is of course the real reason for Elijah's despair. The picture of a prophet so enervated and resigned as to be at the point of contemplating suicide was an extremely bold and thrilling subject for a story teller of the time to attempt. This is truly weakness at its weakest, in fact, the very epitome of weakness.' Gerhard von Rad, *Old Testament Theology*, tr. D. M. G. Stalker, Edinburgh, Oliver and Boyd, 1965, vol. II, p. 19.
19 St John of the Cross, *Complete Works*, ch. I, p. 20.

20 See Tannenbaum, *Biblical Tradition*, p. 120.
21 See, for instance, Aharon Wiener: 'In this borderline situation –
    psychologically, the encounter of the ego with the deeper layers of un-
    conscious – Elijah hears 'the small voice of silence'. He realises that the
    elementary, creative and destructive forces of nature in themselves are not
    God. They are his precursors, symbols and tools of his dynamic effect
    upon the world and upon the fate of the individual. God himself cannot
    be comprehended by the human senses; but in the nothingness of silence
    his word becomes audible.' *The Prophet Elijah*, p. 26.
22 See above, ch. I. p. 16.
23 Though Foster Damon is doubtful: S. Foster Damon, *A Blake Dictionary*,
    Thames and Hudson, 1973, p. 215.
24 See Gershom Scholem, *Kabbalah*, Jerusalem, Keter Publishing House,
    1974, pp. 373–6.
25 For this and other aspects of the chariot I am indebted to Stephen Med-
    calf's paper, 'Coleridge's Vision of the Chariot', delivered at the Con-
    ference on Religion and Literature, Durham University, Sept. 1984.
26 It is possible that some of the attraction of Horne Tooke's *Epea Pteroenta*
    or 'winged words' to Coleridge had its roots in associations with Ezekiel,
    although Tooke's own use of the image is strictly classical and hermetic.
27 Blake, *Complete Writings*, p. 481.
28 In fact, the word 'chariot' (Merkabah) is not used in Ezekiel i, but the
    hermeneutic tradition which interpreted it as such is equally strong in
    both Jewish and Christian thought. See Scholem, *Kabbalah*, p. 373.
29 'A Vision of the Last Judgement', Blake *Complete Writings*, p. 611.
30 Ibid., p. 611.
31 E. M. Forster, *A Passage to India* (1924), Penguin, 1956, pp. 130–2.
32 'Though I speak with the tongues of men and angels, and have not charity,
    I am become as sounding brass, or a tinkling cymbal.' I Corinthians xiii, 1.
33 Tennyson, *In Memoriam*, LVI; Epilogue 128–32.
34 T. S. Kuhn, *The Structure of Scientific Revolutions*, University of Chicago
    Press, 1962.
35 George P. Landow, *Images of Crisis: Literary Iconology, 1750 to the Present*,
    Routledge, 1982, pp. 18–19.
36 Thus Landow argues that the 'transformation of a literal thing (or event)
    . . . permitted the situations of avalanche, shipwreck, or Pompeii to serve
    as cultural codes. They permitted, in other words, members of a particular
    society to communicate something of interest to one another.'
37 Alexander Pope, *An Essay on Criticism*, 1711 pp. 68–73.
38 See Basil Willey on the complex interactions of various 18th century
    meanings of 'nature' in *The Eighteenth Century Background*, Chatto, 1940.
39 A. N. Whitehead, *Science and the Modern World*, New York, 1948, ch. V.
40 I have already written elsewhere on the ambiguity of the climax and
    resolution of the *Ancient Mariner* and *The Wreck of the Deutschland* (see
    Romanticism and Religion pp. 12–17).
41 Mill, *Autobiography*, ch. I.

42 Ibid., p. 30.

43 See Hepworth, *Robert Lowth*, pp. 17–21.

44 Coleridge, had, of course, enjoyed a brilliant, if patchy, academic career, first at Christ's Hospital and then Cambridge. There is no evidence, however, that his precocious learning had in any way contributed to personal growth or maturity – indeed, as the dragoon incident suggests, he was in many ways remarkably immature as a student.

45 See Prickett, 'Dissidents Who Kicked Out at a Rugby Heritage,' *The Times Higher Education Supplement*, 1 August, 1980, p. 10.

46 For a fuller discussion of this see Prickett, *Coleridge and Wordsworth*.

47 M. Pattison, *Memoirs*, 1885, pp. 150–1 ff; pp. 237–44.

48 How desperate this could be we see in Kipling's portrait of the short-lived United Services College, at Westward Ho!, in *Stalky and Co.*, Macmillan, 1899.

49 See J. R. de S. Honey, *Tom Brown's Universe: The Development of the Victorian Public School*, Millington, 1977, pp. 22–30.

50 See Susan Chitty, *The Beast and the Monk*, Hodder and Stoughton, 1974.

51 *Life of Charles Kingsley by his Wife*, ed. F. Kingsley, 7th edn, 1877, Vol. II, p. 161.

52 *The Return to Camelot: Chivalry and the English Gentleman*, New Haven, Yale University Press, 1981; see also R. N. C. Vance, *The Sinews of the Spirit: The Ideal of Christian Manliness in Victorian Literature and Religious Thought*, Cambridge University Press, 1985.

53 See, in addition to Kingsley's *Water Babies*, the fantasy novels of George MacDonald, or Dickens in *Christmas Carol*. For an extended discussion on this theme, see Prickett, *Victorian Fantasy*, Harvester Press/Indiana University Press, 1979.

54 'How to Read', *Literary Essays of Ezra Pound*, Faber, 1954, p. 31.

55 As Crabb Robinson, a close friend of the Wordsworth family, had put it (not unkindly) in a letter to Dorothy Wordsworth in 1826: 'It gives me real pain when I think that some future commentator may possibly hereafter write – "This great poet survived to the fifth decennary of the nineteenth Century, but he appears to have died in the year 1814 as far as life consisted in an active sympathy with the temporal welfare of his fellow creatures." Edith J. Morely (ed.), *The Correspondence of Henry Crabb Robinson with the Wordsworth Circle*, Oxford University Press, 1927, p. 153.

56 See Prickett, 'Peacock's *Four Ages* Recycled'.

57 Thomas Love Peacock, *The Four Ages of Poetry*, ed. H. F. B. Brett-Smith, Percy Reprints, No. 3, Oxford, Blackwell, 1953, p. 9.

58 'it has been shown that it was a deficiency of human reasoning power that gave rise to poetry so sublime that the philosophies which came afterward, the arts of poetry and of criticism, have produced none equal or better, and have even prevented its production.' Vico, *New Science*, p. 120.

59 See, for instance, Robert Forsyth, *Principles of Moral Science*, 1805, Vol. I; Macaulay, 'Milton' (1825), *Literary Essays*, Oxford University Press,

1913, p. 4, also Marilyn Butler, *Peacock Displayed*, Routledge, 1979, pp. 286 ff.

60 Peacock, *Four Ages*, pp. 5–6.

61 Ibid., p. 18.

62 He sent him a copy to Italy.

63 Shelley, *A Defence of Poetry*, pp. 29–30.

64 *Mill on Bentham and Coleridge*, Introduction by F. R. Leavis, Chatto, 1950.

65 See, for instance, Michael Steig, *Dickens and Phiz*, Indiana University Press, 1978; Harry Stone, *Dickens and the Invisible World: Fairy Tales, Fantasy, and Novel Making*, Macmillan, N.Y. 1979; and Prickett, *Victorian Fantasy*, ch. II.

66 D. Lodge, *Modes of Modern Writing*, Ithaca, Cornell University Press, 1977, p. 25.

67 'The Ambiguous Heritage of Frankenstein', *The Endurance of Frankenstein: Essays on Mary Shelley's Novel*, eds. George Levine and U. C. Knoepflmacher, Berkeley, University of California Press, 1979, p. 7.

68 G. Levine, *The Realistic Imagination: English Fiction from 'Frankenstein' to 'Lady Chatterley'*, University of Chicago Press, 1981, p. 7.

69 Ibid., p. 12.

70 The argument of A. D. Nuttall, *Common Sky: Philosophy and the Literary Imagination*, Chattol Sussex University Press, is relevant here.

71 Levine, *Realistic Imagination*, pp. 19–20.

72 Gombrich, *Art and Illusion*.

73 Levine, *Endurance of Frankenstein*, p. 327.

74 J. Wisdom, *Paradox and Discovery*, University of California Press, 1970, pp. 125–6.

75 *The Study of Poetry*, (1880). Originally published as the General Introduction to *The English Poets* edited by T. H. Ward. Arnold, *Complete Prose Works*, vol. IX, p. 161.

76 Arnold, *Maurice de Guerin* (1863), ibid., vol. III,p. 33.

77 Arnold, *The Study of Poetry*, ibid., vol. IX, pp. 161–2.

78 Alasdair MacIntyre, *After Virtue*, Duckworth/Notre Dame University Press, 1981, pp. 80–1.

79 Empson, *Seven Types*, pp. 193–7.

80 Frei, *The Eclipse of Biblical Narrative*, pp. 11 and 16.

81 See above, ch. 2 pp. 82–3; and Frei, *The Eclipse of Biblical Narrative*, p. 142.

82 See above, p. 77.

83 See below, pp. 204–5.

CHAPTER 5

1 Nineham, *Use and Abuse of the Bible*, p. 262.

2 Terry Eagleton, *Literary Theory: An Introduction*, Blackwell, Oxford, 1983, p. 204.

3 Among those not specifically mentioned elsewhere in these pages would be Helen Gardner, *Religion and Literature*, Faber, 1971; Brian Whicker, *The Story-Shaped World*, Athlone Press, 1975; and John Coulson, *Religion and Imagination*, Oxford University Press, 1981.

4 'Romanticism and Classicism', *Speculations*, ed. Herbert Read, 2nd edn, Routlege, 1939, p. 116.

5 I. A. Richards' statement that 'poetry is capable of saving us' has become notorious. See T. S. Eliot's essay 'The Modern Mind' in *The Use of Poetry and the Use of Criticism*, Faber, 1933, with his quotations from Jacques Rivière, and Jacques Maritain's critique of Richards. See also Prickett, *Coleridge and Wordsworth*, pp. 44–5; Richard Foster, *The New Romantics: A Reappraisal of the New Criticism*, Bloomington, Indiana University Press, 1962; David DeLaura,*Hebrew and Hellene in Victorian England*, Austin, University of Texas Press, 1969, pp. xviii-xix; and William A. Madden, 'The Divided Tradition of English Criticism', *PMLA* LXXIII, March 1958, pp. 69–70.

6 Some years ago, in one of the many articles accounting for the superiority of German industrial performance over the British, it was stated that there was no word in German for 'management' – and the concept, therefore, was mercifully alien to German thought. Shortly after reading this I found myself in a large bookshop in Freiburg, and decided to verify this claim. I soon discovered an enormous section devoted to the subject, with English-language works, translations from English, and a substantial native German sector. The word used throughout – and by which the whole department was labelled – was the English word 'management'.

7 Which is not to say, of course, that music cannot be, on occasions, quite as morally relevant.

8 *Les grands traducteurs français*, Genève, Libraire de l'Université, 1963, p. 7.

9 Ricoeur, 'Preface to Bultmann', *Essays*, pp. 50–51.

10 As in Thomas Gainsford's, *The True and Wonderful Historie of Perkin Warbeck*, 1618, the source of John Ford's *The Chronical History of Perkin Warbeck*, 1634.

11 For a critique of emotivist understanding of values, see MacIntyre, *After Virtue*.

12 Blake, *There is No Natural Religion* (1788), section (A) iii, *Complete Writings*, p. 97.

13 Blake, *All Religions are One* (1788), Principle 4, ibid., p. 98.

14 Coleridge, *Aids to Reflection*, p. xvii.

15 See Emmet's review of my *Coleridge and Wordsworth* in the *Review of English Studies*, August 1971, pp. 358–60.

16 Blake, *All Religions are One*, Principle 6, *Complete Writings*, p. 98.

17 Blake, *There is no Natural Religion*, (B) v, ibid., p. 97.

18 Ricoeur, *Essays*, p. 101.

19 See above pp. 85–9; 141–5.

20 A. D. Nuttall, *A New Mimesis: Shakespeare and the Representation of Reality*, Methuen, 1983.

21 Ibid., pp. 147–50.
22 Alter, *Biblical Narrative*, p. 35.
23 Ibid., pp. 125–6; 129.
24 Ibid., p. 128, Alter's translation.
25 Ibid., p. 129.
26 Ibid., p. 155.
27 Nuttall, *A New Mimesis*, pp. 181; 182.
28 A. D. Nuttall, *A Common Sky: Philosophy and the Literary Imagination*, Chatto/Sussex University Press, 1974.
29 See also, E. A. Burtt, *Metaphysical Foundations of Modern Science*, Routledge, 1932.
30 Op. cit., p. 182.
31 Both M. H. Abrams in *The Mirror and the Lamp*, and Raymond Williams in *The Long Revolution*, Chatto, 1961, ch. 1, Part 1, have interesting accounts of this shift in the meaning of *mimesis* from reflection to creation.
32 Nuttall's attack on Locke in *A Common Sky* follows, in essentials, that of Coleridge in 1817: 'The realism common to all mankind is far older and lies infinitely deeper than this hypothetical explanation of perceptions, an explanation skimmed from the mere surface of mechanical philosophy. It is the table itself, which the man of common sense believes himself to see, not the phantom of a table, from which he may argumentatively deduce the reality of a table, which he does not see. If to destroy the reality of all, that we actually behold, be idealism, what can be more egregiously so, than the system of modern metaphysics, which banishes us to a land of shadows, surrounds us with apparitions, and distinguishes truth from illusion only by the majority of those who dream the same dream? "*I* asserted the world was mad" exclaimed poor Lee, "and the world said, that I was mad, and confound them, they outvoted me." ' Coleridge, *Biographia Literaria*, vol. I, p. 179.
33 Auerbach, *Mimesis*, p. 19.
34 M. M. Bakhtin, *The Dialogic Imagination*, ed. Michael Holquist, tr. Caryl Emerson and Michael Holquist, Austin, University of Texas Press, 1981, pp. xix and 272 ff.
35 G. Lukács, *Theory of the Novel*, tr. Anna Bostock, Merlin Press, 1971.
36 Op. cit., p. xxvii.
37 Ibid., p. 47.
38 Ibid., p. xxxiii.
39 Ibid., p. xxviii.
40 'Discourse in the Novel', ibid., p. 271.
41 Ibid., pp. 267–9.
42 Wheeler, *German Aesthetic and Literary Criticism*, p. 3.
43 'Letter about the Novel' (1799), ibid., p. 78.
44 I.e. 'that age of knights, love, and fairytales' in which Schlegel believed the novel had its *Mischgedicht* origins.
45 Wheeler, *German Aesthetic and Literary Criticism*, p. 79.
46 Op. cit. p. 284.

47 See Allon White, 'Bakhtin, Sociolinguistics and Deconstruction', *The Theory of Reading*, ed. Frank Gloversmith, Brighton, Harvester Press, 1984, p. 126.

48 Op. cit. p. 276.

49 I am here, as so often, indebted to Mr Robert Barnes for elucidating some of the complexities of the relationship of biblical languages and their contexts.

50 See above, pp. 31–2.

51 'The language of Haran, whence Abraham is said to have come, was Aramaic . . . Hebrew was the language of Canaan (Isa. 19:18) and was taken over by Israel from the Canaanites, along with their knowledge of agriculture and the pertinent sacrifical rites . . . When during the last three centuries B.C. Hebrew fell gradually into disuse and was supplanted by Aramaic as the vernacular of the Palestinian Jews, this was reversion rather than innovation.' *Language and Imagery of the Bible*, p. 35.

52 'Rhetoric died when the penchant for classifying figures of speech completely supplanted the philosophical sensibility that animated the vast empire of rhetoric, held its parts together, and tied the whole to the *organnon* and to first philosophy.' Ricoeur, *The Rule of Metaphor*, p. 10. For an account of the Aristotelian concept of metaphor see his Introduction, and Study 1: 'Between rhetoric and poetics'.

53 Rev. W. Jones, 'A Course of Lectures on the Figurative Language of Scripture', 1787, p. 325.

54 Jones, 'Lectures', p. 39; pp. 214–17.

55 Ibid., p. 319.

56 See Prickett, *Coleridge and Wordsworth*, ch. 2.

57 Jones, 'Lectures', p. 294.

58 'A Lecture on the Natural Evidences of Christianity', Ibid., pp. 436–7.

59 Ibid., p. 302.

60 See above, ch. 1, n. 36, pp. 247–8.

61 'As philosophy derived much of its influence from the powerful imagery of poetry in the ancient tragedies of Greece; so is the religion of revelation greatly assisted and enforced by its figurative language; always pertinent and instructive: and, on proper occasions, exceedingly sublime and beautiful . . . Philosophy and Poetry differ in this respect; that the one instructs by words, and delivers its precepts literally; the other by the images of things . . . Therefore good poetry, under proper restrictions, is one of the greatest and best works of human art; and has always been accounted divine . . .' Jones, 'Lectures', pp. 297–8.

62 See above, ch. 2, p. 67.

63 Newman, *Grammar of Assent*, p. 372. See also *Romanticism and Religion*, p. 202.

64 Newman, *Grammar of Assent*, p. 251.

65 For a discussion of Kierkegaard's relationship to English Romantic thought see Prickett, *Romanticism and Religion*, Appendix, pp. 268–78.

66 Newman, *Grammar of Assent*, p. 294.

67 Barfield, *Poetic Diction*, p. 30.
68 John Wilson, *Language and Christian Belief*, Macmillan, 1958, pp. 24 ff.
69 See Ch. 2, above, p. 67.
70 Newman, *Grammar of Assent*, p. 203.
71 Such confusion, let it be said, is not confined to theologians; doctors, for instance, have been known to make a similar mistake by equating 'health' and 'sickness' with such quantifiables as temperature, pulse-rate, or urine-sugar.
72 Munroe Beardsley, *Aesthetics*, N.Y., Harcourt Brace, 1958; Max Black, *Models and Metaphors*, Ithaca, Cornell University Press, 1962; Stephen Toulmin, *Foresight and Understanding* Bloomington, Indiana University Press, 1961; Colin Turbane, *The Myth of Metaphor*, New Haven, Yale U.P., 1962; Philip Wheelwright, *Metaphor and Reality*, Bloomington, Indiana University Press, 1962.
73 Berggren, 'Use and Abuse of Metaphor', I, p. 243.
74 Ibid., pp. 243–4.
75 W. Bedell Stanford, *Greek Metaphor Studies in Theory and Practice*, Oxford University Press, 1936, p. 105.
76 Second letter to Thomas Butts, 22 November, 1802, Blake, *Complete Writings* p. 818.
77 J. R. Watson, *Wordsworth's Vital Soul: The Sacred and the Profane in Wordsworth's Poetry*, Macmillan, 1982.
78 Ibid., p. 12. P. Wheelwright, *The Burning Fountain*, Indiana University Press, 1966, pp. 18–19.
79 It is dangerous to base theological arguments upon the rapidly-shifting sands of anthropological hypotheses. Nevertheless, for those with a speculative cast of mind it is worth noticing the point made by Richard Leakey in *The Making of Mankind*, Michael Joseph, 1981, pp. 71–5, that what may have distinguished the ancestors of *homo sapiens* from the other co-existing hominoids about two million years ago was their marginality. Evidence from tooth wear has been interpreted to suggest that *Australopithecus africanus* had a fairly stable habitat in forest areas while the larger *Australopithecus robustus* lived on the more open plains. *Homo erectus*, our putative ancestor, less well equipped for either climbing or running, seems to have followed a more precarious and marginal existence, always under greater threat with no stable habitat or place to call his own.
80 I say 'Wordsworthian' because the distinction is much more clearly marked in later nineteenth-century figures who attribute it to Wordsworth than it is in his own writings. The actual passage in the Preface to the *Lyrical Ballads* is arguably not dissimilar to Berggren.
81 Berggren, 'Use and Abuse of Metaphor', II, pp. 470–71.
82 Ibid., p. 471.
83 Ricoeur, *Rule of Metaphor*, p. 94.
84 Barfield, *Poetic Diction*, p. 48.
85 Ibid., p. 131.

86 Sweet, *Humboldt*, II, pp. 408–9.

87 Ibid., p. 468.

88 There is a story of a Shakespeare scholar strolling through the suburbs of modern Stratford one summer evening musing on the lines from *Hamlet*: 'There is a divinity that shapes our ends/Rough-hew them how we will' (Act V, Sc. ii, 10–11). He encountered two old men cutting a hedge in a somewhat unusual manner, and enquired what they were doing. One of the men replied 'My friend here rough-hews it, and then I shapes the ends ...' Even so, we must presume, did an eccentric Warwickshire gardening practice achieve universal metaphorical status.

89 See, for instance, Roston, *Prophet and Poet*, pp. 25–6. 'It is impossible to translate the phrase "As a mother has mercy upon her children" without losing almost all the effect; for the Hebrew word "to have mercy" is a derivative from the word for "womb".'

90 We recall Ricoeur's division into narration, prophecy, prescriptions, wisdom, and hymns. *Essays on Biblical Interpretation*, pp. 73–89.

91 Ricoeur, *Rule of Metaphor*, pp. 83–90.

92 Ibid., pp. 277, 319.

93 Ibid., p. 319.

94 See Ch. 2, pp. 75–6 above.

95 Ricoeur, *Rule of Metaphor*, p. 222.

96 Ricoeur, *Symbolism of Evil*, tr. Emerson Buchanan, N.Y., Harper and Row, 1967, p. 352.

97 More obvious in French, which has the single Latinate root ('la langue'), than in English, which has both the derived word, 'language', *and* the Anglo-Saxon undifferentiated term 'tongue'.

98 On this point see Gadamer: '. . . it is part of the nature of language that it has a completely unfathomable unselfconsciousness of itself. To that extent, it is not an accident that the use of the concept "language" is a recent development. The word *logos* means not only thought and language, but also concept and law. The appearance of the concept "language" presupposes consciousness of language. But that is only the result of the reflective moment in which the one thinking has reflected out of the unconscious operation of speaking and stands at a distance from himself. The real enigma of language, however, is that we can never really do this completely.' 'Man and Language', *The Scope of Hermeneutical Reflection*, tr. and ed. David E. Linge, University of California Press, 1976, p. 62.

99 'Indirect Language and the Voices of Silence', *Signs*, tr. Richard C. McCleary, Northwestern University Press, 1964, p. 39.

100 Ibid., pp. 44–5.

101 Nuttall, *A New Mimesis*, pp. 19–20.

102 Kirk and Raven, *The Presocratic Philosophers*, pp. 286–97.

103 Ibid., p. 294.

104 Merleau-Ponty, *Signs*, pp. 42–3.

105 Ibid., p. 44.

106 Wheeler, *German Aesthetic and Literary Criticism*, p. 93.
107 Ibid.
108 Ibid., p. 52.
109 Burrow, 'Uses of Philology', pp. 19–20 ff.
110 'Instead of aiming at finding out what a thing really is, and at defining its true nature, methodological nominalism aims at describing how a thing behaves in various circumstances . . . And it sees in our language, and especially in those of its rules which distinguish properly constructed sentences and inferences from a mere heap of words, the great instrument of scientific description; words it considers rather as subsidiary tools for the task, and not as the names of essences . . .' Popper, *Open Society*, vol. I, p. 32.
111 Burrow, 'Uses of Philology', pp. 19–20 ff.
112 Mrs H. Ward, *Robert Elsmere*, ed. Clyde de L. Ryals, Lincoln, Nebraska, University of Nebraska Press (1888), 1967, pp. 276–7.
113 Ibid., p. 317.
114 Jenkyns, *Victorians and Ancient Greece*, Oxford, Blackwell, 1980.
115 John Burrow, *A Liberal Descent*, Cambridge University Press, 1981.
116 Girouard, *The Return to Camelot*, pp. 117–26; Benedict Read, *Victorian Sculpture*, Yale University Press, New Haven, 1982, p. 130, pl. 156.
111 'We are protected from the miraculous by the comforting possibility of rational explanation. To suggest that there could ever be a miracle story capable of breaking through that defence is to suggest that there is a finite limit to man's power to invent. So there comes a time when we grow bored of trying to outrun reason, and instead wonder what happens when we are actually witness to a miracle situaton. This is more difficult especially since it is now less easy to find people who do not believe in hypnotism. The technique used is called "post hypnotic suggestion". It is possible to hypnotise a person, and tell him that he will obey certain commands, or perform some action spontaneously, *after* he has come round from the hypnotic trance. In this way it is possible to confront someone with a miracle and watch his reaction.

A favourite example is to say that a certain person in the room will vanish when one command is given, but will reappear when another is given. So it is possible to present the subject with a human who will vanish and reappear instantly before him. But to your disappointment the subject does not shriek "MY GOD! JOE'S VANISHED!", he merely looks away. If you ask him where Joe is he will not tell you that "he vanished before my very eyes" but will make some very ordinary reply that "Joe went out" or "must have gone". When Joe instantly reappears he will merely say "Ah, there you are". For his mind will cover up the miracle by superimposing a normal exit and return. As far as his conscious mind is concerned he has not witnessed any miracle but simply Joe's comings and goings. The next experiment is to force him to stare directly at the invisible Joe and therefore to see what is behind him. You will find that the subject will think of many good reasons not to cooperate, but if you force him to, say, read a notice while the invisible Joe stands before it, you will be sorry to find that you yourself are unable to see miracles. For the subject will appear perplexed and the suggestion will break down. You have been saved.

No matter how bizarre you make the subject's action under post hypnotic suggestion, you will find that his mind can devise a "rational explanation". A shy young man will stand up in the middle of a lecture and shout "hot stew" without any justification. But if you ask him why, he will be unlikely to say that "dark forces compelled him". If he is rational he will believe that he did it to prove to himself that he was not in an hypnotic trance, or some such reason . . .

A colleague was once privileged to find someone who really did not believe in hypnotism, and still did not believe after many demonstrations. A whole room full of people vanished and reappeared around the subject repeatedly, without his turning a hair. Then my friend remembered a similar case which had been described by a medical hypnotist, and so he caused *half* of a person to disappear. The result was not "oh well, you've convinced me", but something closer to a nervous breakdown.'
Lionel Snell, *S.S.O.T.B.M.E.: An Essay on Magic, its Foundations, Development and Place in Modern Life,* The Mouse that Spins, 29 West Common, Redbourn, Herts. (1975), reprinted 1977, pp. 38–9.

118 'The End of Philosophy and the Task of Thinking', *Martin Heidegger: Basic Writings,* ed. David Farrell Krell (from *On Time and Being,* tr. Joan Stambaugh, N.Y., Harper and Row, 1972), Routledge, 1978, p. 384.

119 See editor's footnote, ibid.

120 Ibid., p. 385.

121 Ibid., p. 386.

122 See John D. Caputo, *Heidegger and Aquinas,* N.Y. Fordham University Press, 1982, ch. I.

123 As Gadamer, who perhaps comes closest to discussing the question satisfactorily, points out, there is a subtle but essential tension behind the common expressions 'the nature of things' and 'the language of things'. For him, as for Nuttall, language presupposes a common sky, a basic agreement about things. The world of things, in a Heideggerian sense, 'speaks' to us if we can listen. For Gadamer, therefore, *neither* the things, nor the human mind with its linguistic conceptualization, has priority. What is prior is the correspondence itself – a point which he sees best illustrated by reference to the function of rhythm in poetry. 'The Nature of Things and the Language of Things', in Gadamer, *Scope of Hermeneutical Reflection,* p. 78.

124 The analogy is, of course, a mathematical one, and does not imply a contradiction. It is, for instance, perfectly easy to conceive of infinite progression within a strictly finite and limited space.

Bibliography

Place of publication is London, unless otherwise specified.

AARSLEFF, Hans, *From Locke to Saussure: Essays on the Study of Language and Intellectual History*, Minneapolis, University of Minnesota Press, 1982.

The Study of Language in England, 1780–1860, Princeton University Press, 1967.

ABRAMS, M. H., *The Mirror and the Lamp*, N.Y., Oxford University Press, 1953 (reprinted N.Y., Norton, 1958).

Natural Supernaturalism, N.Y., Norton, 1973.

ALLEN, Ward (ed.), *Translating for King James*, Allen Lane, The Penguin Press, 1970.

ALTER, Robert, *The Art of Biblical Narrative*, Allen and Unwin, 1981.

ANRICH, E. (ed.), *Die Idee der deutschen Universität: Die fünf Grundschriften aus der Zeit ihrer Neubegründung durch Klassischen Idealismus und romantischen Realismus*, Darmstadt, 1960.

ARISTOTLE, *The Ethics*, tr. J. A. K. Thomson, Penguin, 1955.

ARNOLD, Matthew, *Complete Prose Works*, ed. R. H. Super, University of Michigan Press, 1960–77.

Letters 1848–88, ed. G. W. R. Russell, 2 vols., N.Y., Macmillan, 1900.

Literature and Dogma, popular edn, 1895.

ASBACH-SCHNITKER, Brigitte, *A Linguistic Commentary on John Fearn's 'Anti-Tooke' (1824–7)*, Tübingen, Niemeyer, 1973.

AUERBACH, Erich, *Mimesis*, Princeton University Press, 1953.

BAELZ, Peter, 'A Deliberate Mistake?' *Christ, Faith, and History*, eds. S. W. Sykes and J. P. Clayton, Cambridge University Press, 1972.

BAKHTIN, M. M., *The Dialogic Imagination*, ed. Michael Holquist, trs. Caryl Emerson and Michael Holquist, Austin, University of Texas Press, 1981.

BARFIELD, Owen, *History in English Words*, Faber, 1962.

'The Meaning of "Literal" ', *Metaphor and Symbol*, eds. Basil Cottle and L. C. Knights, Bristol, Butterfield, 1960, reprinted in *The Rediscovery of Meaning*, Middletown, Conn., Wesleyan University Press, 1977.

'The Nature of Meaning', *Seven*, Vol. II, 1981.

Poetic Diction, new edn, Faber, 1952.

Saving the Appearances, N.Y., Harcourt Brace, 1957.

BARTH, J. ROBERT, S. J., *The Symbolic Imagination: Coleridge and the*

283

Romantic Tradition, Princeton University Press, 1977.

BARTHES, Roland, *Image–Music–Text*, Essays selected and translated by Stephen Heath, N.Y., Hill and Wang, 1977.

BASNETT-MCGUIRE, Susan, *Translation Studies*, Methuen, 1980.

BATTISCOMBE, Georgina, *John Keble*, Constable, 1963.

BEARDSLEY, Monroe C., *Aesthetics*, N.Y., Harcourt Bruce, 1958.

(with W. K. Wimsatt), 'The Intentional Fallacy', *Essays in Modern Criticism*, ed. Ray B. West, N.Y., Holt, Rinehart, and Winston, 1952.

BERGGREN, Douglas, 'The Use and Abuse of Metaphor', *Review of Metaphysics*, December 1962, pp. 237–58; and March 1963, pp. 450–72.

BERLIN, Isaiah, *Vico and Herder: Two Studies in the History of Ideas*, Hogarth Press, 1976.

BELL, Quentin, *On Human Finery*, Hogarth Press, 1976.

BLACK, Max, *Models and Metaphors*, Ithaca, Cornell University Press, 1962.

(ed.), *The Importance of Language*, Englewood Cliffs, N.J., Prentice-Hall, 1962.

BLACKWELL, Thomas, *Enquiry into the Life and Writings of Homer*, 1735.

BLAIR, Hugh, *Lectures on Rhetoric and Belles Lettres* (1783), 2 vols., Edinburgh, 1820.

BLAKE, William, *Complete Writings*, ed. Geoffrey Keynes, Oxford University Press, 1966.

BOPP, Franz, 'Analytical Comparison of the Sanskrit, Greek, Latin and Teutonic Languages, shewing the original identity of their grammatical structure' (partial translation of 'Uber das Konjugationsystem der San-skritsprache', 1816), *Annals of Oriental Literature*, Vols. I–III, 1820–1.

BORST, Arno, *Der Turmbau von Babel. Geschichte der Meinungen über Ursprung und Vielfalt der Sprachen und Völker*, 4 vols. in 6, Stuttgart, 1957–63.

BRANTLEY, Richard E., *Locke, Wesley, and the Method of English Romanticism*, Gainsville, University of Florida Press, 1984.

Wordsworth's 'Natural Methodism', New Haven, Yale University Press, 1975.

BRONNER, Leah, *The Stories of Elijah and Elisha*, Leiden, E. J. Brill, 1968.

BROSSES, Charles de, *Traité de la formation méchanique des langues et des principes physiques de l'étymologie*, 2 vols., Paris, 1765.

BROWN, John, *Dissertation on the Rise Union and Power, the Progressions, Separations and Corruptions of Poetry and Music*, 1763.

BROWN, Peter, *Augustine of Hippo*, Faber, 1967.

BUBER, Martin, *The Prophetic Faith*, N.Y., Harper Torchbooks, 1960.

BUNSEN, Christian Karl Josias von, Baron, *God in History, or the Progress of Man's Faith in the Moral Order of the World*, 3 vols., 1868.

Outlines of the Philosophy of Universal History Applied to Language and Religion, 2 vols., tr. S. Winkworth, 1854.

BURKE, Edmund, *A Philsophical Enquiry into the Origin of our Ideas of the Sublime and the Beautiful* (1757), facsimile of 2nd edn, 1759, Menston, Scolar Press, 1970.

BURROW, John, *A Liberal Descent*, Cambridge University Press, 1981.

'Intellectual History: The Poverty of Methodology' (unpublished paper).

'The Uses of Philology in Victorian England', *Ideas and Institutions of Victorian Britain*, ed. Robert Robson, Bell, 1967.

BURTT, E. A., *The Metaphysical Foundations of Modern Science*, Routledge, 1932.

BUSINK, A., *Der Tempel von Jerusalem von Salomo*, Leiden, 1980.

BUTLER, Joseph, *The Analogy of Religion*, 1736.

BUTLER, Marilyn (ed.), *Burke, Paine, Godwin, and the Revolution Controversy*, Cambridge University Press, 1984.

Peacock Displayed, Routledge, 1979.

CAIRD, G. B., *The Language and Imagery of the Bible*, Duckworth, 1980.

CAMBRIDGE HISTORY OF THE BIBLE, eds. R. P. Ackroyd and C. F. Evans, Vol. I, Cambridge University Press, 1970.

CAPUTO, John D., *Heidegger and Aquinas*, N.Y., Fordham University Press, 1982.

CAREY, Edmund, *Les grands traducteurs français*, Genève, Librairie de l'Université, 1963.

CARLYLE, Thomas, *Sartor Resartus*, 1834.

CARROLL, J. S., *Exiles of Eternity*, Hodder, 1903.

CELLIER, Léon, *Fabre d'Olivet: Contribution à l'étude des aspects religieux du Romantisme*, Paris, Nizet, 1953.

CHARITY, A. C., *Events and their Afterlife: The Dialectics of Christian Typology in the Bible and Dante*, Cambridge University Press, 1966.

CHITTY, Susan, *The Beast and the Monk*, Hodder and Stoughton, 1974.

COLERIDGE, J. T., *Memoir of the Rev. John Keble*, 1869.

COLERIDGE, Samuel Taylor, *Aids to Reflection*, ed. T. Fenby, Edinburgh, Grant, 1905.

Anima Poetae, ed. E. H. Coleridge, 1895.

Biographia Literaria, ed. J. Shawcross, 2 vols., Oxford University Press, 1907.

Collected Letters, ed. E. L. Griggs, Oxford University Press, 1956-9.

Confessions of an Inquiring Spirit, 2nd edn, ed. H. N. Coleridge, 1849.

Lay Sermons, ed. R. J. White, Routledge/Princeton University Press, 1972.

Lectures on Politics and Religion (1795), eds. Lewis Patton and Peter Mann, Routledge/Princeton University Press, 1971.

Logic, ed. J. R. de J. Jackson, Routledge/Princeton University Press, 1981.

Notebooks, ed. K. Coburn, Routledge, 1957.

Philosophical Lectures, ed. K. Coburn, Routledge, 1949.

Shakespeare Criticism, ed. T. M. Raysor, 2nd edn, Everyman, 2 vols., 1960.

Table Talk, ed. H. N. Coleridge, 1852.

CONDILLAC, Etienne Bonnot de, *Essay on the Origin of Human Knowledge: A Supplement to Mr Locke's 'Essay on Human Understanding'*, 1756.

COULSON, John, *Newman and the Common Tradition*, Oxford, Clarendon Press, 1970.

Religion and Imagination, Oxford University Press, 1981.

CRAIG, John, *Theologicae Christianae Principia Mathematica*, 1699.

CRAWFORD, Donald W., *Kant's Aesthetic Theory*, University of Wisconsin Press, 1974.

CROCE, Benedetto, *The Philosophy of Giambattista Vico* (1913), tr. R. G.

Collingwood, reissued, N.Y., Russell and Russell, 1964.

CURRIE, Robert, Alan Gilbert and Lee Hursley (eds.), *Churches and Churchgoers: Patterns of Church in the British Isles since 1700,* Oxford University Press, 1977.

DANTE Alighieri, *The Divine Comedy,* tr. John D. Sinclair, 3 vols., N.Y., Oxford University Press, 1939.

DAMON, S. Foster, *A Blake Dictionary,* Thames and Hudson, 1973.

DELAURA, David, *Hebrew and Hellene in Victorian England,* Austin, University of Texas Press, 1969.

DENNIS, John, 'The Grounds of Criticism in Poetry', *Critical Works,* ed. E. N. Hooker, Baltimore, Johns Hopkins Press, 1939.

DERHAM, William, *Astro-Theology,* 1715.

Physico-Theology, 1713.

DONALDSON, J. W., *The New Cratylus,* 1839.

DRONKE, Peter, 'The Procession in Dante's *Purgatorio', Deutsches Dante-Jahrbuch 1978–9.*

DRYDEN, John, 'Preface to Ovid's Epistles' (1680), *Of Dramatic Poesy and Other Critical Essays,* ed. G. Watson, 2 vols., Everyman, 1962.

EAGLETON, Terry, *Literary Theory: An Introduction,* Oxford, Blackwell, 1983.

EICHHORN, Johann Gottfried, *Einleitung in das Alte Testament,* 3 vols., Leipzig, 1780–3.

ELIADE, Mircea, *Australian Religions: An Introduction,* with a Foreword by Victor Turner, Ithaca, Cornell University Press, 1973.

ELIOT, George, *Scenes of Clerical Life,* ed. David Lodge, Penguin, 1973.

ELIOT, T. S., 'The Modern Mind', *The Use of Poetry and the Use of Criticism,* Faber, 1933.

'Tradition and the Individual Talent', *Selected Essays,* 3rd edn, Faber, 1951.

EMERSON, Ralph Waldo, 'Nature' (1836), *Selected Prose and Poetry,* ed. R. L. Cook, N.Y., Holt, Rinehart and Winston, 1950.

EMMET, Dorothy, Review of Stephen Prickett's *Coleridge and Wordsworth, Review of English Studies,* August, 1971.

EMPSON, William, *Seven Types of Ambiguity,* Peregrine (Penguin Books), 1961.

FABRE D'OLIVET, Antoine, *The Hebraic Tongue Restored: and the Meaning of the Hebrew Words Re-established and Proved by their Radical Analysis,* tr. N. L. Redfield, N.Y., Putnam, 1921.

THE FABER BOOK OF MODERN VERSE, ed. Michael Roberts, Faber, 1947.

FARRAR, F. W., *Chapters on Language,* 1865.

Essay on the Origin of Language, 1860.

FARRER, Austin, *The Glass of Vision,* Dacre Press, 1948.

'Poetic Truth', *Reflective Faith,* ed. Charles C. Conti, S.P.C.K., 1972.

A Rebirth of Images, Dacre Press, 1944.

FEARN, John, *Anti-Tooke, or an Analysis of the Principles and Structures of Language* (1824–7), reprinted, with an Introduction by Brigitte Asbach-Schnitker and Preface by Herbert E. Brekle, Stuttgart-Bad Cannstatt, Friedrich Frommann Verlag, 1972.

FEUERBACH, Ludwig, *The Essence of Christianity*, tr. George Eliot, N.Y., Harper Torchbooks, 1957.

FORBES, Duncan, *The Liberal Anglican Idea of History*, Cambridge University Press, 1952.

FORD, John, *The Chronical History of Perkin Warbeck*, 1634.

FORSTER, E. M., *A Passage to India* (1924), Penguin, 1956.

FORSYTH, Robert, *Principles of Moral Science*, 1805.

FOSTER, Richard, *The New Romantics: A Reappraisal of the New Criticism*, Bloomington, Indiana University Press, 1962.

FREI, Hans W., *The Eclipse of Biblical Narrative: A Study in Eighteenth and Nineteenth Century Hermeneutics*, New Haven, Yale University Press, 1974.

FRIEDLÄNDER, Paul, *Plato: An Introduction*, tr. Hans Meyerhoff, Routledge, 1958.

FRUMAN, Norman, *Coleridge: The Damaged Archangel*, Allen and Unwin, 1972

FRYE, Northrop, *The Great Code: The Bible and Literature*, Routledge, 1982.

FULLER, R. C., *Alexander Geddes*, Sheffield, Almond Press, 1983.
'Dr Alexander Geddes: A Forerunner of Biblical Criticism', unpublished Ph.D. thesis, Cambridge University, 1968.

FUNK, Robert W., *Language, Hermeneutics, and the Word of God: The Problem of Language in the the New Testament and Contemporary Theology*, N.Y., Harper and Row, 1966.

GADAMER, Hans-Georg, *The Scope of Hermeneutical Reflection*, tr. and ed. David E. Linge, University of California Press, 1976.

GAINSFORD, Thomas, *The True and Wonderful Historie of Perkin Warbeck*, 1618.

GARDNER, Helen, *Religion and Literature*, Faber, 1971.

GERHARDSON, Birger, 'The Good Samaritan – The Good Shepherd', *Coniectanea Neotestamentica*, Lund, C. W. K. Gleerup, 1958.

GIROUARD, Mark, *The Return to Camelot: Chivalry and the English Gentleman*, New Haven, Yale University Press, 1981.

GOMBRICH, E.H., *Art and Illusion*, Phaidon, 1960.

GRAY, John, *I and II Kings: A Commentary*, revised edn, S.C.M. Press, 1970.

GRAYSTON, Kenneth, 'Confessions of a Biblical Translator', *New Universities Quarterly*, Vol. 33, no. 3, Summer 1979.

GRIMM, Jacob, *Deutsche Grammatik*, 4 vols., Göttingen, 1822–37.

GUTMANN, Joseph, *The Temple of Solomon*, Missoula, Montana, Scholars Press, 1976.

HARDIE, Colin, 'The Symbol of the Gryphon in *Purgatorio* xxxix, 108 and following Cantos', *Centenary Essay on Dante*, by members of the Oxford Dante Society, Oxford, Clarendon Press, 1965.

HARE, Julius C., *Guesses at Truth*, 3rd edn, 1866.

HARRIS, James, *Harmes, or a Philosophical Inquiry Concerning Universal Grammar* (1751), 5th edn, 1794.

HARRISON, J. F. C., *The Second Coming: Popular Millenarianism 1780–1850*, Routledge, 1979.

HARTLEY, David, *Observations on Man, his Frame, his Duties and his Expectations*, 2 vols., 1749.

HEIDEGGER, Martin, 'Hölderlin and the Essence of Poetry', tr. Douglas Scott, *Existence and Being*, Vision Press, 1949.

Martin Heidegger: Basic Writings, ed. David Farrell Krell (from *On Time and Being*, tr. Joan Stambaugh, N.Y., Harper and Row, 1972), Routledge, 1978.

HEPWORTH, Brian, *Robert Lowth*, Boston, Twayne, 1978.

HERDER, Johann Gottfried, 'Esssay on the Origin of Language' (1772), *Herder on Social and Political Culture*, tr. and ed. by F. M. Barnard, Cambridge University Press, 1969.

The Spirit of Hebrew Poetry (Dessau, 1782–3), trans. James Marsh, Burlington, Vermont, 1833.

HOBSBAWM, E. J., *Primitive Rebels: Studies in Archaic Forms of Social Movement in the Nineteenth and Twentieth Centuries*, Manchester University Press, 1959.

HOLLAND, Saba, Lady, *Memoir of the Life of the Rev. Sydney Smith*, 2 vols., 1855.

HONEY, J. R. de S., *Tom Brown's Universe: The Development of the Victorian Public School*, Millington, 1977.

HOPKINS, Gerald Manley, *The Correspondence of G.M. Hopkins and R.W. Dixon*, ed. Abbott, Oxford University Press, 1935.

A Hopkins Reader, ed. John Pick, Oxford University Press, 1953.

HOWES, Thomas, *Critical Observations on Books, Antient and Modern*, 4 vols. (1776–1813); reprinted, New York, Garland, 1972.

HULME, T. E., *Speculations*, ed. Herbert Read, 2nd edn, Routledge, 1936.

HUMBOLDT, Wilhelm von, Baron, *Linguistic Variability and Intellectual Development* (1836), tr. G. C. Buck and F. A. Raven, Miami Linguistics Series no. 9, Coral Gables, Fla., University of Miami Press, 1971.

JACOB, Giles, *An Historical Account of the Lives and Writings of our most Considerable English Poets*, 1720.

JASPER, David, *Coleridge as Poet and Religious Thinker*, Macmillan, 1985.

JENKYNS, Richard, *The Victorians and Ancient Greece*, Oxford, Blackwell, 1980.

JESPERSON, J. O. H., *Language, its Nature, Development and Origin*, Allen and Unwin, 1922.

JONES, Sir William, 'On the Origins and Families of Nations', *Asiatic Researches*, Vol. III, 1799.

'Third Anniversary Discourse, on the Hindus' (1786), *Works of Sir William Jones*, Vol. III, with a life of the author by Lord Teignmouth, 1807.

JONES, Rev. William, 'A Course of Lectures on the Figurative Language of Scripture', 1787.

JUDGE, Edwin A., 'Antike und Christentum: Towards a Definition of the Field', *Aufstieg und Niedergang der Romischen Welt*, eds. Hildegard Temporini and Wolfang Haase, Vol. II, Berlin, de Gruyter, 1979.

KANT, Immanuel, *Critique of Judgement*, tr. James Creed Meredith, Oxford University Press, 1952.

KEATS, John, *Letters*, ed. M. Buxton Forman, 4th edn, Oxford University Press, 1952.

KEBLE, John, *The Christian Year*, 43rd edn, 1851.
Lectures on Poetry, tr. E. K. Francis, 2 vols., Oxford University Press, 1912.

KELLY, Louis G., *The True Interpreter: A History of Translation Theory and Practice in the West*, Oxford, Blackwell, 1979.

KERMODE, Frank, *The Genesis of Secrecy*, Harvard University Press, 1979.

KINGSLEY, F. (ed.), *Life of Charles Kingsley by his Wife*, 2 vols., 7th edn, 1877.

KIPLING, Rudyard, *Stalky and Co.*, Macmillan, 1899.

KIRK, G. S., and RAVEN, J. E. (eds.), *The Presocratic Philosophers*, Cambridge University Press, 1957.

KNIGHT, Gareth, *A History of White Magic*, Mowbray, 1978.

KREBS, W. A., 'The Study of Language in Scotland 1760–1810', unpublished Ph.D. thesis, University of Leeds, 1977.

KUGEL, James L., *The Idea of Biblical Poetry: Parallelism and its History*, New Haven, Yale University Press, 1981.

KUHN, Thomas Samuel, *The Structure of Scientific Revolutions*, University of Chicago Press, 1962.

LAING, R. D., *The Self and Others*, Tavistock Press, 1961.

LAMPE, G. W. H. and WOOLLCOMBE, K. J., *Essays on Typology*, S.C.M. Press, 1957.

LANDOW, George P., *Images of Crisis: Literary Iconology, 1750 to the Present*, Routledge, 1982.
Victorian Types, Victorian Shadows: Biblical Typology in Victorian Literature, Art and Thought, Routledge, 1980.

LASKI, Marganita, *George Eliot and her World*, Thames and Hudson, 1973.

LEACH, Edmund, *Genesis as Myth and Other Essays*, Cape, 1969.

LEAKEY, Richard, *The Making of Mankind*, Michael Joseph, 1981.

LEVERE, Trevor H., *Poetry Realised in Nature: Samuel Taylor Coleridge and Early Nineteenth Century Science*, Cambridge University Press, 1981.

LEVINE, George, 'The Ambiguous Heritage of Frankenstein', *The Endurance of Frankenstein: Essays on Mary Shelley's Novel*, eds. George Levine and U. C. Knoepflmacher, Berkeley, University of California Press, 1979.
The Realistic Imagination: English Fiction from 'Frankenstein' to 'Lady Chatterley', University of Chicago Press, 1981.

LEWIS, C. S., *Fern-Seed and Elephants, and other Essays on Christianity*, ed. Walter Hooper, Collins (Fontana), 1975.
'Is Theology Poetry?', *Screwtape Proposes a Toast*, Collins (Fontana), 1965.

LINDSAY, Jack, *William Blake*, Constable, 1978.

LOCKE, John, *An Essay Concerning Human Understanding*, ed. J. W. Yolton, 2 vols., Everyman, 1961.

LODGE, David, *Modes of Modern Writing*, Ithaca, Cornell University Press, 1977.

LONGINUS, *On the Sublime*, tr. A. O. Prickard (1906), ed. D. A. Russell, Oxford University Press, 1964.

LOWTH, Robert, *Isaiah: A New Translation* (1778), 5th edn, 2 vols., Edinburgh, 1807.

Lectures on the Sacred Poetry of the Hebrews, tr. G. Gregory, 1787.

Short Introduction to English Grammar, 1762.

LUBAC, Henri de, *Exégèse médiévale: les quatre sens de l'Ecriture*, Editions Montaigne, Paris, F. Aubier, 1959–64.

LUKACS, G., *Theory of the Novel*, tr. Anna Bostock, Merlin Press, 1971.

MACAULAY, T. B., 'Milton' (1825), *Literary Essays*, Oxford University Press, 1913.

McCLELLAND, Charles E., *State, Society, and University in Germany 1700–1914*, Cambridge University Press, 1980.

McFARLAND, Thomas, *Coleridge and the Pantheist Tradition*, Oxford, Clarendon Press, 1969.

MACINTYRE, Alasdair, *After Virtue*, Duckworth/Notre Dame University Press, Indiana, 1981.

MACQUARRIE, John, *God-Talk*, S.C.M. Press, 1967.

Principles of Christian Theology, S.C.M. Press, 1974.

MADDEN, William A., 'The Divided Tradition of English Criticism', *PMLA*, LXXIII, March 1958.

MARTIN, B. W., *John Keble, Priest, Professor, Poet*, Croom Helm, 1976.

MARTINDALE, Charles, 'Unlocking the Word-Hoard: In Praise of Metaphrase', *Comparative Criticism*, ed. E. S. Shaffer, Vol. 6, Cambridge University Press, 1984.

MAURICE, Frederick Denison, *The Kingdom of Christ*, 4th edn, 2 vols., 1891.

MEDCALF, Stephen, 'Coleridge's Vision of the Chariot', unpublished paper delivered at the Conference on Religion and Literature, Durham University, 1984.

MEINECKE, Friedrich, *Historism: The Rise of a New Historical Outlook*, tr. J. E. Anderson, Routledge, 1972.

MEINHOLD, Peter, *Luthers Sprachphilosophie*, Berlin, 1958.

MERLEAU-PONTY, Maurice, *Signs*, tr. Richard C. McCleary, Northwestern University Press, 1964.

MICHAELIS, Johann David, *Introduction to the New Testament*, tr. with notes by Herbert Marsh, 1793.

MILL, John Stuart, *Autobiography*, 1873.

Mill on Bentham and Coleridge, Introduction by F. R. Leavis, Chatto, 1950.

'What is Poetry?' (1833) *Mill's Essays on Literature and Society*, ed. J. B. Schneewind, N.Y., Collier–Macmillan, 1965.

MONBODDO, James Burnet, Lord, *Of the Origin and Progress of Language*, 1773–92.

MOORMAN, Mary, *William Wordsworth: The Later Years*, Oxford University Press, 1965.

MORELY, Edith J. (ed.), *The Correspondence of Henry Crabb Robinson with the Wordsworth Circle*, Oxford University Press, 1927.

MORRIS, David B., *The Religious Sublime: Christian Poetry and Critical*

Tradition in Eighteenth Century England, Kentucky University Press, 1972.

MOZLEY, Thomas, *Reminiscences, Chiefly of Oriel College and the Oxford Movement*, 2 vols., 1882.

MÜLLER, Friedrich Max, *Anthropological Religion*, 1892.

Natural Religion, 1889.

Physical Religion, 1891.

Theosophy, as Psychological Religion, 1893.

MURE, G. R. G., *Aristotle*, N.Y., Oxford University Press, 1966.

NEWMAN, John Henry, *Essay on the Development of Christian Doctrine* (1845), Sheed and Ward, 1960.

Essays Critical and Historical, 2 vols., 1846.

A Grammar of Assent (1870), ed. C.F. Harrold, Longman, 1957.

NEWSOME, David, *The Parting of Friends*, Murray, 1966.

NIDA, Eugene A., 'Principles of Translation as Exemplified by Bible Translating', *On Translation*, ed. Reuben A. Brower, Harvard Studies in Comparative Literature, No. 23, Cambridge, Mass., Harvard University Press, 1959.

(with C. Taber), *The Theory and Practice of Translation*, Leiden. E. J. Brill, 1969.

Towards a Science of Translating, Leiden, E. J. Brill, 1969.

NINEHAM, Dennis, *The Use and Abuse of the Bible*, Macmillan, 1976.

NUTTALL, A. D., *A Common Sky: Philosophy and the Literary Imagination*, Chatto/Sussex University Press, 1974.

A New Mimesis: Shakespeare and the Representation of Reality, Methuen, 1983.

Overheard by God, Methuen, 1981.

OATES, Joan, 'The Emergence of Cities in the Near East', *The Cambridge Encylopaedia of Archaeology*, ed. A. Sherratt, Cambridge University Press, 1980.

OLDROYD, Drina, 'Hunting the Griffin in Dante's *Purgatorio*', unpublished paper delivered to the Australasian Language and Literature Association, Melbourne, 1985.

ORSINI, G. N. G., *Coleridge and German Idealism*, Carbondale and Edwardsville, Southern Illinois University Press, 1969.

PALEY, Morton D., 'William Blake, the Prince of the Hebrews, and the Woman Clothed with the Sun', in Morton D. Paley and Michael Phillips (eds.), *William Blake: Essays in Honour of Sir Geoffrey Keynes*, Oxford, Clarendon Press, 1973.

PALEY, William, *Natural Theology*, 1802.

A View of the Evidences of Christianity, 1794.

PALMER, Richard E., *Hermeneutics: Interpretation Theory in Schleiermacher, Dilthey, Heidegger, and Gadamer*, Northwestern University Press, 1969.

PARSONS, James, *The Remains of Japhet* (1767), facsimile reprint, Menston, Scolar Press, 1968.

PATTISON, Mark, 'F. A. Wolf', *Essays*, ed. Nettleship, Vol. I, 1889.

Memoirs, 1885.

Suggestions on Academical Organization with Especial Reference to Oxford, Edinburgh, 1868.

PEACOCK, Thomas Love, *The Four Ages of Poetry*, ed. H. F. B. Brett-Smith, Percy Reprints, No. 3, Oxford, Blackwell, 1921.

PEDERSON, H., *Linguistic Science in the Nineteenth Century*, tr. J. W. Spargo, Cambridge, Mass., Harvard University Press, 1931.

PERCY, Thomas, *Reliques of Ancient English Poetry*, 4th edn, 3 vols., 1794.

PIOZZI, Hester, *British Synonymy*, 2 vols., Dublin, 1794.

POLANYI, Michael, *Personal Knowledge: Towards a Post-Critical Philosophy*, Routledge, 1958.

POLLARD, A. W., *Records of the English Bible*, Oxford University Press, 1911.

POPPER, Sir Karl, *The Open Society and its Enemies*, 4th edn, Routledge, 1962.

PORTER, H. C., 'The Nose of Wax: Scripture and the Spirit from Erasmus to Milton', *Transactions of the Royal Historical Society*, 5th series, Vol. 14, 1964.

POUND, Ezra, *Literary Essays*, Faber, 1954.

PRADO, H., and J. B. VILLALPANDO, *In Ezechielem Explanationes*, 3 vols., Rome, 1596–1605.

PRICKETT, Stephen, *Coleridge and Wordsworth: The Poetry of Growth*, Cambridge University Press, 1970.

'Dissidents Who Kicked Out at a Rugby Heritage', *The Times Higher Education Supplement*, 1 August, 1980.

'Peacock's *Four Ages* Recycled', *British Journal of Aesthetics*, Spring 1982.

Romanticism and Religion: The Tradition of Coleridge and Wordsworth in the Victorian Church, Cambridge University Press, 1976.

Victorian Fantasy, Brighton, Harvester Press/Indiana University Press, 1979.

RAD, Gerhard von, *Old Testament Theology*, tr. D. M. G. Stalker, Edinburgh, Oliver and Boyd, 1965.

'Typological Interpretation of the Old Testament', tr. John Bright, *Essays on Old Testament Hermeneutics*, ed. Claus Westermann (English tr. ed. James Luther Mays), Richmond, Va., John Knox Press, 1966.

RAINE, Kathleen, 'Thomas Taylor in England', *Thomas Taylor the Platonist*, eds. Kathleen Raine and George Mills Harper, Bollingen Foundation/ Princeton University Press, 1969.

RAMSAY, Ian, *Models and Mystery*, Oxford University Press, 1964.

Religious Language, S.C.M. Press, 1957.

RAY, John, *Wisdom of God in Creation*, 1701.

REED, Sampson, *Observations on the Growth of the Mind* (Boston, 1826), reprinted Florida, 1970.

REEVES, Marjorie, and Beatrice HIRSH-REICH, *The 'Figurae' of Joachim of Fiore*, Oxford, Clarendon Press, 1972.

REID, Thomas, *Works*, ed. Sir W. Hamilton, 8th edn, Edinburgh, 1895.

'REPORT OF H.M. COMMISSIONERS appointed to inquire into the State, Discipline, Studies, and Revenues of the University and Colleges of Oxford', *Parliamentary Papers*, XXII, 1852.

RICHARDSON, Alan (ed.), *A Theological Word Book of the Bible*, S.C.M. Press, 1950.

RICHARDSON, Charles, *Illustrations of English Philology*, 1815.

RICOEUR, Paul, *Essays on Biblical Interpretation*, tr. David Pellauer, ed. Lewis S. Mudge, Philadelphia, Fortress Press, 1980.

Freud and Philosophy, tr. D. Savage, New Haven, Yale University Press, 1970.

The Rule of Metaphor, tr. Robert Czerny, with Kathleen McLaughlin and John Costello, S. J., University of Toronto Press, 1977.

The Symbolism of Evil, tr. Emerson Buchanan, N.Y., Harper and Row, 1967.

ROBERTSON, F. W., *Lectures on the Influence of Poetry* (1852), reprinted 1906.

ROBERTSON, J. G., *Studies in the Genesis of Romantic Theory in the Eighteenth Century* (1923), reissued, N.Y., Russell and Russell, 1962.

ROBINSON, H. Wheeler, *Inspiration and Revelation in the Old Testament*, Oxford University Press, 1962.

ROBINSON, J., *The First Book of Kings*, Cambridge University Press, 1972.

ROSENAU, Helen, *Vision of the Temple*, Oresko Books, 1979.

ROSTON, Murray, *Poet and Prophet: The Bible and the Growth of Romanticism*, Faber, 1965.

RUSSELL, Bertrand, *The Principles of Mathematics*, Allen and Unwin, 1903.

SAGOVSKY, Nicholas, *Between Two Worlds: George Tyrrell's Relationship with the Thought of Matthew Arnold*, Cambridge University Press, 1983.

ST AUGUSTINE, *The Confessions*, tr. E. B. Pusey, Everyman, 1966.

ST JOHN OF THE CROSS, *Complete Works*, tr. and ed. E. Allison Peers, Burns and Oates, 1964.

SAYCE, A. H., *Principles of Comparative Philology* (1874–7), 4th edn, 1892.

SCHELLING, F. W. J. von, *On University Studies*, tr. E. S. Morgan, Athens, Ohio, 1966.

SCHILLER, F. C., *On the Aesthetic Education of Man* (1795), trs. R. Snell, Routledge, 1954.

SCHLEGEL, A. W., 'Aus dem Indischen: Ramayana' (1820), *Sämtliche Werke*, ed. E. Böeking, Vol. III, Leipzig, 1846.

SCHLEGEL, F. von, *Uber die Sprache und Weisheit der Indier. Ein Beitrag zur Begründung der Alterthumskunde*, Heidelberg, 1808.

SCHMID, E.A., *Des Lord Monboddo Werk von dem Ursprunge und Fortgange der Sprache übersetzt von E. A. Schmid. Mit einer Vorrede des Herrn Generalsuperintendenten Herder*, Riga, 1784–5.

SCHMIDT, C. B., *Auszug aus Dr R. Lowths . . . Vorlesungen über die heilige Dichtkunst der Hebräer, mit Herders und (Sir William) Jones Grundsätzen verbunden . . . Nebst einigen vermischten Anhängen entworfen* von C. B. Schmidt, Danzig, 1793.

SCHOLEM, Gershom, *Kabbalah*, Jerusalem, Keter Publishing House, 1974.

SCOTT, D. F. S., *Wilhem von Humboldt and the Idea of a University*, Durham University, 1960.

SCRIBLERUS, Martin (Pope?), *The Art of Sinking in Poetry* (1727), ed. E. L. Steeves, N.Y., Russell and Russell, revised edn, 1968.

SCRUTON, Roger, *Kant*, Past Masters Series, Oxford University Press, 1982.

SHAFFER, Elinor, *'Kubla Khan' and 'The Fall of Jerusalem': The Mythological School in Biblical Criticism and Secular Literature 1770–1880*, Cambridge University Press, 1975.

SHELLEY, P. B., *A Defence of Poetry*, Percy Reprints, ed. H. F. B. Brett-Smith, No. 3, Oxford, Blackwell, 1921.

SNELL, Lionel, *S.S.O.T.B.M.E.: An Essay on Magic, it Foundations, Development and Place in Modern Life*, The Mouse that Spins, 29 West Common, Redbourn, Herts. (1975), reprinted 1977.

SPARROW, John, *Mark Pattison and The Idea of a University*, Cambridge University Press, 1967.

STANFORD, W. Bedell, *Greek Metaphor Studies in Theory and Practice*, Oxford University Press, 1936.

STEIG, Michael, *Dickens and Phiz*, Bloomington, Indiana University Press, 1978.

STEINER, George, *After Babel: Aspects of Language and Translation*, Oxford University Press, 1976.

STEWART, Dugald, *Philosophical Essays*, Edinburgh, 1810.

STONE, Harry T., *Dickens and the Invisible World: Fairy Tales, Fantasy, and Novel Making*, N.Y., Macmillan, 1979.

STRACHEY, Lytton, 'Life of Cardinal Manning', *Eminent Victorians*, Chatto, 1918.

SÜSSMILCH, Johann Peter, *Versuch eines Beweises, dass die erste Sprache ihren Ursprung nicht vom Menschen, sondern allein vom Schöpfer erhalten habe*, 1766.

SWEET, Paul R., *Wilhelm von Humboldt: A Biography*, 2 vols., Columbus, Ohio State University Press, 1978–80.

SYDNEY, Sir Philip, *'An Apologie for Poetry'*, Percy Reprints, ed. H. F. B. Brett-Smith, No. 3, Oxford, Blackwell, 1921.

TANNENBAUM, Leslie, *Biblical Tradition in Blake's Early Prophecies: the Great Code of Art*, Princeton University Press, 1982.

THOMPSON, E. P., *The Making of the English Working Class*, Gollancz, 1963.

THOMSON, James, 'Preface to *Winter*' (1726), *Eighteenth Century Critical Essays*, ed. Scott Elledge, Ithaca, N.Y., Cornell University Press, 1961.

TOOKE, John Horne, *The Diversions of Purley*, 2 vols. (1798–1805), reprinted Menston, Scolar Press, 1968.

TOULMIN, Stephen, *Foresight and Understanding*, Bloomington, Indiana University Press, 1961.

TOYNBEE, Paget, *A Dictionary of Proper Names and Notable Matters in the Works of Dante*, Oxford, Clarendon Press, 1898.

TRAPP, Joseph, *Lectures on Poetry* (1742), tr. William Bowyes (asst. William Clarke), reprinted Menston, Scolar Press, 1973.

TRIMMER, Mrs Sarah, *Help to the Unlearned in the Study of the Holy Scriptures*, 1806.

TROMPF, G. W., *Fredrich Max Mueller as a Theorist of Comparative Religion*,

Bombay, Shakuntala Publishing House, 1978.

TRUSLER, John, *The Difference Between Words Esteemed Synonymous in the English Language, and the Proper Choice of them Determined*, 2 vols., 1766.

TURBANE, Colin, *The Myth of Metaphor*, New Haven, Yale University Press, 1962.

TYRRELL, George, *Through Scylla and Charybdis; or The Old Theology and the New*, 1907.

VANCE, R. N. C., *The Sinews of the Spirit: The Ideal of Christian Manliness in Literature and Religious Thought*, Cambridge University Press, 1985.

VICO, Giambattista, *The New Science* revised tr. of 3rd edn (1744), Thomas Goddard Bergin and Max Harrold Frisch, Ithaca N.Y., Cornell University Press, 1968.

WADSWORTH, Michael, 'Making and Interpreting Scripture', *Ways of Reading the Bible*, ed. Wadsworth, Brighton, Harvester Press/New York, Barnes and Noble, 1981.

WARD, Mrs Humphry, *Robert Elsmere*, (1888), ed. Clyde de L. Ryals, Lincoln, Nebraska, University of Nebraska Press, 1967.

WARD, Wilfred, *Life of John Henry Cardinal Newman*, 2 vols., Longman, 1912.

WATSON, J. R., *Wordsworth's Vital Soul: The Sacred and the Profane in Wordsworth's Poetry*, Macmillan, 1982.

WATTS, Isaac, *Horae Lyricae* (1709), 6th edn, 1731.

WESTERMANN, Claus, 'The Interpretation of the Old Testament' tr. Dietrich Ritschl, *Essays on Old Testament Hermeneutics*, ed. Westermann, English tr. ed. J. L. Mays, Richmond, Va., John Knox Press, 1969.

WHEELER, Kathleen M. (ed.), *German Aesthetic and Literary Criticism: The Romantic Ironists and Goethe*, Cambridge University Press, 1984.

WHEELWRIGHT, Philip, *The Burning Fountain*, Bloomington, Indiana University Press, 1966.

Metaphor and Reality, Bloomington, Indiana University Press, 1962.

WHICKER, Brian, *The Story-Shaped World*, Athlone Press, 1975.

WHITEHEAD, A. N., *Science and the Modern World*, N.Y., Mentor Books, 1948.

WHORF, Benjamin Lee, *Language, Thought and Reality*, ed. J. B. Carroll, Cambridge, Mass., M.I.T. Press, 1956.

WIENER, Aharon, *The Prophet Elijah in the Development of Judaism*, Routledge, 1978.

WILES, Maurice, 'Does Christology Rest on a Mistake?', *Christ, Faith, and History*, eds S. W. Sykes and J. P. Clayton, Cambridge University Press, 1972.

Faith and the Mystery of God, S.C.M. Press, 1982.

WILKINS, John, *Essay Towards a Real Character and a Philosophical Language*, 1668.

WILKINSON, John, *Interpretation and Community*, Macmillan, 1963.

WILLEY, Basil, *The Eighteenth Century Background*, Chatto, 1940.

WILLIAMS, Raymond, *The Long Revolution*, Chatto, 1961.

WILLIAMS, Rowland, 'Baron Bunsen's Biblical Researches', *Essays and Reviews*, 1861.

WILSON, John, *Language and Christian Belief*, Macmillan, 1958.

WIMSATT, W. K. Jr, and BEARDSLEY, M. C., 'The Intentional Fallacy', *Essays in Modern Criticism*, ed. Ray B. West, N.Y., Holt, Rinehart and Winston, 1952.

WISDOM, John, *Paradox and Discovery*, University of California Press, 1970.

WITTGENSTEIN, Ludwig, *Philosophical Investigations*, Oxford, Blackwell, 1953.

WOOD, Robert, *On the Original Genius and Writings of Homer*, 1775.

WORDSWORTH, William, 'Preface to the *Lyrical Ballads*', eds. R. L. Brett and A. R. Jones, revised impression, Methuen, 1965.

The Prelude 1799, 1805, 1850, eds. Jonathan Wordsworth, M. H. Abrams, Stephen Gill, Norton, 1979.

Index

Aarsleff, Hans, 55, 253n., 254n., 255n., 257n., 266n., 268n.
Abrams, M. H., 95–100, 124, 144, 248n., 252n., 277n.
Adam, 90–1; language of, 54–5, 57, 59, 123, 126, 132, 216–17, 226, 239, 266n.
Addison, Joseph, 109
Aetherius Society, The, 199
Alain of Lille, 251n.
Allen, Ward, 245n., 249n.
Alter, Robert, 194, 203, 204–9, 211, 244n.
Animal Farm, 215
Aquinas, St Thomas, 163
Aristotle, 29, 37, 43, 45, 46–7, 52, 66, 71, 117, 121, 207, 211, 214, 229, 270n.
Arnold, Matthew, 53, 58, 63–5, 68, 72, 76, 188, 189–94, 196, 206, 215, 218, 256n.
Arnold, Thomas, 54, 181–2, 253n.
Asbach-Schnitker, Brigitte, 268n. 269.
Ast, Friedrich, 23
Athanasius, St, 74
Auerbach, Erich, 7, 81, 209–10, 211, 244
Augustine, St, 3, 14–15, 22, 23, 33, 37–8, 47, 96–9, 104, 131, 132, 211, 216, 246, 247
Austen, June, 185, 187
Ayer, A. J., 82, 220

Bacon, Sir Francis, 184, 216
Baelz, Peter, 73–5
Baird, John Logie, 87

Bakhtin, M. M., 210–11, 212, 213, 214, 235
Barfield, Owen, 85–9, 92, 220, 225, 226, 227, 228, 245n.; *Saving the Appearances*, 86, 245n.; *The Meaning of Literal*, 86; *Poetic Diction*, 257n.
Barnes, Robert, 278n.
Barth, J. Robert, S. J., 270n.
Barthes, Roland, 26–8, 145, 188
Basnett-McGuire, Susan, 250n.
Battiscombe, Georgina, 270n.
Beardsley, Monroe, 221, 226, 249n., 279n.
Beatrice, 151–69, 171–2, 178
Beddoes, Thomas, 115
Bell, Andrew, 181
Bell, Quentin, 248n.
Bentham, Jeremy, 61–2, 185
Berggren, Douglas, 75–6, 221–4, 225, 226, 229, 233, 262n.
Berlin, Isaiah, 51, 54, 110
Bible, *Authorized Version*, 6–10, 30, 110, 234, 236; *Douai*, 9; *Good News Bible*, 4, 9, 10, 31, 111, 228; *Jerusalem*, 8, 16; *New English Bible*, 8, 9, 10, 246; *Pentateuch*, 199, 246; *Revised Standard*, 17; *Rheims*, 9; *Royal*, 15; *Septuagint*, 31–2, 213–14; *Targums*, 213; *Vulgate*, 8, 16, 32, 214; as a linguistic palimpsest 213–14; as poetic, 40–5, 217–18, 229
Black, Max, 221, 222, 279n.
Blackwell, Thomas, 50, 107
Blair, Hugh, 42–3, 109, 114, 115

297

Blake, William, 1, 19, 24, 27, 42, 76, 84, 95, 101, 102, 108, 116–17, 127, 141, 142, 146, 162, 171–3, 183, 201–2, 203, 207, 212, 213, 218, 220, 228, 234, 242, 268n.; *Laocoon*, 116; *Marriage of Heaven and Hell*, 116, 172–3, 201–2; *There is no Natural Religion*, 76, 101; *A Vision of the Last Judgement*, 173
Boehme, Jacob, 54–5, 123, 124, 253n.
Boileau, Nicholas, 38
Bois, John, 9
Bonner, Gerald, 251n.
Bopp, Franz, 56
Borst, Arno, 254n.
Bowden, John, 248n.
Boyle, Robert, 123, 216
Brantley, Richard E., 262n., 263n.
Brekle, Herbert E., 269n.
Bronner, Leah, 245
Brosses, Charles de, 148
Brothers, Richard, 125
Brown, John, 50
Brown, Peter, 247n., 250n.
Browning, Robert, 185
Buber, Martin, 245n.
Bultmann, Rudolf, 35, 69, 72, 249n.
Bunsen, Christian Karl Josias von, Baron, 58–9, 186, 215, 226
Burke, Edmund, 42, 60–1, 63, 109
Burnet, Thomas, 117
Burrow, John, 28, 34–6, 57, 60, 234–6, 239, 255n., 257n.
Burtt, E. A., 277n.
Businck, A., 248n.
Butler, Joseph, 218, 248n.
Butler, Marilyn, 262n., 275n.
Byron, George Gordon, Lord, 173, 183

Caird, G. B., 7, 13, 16, 18, 19–25, 78, 214, 244n., 248n.
Calvin, Jean, 38

Caputo, John D. 282n.
Carey, Edmund, 199
Carlyle, Thomas, 16, 95, 175, 177, 179, 186, 248
Carr, E. H., 207
Carroll, J. B., 267n.
Carroll, J. S., 167
Catullus, Gaius Valerius, 182
Cellier, Léon, 266n.
Cervantes, Miguel de, 82, 212
Charity, A. C., 246n.
Chey, Jocelyn, 244n.
Chitty, Susan, 274n.
Churchill, Winston, 239
Coleridge, Henry Nelson, 5, 146
Coleridge, J. T., 46, 252n.
Coleridge, Samuel Taylor, 1, 4,–6, 17, 19, 25, 30, 33, 34, 43–5, 46, 48–9, 54, 64, 66, 67, 84–5, 92, 93, 94, 115, 116, 117–19, 120, 127, 128, 129, 132–3, 134–48, 153, 168, 176, 179, 180, 185, 191, 193, 196, 201–2, 203, 212, 217–18, 219, 220, 260n., 271n., 277n.; *Aids to Reflection*, 138; *Biographia Literaria*, 44–5, 117–18, 138, 139, 142–3, 147; *Church and State*, 141; *Confessions of an Inquiring Spirit*, 4–5, 244; *Logic*, 137; *Philosophical Lectures*, 137, 146, 147; *Stateman's Manuel*, 43–4, 48, 118, 139
Collingwood, R. G., 221
Collins, William, 179
Comte, Auguste, 186
Condillac, Etienne Bonnot de, 55, 148
Conrad, Joseph, 187, 238
Constable, John, 122
Copernicus, (Nicholas Koppernik), 37
Coulson, John, 258n., 275n.
Cowley, Abraham, 29
Cowper, William, 42, 108
Cozens, John Robert, 122

Crabbe, George, 263n.
Craig, John, 25, 40, 200
Crawford, Donald W., 252n.
Crose, Benedetto, 53, 69, 221
Currie, Robert, 263n.

Damon, S. Foster, 273n.
Dante, Alighieri, 3, 149–73, 175, 178, 184, 188, 193, 212, 223, 242
Darwin, Charles, 37, 148
David, (and Saul) 204, (and Bathsheba) 205, 208–9
DeLaura, David, 276n.
de Maistre, Count Joseph, 54
Dennis, John, 33, 40–5, 57, 60, 68, 70, 71, 107, 108, 109, 184, 196, 201, 228
De Quincey, Thomas, 185
Derham, William, 25
Dickens, Charles, 179, 185, 186, 274n.; *Our Mutual Friend*, 181
Dilthey, Wilhelm, 22, 249n.
Dodd, C. H., 22
Donaldson, J. W., 56
Downes, Andrew, 23
Doyle, Sir Arthur Conan, 187
Dronke, Peter, 156–7
Dryden, John, 29–30, 39, 214

Eagleton, Terry, 197–8
Ebeling, Gerhard, 69, 249n.
Eichhorn, Johann Gottfried, 19, 49, 59, 61, 63, 72, 111, 115, 205, 209, 260n.
Eliade, Mircea, 260n.
Elijah, 6–18, 27, 32, 34–5, 72, 97, 122, 130, 144, 149, 169–71, 174–5, 188, 196, 209, 216, 221, 224, 228, 242, 244–5, 246
Eliot, George, 185, 187, 188, 191, 208; *Scenes of Clerical Life*, 77, 186, 208
Eliot, T. S., 85, 189
Emerson, Ralph Waldo, 136, 268n.
Emmet, Dorothy, 202

Empson, William, 164, 193
Evans, Sir Arthur, 20
Ezekiel, 116, 172–3, 226

Fabre d'Olivet, Antoine, 125–6, 148
Farrar, F. W., 57–8
Farrer, Austin, 19, 79–80, 82, 83, 88, 176, 214, 225
Fearn, John, 268n.
Feuerbach, Ludwig, 53, 63, 95, 145, 174, 186, 191, 192, 258n.
Fichte, Johann Gottlieb, 1, 243n.
Flaxman, John, 127, 172
Fludd, Robert, 124
Ford, John, 276n.
Forbes, Duncan, 255n.
Forster, E. M., *A Passage to India* 174, 187–8
Forster, Georg, 83
Forsyth, Robert, 274n.
Foster, Richard, 276n.
Foucault, Michel, 188
Fowles, John, 189
Frazer, Sir James, 30
Frei, Hans, 2, 17, 18, 76–8, 82, 84, 194, 195, 198, 203, 205, 208, 244n., 247n., 249n.
Frend, William, 115, 116
Freud, Sigmund, 47
Friedländer, Paul, 269n.
Fruman, Norman, 270n.
Frye, Northrop, 21, 24, 70–72, 73, 74, 76, 89, 194, 203, 208, 225, 226
Fuchs, Ernst, 69, 249n.
Fuller, R. C., 265n., 266n.
Funk, Robert W., 2, 198, 244n.

Gabler, Johann Philip, 24–5
Gadamer, Hans Georg, 69, 110, 249n., 280n., 282n.
Gainsford, Thomas, 276n.
Gardner, Helen, 275n.
Geddes, Alexander, 115, 125
Geller, Uri, 239
Gerhardsson, Birger, 23
Gesenius, 19, 49

Gibbon, Edward, 84
Gilbert, Alan, 263n.
Gilgamesh, 75
Girouard, Mark, 182, 239
Gissing, George, 186
Goethe, Johann Wolfgang von, 50, 54, 82
Godwin, William, 95, 116, 134, 139
Gombrich, Sir E. H., 163–4, 165, 187, 223–4
Grass, Günter, 189
Gray, John, 248n.
Grayston, Kenneth, 9–11, 12, 236, 245n.
Gregory the Great, St, 167
Gregory, G., 114, 264n.
Grimm, Jacob, 56, 75
Gutmann, Joseph, 248n.

Hackenborn, Mechtildis von, 158
Halhead, Nathaniel, 125
Hamann, Johann Georg, 50, 53, 54
Hardie, Colin, 156–7
Hardy, Thomas, 176, 187, 215, 263n.
Hare, Francis, 109
Hare, Julius, 56, 84, 265n.
Harris, James, 266n.
Harrison, J. F. C., 262n. 266n.
Hartley, David, 62, 133–4, 136, 137, 147, 216
Hazlitt, William, 136, 185
Hegel, Georg Wilhelm Friedrich, 59, 83
Heidegger, Martin, 68–70, 72, 81, 88, 203, 226, 240–1, 249n.
Hepworth, Brian, 111, 124, 274n.
Heraclitus, 138
Herbert, George, 30, 90–3
Herder, Johann Gottfried, 15, 18, 19, 30, 49–50, 51, 53, 54, 55, 58, 67, 70, 72, 83, 85, 111, 115, 147, 201, 211, 247n.
Hirsch-Reich, Beatrice, 272n.
Hobbs, Thomas, 51, 92, 138
Hobsbawm, E. J., 95

Hogarth, William, 61
Holcroft, Thomas, 116
Hölderlin, Friedrich, 50, 68, 81
Holland, Saba, Lady, 263n.
Hollar, Wenceslaus, 20
Holquist, Michael, 210
Homer, 50, 102, 177–8, 182, 193 (*Iliad*), 209–10, 226
Honey, J. R. de S., 274n.
Hooke, Robert, 124
Hooker, Richard, 10
Hopkins, Gerard Manley, 88, 118–23, 132, 140–1, 146, 176, 179, 207
Horace, 29
Howard, Leonard, 15
Howes, Thomas, 113–14, 115, 116, 117, 125, 130–1, 213
Huet, Pierre Daniel, 38
Hulme, T. E., 198
Humboldt, Wilhelm von, Baron, 1, 2, 30, 56, 58, 59, 68, 83, 197, 211, 227–8, 243n., 270n.
Hume, David, 62, 84, 192, 218, 239
Hursley, Lee, 263n.
Husserl, Edmund, 70
Hutchinson, Roger, 39

Iamblichus, 127
Intentional fallacy, the, 22–4
Irwin, Helen, 270n.
Isaiah, 12, 108, 112, 114, 117
Isidore of Seville, 157

Jacob, 27, 167
Jacob, Giles, 41
Jacobi, Friedrich Heinrich, 54
Jenkyns, Richard, 239, 256n., 262n.
Jeremiah, 61
Jerome, St, 32, 38
Jesperson, J. O. H., 255n.
Joachim of Fiore, 144, 272n.
Job, 60, 75, 80
John of Ephesus, St, 79
Johnson, Joseph, 116

Jones, Sir William, 56, 125, 254n.
Jones, William, (Rev.), 215–17, 221, 278n.
Jonson, Ben, 29
Jowett, Benjamin, 2, 118
Joyce, James, 189
Judge, Edwin A., 243

Kafka, Franz, 189
Kant, Immanuel, 21, 44, 71, 138, 141, 190, 193, 198, 203, 233, 238
Keats, John, 48, 127, 142, 183
Keble, John, 16, 45–9, 56, 62, 67, 123, 131, 140, 148, 170–1, 217, 219, 220, 247–8
Kekulé, von Stradonitz, Friedrich August, 130
Kelly, Louis G., 29, 250n., 259n.
Kermode, Frank, 24
Kierkegaard, Soren, 12, 219
Kimchi, David, 112
Kingsley, Charles, 124, 179, 182, 256n.
Kipling, Rudyard, 274n.
Kirk, G. S., 270n., 281n.
Kleist, Heinrich von, 50
Knight, Gareth, 249n.
Krebs, W. A., 254n., 268n.
Kristeva, Julia, 26
Kugel, James L., 264n.
Kuhn, Hans, 260n.
Kuhn, T. S., 176

Laing, R. D., 272n.
Lamb, Charles, 185
Lampe, G. W. H., 249n., 264n.
Lancaster, Joseph, 181
Landow, George P., 176–7, 267n.
Laski, Marghanita, 260n.
Leach, Edmund, 28
Leakey, Richard, 279n.
Leavis, F. R., 275n.
Leibniz, Gottfried Wilhelm, 54, 211
Lessing, Gotthold Ephraim, 19, 49, 59, 63, 72, 83, 111, 115

Levere, Trevor, 127
Levine, George, 186–7, 189, 206
Lewis, C. S., 80–2, 83, 220
Lindsay, Jack, 95
Locke, John, 29, 38, 45, 62, 89, 93, 132, 135, 147, 206, 216, 233
Lockhart, J. G., 46
Lodge, David, 186
Logos, the, 15, 45, 133, 138–9, 143–4, 148, 170–1, 202, 234
Longinus, 38–41, 108
Lovejoy, A. O., 114
Lowth, Robert, 1, 46, 58, 67, 105–23, 124, 125, 129, 130, 135, 170, 179, 202, 214, 215–16, 217, 220, 228; *Isaiah*, 33, 49, 61, 84, 107, 111, 112, 116, 117; *Sacred Poetry of the Hebrews*, 33, 41–3, 49, 56, 61, 84, 105–13, 116; *Short Introduction to English Grammar* 33, 105
Lubac, Henri de, 246n., 272n.
Lucretius, Titus Carus, 133
Lukács, Georg, 210
Luther, Martin, 54

Macaulay, T. B., 274n.
McClelland, Charles E., 243
MacDonald, George, 274n.
McFarland, Thomas, 257n.
MacIntyre, Alasdair, 192
MacPherson, James, 228
Macquarrie, John, 69, 72–5, 82, 221
Madden, William, A., 276n.
Maimonides, 172
Malraux, André, 230
Marie Antoinette, 160
Maritain, Jacques, 276n.
Marlowe, Christopher, 10, 159
Marsh, Herbert, 116, 265n.
Martin, B. W., 248
Martin, John, 20
Martindale, Charles, 29
Marx, Karl, 53, 88
Matilda of Canossa, 158
Maurice, F. D., 54, 84, 145–6

Mazzini, Giuseppe, 54
Medcalf, Stephen, 248n., 273n.
Meinecke, Friedrich, 106, 110,
   253n., 264n.
Meinhold, Peter, 253n.
Melchizedek, 13
Merleau-Ponty, Maurice, 69, 145,
   230–84
metaphor, theories of, 214–41
   (*passim*); 'metaphorical' and
   'literal' 226–8; 'poetic' as, 228
Michaelis, Johann David, 49, 111,
   112, 115
Michelet, Jules, 54
Mill, James, 61–2, 136
Mill, John Stuart, 61–4, 72, 73,
   179–80, 185, 215
Milton, John, 24, 30, 41, 58, 80,
   102, 120, 160–2, 184; *Paradise
   Lost*, 99, 160, 162, 193
Mimesis, — relation to realism,
   204–12
Monboddo, James Burnett, Lord,
   254n.
Montesquieu, Baron de, 54
Moorman, Mary, 263n., 270n.
Morris, David B., 251n., 252n.,
   268n.
Moses, 12, 15, 38, 41, 126, 149,
   169, 224
Mozley, Thomas, 99–100
Mudge, Lewis S., 260n.
Müller, Friedrich Max, 2, 58–60,
   186, 215, 226
Munchhausen, Gerlach Adolf von,
   1
Mure, G. R. G., 259n.

Napoleon, 130
Nature, 12, 86–8, 93, 95–7, 121–2,
   174–8, 240, as a 'language'
   123–48, 216–17, as 'order' 213
Newman, John Henry, 2, 28, 66–8,
   84, 162, 217–20, 234; *Essay on
   Development of Doctrine*, 66;
   Grammar of Assent, 26, 33–4, 67
Newsom, David, 265n.

Newton, Sir Isaac, 93, 112, 124,
   147, 177, 216, 249n.
Nicholson, Norman, 270n.
Nida, Eugene A., 31–2, 228, 229
Niebuhr, Georg Barthold, 183
Nineham, Dennis, 18–25, 35, 78,
   196, 237, 248n.
Novalis (Friedrich von Hardenberg),
   83, 233
Nuttall, A. D., 204–8, 226, 231,
   258n., 262n., 263n., 277n., 282n.

Oates, Joan, 259n.
Oldroyd, Drina, 272n.
Origen, 246
Orsini, G. N. G., 270n.

Paine, Thomas, 95, 116
Paley, Morton D., 267n.
Paley, William, 25
Palmer, Richard E., 249n.
Palmer, Samuel, 127
Parallelism, 109–10, 118–23
Parsons, James, 253n.
Pattison, Mark, 181, 243, 244
Peacock, Thomas Love, 101, 127,
   183–5
Pederson, H., 255n.
Percy, Thomas, 102
Perrault, Charles, 75
Petrarch, 212
Philo of Alexandria, 199
Philology, 58–60
Piaget, Jean, 237–8
Pighius, Albertus, 251n.
Pilgrim's Progress, the, 80
Pindar, 29, 83
Piozzi, Hester, 269n.
Plato (and Platonism), 66, 68, 71,
   97, 117, 146, 184, 241
Plotinus, 127
Plutarch, 97
'Poetic', the, 49–68, 68–94, 144,
   189–92; Bible as, 40–45, 107–10,
   217–18, 229; extensive vs.
   intensive meanings of, 60–61,

70–2, 201; as healing, 54–9; metaphors, 215–20, 227; primal participation, 60–7, 203, 227; poetic genius, 101, 201–2, 218
Polanyi, Michael, 162
Pollard, A. W., 245
Pope, Alexander, 177, 184; *Windsor Forest*, 97; *Essay on Man*, 147; *Essay on Criticism*, 177
Popper, Sir Karl, 24, 235, 281n.
Porphyry, 97, 127
Porter, H. C., 251n.
Pound, Ezra, 182–3
Prado, H., 248n.
Price, Richard, 116
Prickett, Stephen, 244n., 248n., 250n., 252n., 255n., 258n., 260n., 263n., 267n., 270n., 271n., 273n., 274n., 275n., 278n.
Priestley, Joseph, 116, 124
Psalms, 83, 108–10
pseudo-Philo, 199
Pusey, Edward Bouverie, 2, 115
Pynchon, Thomas, 189

Rad, Gerhard von, 69, 272n.
Radcliffe, Mrs Ann, 187
Rahner, Karl, 67
Raine, Kathleen, 127
Ramsey, Ian, 221, 234
Ramsey, Leopold von, 200, 207
Raven, J. E., 270n., 281n.
Ray, John, 25
Realism, 186–9, 194–5; in relation to biblical narrative, 6–7, 82–3, 203, 206–9
Read, Benedict, 281n.
Reed, Sampson, 132
Reeves, Marjorie, 272n.
Reid, Thomas, 138, 269n.
Richards, I. A., 276n.
Richardson, Alan, 245n., 269n.
Richardson, Charles, 268n.
Ricoeur, Paul, 23, 69–70, 73, 75–6, 78–9, 82, 84–5, 88, 196, 199, 203, 221, 222, 226, 227, 229–30,

232, 280n.; *The Rule of Metaphor*, 75, 221, 232; *Towards a Hermeneutic of the Idea of Revelation*, 76, 229; *Symbolism of Evil*, 229–30, 232
Rig-Veda, the, 59
Rivière, Jacques, 276n.
Robbe-Grillet, Alain, 189
Roberts, Michael, 89–90
Robertson, F. W., 49
Robertson, J. G., 54
Robespierre, Isidore Maximilien de, 130
Robinson, Henry Crabb, 274n.
Robinson, H. Wheeler, 245n.
Robinson, J., 17, 33, 248n.
Rogers, Samuel, 185
Rosenau, Helen, 248n.
Roston, Murray, 111, 280n.
Ruskin, John, 121
Russell, Bertrand, 166
Russell, D. A., 251n.

St John of the Cross, 15, 33, 170, 242, 247
Samuel, 77
Sagovsky, Nicholas, 258n.
Sarraute, Nathalie, 189
Saussure, Ferdinand de, 68, 70, 230, 231, 233
Sayce, A. H., 257n.
Schelling, Friedrich Wilhelm Joseph von, 1, 59, 142–3, 243n.
Schiller, Johann Christophe Friedrich von, 30, 50, 88, 144, 147, 271n.
Schlegel, August Wilhelm von, 56
Schlegel, Friedrich von, 56, 58, 82–3, 211–12
Schleiermacher, Friedrich, 1, 18, 22, 63, 110, 243, 249n.
Schmid, E. A., 254n.
Schmidt, C. B., 49, 56
Scholem, Gershom, 273n.
Scott, D. F. S., 243n.
Scott, Sir Walter, 185, 187

Scruton, Roger, 248n., 252n.
Shaffer, Eleanor, 110, 257n., 265n.
Shakespeare, William, 10, 20, 24, 74, 82, 120, 153–4, 184, 204, 205, 207, 208, 212, 236, 261; *Hamlet*, 261n.; *Henry V*, 153–4; *Henry IV*, ii, 24, 204; *Macbeth*, 215; *Midsummer Night's Dream*, 24
Shelley, Mary, 186
Shelley, P. B., 98, 101–2, 118, 142, 183–4, 185, 186
Sidney, Sir Philip, 10, 102
Sinclair, John, D., 151, 154–5
Smart, Christopher, 42, 108, 115
Snell, Lionel, 239, 281–2n.
Sparks, H. F. D., 250n., 251n.
Sparrow, John, 244n.
Spence, Joseph, 179
Socrates, 71
Solger, Karl, 58
Solomon, 107
Solomon's Temple, 20
Solzhenitzyn, Alexander, 239
Southey, Robert, 1
Spenser, Edmund, 10
Stanford, W. Bedell, 222
Stanley, A. P., 181
Stampfer, Judah, 272n.
Steffens, Henrich, 1, 243n.
Steig, Michael, 275n.
Steinberg, Saul, 164–5
Steiner, George, 21, 26, 29, 32–3, 55, 245n., 262n.
Stendhal, (Henri Beyle), 182–3
Stensen, Sten, 244
Sterne, Lawrence, 206
Stewart, Dugald, 39
Stone, Harry, 275n.
Strachey, Lytton, 248
Strauss, David Friedrich, 192
Süssmilch, Johann Peter, 55
Sweet, Paul R., 243n., 255n., 260n., 279n.
Swift, Jonathan, 184, *Gulliver's Travels* 24

Taber, C. 250n.
Tannenbaum, Leslie, 265n., 272n.
Taylor, Jeremy, 117
Taylor, John, 239
Taylor, Thomas, 127, 139–40
Tennyson, Alfred, Lord, 34, 148, 175–7, 179, 185, 238, 263n.
Thackeray, William Makepeace, 187
Thirlwall, Connop, 56
Thomasius, Jacob, 1
Thompson, E. P., 96, 239
Thomson, James, 41, 52, 57
Thornton, L. S., 264n.
Tieck, Ludwig, 58, 82
Tiresias, 168
Tooke, John Horne, 56, 134–8, 147, 273n.
Toulmin, Stephen, 279n.
Toynbee, Paget, 272n.
Trapp, Joseph, 41, 57, 114
Trench, Richard Chenevix, 136
Trilling, Lionel, 22
Trimmer, Mrs Sarah, 15, 33, 105–6, 247
Trollope, Anthony, 187
Trompf, Garry, 60
Trusler, John, 269n.
Turbane, Colin, 279n.
Turner, Victor, 260n.
typology, 14–16, 47–8, 127–30, 228
Tyrrell, George 65–6

Usener, Hermann, 1
Ussher, James, 40, 200

Vallon, Annette, 180
Vanbrugh, Sir John, 4, 20
Vance, R. N. C., 274n.
Vico, Giambattista, 50–4, 61, 64, 67, 69, 70–1, 85, 147, 183, 184, 191–2, 196, 200, 203, 221, 225, 233
Villalpando, Juan Bautista, 20, 248n.
Villon, François, 182

Virgil, 29, 43, 149–69, 177–8
Voss, Johann Heinrich, 50, 83

Wadsworth, Michael, 246
Waller, Edmund, 29
Ward, Mrs Humphry, *Robert Elsmere*, 237–9, 240
Ward, Wilfred, 258n.
Warton, Joseph, 179
Warton, Thomas, 179
Watson, J. R., 224–5
Watts, Isaac, 38, 41, 140
Webster, Noah, 136
Wesley, Charles, 91–3
Westermann, Klaus, 245
Wheelwright, Philip, 224, 279n.
Whicker, Brian, 275n.
White, Allon, 278n.
Whitehead, A. N., 178
Whittier, John Greenleaf, 170–1
Whorf, Benjamin Lee, 126
Wieland, C. M., 50
Wiener, Aharon, 244, 246, 273n.
Wiles, Maurice, 17, 34
Willey, Basil, 273n.
Williams, Charles, 220
Williams, Raymond, 277n.
Williams, Rowland, 256n.
Wilkins, Sir Charles, 125

Wilkins, John, 25, 33, 40, 124, 200, 266n.
Wilkinson, John, 246n., 249n.
Wilson, John, 220
Wimsatt, W. K., 24
Winckelmann, Johann Joachim, 88
Wisdom, John, 188
Wittgenstein, Ludwig, 82, 220, 258n.
Wolf, Emil, 239
Wolf, Friedrich August, 23, 243n.
Wollstonecraft, Mary, 116, 127
Wood, Robert, 50, 107
Woolf, Virginia, 189
Wordsworth, Dorothy, 100, 180
Wordsworth, William, 1, 34, 42, 45–6, 59, 61, 62, 64, 70, 85, 87, 96–100, 102–4, 108, 115, 118, 127, 128–31, 139, 140, 143, 147, 148, 170, 175, 177, 179–81, 183, 186, 189, 203, 220, 224–5
Wyatt, Sir Thomas, 7
Wyle, Nicholas von, 245

Young, Edward, 179

Zeno (of Elea), 230–1, 232, 233
Zola, Emile, 186